"Ethics are the cornerstone to good clinic°¹
clinical needs of patients are paramou
that across cultures, rights of individua
respected. Issues related to privacy and
care systems and cultures, however, ethı   ...ount.
The success of the previous two editions   volume indicates the need for continuing to deliver   ᵥare services in an
appropriate and ethical manner. Editors and ᵢ   ᵤ are to be congratulated for
their vision and effort in highlighting challenges and potential ways forward
ensuring that clinicians approach their practice in an ethical framework. This
volume will be of great interest to mental health professionals."
– **Professor Dinesh Bhugra**, CBE, President, BMA (2018–2019),
President World Psychiatric Association (2014–2017), President,
The Royal College of Psychiatrists (2008–2011)

"As a trainee psychotherapist, the changing landscape and challenges faced in
clinical practice can feel overwhelming and hard to navigate. However, having
such a comprehensive, accessible and informative book like this is invaluable
to professional development. This is a well-thought and well-crafted book,
which attends to numerous dilemmas that clinicians encounter. It also acts as
a guideline for trainees to ensure that an ethical framework is adopted at all
times throughout training and clinical practice. As a trainee therapist, it is vital
to have a book like this to refer to as it offers trustworthy guidance on a range
of important topics that need careful consideration."
– **Martina Kehoe**, Trainee, MSc, Integrative Psychotherapy

"Ethics are the foundation of therapeutic practice. In order to navigate the
unique and complex challenges presented to practitioners, a robust understanding of ethics in practice is essential. This considered edition brings together
notable voices from a variety of perspectives, presenting a comprehensive analysis of ethics in contemporary psychotherapeutic work. This publication is
one of those must have references for all practitioners at every level."
– **Bee MacBean**, MBACP Registered Counsellor/Psychotherapist

"The *Handbook* consists of accessible, concise overviews of an incredibly
comprehensive range of professional issues. As such, it will be highly relevant
to a broad audience of counsellors, psychotherapists, psychiatrists and clinical
and counselling psychologists. This third edition has been updated to take
account of recent UK professional body practice and ethical guidelines and
also includes a number of new chapters including ones on service user involvement and social inclusion issues. As with previous editions, it will undoubtedly
prove invaluable to trainees and highly experienced practitioners alike."
– **David Murphy**, President, British Psychological Society (2019–2020)

The Handbook of Professional, Ethical and Research Practice for Psychologists, Counsellors, Psychotherapists and Psychiatrists

This exciting new edition provides an overview of the main professional, ethical and research issues that are required knowledge for counsellors, therapists, psychologists and psychiatrists engaging in therapeutic or clinical work. These issues form part of the curriculum and practice requirements of all the major counselling, psychotherapy, psychology and psychiatry professional organisations (including BACP, BPS, HCPC, RCP, UKCP, IACP, IPS and IAHIP).

Divided into six clearly defined sections, this book will provide a comprehensive overview of all the major professional practice and ethical issues in one edited volume. The authors are well-known experts in their fields and their work has been brought together with clarity and helpful features, including reflective questions and case vignettes. This new edition has also been updated to include content on social justice, community psychology and professional guidelines, reflecting the latest academic research and clinical developments.

This book is unique in the breadth of issues covered and its focus on therapeutic practice. It will be of interest to practitioners and students of psychotherapy, counselling and psychiatry.

Professor Rachel Tribe works at the School of Psychology, University of East London. She is a Fellow of the British Psychological Society. She is an active clinician and is involved in national and international consultancy, training and research. She has published widely and regularly contributes to conferences and workshops around the world.

Dr Jean Morrissey works at the School of Nursing & Midwifery, Trinity College Dublin. She is a registered counsellor/psychotherapist and clinical supervisor (BACP and IACP) and has worked for many years as a clinician, supervisor and educator.

The Handbook of Professional, Ethical and Research Practice for Psychologists, Counsellors, Psychotherapists and Psychiatrists

Third Edition

Edited by
Rachel Tribe and Jean Morrissey

LONDON AND NEW YORK

Third edition published 2020
by Routledge
2 Park Square, Milton Park, Abingdon, Oxon, OX14 4RN

and by Routledge

52 Vanderbilt Avenue, New York, NY 10017

Routledge is an imprint of the Taylor & Francis Group, an informa business

[First edition published by Routledge 2004]

[Second edition published by Routledge 2015]

British Library Cataloguing-in-Publication Data
A catalogue record for this book is available from the British Library

Library of Congress Cataloging-in-Publication Data
Names: Tribe, Rachel, editor. | Morrissey, Jean, editor.
Title: The handbook of professional, ethical and research practice for psychologists, counsellors, psychotherapists and psychiatrists / edited by Rachel Tribe and Jean Morrissey.
Description: 3rd edition. | Abingdon, Oxon ; New York, NY : Routledge, 2020. | Includes bibliographical references and index.
Identifiers: LCCN 2019053715 (print) | LCCN 2019053716 (ebook) | ISBN 9781138352070 (hardback) | ISBN 9781138352087 (paperback) | ISBN 9780429428838 (ebook)
Subjects: LCSH: Psychologists–Professional ethics. | Counselors–Professional ethics. | Psychotherapists–Professional ethics.
Classification: LCC BF76.4 .H365 2020 (print) | LCC BF76.4 (ebook) | DDC 174/.915–dc23
LC record available at https://lccn.loc.gov/2019053715
LC ebook record available at https://lccn.loc.gov/2019053716

ISBN: 978-1-138-35207-0 (hbk)
ISBN: 978-1-138-35208-7 (pbk)
ISBN: 978-0-429-42883-8 (ebk)

Typeset in Times New Roman
by Swales & Willis, Exeter, Devon, UK

Contents

Illustrations

Tables

Box

Figures

Contributors

Editors

Rachel Tribe is employed at the School of Psychology at the University of East London. She is a Fellow of the British Psychological Society and the Royal Society of Arts. She is a Health and Care Professions Council registered Counselling and Organisational psychologist. She was given the British Psychological Society's Ethics Committee's Award for Promoting Equality of Opportunity in Psychology in 2014. She is an active clinician and is involved in national and international consultancy, training and research. She has published widely and regularly contributes to conferences and workshops for a range of mental health professionals.

Jean Morrissey is an Assistant Professor in the School of Nursing, Trinity College Dublin. She is also a registered counsellor/psychotherapist and clinical supervisor (BACP and IACP) and has worked for many years as a clinician, educator and supervisor in both private practice, adult mental health (NHS) and higher education in the UK and Hong Kong. She is an active clinician, supervisor and researcher in the area of self-harm and suicidology, clinical supervision. She has published widely and regularly contributes to conferences and workshops for a range of mental health professionals.

Authors

Nicola Barden is a Professional Fellow at the University of Winchester, where from 2013 to 2018 she was the Director of Student Services. Prior to this she led counselling and mental health teams at the Universities of Portsmouth and Aston, and from 2012 to 2018 she was the Secretary of the Mental Wellbeing in Higher Education Working Group. She has over 30 years of experience as a counsellor and psychotherapist, She has contributed to the work of the British Association for Counselling and Psychotherapy (BACP) as Chair of their Accreditation and then Professional Standards

Committee before becoming Chair of the Association from 2005 to 2008. She remains a BACP Fellow.

Haneyeh Belyani is a Chartered Counselling Psychologist. Her work with vulnerable individuals across a range of different settings led to her interest and specialism in working with trauma in child and adult populations. Following her previously held position of Senior Lecturer on the Professional Doctorate in Counselling Psychology at the University of East London, Haneyeh continues to contribute to the teaching and the clinical supervision of trainees. Alongside her private practice, she provides training and consultation to fostering agencies and children's homes and is currently the Clinical Director and Lead of a secondary school-based therapy service in one of London's most diverse boroughs.

Lucia Berdondini is a Senior Lecturer and Programme Leader of MSc International Humanitarian Psychosocial Intervention at the School of Psychology, University of East London. She is also a BACP accredited Gestalt psychotherapist and has been practicing for the past 15 years with individuals and groups running a small private practice. She is particularly interested in Psychology of Disasters and Humanitarian Projects and has focused her professional activity on developing counselling training courses in countries in war and post conflict, such as Afghanistan, India and Angola.

Angela Byrne is a Clinical Psychologist working in a service to improve accessibility and cultural relevance of psychological therapy to communities in Tower Hamlets, East London. She also works as a clinical supervisor with Derman, a Hackney-based charity for the wellbeing of the Kurdish and Turkish communities.

Ruth Caleb MBE is a wellbeing consultant and trainer who specialises in the mental health and wellbeing of students and staff in higher education. She is also a supervisor and tutor on the Metanoia Institute/Middlesex University Doctoral Psychotherapy and Counselling Psychology programmes. She was Head of Counselling at Brunel University London from 1999 to 2017 and Chair of the Mental Wellbeing in Higher Education Working Group from 2012 to 2018. She has worked strategically at a national level, as a member of Universities UK's Mental Health in HE programme working group, and informing All-Party Parliamentary Group meetings and parliamentary debates on student wellbeing.

Michael Carroll is a retired counselling psychologist who worked with individuals teams and organisations. He was a supervisor, executive coach and trainer who taught at University and worked internationally.

Maria Castro Romero is a narrative and community psychologist, Senior Lecturer in Clinical Psychology at the University of East London since 2009. Before this, she worked as a Highly Specialist Clinical Psychologist in NHS

Mental Health for Older People Services. Maria has an interest in teaching-learning as a dialogical process, and in collaborative and participative research that will contribute to a psychology for social justice. She has shared her expertise in critical pedagogy, community and liberation psychology praxis through teaching, publications and conference presentations in the UK, France, Spain, Brazil and Cuba.

Mary Creaner is an Assistant Professor with the Doctorate in Counselling Psychology and Director of the MSc in Clinical Supervision, Trinity College, the University of Dublin, Ireland. She is an accredited therapist and supervisor with the Irish Association for Counselling and Psychotherapy and a member of the American Psychological Association.

Thomas Elton joined the BPS as Professional Development Manager in December 2014, with a remit of progressing Professional Development opportunities to members. He has over 15 years' experience and a successful track record of leading and developing CPD programmes; strategic and operational planning in educational settings; and delivering high quality professional development and training.

Hannah Farndon is Policy Advisor (Professional Practice) for the British Psychological Society. She supported the working group that revised the Society's Practice Guidelines, published in 2017. Hannah studied Forensic Psychology and started her career as an Intelligence Analyst with Leicestershire Police before joining the Society in 2016.

Lorna Farquharson is a BPS Chartered Psychologist, HCPC registered Clinical Psychologist and a Fellow of the Higher Education Academy. She has extensive experience of working in the NHS, as well as advising on national quality improvement projects that relate to psychological therapies. She has published in a range of clinical areas and is currently an Academic Tutor on the Professional Doctorate in Clinical Psychology at the University of East London.

Nicola Gale is an HCPC Registered Psychologist, a Chartered Psychologist with the British Psychological Society, and was the Society's President from 2017 to 2018. She chaired the working group that revised the Society's Practice Guidelines, published in 2017. Nicola's current post is in the Department of Psychology at City, University of London, where her teaching focuses on professional standards of practice in psychology, diversity, equality and inclusion, and clinical practice and supervision. She has been clinical lead and head of service for an occupational health psychology service in the NHS, where the work had both a clinical mental health and organisational focus. Nicola's early career was in organisational development and training, management consultancy and accountancy. She has worked in different industries and on international projects.

Kenneth Gannon is the Research Director of the Professional Doctorate in Clinical Psychology at the University of East London. Following his PhD in Trinity College, Dublin he undertook training in clinical psychology in Dublin and later carried out post-doctoral research in University College London before joining the School of Medicine at Queen Mary University of London as lecturer in behavioural science. His research interests lie in the area of health psychology, particularly men's health, and in issues related to the relationships between health, human rights and research ethics.

Israel González-Urbieta is a physician at the Psychiatry Department at National University of Asunción, School of Medical Sciences (Paraguay). His areas of interest are psychopharmacology, physiopathology of mental disorders, forensic psychiatry, public mental health, cultural psychiatry and health and human rights.

Afreen Huq AFBPsS is a retired Clinical and Neuropsychologist, having worked in the NHS for 30 years. She is a passionate advocate for older adults, working with diversity, maintaining their personhood and addressing social inequalities. She is committed to championing the rights of others by mentoring, supporting and empowering people.

Peter Jenkins is a registered counsellor, trainer, supervisor and researcher. He has been a member of both the BACP Professional Conduct Committee and the UKCP Ethics Committee. He has written extensively on legal, ethical and professional aspects of counselling and psychotherapy. His latest book is *Professional Practice in Counselling and Psychotherapy: Ethics and the Law* (Sage, 2017).

Brian Linfield MBE JP, Lay Chairman United Kingdom Council Psychotherapy Professional Conduct Committee, is a specialist Presiding Lay Magistrate sitting in the family court. He has two other Judicial Appointments, he sits as a disability-qualified panel member in the Social Entitlement Chamber and also as a Specialist Member of the Mental Health Tribunal in the Health, Education and Social Care Chamber. He is a retired Civil Servant. Brian had a 15-year background of statutory regulation within the water industry for which he was honoured with his MBE and was a regional lay chairman for complaints within the NHS.

Claire Marshall is a Chartered Counselling Psychologist with 12 years of experience and an extensive background in organisational management, teaching, research and psychological interventions. Her work has contributed to projects running in collaboration with bodies such as the United Nations and the European Commission. Currently faculty member of the Doctorate in Counselling Psychology at the University of East London, and the New School of Psychotherapy and Counselling. Her special interests include: humanitarian operations in conflict and post-conflict settings and responses to forced migration from state and non-state actors, with a particular focus on psychosocial policy and interventions.

Maureen McIntosh [AFBPsS] is a Chartered Senior Counselling Psychologist who works with older adults. She is a Mindfulness Teacher, co-editor of the book *Leadership and Diversity*, an Associate Fellow of the BPS and she was a previous BPS Chair of the Division of Counselling Psychology (2016–2018).

Sarah Niblock is Chief Executive of the UK Council for Psychotherapy. Sarah joined UKCP from the university sector where she was a professor and senior manager. With a PhD in psychoanalytic theory and popular culture, she is the author of several books and peer-reviewed journal articles on ethics, media and methodology. Alongside this, she her work as a journalist, broadcaster and commentator on psychotherapy in the UK and globally.

Colman Noctor is a Child and Adolescent Psychoanalytical Psychotherapist with over 20 years of experience working with young people and their families. Colman is also an Adjunct Assistant Professor in Trinity College Dublin and an Advanced Nurse Practitioner in St Patrick's Mental Health Services, Dublin. Colman has a MSc in Child and Adolescent Psychoanalytical Psychotherapy and completed his Doctorate in Psychotherapy by researching the impact of social media on mental wellbeing. Colman is also the author of the book *Cop On*, which is a parenting guide for the technological age.

Trishna Patel is the Deputy Research Director on the Professional Doctorate in Clinical Psychology at the University of East London. She holds an honorary contract with North East London NHS Foundation Trust, where, in partnership with clinicians, she has set up a programme of research aimed at improving psychological health services to ensure that they foreground service user perspectives and maximise service user participation in terms of nature and frequency of care.

Neil Rees is a Consultant Clinical Psychologist and the Programme Director (Clinical) of the Professional Doctorate in Clinical Psychology at the University of East London. He also works in the NHS at the Child and Family Consultation Service in Newham, East London. Other activities include psycho-social emergency response overseas and dissemination activities relating to the experiences of people in the sexual minority (including contributing to the BPS guidelines for psychologists working with sexual and gender minority clients and being executive producer of the film *Homoworld*.

Rachel Smith works as a Clinical Psychologist in the NHS and a Clinical Tutor on the Professional Doctorate in Clinical Psychology at the University of East London. Within the NHS she has worked in a variety of forensic settings over the last ten years and has a particular interest in family therapy, service user involvement, recovery approaches and working to address social inequalities.

Julio Torales is Professor of Psychiatry and Medical Psychology, and Head of the Standards Department (Research Directorate) at National University of Asunción, School of Medical Sciences (Paraguay). Professor Torales is categorized as a Level 1 Researcher of the National Council of Science and Technology (Conacyt) of Paraguay. His areas of interest are psychodermatology, epidemiology of mental disorders, public mental health, health and human rights, medical education, research methodology, educational and curriculum theory, and teaching methods.

Premila Trivedi is a British Indian psychiatric service user who has personally experienced various forms of counselling and psychotherapy over the years, both within and outwith statutory health services. She pro-actively uses her 'lived experience' in her work as a writer and a trainer, focusing specifically on service user perspectives, in particular those of people from Black and ethnic minority communities.

Allan Winthrop is a Consultant Counselling Psychologist who divides his time between working as a Senior Partner in Independent Psychological Services LLP and as Lead Psychologist for an NHS Specialist Pain Management/Chronic Fatigue Service. Previously, for 13 years, he was Director of the Doctorate in Counselling Psychology and Clinical Director of the Psychological Therapies Clinic at Teesside University. As part of his role in Independent Psychological Services LLP he regularly undertakes work as an Expert Witness.

Acknowledgements

Rachel Tribe would like to dedicate this book to the memory of her mother, Prue Tribe, and her sister, Maureen Kenyon, both of whom sadly passed away in 2019. Their kindness, warmth, compassion, resourcefulness and good humour will be remembered by all those who knew them.

Jean Morrissey would like to dedicate this book to the memory of Roslyn Sharman, a colleague and friend who always made her laugh.

We would also like to thank all the clients, organisations, trainees and contributors who have stimulated our interest and challenged our thinking in new and diverse ways.

Part 1

Professional practice and ethical considerations

Chapter 1

Introduction

Rachel Tribe and Jean Morrissey

This 3rd edition of the *Handbook of Professional, Ethical and Research Practice for Psychologists, Counsellors, Psychotherapists and Psychiatrists*, has been updated and enhanced in line with developments in the external environment. Changes have been made that include new practice guidelines being issued by several professional organisations, the expanding role of social media and the latest research. Professional, ethical and research practice issues that are experienced in a fast changing and complex landscape are of concern to all practitioners and service users/experts by experience, regardless of the therapeutic or clinical context or the modality used. The need to be an effective, ethical and socially responsible practitioner is a central requirement of clinicians irrespective of their professional grouping. In an increasingly multifaceted and litigious environment, practitioners may face a range of perplexing demands and issues that can feel challenging, anxiety provoking and, on occasions, isolating. Preparation, knowledge, understanding and reflection are key to dealing with these professional and personal demands. It can feel difficult to keep abreast of all developments, be familiar with up to date research and any current policy changes taking place.

This book contains chapters written by counsellors, psychologists, psychotherapists and psychiatrists. New additions to the book include chapters detailing the new challenges for professional ethics and good practice guidelines, the possible adverse effects of therapy, conducting research in therapeutic practice settings, Continuing Professional Development (CPD), Social Justice and Community Psychology. The book has six sections these are; Professional and practice and ethical considerations, Legal considerations and responsibilities, Clinical considerations and responsibilities, Working with diversity: professional practice and ethical considerations, Research, supervision and training and Social inclusion. Each chapter contains a range of clinical vignettes to illustrate the points made as well as four reflective questions which can be considered by individuals, teams, supervision groups or in lectures, workshops and seminars. We hope that the handbook will provide guidance to practitioners whether they are very experienced clinicians, researchers or just starting out as trainees.

Significantly, the book starts with an important chapter which sets the tone for the book; this is written by a service user/expert by experience who reflects on her experience of using a range of therapeutic services. She also challenges the reader to consider how the voice of the service user is often not heard, is marginalised, or is considered in a tokenistic manner. Some of the issues raised are those which practitioners may ignore and/or fail to consider adequately. The author raises a number of seminal issues which, practitioners will find helpful to consider if they are to work with experts by experience effectively and ethically and to meet best practice guidelines.

Professional, ethical and research questions are often multi-dimensional and changes in the environment require continuous reflection and discussion with supervisors or consultation with guidelines. The latter is illustrated in the contributions from authors from the British Psychological Society and the United Kingdom Council for Psychotherapy, who reflect upon the development of new codes of professional and ethical practice which their organisations have recently published. For example, the British Psychological Society (BPS) updated their code of ethics and conduct in 2018 and their Practice Guidelines in 2017, the United Kingdom Council for Psychotherapy (UKCP) are currently undertaking a second consultation with their members on their draft Code of Ethics and Practice. In July, 2018 the British Association for Counselling and Psychotherapy launched a new version of their ethical framework, whilst the Royal College of Psychiatrists issued new guidance in 2017 on confidentiality and information-sharing. We invited the BACP to contribute to the chapter on guidelines, unfortunately the timing coincided with them undertaking a major reorganisation around their professional and ethical codes and therefore they had to decline this invitation.

Internationally, the American Counseling Association updated their guidance in 2015, whilst the Canadian Counselling and Psychotherapy Association updated their standards of practice in 2015. Changes in the environment are occurring on a global scale and professional, ethical and research practice requires ongoing attention to ensure best practice is followed and that service users requirements are foregrounded. The importance of the psychological contract is then discussed and how the psychological contract differs from an overt contract is reviewed. This refers to the hidden contract and contains the personal assumptions, expectations and presumptions that influence everyone, which underpin our clinical work, the relationships with the people that use our services as well as the relationships experts by experience have with clinicians. A psychological contract is also in operation in the relationship between individual clinicians and the organisations or clinics they work with. This chapter details the importance of actively considering these to ensure that ethical, professional and research practice guidelines are upheld.

The second section of the handbook on legal considerations and responsibilities, discusses issues relating to client confidentiality and data protection, with reference to legal and clinical requirements. The chapter also examines what is meant by the public interest, disclosures and access to information by the courts. It discusses why it is important for clinicians to be cognisant of statutory duties alongside clinical responsibilities. The chapter on the legal context of therapy details the legal parameters of clinical work generally and includes a description of the structure of the legal system and summarises negligence case, contract, statute, mental health and laws relating to children. A further chapter on Writing a report for use in court and appearing in court as a health professional or expert witness provides an introduction to medico-legal report writing. It also covers such issues as the different types of report that may be requested and discusses issues the practitioner needs to be cognisant of in advance of, during the writing of and in presenting the report and provides a possible template for a report and has a section on appearing in court.

In the third section of the handbook on clinical consideration and responsibilities, the chapter on complaints explores a number of the professional ethical issues associated with complaints including having a complaint made against you and the impact for the practitioner as well as triggers for complaints. The next chapter looks at the vital issue of the fitness of the clinician to practice. Issues relating to fitness to practice are complex, but are an important ethical and professional issue and one that many professionals will have to consider themselves or in their role as colleagues, students or supervisors at some points during their career, either when they may personally experience some of life's difficulties or when a colleague is giving cause for concern. This chapter looks at the associated challenges of definition, examines the related ethical and professional frameworks, and discusses common factors as well as issues of responsibilities and finally taking action. This is followed by the chapter on social media, which addresses the often overlooked issues relating to the role of social media in therapy. The role of social media in a therapeutic context requires consideration from many angles and is one area that is changing faster than many others. It is one that practitioners who are not so active in or conversant with recent developments in social media may ignore at their peril. The divisions between digital and non-digital therapy is becoming increasingly complex, with issues such as personal social media accounts, the storage of records and privacy, confidentiality and informed consent in social media use. The next chapter looks at the under researched issue of the possible adverse effects of therapy. It examines definitions of adverse effects before moving on to consider how these may be identified, understood and worked with. It also considers the strategies that can be used by practitioners to address adverse effects and the implications of being mindful of these to ensure that professional, ethical and research practice standards are upheld. It also provides some data showing how older adults are often not referred for therapy although when they do the results are good.

The fourth section of the handbook on working with diversity – professional, practice ethical and research consideration starts with a chapter on working with children and adolescents. This focuses on the issue of minors being legally positioned differently and how this may impact upon the thera-peutic relationship, the role of the clinician and the relationship of the clinician with the service users' families. It explores some of the complexities that may be connected with multiple agency work, specifically the issue of therapeutic disclosures and confidentiality when working with young people. Moving to the other end of the age range, the next chapter focuses on professional and ethical issues with older adults. The issues of ageism, stigma, service usage and age discrimination are discussed in relation to mental health and thera-peutic services offered. Practitioners are asked to question their own views and assumptions about older adults and therapy. There has frequently been a prevailing discourse that older adults will not benefit from talking therapies although evidence disproves this. A variety of links to guidelines and docu-ments are provided. The issue of elder abuse is foregrounded and the need for all practitioners to be mindful of this. An important chapter on working with lesbian, gay, bisexual and transgender people is also included. This chapter, like the previous one, asks the reader to reflect upon their own views and posi-tioning in relation to the client group being considered. It draws attention to the common humanity of all people as well as the diversity of the lesbian, gay, bisexual and transgender community/ies. It also explores the marginalisation that LGBT people face in the wider society and the potential impact of this on mental health and wellbeing. The final chapter in this section is on Profes-sional and ethical practice in a multicultural and multiethnic society and this examines the concept of culture and cultural competence. It draws on a range of national and international guidelines and explores racism and potential racist dynamics in the clinical relationship.

The fifth section in the handbook is on research, supervision training and Continuous Professional Development (CPD) and learning. The first chapter in this section is on research in therapeutic practice settings: ethical consider-ations and it reviews the reciprocal and often unrecognised but vital and inter-active relationship between research and practice in therapeutic training and all aspects of practice including service development and health related policy. It discusses how research and practice are often seen as separate which fails to account for the importance of each to the other and the informative and symbi-otic relationship they have. The chapter also details the importance of research in every aspect of clinical work. The chapter then reviews a range of ways to undertake research in organisations offering therapy and reviews some the practical, methodological and ethical challenges as well as the opportunities and possible important outcomes of undertaking this work. This is followed by a chapter on evidence based practice – the ethical dimension. This chapter deconstructs what is meant by evidence-based practice, it examines its epis-temological basis, its values and discusses the competing interests in evidence based practice. It then examines how applicable the evidence is, as well as considering how complete and unbiased the evidence base is. It reviews the ethical, professional and research issues at the micro, meso and macro levels and discusses the complex challenges involved in making the best use of resources when delivering the best care while not losing site of the multifaceted needs of individuals. The next chapter is on the issue of personal therapy for therapists, the chapter examines and comments upon the related ethical and professional issues. Some professional groupings view personal therapy as essential to the personal and professional training and the development of the practitioner, whilst a few do not see it as essential. This chapter looks at the evidence for and against and the differing rationales. It also examines accounts of personal therapy and also at the context and complexity of referrals and differences in professional trainings. The next chapter discusses teaching ethics for professional practice and will be an essential chapter for anyone teaching ethical, professional and research practice. This chapter briefly reviews the dominant professional ethical codes which are in existence in parts of Europe to show how professional ethical codes develop from specific contexts. The chapter links the personal and professional development of the trainee and considers how to measure programme requirements and outcomes in relation to ethics and ethical practice. The author argues that developing as an ethical professional is intrinsically interlinked with developing critical thinking, including reflective practice. It stresses the importance of thinking of the ethics implicit in all aspects of psychological, psychiatric and therapeutic knowledge and their practical applications rather than passively assuming everything is contained in an ethical code. The fifth section then includes a chapter on training supervision, which plays an integral part in the process of becoming a counsellor, psychologist or psychotherapist and a required contributory component of continuing professional development. Essentially an educative process, the role of supervision carries a responsibility to the needs of the client, supervisee and public as well as the profession. While the chapter focuses on training supervision, the complexity of such relationships and responsibilities as well as the power differential involved, including issues of confidentiality, competency, dual relationships and clinical accountability, which will be of relevance to qualified therapists either in their role of supervisor, supervisee or both. This is followed by a chapter, which details trainee perspectives' on professional and ethical issues. It explores the issues that a particular group of trainees viewed as important and which caused them concern. These issues included how to consider and integrate their own personal values with their professional role. It includes a variety of issues including being given gifts, whistle blowing, levels of competence and issues relating to personal and professional boundaries. The next chapter provides a range of really helpful clinical vignettes and reflective questions, which presents the reader with different professional and ethical issues. The material provides the reader with material to stimulate ongoing reflection, discussion and learning about the every-day professional and ethical challenges that may confront any trainee, clinician, supervisor and/or trainer within an ever-changing context. The final chapter in this section is on the issue of Continuing Professional Development (CPD). It examines how different organisations describe CPD and define its role. The CPD cycle is presented and discusses how CPD activities may be selected. The chapter identifies why CPD is important in ensuring that professional, ethical and research practice is of a high standard. It also examines the challenges and limitations associated with it, including measuring the impact on clinical practice.

The sixth section of the book is on social inclusion. The first chapter of this section is on social justice. The chapter looks at the term and what it is understood to mean. It then looks at social justice in practice and at the different potential levels of action and offers a range of suggestions in relation to this. It also discusses the therapeutic gaze, issues of accessibility and engagement, and importantly the practitioner's own position in relation to power. The final chapter in the section is on community psychology, a developing and important area of practice which also raises professional, ethical and research issues and where the focus is a little different. The chapter shows how community psychology provides a different understanding in comparison to the individual internalizing models more usually used by practitioners in high income countries and discusses how practitioners may consider these to ensure that they work ethically and are clear about their objectives.

Chapter 2

Service user involvement, ethics and power in therapy services

Premila Trivedi

After many years of campaigning by mental health service users[1] (Campbell, 2008) and recognition of its importance by policy makers and service providers (Department of Health (DOH) (2012, 1999); Thornicroft & Tansella, 2005), service user involvement is now a prominent feature in many areas of mental health. Service users (who might previously have been regarded as too ill to constructively critique services) are now acknowledged as having crucial experiential expertise that should be used to develop and improve services (NHS England, 2014). Service user involvement (while not without its issues (Ocloo & Matthews, 2016; Omeni et al., 2014) is now therefore considered to play a vital role in service development (Noorani, 2013; Omeni et al., 2014), with many services now moving to co-production, where power and decision-making is ostensibly shared by service users and providers as they work to bring together different types of knowledge and skills, based on their respective lived and professional experience (Boyle & Harris, 2009).

In psychology-specific services, the extent of service user involvement varies. For example, while service users are now involved in many professional training courses (Townend et al., 2008), an increasing number in research programmes (Hamilton et al., 2011; Morris, 2005; Shippee et al., 2015) and some in service and policy development (Hutchinson et al., 2012; Sheldon & Harding, 2010; Slade, 1994), there appears to be little direct evidence in the literature of user involvement in clinical settings. In one of the few references that was found (Healy & Boyd, 2012: 15), the authors clearly stressed the importance of user involvement and set 'a challenge to colleagues working in other psychotherapy service settings to seek to find the value for themselves in involving and listening to the views of service users'.

When I (as a mental health service user who has used various forms of counselling and therapy services) was invited by the editors of this book to contribute a chapter from a service user perspective, it seemed to be an ideal opportunity to flag up the lack of service user involvement in clinical therapy services and the potential benefits I believe this could bring. My aim here is therefore to raise awareness of these issues and promote open discussion and debate so that a way forward for user involvement may be found in clinical therapy just as it has in other areas of mental health (Omeni et al., 2014). Throughout this chapter, I will draw on my personal lived experience of using therapy services and of trying to promote user involvement in such services. Where relevant, I will also refer to my experience of user involvement in other areas of mental health (Trivedi, 2015, 2008, 1996; Trivedi & Wykes, 2002).

Putting personal experience into context

The central tenet of service user involvement is the concept of 'lived experience, based on two principles' (Bland & Tullgren, 2015: 43):

- That a focus on lived experience acknowledges the service user as expert in their own mental health problems/illness.
- That 'lived experience' is the service user's own view of their mental health from the inside looking out and focuses on how their mental health affect their life as a whole and how to best manage this. In contrast, 'mental illness' is mostly seen as a set of symptoms, which clinicians from the outside look in on in order to assess, diagnose and then correct.

As a long-term mental health service user with lived experience, I like many others, have always highly valued 'talking therapies' (McHugh et al., 2013) as a way of making sense of my experiences and managing the ups and downs of my life. I therefore fought hard over the years for access to counselling and therapy and was lucky enough to have been referred (or self-referred) to various forms of therapy at different times, both within statutory, voluntary and private sector services. All seemed to serve a function for me at the time, but looking back realistically, I feel I very rarely found the precious therapeutic space I was really looking for. It was not until I eventually found more flexible and collaborative therapy that I began to realise how constrained I had felt within the often rigid systems of therapy I found myself in. Trying to figure this out, I have concluded that this could have been because of:

- **Me**: I have been told more than once that my frustration with therapy has ultimately been down to me and because of my inability to use therapy appropriately, my unrealistic expectations, my intransigence and my lack of appreciation of the therapy I was being given. I freely admit I am not an easy person to work with and I have no doubt that some of this is true, but the fact that I did eventually find very enabling therapy and made real progress makes me wonder if there was also something else going on that made therapeutic progress so elusive for me.
- **The therapist**: I knew I didn't want to blame individual therapists because (mostly) they seemed very well-meaning and sincere in their desire to help, and several stuck with me through some very challenging times. But

often that wasn't enough to get me to really open up to them or truly feel safe in the therapy room.

- **The systems and structures within which therapists' work**: these seemed to so often be rigid and almost authoritarian and sometimes left me wondering if therapy services were more about upholding their professional status in order to prove their credibility, rather than responding to us service users as unique beings, each in our own cultural social and political context. Too often it felt like I was in a mad-making system, where you were led to believe that the focus was on you as an individual but then attempts were made to fit you into the structure of the system. For those who *can* fit in, counselling and therapy can no doubt be hugely beneficial. But maybe that was why I was so often frustrated, because in therapy just as in life, I (as a British Asian with very confusing cross-cultural issues) somehow couldn't make myself fit into others' expected norms.

Also, just as in real life, it seemed impossible to share my feelings of frustration and confusion with most of the therapists I encountered. Too often, I ended up feeling guilty about my lack of progress in therapy and even a total failure. Me trying to blame my therapist or 'services' for this would only be seen as further evidence of my pathological destructiveness and sabotaging of those trying to help me.

Maddeningly though, during the same period of time, I was finding that in other areas of mental health, services (e.g. in acute care) were taking up user involvement and proactively seeking open communication and feedback from service users. In response to this, and crucially as part of a supportive user group, I found myself working on many service user initiatives over the years focusing on clinical services, research and training of mental health professionals (Trivedi, 2008, 1996; Trivedi & Wykes, 2002). However, in terms of 'talking therapies', I was struck by how rarely service user involvement seemed to come up. I myself was reluctant at first to bring this up in our user group, because those of us in therapy were always considered by our peers to be very privileged, so it never felt right to raise issues about therapy services when other's issues re restraint or forced medication seemed so much more important. Furthermore, therapy always seemed to me to be a bit of a secret enterprise, carried out in the often sealed box of the therapy room and should not be discussed outside those confines. On reflection, I wonder if the feeling of such secret-ness is, at least in part, an ethical issue, especially when combined with the imbalance of power relations inherent in therapy.

Therapy, ethics and service user involvement

While counselling and therapy can undoubtedly be very beneficial to service users, professional bodies and therapy services have acknowledged that there may also be potential risks in these treatments and have established the crucial need for ethical codes of conduct (Crawford et al., 2016). Ethical codes, with their general principles of autonomy, beneficence, non-maleficence and distributive justice, are essentially about preventing harm to service users, harm that could occur because of the private nature of therapy and the inevitable imbalance of power between therapists and service users. When assessing adherence to ethical codes, it is obvious that service users themselves are in the most authentic position to provide feedback on this, most usefully within a user involvement framework. As Dr Alison Faulkner, a much-respected service user/survivor activist and researcher in mental health, has stated

> The very nature of psychotherapy (e.g. it is a private enterprise and non-explicit) means that it is vital to hear the views of the patient/client about what they think is going on, what they value or do not value if we want to demonstrate the efficacy of psychotherapy and improve its provision.
>
> (Faulkner, 2004)

If assessment of ethics is carried out purely by service providers, there are chances that important grass-roots issues may be missed. As Healy and Boyd state (2012: 27) 'Service users can often see the obvious in situations where professionals can only see what they expect to see. We suggest that it is always in the interests of patients and therapists to be aware of the obvious in life'.

Involving service users in monitoring and evaluating ethics and then working together with them to improve ethical practice would, undoubtedly, be beneficial to therapy services (Dierckx de Casterlé et al., 2011). But how often do we see these services proactively seeking out the voices of service users, encouraging and enabling them *to honestly speak for themselves* regarding their experience of therapy and any ethical concerns they might have? How often do services acknowledge the experiential expertise of their service users and try to redress power imbalances by giving them the authority to help improve clinical practice and develop services that more appropriately meet the needs of the service users they are there to serve? And how often do service users in therapy feel valued as rational human beings, capable of being objective and constructively critical about the services they have received, just as they are encouraged to do during user involvement in other areas of mental health?

The lack of user involvement in clinical therapy services

As Millar and colleagues (2015: 216) point out,

> user involvement: an active partnership between service users and mental health professionals in decision making regarding the planning, implementation and evaluation of mental health policy, services, education, training

and research, employs a person-centred approach, with bidirectional infor-mation flow, power sharing and access to advocacy at a personal, service and/or societal level.

While service user involvement has become commonplace in many mental health services and many professional bodies have developed clear user involvement policies, in clinical therapy services, user involvement seems to be much less established. Professional bodies such as BACP and UKCP do not have user involvement policies and while a search of the literature did find some reference to user involvement (Healy & Boyd, 2012), these were very sparse. Furthermore, service users who have tried to raise the issue of service user involvement in these services have reported their attempts often being met with indifference or frank resistance (personal communication, 2018). Often service providers respond to these users by saying that they already take account of their service user views, e.g. when collecting and using client feed-back at the end of periods of therapy. However, it needs to be appreciated that feedback (collected from individual service users on the service provider's terms generally at a single point in time) may be very different to the views and ideas developed in user involvement settings.

In these settings, time and space is ideally built in for service users to come together to share their experiences, check them out with their peers, reflect on them over a period of time and then collectively come up with creative ideas as to how practice could be improved. In many ways this process could be said to be similar to reflective practice in professional peer supervision sessions, which services value highly. However, how often are we users of therapy services enabled to experience such 'peer supervision' and are explicitly given the author-ity to contribute directly and meaningfully to service development? On the rare occasions when service users have directly been involved, e.g. as researchers in the evaluation of therapy services, the outcomes have been very positive, with services learning, through the process, how best to use service user experience and skills to improve service (Morris, 2005). So why don't therapy services appear to take advantage of this more? And why, in my experience, do they try to stop us in our tracks when we try to raise the importance of user involvement?

The challenge of getting our voice heard

As someone who has long been involved in user involvement in other areas of mental health, I wonder if the way therapy services seem to respond to calls for user involvement are particularly resistant or harsh. Variously, service users have been told (personal communication) that:

- Since therapy is based on the complexity and sometimes messiness of human relationships, it would be very hard to disentangle a clear service user voice that could dispassionately comment on therapy services.

- Criticisms of therapy often come from users' misperceiving people and situations and/or those with an 'axe to grind' and may therefore say more about their psychological deficits than the reality of their therapeutic experience.
- Service users' views are likely to be part of a transference that can persist long after therapy has ended, implying that users are trapped in some sort of psychological phenomena that prevents them ever being 'real' human beings capable of coherent and dispassionate thought.
- Service users may be too vulnerable to participate in user involvement activities, thus negating their right to reflect and discuss their therapy out with the safety (closed box) of the therapy room.
- Therapy services do not require user involvement since most therapists go through their own grass-roots experience of therapy and their knowledge of this lived experience automatically gets built in when they contribute to the development of services and practices. But is this lived experience, undergone in the context of professional knowledge and understanding of how therapy is meant to work, really the same as 'lay' lived experience, where the absence of knowledge and understanding can alert us to issues which may come to be taken for granted by professionals as a result of intense training and CPD. The value of this does not seem to be recognized and, in fact, our voices and views are often dismissed primarily because we do not know enough about therapy systems and practice.
- Perhaps most galling of all, that users should be grateful that they got access to precious talking therapies on the NHS, rather than questioning the process, models or therapists involved.

Responses such as these and a resistance to user involvement can create, for service users, a mad-making situation where (while we may feel that therapy has really helped us move on and be more in control of our lives) we are denied the opportunity to ever be in an autonomous, adult relationship with services or have a constructively critical view on the input we have received. I have no doubt some of the above arguments against involving service users hold true, but I cannot believe that a discipline as intellectually and psychologically able as therapy cannot find a way to overcome or work meaningfully in user involvement with service users. Other mental health services, such as forensic services, have had to face equally (albeit different) challenges to harness the experiential expertise of their service users, so surely this can be done in therapy too? Maybe what is needed is a change in attitude and culture with regard to service users and the possibility of creating a shift in power relations if user involvement is to become a reality and fulfil its potential?

Power in therapy and user involvement settings

Power is a key issue in both psychotherapy services and in user involvement, yet rarely seems to be explicitly discussed in clinical settings, maybe because power tends to be viewed as an uncomfortable concept, a structural, monolithic force that rests in the hands of the service and considered to be necessarily negative for the service user. Gillian Proctor in her excellent book *The Dynamics of Power in Counselling and Psychotherapy* (Proctor, 2002) proposes a rather more hopeful view of power. While she stresses the importance of acknowledging power and the inescapability of imbalanced power relations between service providers and service users in clinical therapy settings, she describes a much more flexible concept of power, where power is not seen as a static thing but rather as dynamic and being 'present in the relationship rather than being in the possession of one person, bi-directional, may be influenced by outside factors, and can be potentially negative or positive' (Proctor, 2002: 136). Proctor goes on to suggest there are different forms of power, i.e. power-over (which is coercive and negative and can be used quickly without too much thought or expertise) and power-with (which is collaborative, positive and productive, but requiring more time, skill and sensitivity). This reminds me very much of how power has been used when I have tried to advocate for service user involvement in therapy settings, e.g. a power-over response by services when they claim that service users' views would not be credible because of transference, etc. I now realise how, this in turn, resulted in me attempting to resist such power-over by withdrawing and refusing to engage further (or become intransigent as they would call it).

This is also very resonant of how I have often been in clinical settings when experiencing power-over (Trivedi, 2015), e.g. when my therapist repeatedly interpreted something in a completely un-understanding way and seemed more wedded to fitting me into their theoretical therapy model rather than seeing me as me in my cultural context. In this and many other examples, I tended to respond in negative (for me) ways, which I now see could be a way of my resisting the therapist's power-over, e.g. by withdrawing completely or adopting a false (more understandable to the therapist) cultural self. Responding in this clearly negative way became rather a pattern for me, and it was not until I experienced power being used in a different, more positive power-with form that I realised I suddenly didn't have to resort to my sometimes rather pathetic attempts at resistance to my therapist's power-over. Up to then, I think I had come to believe that power-over was the norm in therapy, but now the situation felt very different; power distribution was still very imbalanced but the way in which power was being used was very different and resulted in a much more positive relationship and outcome.

Another aspect of Proctor's concept of power is the way she describes power as not only the authority arising from the roles of the therapist and service user (role power) but also as societal and historical power. The former arises from one's structural position in society (e.g. because of class, gender, ethnicity, age, education, etc.) and the latter from one's personal history (with respect to experiences of power, oppression and powerlessness). In my personal therapy, I usually knew very little about the societal or historical position of my therapist, though I often could deduce something from, e.g. their personal demeanour, appearance, accent, attitudes and the organization they had chosen to work in. Being aware of such societal power could perhaps explain why I had fared better clinically with particular therapists than with others, e.g. because of class, ethnic or political similarities. However, my experiences were never quite as clear cut as that, because there was definitely one occasion when there was a very marked difference in societal power between myself and my therapist, yet I would count him among the best therapists I have ever encountered. Similarly, in user involvement, I often felt uncomfortable with service managers who tended to be white, super-confident and middle class. Yet, one of the most positive experiences I have had was of working as part of a vociferous Black user group with a White service manager who worked very collaboratively with us by using power-with to bring about real improvements on a particular acute ward.

Clearly, then, the way in which power and power relations can impact on relationships (whether in therapy or user involvement settings) is complex (Proctor, 2002; Zur, 2014). In user involvement, I know from other areas of mental health, that for involvement to develop productively, the power differential between service providers and service users and the way power is used must be able to change when moving from the clinical into the user involvement setting. In the best situations (e.g. in co-production), role power should become more equal (with service users being given the authority to make decisions and work equitably with service providers to improve services) and used by both parties in a power-with way if desired outcomes are to be achieved. Developing this sort of change in power relations between clinical and involvement settings is not easy. In counselling and therapy services, where the clinical therapeutic relationship (with its inevitable power imbalance) can seem to become almost sacred, I wonder if there is a tendency for this to spill over into user involvement situations and/or a reluctance for services to adopt a more equally balanced power relationship? So how could such change be enabled to happen and how could therapy services and service users work equitably to bring together lived and professional experience in synergistic ways.

Developing a change in power relationships in clinical settings through user involvement

Using Proctor's concept of power could be useful in this respect by identifying issues that need addressing, considering what type of power is operating in the situation and how it is being used, aiming to maximise power-with (collaboration) and minimise power-over (coercion). Table 2.1 gives some examples of how this might work; all the examples given are very simple, but often in clinical and user involvement settings this is what the issues are often like; small things that can build up cumulatively to have an ultimately detrimental effect

Table 2.1 Examples of some of the issues flagged up during a user involvement exercise to identify and address users' issues in clinical settings

Stage	Issue: therapist using power-over	Impact on service user	Address by: therapists using power-with
Following referral	• Therapist gives no indication as to what they already know about service user.	• Can become suspicious of what has/has not been said about them, leading to feeling that others have inside knowledge of them that cannot/must not be shared. • Confusion as to where or how to proceed.	• Therapist shares referral letter/notes with service user (having informed referrer they will do this. • Is prepared to discuss any issues that may arise. • Allows service user make informed choice as to where they want to begin.
At assessment	• Assessment is very structured.	• May feel assessment is like an exam that they must pass in order to gain access to precious/hard won therapy. • May adopt a 'false self' in order to 'pass' and feel compelled to 'play the game'.	• Ensures assessment is user-friendly AND assessment made in range of ways as appropriate for particular service user.
During therapy	• Not acknowledging or saying hello when collecting service user for session. • Never using their name within session.	• May feel non-existent/invalidated when outside the therapy room, like a dog just being expected to follow its master. • May feel not recognized as them within the session.	• Acknowledges service user and greets warmly. • Make effort to use person's pre-ferred name (when appropriate).

(Continued)

Table 2.1 (Cont.)

Stage	Issue: therapist using power-over	Impact on service user	Address by: therapists using power-with
During therapy	• Chastising service user for breaking rules of therapy, even though these have never been made explicit, e.g. service user emailing between sessions.	• May feel sense of unfairness, being treated like a child. • May feel angry because rules never explained. in first place. • issue turns from user needing to share something to user being reprimanded.	• Makes sure rules are clear from the start. • Ensures rules are not so rigid that service user can't express themselves in their own preferred way. • Doesn't lose the point of why rule was broken.
During therapy	• Remaining very silent even when service user says this makes them feel very uncomfortable.	• May feel trapped, very uncomfortable, confused as to what silence means, e.g. indifference, boredom, anger. • Not knowing if they are being genuinely heard, especially after plucking up courage to say how silence makes them feel.	• Is aware of person in front of them rather than rigidly sticking to the rules of your therapy model (especially at the beginning). • Explains purpose of silence and don't insist on this if service user clearly finds this intolerable.
During therapy	• Thinking they have adequate cultural awareness and knowledge and not able or willing to ask for specific information that applies to service user. • Unclear how to respond to user raising issues of racism, moves on to other issues.	• May feel no point in bringing up race/culture issues if therapist clearly doesn't 'get it' and makes no effort to clarify. • May feel any mention of racism is not taken seriously, detects uncomfortableness in therapist and thinks they should keep off this topic.	• Asks if they don't understand cultural issues – it can be empowering for service user to teach you something about their specific context. • Doesn't just make assumptions or stereotype. • Responds explicitly and without embarrassment to issues of racism.

At ending	• Insists that service user must be angry regarding ending, allowing no real space to explore any other feelings or reflections.	• Angry at being told how they must be feeling. • Frustrated as any talk of ending leads to an assumption of anger. • No opportunity to talk about other equally important feelings.	• Is open to range of feelings at ending.
At ending	• Gives no or very little feedback as to what progress has been made.	• Angry and sense of unreality at not knowing how therapist feels therapy has gone. • Feeling unsure as to what has been achieved through therapy. • Secrecy raising its head again.	• Gives service user full copy of report/review. • Is open to discussing it, after service user has had an opportunity to reflect. • Provides opportunity for service user to feed-back 3–6 months later.

on therapy and the therapeutic relationship. It is often only when one genuinely experiences power-with (as I have been fortunate enough to do) that one realises the impact power-over can have.

Conclusion

In this chapter, I have used the opportunity of writing as a service user to consider the importance of user involvement in counselling and therapy services if such services are to maintain high ethical standards and become more appropriate and relevant to the populations they are there to serve. In making my plea for more user involvement in therapy services, I acknowledge that this is not necessarily going to be easy and challenges will exist. But I am trying to keep confidence in therapy services and hope that they will be able to work collaboratively with service users to find a way round the issues and make user involvement a practical reality.

Acknowledgements

I would like to thank all those who have encouraged and supported me to write about user involvement in therapy services, in particular Alison Faulkner, Angela Sweeney and Catherine Jackson. Also to Gillian Proctor, for helping me be clearer about the complexity of power dynamics in clinical settings. Finally, to the editors of this book for giving me this valuable opportunity and working with me so patiently throughout the sometimes painful process of putting this chapter together.

Reflective questions

1. How could you use your power more positively at different stages in your service, e.g. referral, assessment, therapeutic interaction, ending, evaluation?
2. In what ways do you currently collect feedback on your service delivery, i.e. who is involved, how and when do you collect feedback and how do you (both as an individual and a service) practically use this?
3. Would you personally be prepared to adapt your clinical practice to meet the expressed needs of your service users (i.e. as expressed by them) and so enable user involvement to develop?
4. How might you facilitate/support people who use your service feel able to give you authentic feedback about their treatment/therapy?

Note

1   In mental health, different terms are often used to describe the same thing, with each term communicating different values and political perspectives, e.g. those on the receiving end of services may refer to themselves as service users, clients, consumers, survivors, resistors (McLaughlin, 2009). In user involvement, terms such as user participation, partnership working, or co-production are often used. In this chapter, I have chosen to use the commonly used terms 'service user' and 'user involvement' since here I am talking largely in the context of professional services where these terms are still most commonly used.

References

Bland, R., & Tullgren, A. (2015) Lived experience of mental illness. In J. Fitzgerald, & G. Byrne (Eds). *Psychosocial Dimensions in Medicine*. Melbourne, Australia: (IP Communications), pp. 43–56.

Boyle, D., & Harris, M. (2009) *The Challenge of Co-Production*. London: New Economics Foundation.

Campbell, P. (2008) Service user involvement. In P.L. Theo Stickley, & T. Basset (Eds). *Learning About Mental Health Practice*. London: Wiley. pp. 291–310.

Crawford, M.J., Thana, L., Farquharson, L., Palmer, L., Hancock, E., Bassett, P., Clarke, J., & Parry, G.D. (2016) Patient experience of negative effects of psychological treatment: Results of a national survey. *The British Journal of Psychiatry*, 208(3), 260–265.

Department of Health. (1999) *National Service Framework for Mental Health*. London: HMSO.

Department of Health. (2012) *Health and Social Care Act 2012 (incl. fact sheets)*. London: HMSO.

Dierckx de Casterlé, B., Verhaeghe, S.T., Kars, M.C., Coolbrandt, A., Stevens, M., Stubbe, M., Deweirdt, N., Vincke, J., & Grypdonck, M. (2011) Researching lived experience in health care: Significance for care ethics. *Nursing Ethics*, 18(2), 232–242.

Faulkner, A. (2004) Challenging the orthodoxy: Genuine user involvement in psychotherapy research, *Part of Conference Workshop on Consumer Perspectives at The 35th Annual Meeting of the Society for Psychotherapy Research*, Rome.

Hamilton, S., Hicks, A., Sayers, R., Faulkner, A., Larsen, J., Patterson, S., & Pinfold, V. (2011) *A User-Focused Evaluation of IAPT Services in London*. London, UK: Report for Commissioning Support for London, Rethink March 2011.

Healy, K., & Boyd, C. (2012) Seeking and using service user input to improve clinical services. *Group Analysis*, 45(1), 15–27.

Hutchinson, A., Atkinson, P., Bellanger-Jones, C., Clemson, H., Chadwick, P., Colerick, G., & Richards, M. (2012) Involving service users' stories in developing mental health services: The process of capturing, enabling and supporting service users' expertise and experiences. *FoNS Improvement Insights*, 8(9), 1–82.

McLaughlin, H. (2009) What's in a name: 'Client', 'patient', 'customer', 'consumer', 'expert by experience', 'service user' – what's next? *The British Journal of Social Work*, 39(6), 1101–1117.

McHugh, R.K., Whitton, S.W., Peckham, A.D., Welge, J.A., & Otto, M.W. (2013) Patient preference for psychological vs. pharmacological treatment of psychiatric disorders: A meta-analytic review. *The Journal of Clinical Psychiatry*, 74(6), 595–602.

Millar, S.L., Chambers, M., & Giles, M. (2015) Service user involvement in mental health care: An evolutionary concept analysis. *Health Expectations*, 19, 209–221.

Morris, B. (2005) *Discovering Bits and Pieces of Me: Women's Experiences of Psychoanalytical Psychotherapy*. London: Women's Therapy Centre.

National Health Service (NHS) England. (2014) Five *Year Forward Plan*. London: HMSO.

Noorani, T. (2013) Service user involvement, authority and the 'expert-by-experience' in mental health. *Journal of Political Power*, 6(1), 49–68.

Ocloo, J., & Matthews, R. (2016) From tokenism to empowerment: Progressing patient and public involvement in healthcare improvement. *BMJ Quality Safety*, 25, 626–632.

Omeni, E., Barnes, M., MacDonald, D., Crawford, M., & Rose, D. (2014) Service user involvement: Impact and participation: A survey of service user and staff perspectives. *BMC Health Services Research*, 14(1), 491.

Proctor, G. (2002) *The Dynamics of Power in Counselling and Psychotherapy: Ethics, Politics and Practice*. Ross-on-Wye: PCCS Books.

Sheldon, K., & Harding, E. (2010) *Good Practice Guidelines to support the involvement of Service Users and Carers in Clinical Psychology Services*. Leicester, UK: BPS.

Shippee, N.D., Domecq Garces, J.P., Prutsky Lopez, G.J., Wang, Z., Elraiyah, T.A., Nabhan, M., Brito, J.P., Boehmer, K., Hasan, R., Firwana, B., & Erwin, P.J. (2015) Patient and service user engagement in research: A systematic review and synthesized framework. *Health Expectations*, 18(5), 1151–1166.

Slade, M. (1994) Needs assessment: Involvement of staff and users will help to meet needs. *The British Journal of Psychiatry*, 165(3), 293–296.

Thornicroft, G., & Tansella, M. (2005) Growing recognition of the importance of service user involvement in mental health service planning and evaluation. *Epidemiol Psichiatr Soc*, 14(1), 1–3.

Townend, M., Tew, J., Grant, A., & Repper, J. (2008) Involvement of service users in education and training: A review of the literature and exploration of the implications for the education and training of psychological therapists. *Journal of Mental Health*, 17 (1), 65–78.

Trivedi, P. (1996) Partners not Adversaries. *Nursing Times*, 92(21), 59–60.

Trivedi, P., & Wykes, T. (2002) From passive subjects to equal partners - user involvement in research. *British Journal of Psychiatry*, 181, 468–472.

Trivedi, P. (2008) Black user involvement – rhetoric or reality? In S. Fernando, & F. Keating (Eds.). *Mental Health in a Multi-Ethnic Society*, 2nd edition. London: Routledge. pp. 136–147.

Trivedi, P. (2015) Who holds the power? *Therapy Today*, 26(5), 4–5.

Zur, O., (2014) Re-thinking the 'power differential' myth and exploring the moral, ethical, professional, and clinical issues of power in therapy. *Power in psychotherapy and counselling. The Zur Institute* Available at: www.zurinstitute.com/power_in_therapy.html

Chapter 3

Psychological contracts

Hidden agreements in life and at work

Michael Carroll and Rachel Tribe

This chapter will review what is meant by the term the psychological contract. It will critically evaluate how these contracts can influence our personal relationships and expectations, as well as our interactions with clients/service users/experts by experience, as well as, our relationships with organisations and employers and vice versa. The term psychological contract refers to the covert and usually unspoken and unwritten assumptions, beliefs, expectations and presumptions that influence and pervade all relationships (George, 2009). It is seen as so important by the Chartered Institute for Personnel Development, that in 2018 they issued guidance on the psychological contract. On an individual level the psychological contract belongs to our inner beliefs, which often remains buried in our unconscious. They also reside in the collective memories, expectations and culture of families and organisations: they are silent, hidden, powerful inherited influences on attitudes and behaviours.

With regard to organisations,

> On its own, the legal contract of employment offers a limited representation of the employment relationship, with workers contributing little to its terms beyond accepting them. In this sense, the psychological contract may be more influential as it describes the perceptions of the relationship between employers and workers and influences how people behave from day to day. At its core, the psychological contract is built on the everyday actions and statements made by one party – and how they are perceived and interpreted by the other. It's intangible by nature, unlike the legal contract of employment signed by employers and workers.
>
> (Chartered Institute of Personnel Development, 2018: 1)

Often, unaware of their existence, we don't notice how our beliefs about the psychological contract leak into our view of the world and how they can cause problems or misunderstandings in our personal relationships or our relationship with our employer (Payne et al., 2014). We are usually unaware of where they come from and who is responsible for them. Our internalised psychological contracts often lead us to blame others for things they are unaware of, and did not agree to (Rodwell & Gulyas, 2013). Griep et al. (2018) claim that counter-productive work behaviour may be brought about in some situations by what people perceive as a psychological contract breach and feelings of abuse. For example, in the work context, annual leave entitlement is written into employment contracts, but this ignores the psychological contract, to which people often pay more attention. The psychological contract consists of the unwritten rules that are created by employers relating to, those things which we feel to be expected in our workplace. Knight (2018) refers to a study conducted by British Airways in 2017, they surveyed 2,000 people and found that one-third of people employed in Britain did not take all their annual leave in the preceding year, giving their employers four free days of their time in that year. It appears that the prevailing psychological contract and organisational culture contained a view about holiday entitlement; this was absorbed by workers, who felt unable to take all their holiday entitlement despite being authorised to take it. 16% of participants reported that they felt guilty for using all their holiday allowance and others reported that they were too busy.

Vignette I

Scott works as an administrator in a busy Improving Access to Psychological Therapies (IAPT) service. His contract states that he begins work at 8.30 and finishes at 4.15. Faced with the morning rush of getting his children to school for 8.15 and then catching the train to work has proved complicated. He begins coming into work for a 9.00 start; and when no one objects, moves his start time again to 9.15, before finally settling on 9.30, this reduces his stress levels and solves all his domestic and travel difficulties. Being a conscientious employee, he works an extra 30 minutes at lunch time, and a further 30 minutes at the end of the day. His boss, a good natured and conflict avoidant person, allows this ad hoc solution to continue for four months. Since no one has objected to his new timetable arrangements Scott assumes that all is fine. The other administrator in the service assumes Stuart has worked out a new start/finish time with his boss, and his boss assumes his old contract is still in place – with this as a temporary arrangement to deal with a temporary problem. The new arrangement does not appear to be causing any issues for anyone. All is well until a new manager is appointed who challenges Scott about his timekeeping. This results in Scott taking out a complaint of bullying and harassment against his new boss.

This fictitious case study illustrates some of the negative impacts of a psychological contract. Scott has, in effect, created a psychological contract with his employer; with nothing written down, negotiated, discussed or agreed he believes he can reset his start and finish times at work as long as he can fulfil his contracted hours of work and no one disagrees. Unaware that he has created a new contract (psychological though it is), he has not noticed how binding he has made this contract on others. His new boss, unwittingly, breaks the psychological contract by enforcing the original, legal contract. Scott plunges into all the feelings and reactions that come when people feel a contract has been broken (in any area of their life) – disappointment, rejection, abandonment and injustice. It could be argued that the organisation has colluded with Scott's psychological contract by not challenging or clarifying his behaviour earlier. Probably both parties are to blame for the unfortunate state of affairs that eventually sours all the relationships involved. In the mediation that follows Scott, his co-workers and his new manager all come to understand how psychological contracts work. This insight allows them to come to new, open, clearly negotiated arrangements with which they are all happy.

The example of Scott might lead us to think that psychological contracts are only individual creations, this is not the case. Psychological contracts are also co-created (between two or more people) and organisationally (or family) designed and enacted (Mai et al., 2016; Zhao et al., 2007).

Vignette 2

Humanitarian incorporated is an international firm working around the world. They have a standard written contract with their employees that the normal working week is 35 hours. Staff know, however, that working 35 hours alone is totally inadequate for undertaking this work adequately or for progression in the organisation. This is not written down anywhere, but is known by all. Most people entered the organisation as they wanted to be of service to others. Humanitarian Incorporated is a mass of psychological contracts. These are 'held' in the ethos and culture of the organisation rather than captured in contracts and written policies.

Most organisations have psychological contracts with their employees (Conway et al, 2007). These are often non-negotiable aspects of the culture and may be summarised as the unwritten rules of the work place (George, 2009). Such an environment is full of psychological messages about what is expected (Lee et al., 2011). The psychological contract was known to all staff at Humanitarian Incorporated; those who choose to ignore it found themselves labelled as not committed or not really fitting in with the ethos of the organisation.

- What are some of the components of the psychological contract in operation where you work?

The roots of psychological contracts

Psychological contracts are developed early in life and weave their way subtly into all relationships. From an early age, children create sets of untested assumptions (sometimes called beliefs, myths or schemas), which direct their way of being in the world. We can define these beliefs as systems of beliefs that determine, and are determined by, feelings and behaviours. These attitudes or assumptions are generally unexpressed directly and run beneath the surfaces of life and consciousness. They are sets of untested assumptions that develop outside of awareness but which greatly impact upon relationships, interactions, roles and patterns in the family. Therapy often starts by bringing these assumptions to the surface to break their invisible hold over the family dynamics.

Children usually see their caretakers as all-powerful, nurturing and available. From these foundations it is not unusual for children to create psychological formulae in regard to their parents, for example:

- My parents will never die
- My parents will be around to meet all my needs
- Their explanations of my life's complexities are correct.

Building a life on such foundations, unconscious and unspoken as they are, inevitably results in problems, for example, when a parent dies. In addition to all the normal grief there can be a deep sense of anger, abandonment, rejection, betrayal and aloneness (Worden, 2002). From this basis in early childhood other psychological contracts emerge; hidden, inherited and powerful. Formed in the early relationships of the family, they become powerful unquestioned anchors in life, in relationships and at work.

Individuals will hold different types of assumptions developed through their familial upbringing resulting in both complementary and conflicting psychological contracts that impact relationships profoundly. Life stages can also create new assumptions; teenagers often assume that they have a sort of psychological deal with life that brings immunity from the consequences of actions. All of these psychological contracts shape our lives and our view of life (George, 2009).

Vignette 3

Shamil is furious. Angry tears stream down his face. How could they do this to me after all I have given them? I gave them the best 10 years of my life! I was in the office every morning at 7.30 am, never once left before 7.30 in the evening ... I lost the best year of my children's lives ... and now, now they do this to me?'

Shamil has been made redundant as Managing Director with a large bank. 'Clearly, they were poor employers,' I say, 'they didn't treat you well and they didn't give you the redundancy package you deserve'.

'Not at all!' Shamil interrupts. 'They were terrific employers.'

'Why are you so angry then?' I probe. As we work with the anger Shamil comes to realise, slowly, that his negative feelings are not because the company broke its contracts or treated its employees poorly. I will always remember Shamil's words; 'I will never get into that kind of relationship with an organisation again.' Shamil has discovered the power of the psychological contract. He is angry and betrayed, not because the company has broken its contract with him or treated him badly, but because he has worked out a psychological contract with them (albeit one they knew nothing about) that the bank would not make him redundant if he was conscientious and dedicated. Shamil had unwittingly recreated an old psychological contract that went back to his childhood – that if he pleases his parents, and goes that extra mile, they will never leave him.

Contracts

Contracts (overt and covert) underpin all relationships; one-to-one, team and organisational. They contain the agreements, conscious and unconscious, and the rules and procedures that guide all of the parties. Overall, contracts revolve around:

- 'exchange' (we do things *for* each other)
- 'reciprocity' (*two-way* arrangements)
- 'choice' (we *freely* enter this arrangement)
- 'predictability' (we have some *guarantees* that this will happen)
- 'future' (we *will* do)
- 'responsibility' (I will be responsible for X if you take accountability for Y).

While overt contracts attempt to articulate these elements, either verbally or in written form, words and gestures are always open to interpretation. *It is because of this openness to interpretation that the psychological contract is part of all contracts.* Individuals bring to their contracts and agreements their own assumptions, beliefs and expectations, most of which will be unspoken and un-negotiated, (Robinson & Rousseau, 1994). This part of contracts is called the 'psychological contract', the subjective side that contains our hidden agendas in respect to the covert contract (Rousseau, 1995).

The psychological contract

Psychological contracts are much more prevalent than overt, articulated, negotiated or agreed contracts. In our minds we work out an agreement with another person, a team or an organisation and thereafter it has all the emotional force of a binding agreement. Rousseau and Schalk (2000) define the psychological contract as 'an *individual's interpretation* of an exchange of promises that is mutually agreed on and voluntarily made between two or more parties.' (p. 284). There is usually a psychological contract in place when you hear such phrases as ... 'But I had expected you to ... I thought we would ... I understood it to mean that ... I hoped ... anyone can see this is what should be done ... I believed that ... I assumed ... .' When a person or an organisation does not keep the promises I have made on their behalf it results in more pain and distress than if they had broken an actual contract. Sills (2006) points out that failed or discontinued treatment in counselling is largely caused by a difference in expectations between participants i.e., differences in the understanding of the psychological contract.

Ordinary, everyday relationships can be filled with unspoken psychological contracts. These are often revealed by the assumptions on which they are based.

When Jane married John she assumed:

*   They would have children
*   They would spend their free time together
*   His mother would eventually come to accept her
*   They would share the chores around the house
*   John would learn to cook.

It came as quite a surprise for her to learn that John had other assumptions:

*   That Jane would do the cooking and the house chores (as his mother had)
*   That he wouldn't need to learn to cook
*   That he would still continue with his golf and enjoy long weekends away
*   That children would destroy their lifestyles and interfere in their plans to traveland/or live abroad for a few years
*   That his mother would eventually come and live with them as he had promised hershe would not end up in a home for older adults.

You can see how the seeds of conflict have already been sown by two people who have not gone 'assumption hunting' when it might have been very useful.

Contracts are like icebergs; the formal, agreed and overt contract is the part that is visible above water; while the unseen, un-negotiated psychological contract is the part beneath (Hewson, 1999). Like icebergs, the part below water is always much larger than the part above, and much more dangerous. Understanding psychological contracts for individuals, teams and organisations is a key concept in fostering and enhancing healthy relationships. Not being aware of their existence and their power often leaves people confused as to why certain behaviours and attitudes take place and can lead to dissatisfaction (Turnley & Feldman, 2000).

For example, a client comes for counselling expecting the practitioner to provide answers as to why his relationships at work continually break down. Unaware of this unspoken psychological contract the practitioner works to facilitate insight into the client's past that might contribute to their present situation. This results in frustration for the client who continually asks the practitioner what they should do. Eventually, the client terminates the sessions as their expectations are not being met.

It is not what is written or said that makes up the psychological contract but how it is understood by both parties. Rousseau (1995: 9) writes 'The psychological contract is individual beliefs, shaped by the organisation, regarding terms of an exchange agreement'. The subjective side of the contract (the psychological meaning it has) does not come solely from within the individual, but is subtly shaped by outside factors. Contracts, in general, and the psychological contract in particular, are 'promises about the future' (Rousseau, 1995: xi). Like all promises they can 'lead us on'. They can imply, hint and even encourage hidden expectations. Psychological contracts are influenced by society, culture, race, religion and a variety of sociological, economic and environmental factors.

The psychological contract at work in organisations

Let us examine several interrelated psychological contracts as they pertain to a counselling facility within an organisational setting. George is an experienced counsellor who works as an associate for an Employee Assistance Programme (EAP). He sees clients in his office, employees who are referred through the EAP for an organisation called AVEC. Part of George's contact with the EAP is that he engages in clinical supervision for his work, and his supervisor Fred provides an annual supervisor report to the EAP. The Supervisor has no other contact with anyone in this counselling system other than George. There is also an EAP case manager, Jo, who oversees counselling cases and who is point-of-contact for George if there are any administrative or clinical decisions to be made regarding clients (e.g. requests for additional counselling sessions, onward referrals for specialist help or where crisis intervention is required. Figure 3.1 below illustrates the eightfold psychological contracts that occur when a client (Mandy) comes to George from the company's EAP for counselling.

In the counselling arrangement given in Figure 3.1 there are eight overt contracts:

1. The sessional employment contract between George and the EAP
2. The counselling contract between George and the individual employee, Mandy
3. The supervision contract between George and his supervisor Fred
4. The contract between Fred and the EAP
5. The contract between George and the EAP case manager Jo
6. The contract between the EAP case manager Jo and the EAP
7. The contract between the EAP and the company AVEC
8. The employment contract between the company AVEC and the individual employee, Mandy who is the client.

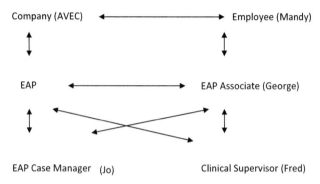

Figure 3.1 Eight contracts at work in an EAP Counselling System

While there are eight overt contracts, there is twice that number of psychological contracts (16) at play. So while George and the EAP have a written contract, they will each also have a very different psychological contract with one another. This counselling room in George's home is ghosted with the presences of these 16 systemic psychological contracts.

• What might these psychological look like and how might they impact upon the counselling work?

Psychological contracts – interpretative filters

Psychological contracts consist of the internal agreements we make consciously and unconsciously with the people, teams and organisations in our world. Those agreements are built on beliefs and assumptions about us, others and reality. We see, and interpret what we see, through filters, some of which derive from psychological contracts. They are our unique, defined way of organising our knowledge of ourselves and our realities. We therefore need to take account of them and try and ensure that we are as aware of them as possible. One way of doing this is through what has been called reflective practice. This has been defined as 'the capacity to reflect on action so as to engage in a process of continuous learning' (Social Care Institute for Excellence (SCIE, 2018)

Our ability to reflect will also influence the psychological contract. Critical reflection is a key to understanding our ways of making meaning and our awareness of our expectations. The absence of reflection leaves individuals and groups prone to mindless routines – our underlying assumptions are never questioned. Likewise our own unresolved issues, past experience and styles of relationship result in patterns that create and reinforce our inherent expectations and assumptions. Psychological contracts are a result of an interweaving of all of these elements; hence their power and complexity.

Managing the psychological contract

Difficulties within psychological contracts can result in formal and informal complaints, legal actions and breakdowns in professional and personal relationships (Aggarwal & Bhargava, 2010). It is imperative to examine how practitioners, supervisors and clients can 'manage' this side of the contract.

Hewson (1999) articulates helpful ways of managing the psychological contract in a healthy manner:

- All parties are involved actively in developing the contract
- The contract provides a unified perception of what the end goal is
- Contracting creates a guard against the abuse of power and all participants are aware of and manage the boundaries of power
- Overt contracts are designed to minimise covert agendas
- Transparency, honesty, openness and dialogue are built into contracting
- Contracts are often developmental (they need to change over time, e.g. in marriage) and need to have renegotiation built in
- Contracts are emotional arenas as well as rational agreements
- The social, political, organisational and professional contexts in which contracts are lived and played out (seeing the big picture) are important
- Subtle shifts in expectations must be articulated
- Tracking the relationships to see if any new needs emerge (e.g. transference issues in therapeutic work)

From these structural and qualitative criteria we have generated four ways in which the psychological contract can be identified and addressed so that it can be a healthy part of the contract relationship.

1. Understanding and challenging assumptions

As Kline, (2009: 87) explains

> assumptions are not dry. They sound it, but in the actual they are very powerful belongings. The presence of assumptions at the very core of our lives is actually a vital organising concept. Searching for them competes hands down with the best forensic thriller you couldn't put down.

Psychological contracts are built on assumptions and intertwining sets of assumptions. Getting in touch with them and easing their hold on us to exchange them for more useful and effective ones is not easy. Brookfield (2012) notes how people can identify and change unhelpful assumptions. Some of these include:

- moving from judgement to curiosity
- thinking how we co-create assumptions
- looking at how systems build assumptions
- reviewing how our commitments bring lots of assumptions and embed them in our lives (e.g. political or religious affiliations)
- examining how expectations are often based on assumptions
- considering how fundamentalist approaches are prone to deep assumptions
- discovering that parts of us which are difficult to accept might help us uncover assumptions
- contextualising our assumptions
- questioning inherited assumptions
- considering conclusions we come to from underpinning assumptions
- unravelling layers of assumptions
- allowing time for assumptions to come to light.

2. Transactional analysis
By using a very simple version of Transactional Analysis (Berne, 1966) it is possible to get individuals to take a stand from within one of the ego-states/positions, and then speak their needs and expectations from that position. These basic tools of TA can be learnt in minutes:

- There are three positions we can speak or listen from. The Child state is that part of us (still alive within us) that remains the child and reacts as a child; the Adult state is that reasonable, rational side from which we make adult decisions; and the Parent state is that set of injunctions our parents used on us.
- We can move through these three states depending on the situation and what happens to us, e.g. a manager can move into Child state and sulk as a result of a comment made, be in Parent state by telling off an employee and be in Adult state by working with others to make a decision.
- Complications can arise when we talk to each other across and between the states (e.g. Adult to Child, or Parent to Adult, Child to Adult, Child to Child, etc.).

This simple scheme is very useful in that it utilises role-play in different scenarios; e.g. Carroll (2015: 28) will act out as a new employee coming to the manager from the Child state and make statements such as:

I am thrilled to be here and know this job will be great fun! I wonder if it is possible for me to be your favourite employee? In fact, it would be truly marvellous if I could be the only employee you look after. Also, until I get up to speed, could you be available for me anytime I need you? I would like you to have all the answers so that when I am stuck you will offer me a solution.

Participants always laugh at this role-play. It puts into words how they might think if they were a child-employee and could articulate their needs. Carroll (2015) emphasises the point that the child is *always* still alive and active within us. While none of us would put the above 'irrational needs' into words, these same needs are often played out in the transactions we go through at work. Issues of envy and jealousy, favouritism, patronage, bullying, harassment and cliques are often Child states played out in the adult arena of work.

This exercise is very powerful for bringing out into the open and articulating hidden agendas (the psychological contract) in a startling and vivid manner. It makes explicit the hidden assumptions and expectations we bring to relationships and organisations.

3. Scenario planning
A third way of identifying and managing psychological contracts is through scenario planning or scenario learning. No one knows the future and it is unpredictable; but we constantly try. Our guesses profoundly influence our attitudes to ourselves, life situations and others, for example:

We'll live happily ever after!
I will have a job here for life.
I will be promoted.
People in my family work at their relationships, divorce is failure.
People from my family are not artistic.
I will be the parent of three children

Scenarios anticipate possible futures. Scenario planning is about imagining possible futures so that we are ready for whatever happens. Companies frequently undertake a SWOT (strengths, weaknesses, opportunities and threats) and PEST (political, economic, social and technological) analyses which form part of scenario planning.

Rather than attempt to *predict* the future it makes more to sense to ask the 'what ... if?' sorts of questions;
What if ... you were to get ill and couldn't work anymore?
What if ... you took a year's sabbatical and set off around the world?
What if ... you move house?
What if ... your most significant relationship breaks down?

What if ... you live to be 70, 80, 90?

The 'miracle question' of de Shazer (1988) is an example of scenario learning. You imagine that you wake up tomorrow morning and a miracle has happened; your problem has miraculously disappeared. What would be different? It's a simulation game – the service user imagines a single day without the problem shaping and tainting every part of life. So clients can learn by imagining and simulating life without problems or symptoms. 'Imagine you and your partner are talking again and in a healthy, mature relationship – what is different from the present?' This is why armies play games; simulation games are ways of anticipating what a potential enemy might do. Pilots also learn by simulation before they tackle real flying. Training as a therapist or psychologist often involves role playing scenarios with other students or tutors.

In devising possible futures we create narratives that reveal our hidden psychological contracts playing out in the future. Playing out such scenarios allows us to consider, articulate, talk through issues in the individual, couple, family, team or organisational relationship; the psychological contract.

4. 'What are we not talking about?'

A fourth way of managing psychological contracts is to review relationships with a particular question; 'What are we *not* talking about?' This incisive question enables participants in relationships (pairs, teams, organisations) to look at some of the difficult areas of the relationship that will contain unspoken elements. It is here that the psychological contract content most often appears.

In your relationship, family or work context:

* What can you talk about there that will be easy?
* What can you talk about, but only with some difficulty?
* What can you not talk about?

Conclusion

This chapter has concentrated on understanding the content and process of the psychological contract and the subjective interpretation of that contract. Concentrating solely on the overt, agreed, written or verbal contract fails to account for why people may feel let down, confused, betrayed or hurt, even when the overt contract has not been broken. In many ways it is the psychological contract that is the most important part of any contract for this is the lived 'reality' for most people. Awareness of the existence and implications of psychological contracts helps practitioners stay in touch with the unconscious, unarticulated needs and expectations of clients and themselves, as well as their own relationships with clients, organisations and employers. Considering our own psychological contracts and helping clients articulate these expectations allows both parties to start to deal with them.

Reflective questions

1. Can you describe some elements of the psychological contract that is in operation within your family of origin?
2. How might you deal with the unreasonable demands made on you as a result of a 'psychological contract' someone has with you?
3. How might organisations manage the psychological contracts with their staff to the benefit of themselves?
4. Describe a psychological contract another person or organisation has with you. How can you manage that contract so that it doesn't impact negatively on the relationships involved?

References

Aggarwal, U., & Bhargava, S. (2010) Predictors and outcomes of relational and transactional psychological contract. *Psychological Studies*, 55(3), 195–207.

Berne, E. (1966) *Principles of Group Treatment*. New York: Grove Press. Reprinted, 1994, by Shea Press, Merlo Park.

Brookfield, S.D. (2012) *Teaching for Critical Thinking; Tools and Techniques to help Students Question their Assumptions*. San Francisco: Wiley.

Carroll, M. (2015) Psychological contracts: Hidden agreements in life and at work. In R. Tribe, & J. Morrissey (Eds.). *The Handbook of Professional and Ethical Practice for Psychologists, Counsellors and Psychotherapists*. London: Routledge. pp. 19–31.

Chartered Institute of Personnel Development (2018) Available at: www.cipd.co.uk/knowledge/fundamentals/relations/employees/psychological-factsheet Accessed 30 June 2018.

Conway, N., & Briner, R.B. (2007) *Understanding Psychological Contracts at Work*. Oxford: Oxford University Press.

de Shazer, S. (1988) *Clues: Investigating Solutions in Brief Therapy*. New York: Norton.

George, C. (2009) *The Psychological Contract*. Maidenhead, Berkshire: McGraw Hill Open University Press.

Griep, Y., Vantilborgh, T., & Jones, S.K. (2018) The relationship between psychological contract breach and counterproductive work behavior in social enterprises: Do paid employees and volunteers differ? *Economic and Industrial Democracy*, 10.1177/0143831X17744029 Accessed 28 May 2018.

Hewson, J. (1999) Training supervisors how to contract in supervision. In E. Holloway, & M. Carroll (Eds.). *Training Counselling Supervisors*. London: Sage. pp. 67–91.

Kline, N. (2009) *More Time to Think*. Pool-in-Wharfedale: Fisher King Publisher.

Knight, (2018) Available at: http://mediacentre.britishairways.com/pressrelease/details/86/2017-228/9110 Accessed 23 April 2018.

Lee, C., Liu, J., Rousseau, D., Hui, C., & Chen, Z. (2011) Inducements, contributions and fulfilment in new employee psychological contracts. *Human Resources Management*, 50(2), 201–226.

Mai, K., Ellis, A., Christian, J., & Porter, C. (2016) Examining the effects of turnover intentions on organizational citizenship behaviours and deviance behaviours: A psychological contract approach. *Journal of Applied Psychology*, 101(8), 1067–1081.

Payne, S., Culbertson, S., Lopez, Y., Boswell, W., & Barger, E. (2014) Contract breach as a trigger for adjustment to the psychological contract during the first year of employment. *Journal of Occupational and Organizational Psychology*, 88(1), 41–60.

Robinson, S.L., & Rousseau, D.M. (1994) Violating the psychological contract: Not the exception but the norm. *Journal of Organizational Behavior*, 15(3), 245–259.

Rodwell, J., & Gulyas, A. (2013) The impact of the psychological contract, justice and individual differences: nurses take it personally when employers break promises. *Journal of Advanced Nursing*, 69(12), 2774–2785.

Rousseau, D.M. (1995) *Psychological Contracts in Organisations; Understanding Written and UnWritten Agreements*. Thousand Oaks, CA: Sage.

Rousseau, D.M., & Schalk, R. (Eds) (2000) Psychological *Contracts in Employment; Cross-National Perspectives*. Thousand Oaks, CA: Sage.

Sills, C. (Ed.) (2006) *Contracts in Counselling & Psychotherapy*. London: Sage.

Social Care Institute for Excellence (2018) Available at: www.scie.org.uk/workforce/induction/standards/cis02_personaldevelopment.asp

Turnley, W.H., & Feldman, D.C. (2000) Re-examining the effects of psychological contract violations: Unmet expectations and job dissatisfaction as mediators. *Journal of Organizational Behavior*, 21, 25–42.

Worden, W. (2002) *Children and Grief: When a Parent Dies*. New York: Guildford Press.

Zhao, H.A.O., Wayne, S.J., Glibkowski, B.C., & Bravo, J. (2007) The impact of contract breach on work-related outcomes: A meta-analysis. *Personnel Psychology*, 60(3), 647–680.

Chapter 4

New challenges for professional ethics and good practice guidelines for psychologists, psychotherapists and therapists

Hannah Farndon, Nicola Gale and Sarah Niblock

This chapter discusses the processes and issues that representatives from two different professional organisations have considered and addressed in their guidelines. The first section of the chapter is written by Hannah Farndon and Nicola Gale from the British Psychological Society (BPS) and the second section is by Sarah Niblock of the United Kingdom Council for Psychotherapy (UKCP). While there are similarities in their approaches there are also differences in how the task has been approached. The two organisations are at differing points in the cycle of updating their guidelines on professional, ethical and research practice. Both organisations draw attention to the changing environment and the associated range of challenges and also raise the issue of why things go wrong.

Hannah Farndon and Nicola Gale – the British Psychological Society's Practice Guidelines

Practice guidelines for psychologists define good practice, they support decision making, offer clarity of expectations, underpin teaching and contribute to good governance of services by helping to benchmark standards. Sitting underneath the Code of Ethics and Conduct (BPS, 2018), and alongside the Code of Human Research Ethics (BPS, 2014), the British Psychological Society's Practice Guidelines ('the Guidelines') (BPS, 2017a) is one of the core guidance documents the Society publishes which underpin the work of psychologists.

Ethical and good practice standards rarely stand still, and this is certainly true for psychologists. Societal needs, norms and expectations change, sometimes rapidly and unexpectedly. Professional challenges therefore change too, and new areas of concern emerge. It is important that the Guidelines are informed by users and keep pace with change, or both client and professional are done a disservice. The Guidelines cover areas core to the good practice of psychology in all contexts including making and maintaining agreements, so both professional and client have clear expectations; informed consent, including where clients may need help with this process; managing data and confidentiality, including when psychologists may be obliged to consider breaching confidentiality. These areas, while familiar, bear revisiting to ensure practice remains of a high standard and important points are not overlooked in the pressures of day to day work. The main focus of this chapter, however, is on areas of practice that are changing due to untoward incidents, shifts in societal expectations or in the legal and regulatory framework.

Response to changing context

Psychology is not alone in being challenged by significant shifts in societal expectations. All professions are expected to run safe, effective quality services where client experience is positive and staff well-being is supported to allow them to deliver the quality of service that is expected. Service delivery is underpinned by clinical governance, described by the Department of Health (2000: 1) as 'a framework through which NHS organisations are accountable for continuously improving the quality of their services and safeguarding high standards of care by creating an environment in which excellence in clinical care will flourish'. Since that report encouraging learning from adverse events, high profile failings in care, criminal acts, and regular adverse occurrences that cause harm remain testament to ongoing need. The Guidelines therefore address important current issues including dealing with increased pressures in the workplace; responding to raised public and regulatory expectations of professionals including cases of non-recent sexual abuse, modern slavery and the legislation around terrorism; and the growing focus on social justice and inclusion.

Challenges in the workplace

Pressures on service delivery, caseloads, targets, doing more with less, and raised expectations to report and take action when things are wrong, have meant there is a need for support with working environment and relationships, setting expectations of appropriate workplace behaviour and addressing harassment and bullying. These aspects are perhaps best considered in the context of the systemic work psychologists do on workplace culture and positive managerial and leadership behaviours.

One area of reported difficulty is the quality of the working environment and safety. This includes the physical setting in which psychological work is done, where psychologists can experience what feels like undue pressure from employers to work in sub optimal conditions, especially in services which are under resourced. Many psychologists, in line with the drive to provide community and home-based services wherever possible, now practise as lone workers and may visit clients in their own homes. This raises the need for psychologists to think about keeping safe, have a plan and stick to it. It is also becoming increasingly common for psychologists to make use of the internet and technology. These require the psychologist to ensure that the network used is as secure as reasonably possible and, as far as is feasible, assures privacy to their clients. This is discussed further in Chapter 11 of this book.

One of the most demanding aspects of practice, however, is for psychologists who may experience problems with those they work alongside through harassment or bullying. Bullying may be explicit and therefore obvious, or an experience recognised only by the recipient and harder to notice by others. Bullying may be vertical (i.e. between managers/supervisors and staff) or horizontal (i.e. between colleagues). Clients may also experience bullying by professionals. While bullying may involve a misuse of power and be committed by a manager, supervisor or senior colleagues, it is not uncommon for senior staff to be bullied by those whose work they oversee (Hoel et al., 2001). Harassment can be defined as unwanted actions or comments, which may be related to age, disability, gender, sexual orientation, religion or any other personal characteristic of the recipient. The following vignette illustrates some of the issues that can arise.

Vignette 1

The psychological services in this particular area have in recent years undergone several reorganisations. Staff are now working from different geographical bases, as services have been reconfigured. For many this has meant personal disruption in terms of family commitments and ability to manage work life balance. Some are working in the community, and with the numbers of clients on their caseload struggle to get back to the team base at all. The leadership of the service has changed, several senior staff have moved on and posts have been down-banded as a result. The new head of service is from a different professional background and is not a psychologist. A number of the psychologists and other professionals are assertively challenging management decisions in team meetings, and splits are becoming apparent in the teams.

When things go wrong

When things do go wrong, there is a need for supportive guidance on what to do. Whistleblowing has come to the fore in recent years due to high profile failures particularly in healthcare, and the long term and systematic failures to address the poor practices subsequently revealed. Whistleblowing is the disclosure of wrong doing (beyond normal managerial channels) and is important as it is a critical way not only of seeking justice for the individual or individuals affected, but also of developing inside information within organisations about incorrect or unfair practices (Miceli et al., 2008), thereby increasing the evidence required for corrective action to take place.

A whistle-blower is protected by law (the Public Interest (Disclosure) Act 1998) in specific circumstances defined by law. Whistleblowing is a complex legal area and it is important that anyone considering it seeks appropriate advice, for example from an accredited trade union representative or helpline. The Health and Social Care Act 2008 (Regulated Activities) Regulations 2014 duty of candour (regulation 20) is now pretty universal across healthcare professions and requires all health and adult social care providers registered with the Care Quality Commission to be open with people when things go wrong. Dealing with, and providing support when a complaint has been made, is also an increasingly regular part of providing healthcare services.

Reflective question

1.   When is it appropriate to consider whistleblowing, and what are some of the important considerations before doing so?

Current societal challenges

The issue of safeguarding has become more salient in recent times. Traditionally thought of as child protection, it has for some time encompassed vulnerable adults and is recognised as a matter for everyone not just those working with children directly (HM Government, 2015). In response to growing societal awareness of the issues, expectations of how psychologists should respond in cases of historical sexual abuse has changed. Modern slavery is also now a matter that practitioners need to be familiar with. Modern Slavery is a serious crime, encompassing slavery, servitude, and forced or compulsory labour and human trafficking. A challenging area for many practitioners too is responding to terrorism and extremism. All these are now addressed in the Guidelines.

Given the number of high profile cases, across national boundaries, social and professional spheres, societal awareness of sexual abuse and its impact across the lifespan is now higher probably than at any other time. There is a growing recognition that a disclosure of non-recent abuse may reveal current risks to others from an alleged perpetrator. This may place psychologists in complex positions when trying to negotiate and balance their duties and responsibilities. Psychologists who work with adult clients who disclose non-recent sexual abuse, should recognise that there may be current and ongoing risks posed by the alleged perpetrator to others. Not sharing concerns beyond the consulting room could mean that children and young people could be at risk. The following vignette illustrates how these issues might arise in psychological practice.

Vignette 2

A client is referred to psychological services. She has a history of brief engagement with services, then does not return, then sometime later re-presents. She describes longstanding difficulties in maintaining relationships, impulsive behaviours that cause her detriment, and at times heavy substance use. She has in the past alleged historical abuse, then withdrawn the allegation. This time, she has started to build a therapeutic alliance with the newly qualified psychologist she is seeing and has talked more about past abuse.

Reflective question

1. What responsibilities does the psychologist have in relation to the alleged non-recent abuse, and what are the professional issues that arise?

The Counter-Terrorism and Security Act (2015) places a duty on certain bodies to have 'due regard to the need to prevent people from being drawn into terrorism'. Depending on where the psychologist works, these duties may have relevance. This is a contentious area of practice. Psychologists should ensure they focus on their core role, working in a non-stigmatising way, and avoiding profiling based on characteristics such as race, religion, ethnicity or any other aspect. Psychologists should carefully weigh relevant professional obligations and seek and follow appropriate local and employer guidance.

Equality, diversity and inclusion

Equality, diversity and inclusion (EDI) underpin the Guidelines as the bedrock of practice. EDI should permeate all aspects of practice from a specific focus in policies, in training, recruitment, service design and delivery, and advocating for those less able to do so, through to active promotion of a culture of equality and inclusion as core to all the profession does (BPS, 2017b). The Guidelines support inclusion in psychological practice such as working with cultural difference; with people of faith, religion and spirituality; with sexual and gender minorities; and with people who may be socially excluded. Specific guidance is also provided when working with people who may be vulnerable because of their situation such as unemployment. It is expected that all psychologists will have the necessary skills and abilities to work with all sections of the community.

Special consideration is needed when working with people who may be socially excluded.

Social exclusion refers to the extent to which individuals are denied access to the prevailing social system and the right to participate in key areas of social, economic and cultural life. Exclusion is typically a result of poverty and/or belonging to a social minority group and is not a matter of choice. The impact of social exclusion leads to the perpetuation of cycles of inequality for individuals and groups in terms of income, health, opportunity, relationships and life-span. Social inclusion is the process where the needs of all members of communities and the groups which constitute them are recognised, prioritised and met, resulting in these individuals feeling valued and respected. Promoting social inclusion is a broader task than promoting equality and tackling discrimination and stigma. It requires psychology professionals to address wider structural issues in society which maintain excluding processes and power differentials.

An important part of upholding equality, diversity and inclusion in practice is to work in genuine and respectful collaboration with those whom the psychologist's service serves. Psychologists should develop services, policies and guidelines in collaboration with the people who use their services. The following vignette aims to provoke thinking about how genuine collaboration can be achieved.

Vignette 3

The organisation you work for is redefining what psychology services it offers, how those are accessed, and developing new policies for equality, diversity and inclusion. This is in part a response to changes in commissioning requirements, and also pressure from existing service users, some of which has been in the form of complaints.

- Who needs to be involved and what should be included in the equality, diversity and inclusion policy?

Guidelines such as these in all walks of life can often seem straightforward and considered to be 'common sense'. So why is it that adverse incidents continue to occur throughout the human services professions? One important aspect to consider is the various competing biases that impact upon adherence to standards of good practice. These are considered further in the BPS Code of Ethics and Conduct (BPS, 2018), and include salience, what comes to mind; how humans tend to look for confirmatory evidence for our existing beliefs and ignore other evidence; behaviours aimed at avoidance of loss; the impact of likelihood of something coming to light on choice of action; desire not to disrupt existing belief systems. Particularly in a work context, aspects such as power, reward, organisational pressures such as targets, and team relationships, can have an impact on whether a practitioner feels motivated and able to follow an appropriate course. This leads on to the importance of reflection on practice to maximise beneficial outcomes.

Sarah Niblock – guidelines – UKCP

At the time of writing, the UK Council for Psychotherapy (UKCP) is launching a second consultation with its members on the latest iteration of our Code of Ethics and Professional Practice. A group of UKCP therapists from a range of modalities steered by the lay chair of the committee have prepared the new guidance. One of the UKCP's remits is to regulate our members, one of the hallmarks of our quality and credibility in safeguarding the public. The new Code contains remarkably few directive dos and don'ts. This is because, however written or prescribed, standards, codes and guidelines can only ever act as a guide and cannot cover every possible eventuality. That said, in drafting the document, the UKCP is highly mindful of two key challenges. First, how can a succinct Code reflect the sheer plurality of practice across our organisation while still being enforceable through our complaints process? As well as providing professional support to our members, we are regulators and consider breaches of the Code which raise concerns about a member's suitability to be on the UKCP register without any restrictions or conditions. Therefore we have a remit to provide guidance for members in ethical decision making while at the same time being very explicit about what behaviours are not permissible. It is essential that all our members support and adhere to the Code, because it forms the backbone of our regulatory function. Second, how do we present those clear and practical issues of conduct, ones that cannot be open to interpretation, in such a way that we do not stray into overly defining – and potentially manualising – psychotherapy?

In its current iteration, which may of course change through consultation, the Code sets out non-negotiable points of practice, which include not having sexual contact with clients, not accepting gifts or other favours, maintaining confidentiality, and securing regular supervision and undertaking ongoing and regular professional development. There have been no new additions since the previous 2009 iteration of the UKCP code. Where the UKCP ethics committee feels there might be specialist detail needed, such as on research ethics, safeguarding, gender and sexuality or torture for instance, we will build a repository of specific guidelines along with learning, development and engagement opportunities for our members.

Balancing virtue ethics and regulation

Maintaining a healthy balance of ethical thinking alongside a rigorous, unambiguous regulatory Code is challenging but essential. From the time of Aristotle, philosophers have emphasised ethical decision making as resting with the individual; that ethics must be personal, a matter of free choice rather than merely conformity to institutional or other group norms (Merrill, 1996). That said, our concepts of ethics cannot be divorced from organisational requirements any more than from cultures, from religions, philosophies and other factors that have shaped them. Primary ethical values are transmitted to any culture's members by parenting and socialisation, education and religion. Secondary factors affecting ethical behaviour including organisational and professional ethos and requirements (Pitta et al., 1999).

The UKCP is not alone in applying a virtue ethics approach to supporting and educating members in thinking through dilemmas. It is an approach favoured in other applied sectors, such as business, where organisations need to build and sustain trust among a range of stakeholders, be they staff, clients, suppliers and board members. Virtue ethics emphasises moral character in contrast to deontological approaches that foreground duties or rules (Smith, 2017; Van Hooft, 2014; Van Welfel, 2015). It is intended to create a clear, decisive ethos and character for UKCP registrants by highlighting the central principles of professional ethics. In our ethical guidelines, we outline seven headline principles, which we regard as fundamental to good ethical practice.

Avoiding harm

The duty of care is central to professional practice. Members' overriding priority must be to avoid harm and damage to clients.

Benevolence

The object of therapy is to exercise professional knowledge and skills so as to do good.

Candour

Members must be open and transparent with all relevant people. When things do not proceed as they should, members should be proactive in providing information about what has happened. Members must provide full, truthful information, give reasonable support and, where appropriate, apologise.

Competence

Members must ensure they are capable of delivering the standards of competence appropriate to their area(s) of practice, education or research, and that their standards of proficiency and performance match their competence.

Honesty

Professional relationships are founded in trust. Trust will be compromised if there is not honesty on both sides. Members must justify the trust placed in them, and in the profession, by acting with honesty and integrity at all times.

Human rights and social justice

Members must act in all circumstances to promote equality and celebrate diversity.

Personal accountability

Members are personally accountable for their conduct, actions and professional practice.

These principles are intended to stimulate thinking about and encourage engagement with ethical dilemmas. Through UKCP'S internal media, our conferences and networking, we encourage practitioners to contribute ideas about the challenging issues that confront them in their day to day practice. However, side by side with that must sit unambiguous statements on conduct that can be tested and measured in a complaint case. Our Code must be a separate document that sets out non-negotiable rules but we intend that, through a deeper processes of engagement, our members will have the necessary resources to avoid falling foul of the Code.

The dangers of manualising ethics

There is always the risk that the professionalization of psychotherapy, as with other professions, can detach ethical conduct from individual values. Ethics, both in their content and their maintenance, are in danger of becoming institutionalised instead of internalised by practitioners. Ethics can drift into an ongoing negotiation between two sides of professionalism: between the organisational demands of the accrediting body on one hand and the values and identity of the practitioner on the other. Jungers and Gregoire (2013: 5) point out that ethical principles help therapists contemplate obligations to client well-being because the principles 'provide a bridge between ethical theory and practical guidance'.

While there are some practical steps that can help build ethical accountability, starting with the individual therapist and radiating out to the profession as well as vice versa, it is vital that the welfare of the client is uppermost. A strong foundation must be built through education and training and psychotherapists must continue to converse about ethics through their careers. Codes and guidelines can only help in practice if the practitioner already has firm enough foundations of self-awareness, study, reflection and skills to take the weight of tough decision making. Those foundations must be laid carefully from the outset, layer upon layer, and once laid they must be checked and assessed frequently if they are to withstand the inevitable tests or challenges psychotherapists will face in their career.

In training, and indeed long after, students must reflect honestly on why they wish to be a psychotherapist; what are their motivations, what do they see as the profession's role in society and what are their own values and feelings? Here ethics codes can be thought of as a practice theory negotiation between the individual therapist and their client against a backdrop of fluid and dynamic contexts, within which they work. Practice theory, while generally thought of as relating to the inter relationship and negotiations between individuals and society, is not a unified theory or school of thought. There is no singular approach, instead it emerges from the coming together of several distinct scholarly traditions' that 'comprise a complicated network of similarities and dissimilarities' (Nicolini, 2012: 8). That is not to say that there should be no rules, rather that the moment of their application is an active negotiation by the therapist drawing upon their experience, training and understanding of the Code.

We train and educate our members to be lifelong critically reflexive practitioners through a combination of classroom based scenario work, study of texts and critical practice throughout their Diploma, Masters and Doctoral levels of study. This immersion can last anything from degree level for psychotherapeutic counsellors to a minimum of four years for postgraduate psychotherapy training. By exploring these aspects in depth, whether through immersion in academic or scholarly work, discussion in a seminar room or through self-reflection and debate with others in the field, the entrant will begin to develop a deeper critical vocabulary to articulate their relationship to the material in the consulting room within the remit of the Code. It is reflexivity that makes any practitioner in psychotherapy 'be able' to do the job, rather than just 'know how' (Niblock, 2007). The benefit of pre-entry education in ethics within training is that it offers a space for students to explore options and take risks while minimizing any future harm to their clients, themselves and others.

At the institutional level, various attempts have been made to adapt models of personal moral development (Gilligan, 1977; Kohlberg, 1931; Piaget, 1932) to organisational ethics (Logsdon & Yuthas, 1997; Petrick & Manning, 1990; Sridhar & Camburn, 1993) are among those who have applied Kohlberg's six stages of moral development to organisations based on stakeholder engagement. Coleman (2000), a former ethics officer with a technology company, identified a different, six-stage approach to achieving ethical progress in an organisation, specifically (1) commitment, (2) formulation, (3) action and feedback, (4) re-evaluation, (5) total ethical culture, and (6) total alignment and integration. He describes each level as 'more ingrained, more naturally integrated, than the one before …' (2000: 1F) as organisations' attempts to manage ethics become more sophisticated over time. While the process of achieving ethical coherence individually and professionally is captured, what is not clear is how to map a virtue ethics approach onto a robust regulatory Code for which the UKCP is accountable.

Negotiating ethics in pluralistic organisations

To fulfil our role as a regulator our Code must be explicit and that balance is a hard one to strike in a multi-disciplinary context. A rulebook couldn't possibly cover every situation or modality; clearly, a major challenge for practitioners is that ethical standards and guidelines can never stand still or embrace plurality if they go into acute detail. They have always been and continue to be evolving due to changes in society, culture, the professional contexts in which we work and innovations in modalities of practice. These may include the distinctions between individual, couple and group therapies and the introduction of new methods. Too many details in a Code of professional practice can result in many loopholes and challenges, slowing progress and making it harder to apply (Office of the Parliamentary Counsel, 2013).

Psychotherapists of all modalities must, alongside their clients, accommodate being at the nexus of an array of influences; internal influences such as occupational, contractual, employment matters and external such as regulatory requirements, government policy, the legal context and of course the cultures in which they and their clients live. Now, in the second decade of the twenty-first century, tectonic plates of digital transformation, artificial intelligence alongside local national and global shifts in the socio-cultural and socio-economic and environmental contexts are impacting to an ever-greater degree (Orange, 2016). The format affords us the flexibility and agility to create, review and regularly update best-practice guidelines on specific issues, as broad ranging as social media to torture.

Conclusion

While conformity to professional behavioural expectations is embedded in codes and guidelines, psychotherapy by its very nature must be shifting and dynamic to mirror the rapid changes within the practice, within the client's context and that of society in which the work takes place. Therefore, no code or guideline can ever be said to be an expert body of knowledge. For psychotherapy practitioners, ultimately ethics is about protecting and enshrining their relationship of trust with their clients. UKCP must ensure a profession the public can have faith in, that any complaint made will be examined and if there is any merit in the claim and it is against our regulations then we will take action that can result in the therapist being struck off. While upholding the highest values and serving as an aid to ethical thinking, our new Code must be practical and realistic because these are ethics with consequences.

Reflective questions

1. What are the emerging challenges in your context of practice that you need to be thinking about and considering how to respond?
2. How effectively are you using Practice Guidelines, and other relevant legal, ethical, policy, and relevant context specific guidance, in your work?

3. What are the legal duties in relation to 'Prevent', www.gov.uk/gov
   ernment/publications/prevent-duty-guidance and how do you understand the intersection between the Prevent duty and working in
   a non-stigmatising way?
4. What are some of the key issues facing psychological services as
   a whole, and how can teams and service leads work together to continue to deliver a safe, effective and valued service?

References

British Psychological Society. (2014). *Code of Human Research Ethics*. Leicester: Author. Available at: www.bps.org.uk/news-and-policy/bps-code-human-research-ethics-2nd-edition-2014 Accessed 8 July 2018.

British Psychological Society. (2017a). *Practice Guidelines*. Leicester: Author. Available at: www.bps.org.uk/news-and-policy/practice-guidelines Accessed 8 July 2018.

British Psychological Society. (2017b) *Declaration on Equality, Diversity and Inclusion*. Leicester: Author. Available at: www.bps.org.uk/sites/bps.org.uk/files/News%20-%20Files/INF278%20Declaration%20on%20equality%20v3.pdf Accessed 8 July 2018.

British Psychological Society. (2018) *Code of Ethics and Conduct*. Leicester: Author. Available at: www.bps.org.uk/news-and-policy/bps-code-ethics-and-conduct Accessed 8 July 2018.

Coleman, G. (2000) The six levels of a totally aligned ethics culture. *Paper presented at Managing Ethics in Organisations Conference*. Waltham, MA: Centre for Business Ethics. cited in Rossouw, G.J and Van Vuuren, L.J. (2003) Modes of managing morality; a descriptive model of strategies for managing ethics. *Journal of Business Ethics*, 46 (4), 389–402.

Department of Health. (2000) *An Organisation with a Memory. Report of an Expert Group on Learning from Adverse Events in the NHS*. London: The Stationery Office. Available at: webarchive.nationalarchives.gov.uk/20130107105354/www.dh.gov.uk/prod_consum_dh/groups/dh_digitalassets/@dh/@en/documents/digitalasset/dh_4065086.pdf Accessed 8 July 2018.

Gilligan, C. (1977) In a different voice: Women's conceptions of self and morality. *Harvard Educational Review*, 47(4), 481–517.

HM Government. (2015). Working together to safeguard children: A guide to inter-agency working to safeguard and promote the welfare of children. Available at: https://assets.publishing.service.gov.uk/government/uploads/system/uploads/attachment_data/file/592101/Working_Together_to_Safeguard_Children_20170213.pdf Accessed 14 July 2018.

Hoel, H., Cooper, C., & Faragher, B. (2001) The experience of bullying in Great Britain: The impact of organizational status. *European Journal of Work and Organizational Psychology*, 10(4), 443–465.

Jungers, C., & Gregoire, J. (Eds.) (2013) *Counseling Ethics: Philosophical and Professional Foundations*. New York: Springer.

Kohlberg, L. (1931) *The Philosophy of Moral Development: Moral Stages and the Idea of Justice (Vol. 1)*. San Francisco, CA: Harper and Row.

Logsdon, J.M., & Yuthas, K. (1997) Corporate social performance, stakeholder orientation, and organisational moral development. *Journal of Business Ethics*, 16(12–13), 1213–1226.

Merrill, J. (1996) *Existential Journalism*. Ames, IA: Iowa State University Press.

Miceli, M., Near, J., & Dworkin, T. (2008) *Whistleblowing in Organizations*. New York: Routeledge and Lawrence Erlbaum Associates.

Niblock, S. (2007) From 'knowing how' to 'being able': Negotiating the meanings of reflective practice and reflexive research in journalism studies. *Journalism Practice*, 1 (1), 20–32.

Nicolini, D. (2012) *Practice Theory, Work, and Organization: An Introduction*. Oxford: Oxford University Press.

Office of the Parliamentary Counsel. (2013) Research and analysis: When laws become too complex. Available at: www.gov.uk/government/publications/when-laws-become-too-complex/when-laws-become-too-complex Accessed 27 July 2018.

Orange, D. (2016) *Climate Crisis, Psychoanalysis and Radical Ethics*. London: Routledge.

Petrick, J.A., & Manning, G.E. (1990) Developing an ethical climate for excellence. *The Journal for Quality and Participation*, 14(2), 85–87.

Piaget, J. (1932) *The Moral Judgement of the Child*. London: Kegan, Paul, Trench, Tubner & Co.

Pitta, D.A., Fung, H.G., & Isberg, S. (1999) Ethical issues across cultures: Managing the differing perspectives of China and the USA. *Journal of Consumer Marketing*, 16(3), 240–256.

Public Interest Disclosure Act. (1998) (UK). Available at: www.legislation.gov.uk/ukpga/1998/23/contents Accessed 16 January 2019.

Smith, R.S. (2017) *Virtue Ethics and Moral Knowledge: The philosophy of language after MacIntyre and Hauerwas*. London: Routledge.

Sridhar, B.S., & Camburn, A. (1993) Stages of moral development of corporations. *Journal of Business Ethics*, 12(9), 727–739.

The Health and Social Care Act. (2008) *(Regulated Activities) Regulations 2014 Part 3 Section 2 Regulation 20 (UK)*. Available at: www.legislation.gov.uk/ukdsi/2014/9780111117613/contents Accessed 16 January 2019.

UKCP. (2009) Ethical principles and code of professional conduct. Available at: www.psychotherapy.org.uk/wp-content/uploads/2018/10/UKCP-Ethical-Principles-and-Code-of-Professional-Conduct.pdf Accessed 21 February 2019.

Van Hooft, S. (2014) *Understanding Virtue Ethics*. London: Routledge.

Van Welfel, E.R. (2015) *Ethics in Counseling and Psychotherapy*. Independence, KY: Cengage Learning.

Part 2

Legal considerations and responsibilities

Chapter 5

Client confidentiality and data protection

Peter Jenkins

The concept of respect for client confidentiality is a value of central importance to therapeutic practice regardless of context, but it is also one which seems to be increasingly under siege. All training courses will place heavy emphasis on the crucial necessity of maintaining client confidentiality. However, the difficulties of translating this into day to day practice are often left to the individual practitioner to negotiate for themselves, relying upon guidance of somewhat variable quality from their employing organisation. Some of the resultant problems arise from the fact that confidentiality may well be a key value informing ethical practice, but it is also one, which is heavily constrained by contextual factors. These factors can include employment, such as whether the therapist is working in a statutory or voluntary agency or is working in private practice. Issues relating to client confidentiality, data protection and research are briefly identified below and discussed further in section V of this book.

Confidentiality is, at the same time, a *legal* concept, with many different connotations. The deceptively simple concept of keeping client information 'confidential' is often beset with challenges or constraints, which makes this a highly problematic issue to work with in actual practice. This chapter falls into two parts. In the first, the emphasis will be on the role of the therapist as *custodian of sensitive client personal information*, i.e. in *deciding* whether to *maintain confidentiality or to disclose client information*. It will attempt to outline some of the key features of the law relating to client confidentiality, and to identify some of the situations, which may present major challenges to therapists on this issue. The notion of confidentiality will be contrasted with other legal concepts, such as privilege and the public interest. Additional duties and requirements placed upon the therapist under data protection law will also be explored. The second part of the chapter will identify routes whereby agencies *external* to the therapeutic relationship can gain access to client material, by *overriding, if necessary, the therapist's ethical duty to protect sensitive client information*. Thus, access can be variously sought by the client, by an employer, by the police, or by the courts. Steps that therapists can take to resist these encroachments of therapeutic confidentiality, if necessary, will be briefly outlined.

Therapy and confidentiality

Therapists need to know about the legal protection for, and limits to, confidentiality for several reasons. First, in order to defend client confidential material in a robust manner from unauthorised attempts at access, for example, by managers, funding committees, or clients' partners, or parents. Second, to convey accurately to the client any limits to confidentiality imposed by the law, as well as by agency practice, such as supervision. Third, to facilitate the client's provision of explicit consent to record-keeping, and their exercise of enhanced rights, such as access, under data protection law, such as the General Data Protection Regulation (discussed below). Finally, practitioners engaged in research are required by ethical codes to protect the privacy and confidentiality of research participants, via demonstrating rigorous attention to issues, such as informed consent, data security and the anonymization of research data, in order to avoid causing harm to subjects and compromising the integrity of the research (BACP, 2018; BPS, 2014).

Public interest in maintaining confidentiality

In terms of ethical practice, maintaining client confidentiality can be framed within wider principles such as fidelity and the keeping of trust with the client (BACP, 2018). These concepts may then be translated into the specific requirements of professional codes of practice (HCPC, 2016). At this initial point at least, there is a close correspondence between ethical and legal principles. The legal concept of confidentiality is based on the idea of equity, or fairness, insofar as a person who has received information in confidence should not then make unfair use of it. The common law duty of confidence arises where it would be a reasonable expectation to keep information private. Examples here could include a relationship of trust between a doctor and patient, between friends, or between a therapist and client. Unjustifiable breach of such confidence, for example by publishing deeply private material, could result in court action by the party suffering the damaging effects of such disclosure. Confidentiality can also be protected by being written into the express terms of a therapeutic contract, for example by preventing the unauthorised disclosure of innovative therapeutic techniques. However, an expectation of confidentiality will generally be assumed to apply to therapists in their therapeutic work, even if not written as a specific term of a contract.

Overall, the law takes the protection of confidentiality as a serious matter, but there are clear limits to what can be kept confidential. There is no requirement to keep confidential material, which is of a trivial nature, already in the public domain, or where the public interest in disclosure outweighs the public interest in keeping material confidential. The 'public interest' here refers to the court's conception of what is for the 'public good', namely what is in the interest of society as a whole. While therapists are well versed in the idea of confidentiality, as part of their professional training and practice, they are often less familiar with the wider and more authoritative concept of the *public interest*. The public interest, as determined by judges with reference to past case law, may be to *prevent* publication of confidential information, or to order its disclosure to the court.

What is clear is that therapists cannot protect client information simply by referring to a duty of confidentiality, as the public interest holds decisive authority. Consequently, the notion of *privilege* is attractive to for many therapists, as this would enable therapists to protect client confidentiality, even in the face of public interest demands for disclosure. However, unlike some of their counterparts in the US, therapists do not possess privilege in the UK. Privilege is the legal authority to protect client confidentiality from court demands for the release of therapeutic records, or to resist demands for the therapist to appear as a witness in a court of law, a status currently held by therapists in the US in relation to federal courts. The main professional group in the UK, which does possess privilege, or more accurately whose *clients* possess it, are lawyers. This is in order to facilitate the essential processes of providing legal advice and representation.

Public interest in requiring disclosure

Despite the arguments of certain schools of therapy, confidentiality of client material cannot be guaranteed to be *absolute*. While the public interest is generally very protective of confidentiality, it can also *justify*, or even *require*, that confidential client information be disclosed, albeit in a professional and accountable manner. The situations where the therapist is faced with the need to disclose client information without consent often involve a perceived threat of harm, to the client, to the therapist, or agency, or to a third party, such as to a partner, or child.

With regard to threat of self-harm or suicide, any limits to confidentiality may already be part of the therapeutic agreement/contract for work with the client. Client consent to disclosure in this situation would therefore protect the therapist from any future claim for breach of confidence. It becomes more problematic, however, if the therapist is seeking to inform a third party, such as the client's GP, for example, *without* first obtaining client consent. This would presumably be on the basis that it is in the public interest to prevent self-harm, suicide and the associated possible risk of harm to other members of the family. The courts may well favour the therapist's public interest defence for breaking confidentiality, but this cannot be known for certain without more extensive reported case law on this topic. In England and Wales, there is the example of the *Egdell* case, where a psychiatrist breached client confidentiality in order to alert the authorities to what was perceived to be a substantial risk to the public posed by a prisoner seeking early release. The psychiatrist's ultimately successful defence against the client's legal action for breach of confidence was made on the basis of the public interest. However, breaking client confidentiality on the basis of the assumed public interest is not a risk-free enterprise, as the public interest cannot be known with absolute certainty in advance. It is, therefore, generally advisable for the therapist to take informed legal advice, *before* breaking client confidentiality on a public interest basis.

The public interest generally lies in the prevention of crime, or even, as some judges have claimed, in the prevention of antisocial behaviour. The therapist, as with any citizen, is not legally required to report crime (outside of Northern Ireland), or the threat of crime, but can *choose* to do so in the public interest. Furthermore, employed therapists may report abusive practice by colleagues to their own employer, as a protected disclosure under the Public Interest Disclosure Act 1998.

Reporting allegations of child abuse can raise particularly acute dilemmas for therapists, where there may be a conflict between a duty of confidentiality to the client, and a wider public duty to protect vulnerable children from harm. It can be made more complex still, where the client is a child alleging abuse by family, or caretakers, but who insists that no action be taken as yet. Therapists are not under a general legal requirement to report child abuse to the authorities in England and Wales. However, therapists and other practitioners regulated by the Health and Care Professions Council (HCPC) are subject to certain forms of mandatory reporting, as in the case of Female Genital Mutilation, under the terms of their statutory registration. In addition, practitioner psychologists regulated by the Health and Care Professions Council are required to 'identify and minimise risk', relating to service users, carers and colleagues, by taking appropriate action, such as reporting abuse or risk of harm (HCPC, 2016: 8, 10).

Section 47 of the Children Act 1989 imposes a duty on the local authority to investigate situations where a child, i.e. a person under the age of 18, is suffering, or is likely to suffer, 'significant harm'. Therapists working for statutory organisations in health, education and social services will be bound by their contract of employment to follow child protection guidelines, based on the key document *Working Together* (Department for Education, 2015). These guidelines will also apply to therapists working in voluntary organisations, which have subscribed to reporting procedures devised by the Local Safeguarding Children Board. However, the obligation to report abuse is based here on a therapist's *contract of employment*, rather than any more general mandatory reporting requirement, such as applies to most childcare and healthcare professionals in the US (see fictional clinical/legal scenario below). Hence therapists in England and Wales who work in private practice, or for voluntary organisations outside the immediate ambit of the *Working Together* framework, are not bound by law to report abuse, although the ethical and moral pressures to do so may be considerable. Once again, the therapist could employ a public interest defence for breaking client confidentiality, with some confidence in it being recognised as valid by the courts, in the unlikely event of ever being legally challenged by a client.

Vignette I

Joan was a counsellor working for student services in a College of Further Education. The college managers introduced a new safeguarding procedure, whereby *all* suspected child abuse had to be reported to a named person within two hours, or the employee would face disciplinary proceedings. Joan's (forcefully expressed view) was that this policy seriously compromised the client's right to confidentiality, as these were often mature youngsters, with perhaps compelling reasons for not wanting their past abusive experiences to be reported to social services. She felt that the blanket reporting procedure was also flawed, in putting her in an identical position to that of a lecturer, or any other college employee, by taking no account of her ethical duty of confidentiality, or her commitment to a professional code of conduct.

What are your views on this situation and what informed your thinking here?

Statutory duties to disclose client information

The law generally seeks to protect client information from unauthorised disclosure without consent, as has been outlined. In rare cases, therapists can seek to use a public interest argument, where they disclose information about clients presenting a risk to themselves, or to third parties. In the case of child protection, therapists may be under a specific obligation of their contract of employment to follow child protection reporting guidelines, as opposed to any general mandatory requirement to report alleged abuse. There are currently two situations where therapists are under a statutory obligation to report client information to the authorities. Under the Drug Trafficking Act 1994, any citizen is required by law to pass on information obtained as part of their business, trade, or profession, about drug money laundering, with a particular relevance, presumably, for those involved in banking and financial services.

There is a further specific duty to disclose information to the authorities about terrorism, under the Terrorism Act 2000. Furthermore, there is a duty under the Act not to prejudice investigation by disclosure to any other person. A therapist would therefore be obliged *not* to inform the client that they had informed the authorities, in order to avoid being prosecuted. Terrorism is closely defined for the purposes of the Act, as involving serious violence to property, or persons, a risk to life or health, safety, or electronic systems. Information about actual, or planned, terrorist activities needs to be reported as soon as is reasonably practicable to the authorities, or where appropriate procedures exist, to the therapist's employers.

Statutory duties to protect client confidentiality

There is strong statutory protection for client confidentiality. The Data Protection Act 2018, considered in more detail below, puts in place very clear and specific protection for client personal data, and for the more sensitive kinds of personal data likely to be explored in therapy. Unauthorised disclosure, or disclosure, without client consent or proper legal authority, is a criminal offence, under s.170 of the Act. Finally, Article 8 of the Human Rights Act 1998 endorsed the client's right to, if not to confidentiality or privacy *per se*, then, at the very least, to the right to *respect* for the citizen's 'private and family life, his home and his correspondence', and to protection from any unauthorised interference by a public authority with the exercise of these rights. In the undervalued *Campbell* case, the House of Lords ruled, significantly, that therapy was akin to medical treatment, in terms of its entitlement to *privacy*. Therapy was seen to be essentially a *private* matter, and not to be disclosed, for example via press reporting, without explicit client consent (*Campbell v MGN Ltd* [2004]).

The previous Data Protection Act (DPA) 1998 represented a major shift in perspectives on a number of themes, which lie at the very heart of the therapeutic enterprise. Citizens possess rights to know what forms of personal data are being processed about them, to give, or withhold, consent to its processing, and to gain compensation for inaccurate, or damaging, recording. The Act extended earlier rights of access to computerised information to most forms of manual recording, building on already established rights with regard to social work, education and health records. Taken together with the Human Rights Act 1998, and the Freedom of Information Act 2000, the Data Protection Act 1998 marked the opening of a new period of transparency and professional accountability in the handling of personal information. This shift is endorsed by statutory regulation, in the form of Health and Care Professions Council Standard 10: 'Keep accurate records/Keep records secure' (HCPC, 2016: 10). In 2012, a clinical psychologist was struck off by the regulatory body, for breaching the then current version of this particular standard (HCPC, 2012).

General data protection regulation

The DPA 1998 has been replaced by the General Data Protection Regulation (GDPR), effective from May 2018, and the Data Protection Act 2018. The General Data Protection Regulation now provides the central legal framework governing the recording and communication of client data. It refines and updates some earlier definitions of key terms, in order to adapt to a rapidly changing electronic environment for data and its protection (Jenkins, 2018). 'Personal data' relates to information concerning an identifiable living individual, now extended to include potential identifiers, such as an IP address for a computer, tablet or laptop. A key operational distinction is made between 'data controllers' and 'data processors', but both carry additional responsibilities for processing data and also carry enhanced liability for errors and data breaches. A data controller 'says how and why personal data is processed and the processor acts on the controller's behalf' (ICO, 2017: 3). The keynotes of the GDPR relate to *transparency and accountability* in the handling of personal data. This is to be achieved by a renewed emphasis on demonstrating that consent has been obtained for recording and disclosing the personal data of clients. Consent is defined as 'a freely given, specific, informed and unambiguous indication of the individual's wishes' (ICO, 2017: 10), i.e. processing depends upon an active affirmation and agreement by the client, rather than being assumed from a passive failure to opt-out of such processing. *Transparency* is underpinned by demonstrating compliance with core data protection principles, issuing data privacy notices where required, and facilitating client access to records without charge. *Accountability* is maintained by larger organisations appointing a Data Protection Officer to oversee policy and practice, and, more generally, by the ICO monitoring compliance, with provision for imposing substantial fines and other sanctions in the event of serious breaches of the law.

The data protection legislation protects client confidentiality regarding use of personal data in a number of specific ways. Personal data, as indicated, refers to information relating to an identifiable living person, and data processing generally requires client consent. Certain types of personal information previously deemed as 'sensitive', including information on a client's mental, or physical health, or sex life, are now defined as 'special categories' of personal data, requiring *explicit* consent. Handling and communicating client, or 'data subject,' personal data is governed by relatively clear principles of data processing (see Box 5.1).

BOX 5.1 General Data Protection Regulation: revised data processing principles

Personal data is to be:

1. processed lawfully, fairly and in a transparent manner;
2. collected for specified, explicit and legitimate purposes;
3. accurate and, where necessary, kept up to date;
4. kept in identifiable form no longer than is necessary for data processing purposes;
5. processed with appropriate security of the personal data;
6. with the data controller holding responsibility for compliance with these principles.

(Adapted from Information Commission's Officer (ICO), 2017: 7)

However, over the past decade, the actual detail of day-to-day client recording has involved reference to increasingly complex and somewhat arcane regulations. Even the injunction to keep records 'no longer than is necessary', for example, can raise real anxieties amongst therapists and their managers, in the absence of statutory requirements, or established agency protocols, with a clear rationale for the retention and destruction of records (Bond & Mitchels, 2015).

Data protection law has reframed the already existing common law protection for client confidentiality outlined above. Disclosure of personal data is an offence, unless it is required by law, necessary for the prevention of crime, or is made with the consent of the data subject. Disclosure of personal data in the public interest remains a valid ground, based on already well-established legal principles.

The major thrust of data protection law extended the principles of accountability and transparency to previously unregulated forms of data handling, such as manual records kept in relevant filing systems, and to electronic recording, such as audio and video tapes. In effect, the law redefined therapeutic recording as a *public*, rather than a purely *personal and private*, activity. The onus was firmly placed upon therapists and their agencies to take control of what may well have been previously multiple and often unregulated forms of recording. This might well include official agency records, ongoing records of therapy, notes for supervision and allegedly *private* reflective recordings, kept outside of formal agency processes. For clearly, if the client is unaware of the very existence of therapeutic process notes in addition to any more formal records retained by the agency, then he or she is not in any position to exercise their rights of consent, inspection and challenge under data protection law.

Access to confidential client material

The first part of this chapter has focused on the role of the therapist as *custodian of sensitive client information*, bound in this role by legal responsibilities and options available under common law and statute. This second part now turns to explore some of the situations where access to client material can be gained *without* the therapist's agreement or discretion, in effect via *legally enforced disclosure*. Access to confidential client material may be sought by the client, by an employer, by solicitors acting for the client, by the police investigating alleged crime, and by the courts in the course of legal proceedings, both civil and criminal (Jenkins, 2007).

An employer may seek access to a client's records for the purposes of audit or evaluation, or to appraise risk of damage to property, or harm to other staff, or to the public. In the case of audit, there should be provision for evaluation on the basis of suitably anonymised data, which does not infringe client confidentiality. Disclosure of identifiable client information to employers should be on the basis of prior client consent. Thus, in employee counselling, or occupational health settings, clients need to be forewarned if confidentiality is limited, on the basis of a clear contractual agreement between client, therapist, counselling agency and employer. Many counselling agencies have explicit provision for therapist disclosure of criminal activity, alcohol or drug dependency, where there is a perceived risk to other staff, or to the public. Client consent, or agreement to a contractual term, will protect the therapist and agency in this situation from legal challenge.

Of course, one of the possible interested parties wanting to gain access to records of therapy may well be the client him or herself. However, some therapists may well find a request by a current, or former, client for access to their records as being somehow intrusive, or disruptive, of the therapeutic process. It may perhaps be thought to indicate a sense of mistrust of the therapist, or a possible challenge to the therapist's competence, or represent some unspoken or unfinished business (see vignette 2). However, putting such interpretation aside for the moment, the client generally has a right of free access to their record of therapy under the General Data Protection Regulation, in an understandable and permanent form. Access to third party material on file may be restricted to protect the latter's right to confidentiality, but the law no longer provides an absolute protection for such information (see fictional clinical/legal scenario below).

Vignette 2

Paul was a troubled young man, who received counselling from a small voluntary agency, for problems of low self-esteem and difficulties in forming relationships. Six weeks after abruptly ending the counselling, he asked for access to his files, under the General Data Protection Regulation. Adam, the counsellor, was initially resistant to this request. The agency's management committee took the view that the client had a legal right of access to the agency's own, somewhat brief, records, and also to any more detailed record of the content of the therapy made by the counsellor and held in the same file. Adam arranged a session to go through the notes with Paul, in what turned into a difficult and inconclusive meeting. Paul then requested access to the notes of *supervision* relating to him, as made by Adam's supervisor. After taking advice, the agency refused access to the supervisor's notes, on the grounds that all supervision in the agency was based on the principle of client anonymity, and that these notes therefore fell outside the ambit of the data protection law.

In some cases, client access may be sought in the context of preparing for a complaint to the therapist's employer, or professional association. In many situations, access may be sought in the context of legal proceedings, where records of therapy are thought to be useful evidence in support of a claim for damages, or a criminal prosecution. Solicitors do not generally have legal authority to enforce disclosure of client records, without a court order, or a signed client consent form. Certain counselling agencies take a firm stance in responding to requests made by a solicitor for release of records, based on a policy of *only* releasing records under a court order. Of course, a client and their solicitor can easily circumvent this, by seeking access as a data subject, under data protection law, rather than by going through the process of seeking a court order for disclosure.

The police, as part of a criminal investigation, prior to court proceedings may also seek access. The law provides somewhat rare protection for records of therapy in this specific situation. Under s.12 of the Police and Criminal Evidence Act 1984, records of therapy are classed as 'excluded material', requiring a Warrant authorised by a Circuit Judge, before the police can seize them as evidence.

Access to confidential client material by the courts

Therapists do not possess privilege and must comply with a court order for release of records for use by the courts. This is on the public interest basis, namely that the courts require the fullest access to material, which may be of evidential value in deciding a case. Any records that are in the ownership possession or control of the therapist, including 'second sets' of notes, such as process notes, are due to be disclosed, under the penalty of contempt of court for failure to comply. Where the therapist no longer has the notes, or did not keep any written records, then the court may issue a witness summons for the therapist to give evidence in person.

A therapist cannot simply refuse to comply with an order for disclosure, on the basis of an ethical commitment to client confidentiality, any more than a medical practitioner can. However, case law seems rather to contradict this, in the instance of Dr Anne Hayman, a psychoanalyst, who declined to answer questions put to her in court, even at the risk of going to prison for contempt of court. She presented a coherent and forceful argument that *any* disclosure of client material would be both counter-therapeutic and a breach of client confidentiality (Hayman, 2002). In this case, the judge accepted her arguments. However, this was on the basis of judicial discretion, rather than establishing a formal legal precedent for others to follow.

Client records released to the court are used as evidence in an adversarial process, where both sets of legal representatives have access to confidential material. Clients may not fully appreciate that their records are used in a highly selective, and frequently challenging, way, in order to further the interests of the case. It is not usually possible for the release of records to be controlled by the client, on the grounds that some material is too sensitive, or potentially damaging to their case. Opposing solicitors will be alert to material, which indicates prior psychological problems, alcohol or drug dependence, previous sexual history, inconsistency in recorded narratives, or any other material, which tends to undermine the credibility of the client as witness.

While therapists need to comply with a court order for disclosure of records, there are certain limited steps that can be taken to protect client confidentiality from total breach in the public environment of the court. Disclosure of records should be limited to 'the necessity of the case' in civil proceedings, for example, rather than give solicitors a free reign, in trawling through evidence of limited relevance to the case in hand. A case can be made to the judge via a formal letter, or by a case put by a legal representative, for records to be perused by the judge in chambers, with a view to excluding irrelevant material from disclosure. This can be successful in limiting, or avoiding, disclosure of client information, which is highly sensitive, but also not material to the case. Therapists faced with this situation need to take advice from their employer's legal department, if one exists, or their professional association, or professional indemnity insurance company. In many cases, the cost of legal representation is covered by professional indemnity insurance policies, even though the therapist is technically a *witness*, rather than an actual party, to the case.

Conclusion

It will be seen that therapists work in a complex matrix of countervailing legal duties regarding client confidentiality, made up of many factors. A decision to disclose client information, or *not* to disclose, needs to be based on a close consideration of specific factors, such as client consent, contractual limitations to confidentiality, the therapist's own contract of employment, the strength of a public interest argument case for disclosure, and, more rarely, actual statutory obligations to disclose. There are also the assumed duties of confidence arising from the nature of the therapeutic relationship and from the express, or implied, terms of any contract for such work. Client confidentiality has additional protection under statute, such as data protection and human rights law. The therapist's role as custodian of sensitive personal information can be further challenged by rights of client access, and by the court's authority. Therapists do not possess privilege and need to be aware of the very limited means available for defending confidentiality under the threat of legally enforced disclosure.

Reflective questions

1. How might you construct an ethically based argument for *not* breaching client confidentiality in cases of potential harm by a client to self or to a third party?
2. How far should therapy be considered as a 'special case', i.e. exempt from the requirement to comply with court orders for disclosure of client records?
3. To what extent might the impact of limited confidentiality, or of court access to records, undermine or assist the therapeutic process?
4. Regardless of specific data protection requirements, what are the ethical arguments for and against client access to records of therapy?

Note

1 Acts of Parliament and Statutory Instruments can be downloaded from www.legisla tion.gov.uk.

References

Bond, T., & Mitchels, B. (2015) *Confidentiality and Record Keeping in Counselling and Psychotherapy*, 2nd edition. London: Sage/BACP.

British Association for Counselling and Psychotherapy (BACP). (2018) *Ethical Framework for the Counselling Professions*. Lutterworth: BACP.

British Psychological Society (BPS). (2014) *Code of Human Research Ethics*, 2nd edition. Leicester: BPS.

Department for Education (DfE). (2015) *Working Together to Safeguard Children: A Guide for Inter-Agency Working to Safeguard and Promote the Welfare of Children*. London: Stationery Office.

Hayman, A. (2002) Psychoanalyst subpoenaed. In P. Jenkins (Ed.). *Legal Issues in Counselling and Psychotherapy*. London: Sage, pp. 21–23.

Health Professions Council (HPC). 2010 https://www.hcpc-uk.org/ Accessed 10/9/12.

Health and Care Professions Council (HCPC). (2016) *Standards of Conduct, Performance and Ethics*. London: HCPC.

Information Commissioner's Office (ICO). (2017) *Overview of the General Data Protection Regulation*. ICO: Wilmslow.

Jenkins, P. (2007) *Counselling, Psychotherapy and the Law*, 2nd edition. London: Sage.

Jenkins, P. (2018) An upgrade for data privacy? *Counselling at Work*, 95(January), 22–27. www.bacp.co.uk/bacp-journals/bacp-workplace/january-2018/an-upgrade-for-data-privacy/.

Legal references

Campbell v MGN Ltd [2004] UKHL 22

Durant v Financial Services Authority [2003] EWCA Civ 1746

W v Egdell [1990] Ch 359, [1990] 1All ER 835

Legal references: regulations

General Data Protection Regulation (GDPR)

Legal references: statute[1]

Children Act 1989

Data Protection Act 1998, 2018

Drug Trafficking Act 1994

Freedom of Information Act 2000

Human Rights Act 1998

Police and Criminal Evidence Act 1984

Public Interest Disclosure Act 1998

Terrorism Act 2000

Chapter 6

The legal context of therapy

Peter Jenkins

Therapists are increasingly aware that their practice is bounded by the law, as well as by ethical and professional considerations. This may be because their work takes place within a statutory setting, such as health or social services, or via the impact of quasi-legal concepts such as contracts and confidentiality, or arising from a growing recognition of issues such as litigation, liability and negligence. In addition, some therapists, i.e. psychologists, are subject to statutory regulation, via the Health and Care Professions Council. Statutory changes, such as the introduction of human rights and data protection law, have had a major impact of therapeutic practice, which it is no longer possible to ignore. Therapists working with risk are also conscious of the interface of their practice with the law in the form of key pieces of legislation, such as the Mental Health Act 1983 and the Children Act 1989. However, therapists are often uncertain about the nature of their legal responsibilities, unsure about the legal parameters of their work and may be subject to conflicting advice, or guidance, about their actual duties regarding compliance with the law.

Therapists and other practitioners regulated by the Health and Care Professions Council (HCPC), for example, are subject to a mandatory duty to report Female Genital Mutilation, under the terms of their statutory registration. The HCPC, however, does not provide legal advice as such to its registrants. The British Psychological Society (BPS) briefly outlines certain legal requirements applying to its members in its *Practice Guidelines* (BPS, 2017), and also provides some sector-specific guidance, for example, on record-keeping (Newton, 2008). The United Kingdom Council for Psychotherapy (UKCP) provides outline information on compliance with the General Data Protection Regulation (GDPR) (www.psychotherapy.org.uk/registers-standards/gdpr/). Legal resources for its members are provided by the British Association for Counselling and Psychotherapy (www.bacp.co.uk/ethical_framework/newGPG.php). The latter resources have been subject to a detailed critique, particularly in relation to the understanding and model of therapeutic contract advanced there (Jenkins, 2016).

This chapter attempts to set out a brief overview of the law with particular relevance to therapeutic practice (for more detailed coverage see Jenkins, 2007). The term law relates to all systems of civil and criminal law, including statute, common and case law. In the UK, there are significant differences between the legal systems operating in Northern Ireland, Scotland and England and Wales. The focus here will be on the law relating to England and Wales. The legal system includes statutes, i.e. Acts of Parliament, such as the Data Protection Act 2018. In turn, Acts rely upon additional guidelines, in the form of Codes of Practice, secondary legislation, such as Statutory Instruments and authoritative guidance and regulations. Common law, on the other hand, is the system of law built up over centuries, devised by judges on an empirical basis. This derives from legal custom and practice, rather than from the formal political process, in Parliament. Principles of common law have particular relevance to therapy in areas such as confidence, contract and negligence. Case law provides key markers in the process of debate and decision making. Specific cases embody key principles, which may then be translated into legislation, or referred to as precedents, in deciding complex and contentious cases. The *Gaskin* case, for example, held a key position in case law, as opening the doors to client access to files. Graham Gaskin, a young man formerly in care of Liverpool Social Services, brought a case against the UK government, at the European Court of Human Rights. His partial success with the case then led to major changes in the law. Legislation introduced the principle of client, or data subject, access to files, formerly considered as protected from access on the grounds of confidentiality.

Structure of the legal system

There is a major divide within the legal system between civil and criminal law. The criminal law operates to punish breaches of law within the wider community, and requires a correspondingly high threshold for proof of guilt. Therapists may have some contact with the criminal law, but are much more likely to need to know at least the basic features of civil law. Civil law provides remedies for resolving disputes between individuals, such as over property, in child and family proceedings, and concerning the protection of individuals' interests, such as privacy and rights under contract. Cases are proven on a less exacting standard, namely 'on the balance of probabilities'.

The area of tort, or negligence law, has particular relevance to therapists. This is a branch of law, developed since a key case in the 1930s, concerning the limits of professional responsibility to others, including clients. (The term tort comes from the French word for 'wrong'.) Under this law, individual citizens have a responsibility to avoid harming their neighbours by any careless act, or omission. In a therapeutic relationship, the practitioner has a similar legal obligation to avoid harming the client. Therapists are often quite wary of the threat of being sued by clients on this basis, although the actual obstacles facing clients in bringing a case of this kind are, in fact, substantial.

A client bringing a case of negligence against a therapist needs to establish three conditions. First, that the therapist owed a *duty of care* to the client. Second, that there was a *breach* of that duty. Third, and most difficult to prove in court, that the breach *directly* caused foreseeable harm to the client, as a result. Negligence law relating to therapists is an offshoot of law relating to medical negligence, presumably because the roots of therapeutic practice, such as psychoanalysis, can be traced in part to medicine. Medical negligence is a well-established and fast growing field of litigation. However, even here, it is markedly difficult for patients to win cases, given the complexity of medical practice and the range of alternative viewpoints that there may be on the appropriateness of any given clinical procedure. In contrast, negligence action against therapists in the UK is almost unknown, at least in terms of successful reported cases, although an unknown number may be settled out of court (see Vignette 1).

There are a number of reasons for the relative lack of reported successful cases against therapists on the grounds of negligence. The client needs to prove that the damage caused by the therapist was of a high standard, constituting a psychiatric injury, such as clinical depression, rather than simple anger, or dissatisfaction. The key problem, in lawyers' terminology, lies in establishing *proof of causation*. The client may be diagnosed as having depression after a course of therapy, but the court needs to be convinced that the therapist actually *caused* this to develop, through serious breaches of professional conduct. The defending solicitor could well point out that the client already had a predisposition to depression, or had showed signs of depressive thinking, even *before* starting counselling. This approach makes it much harder to pin responsibility for the client's worsened emotional state *solely* on the actions of the therapist. Proving causation in the case of psychological matters is not at all easy, although there is now an emerging specialism in the field of cases brought against employers for 'workplace stress' (Jenkins, 2010).

Negligence case law

It is rare for clients to win negligence cases against therapists in England and Wales, although there is now a burgeoning case law for such actions in the US. The key case relating for therapist negligence in England and Wales is that of *Werner v Landau*. In this case, a client brought a legal action against her former therapist; arising out of the latter's attempts to combine psychoanalysis with a social relationship. There were two periods of therapy, separated by a time when the therapist and client had a social relationship, including sending letters, making a visit to the client's flat and holding discussion about a proposed holiday together. The social contact was necessary, according to the therapist, in view of the client's deep emotional attachment to him, and to avoid the client falling into an anxiety neurosis. On ending therapy for the second time, the client made a suicide attempt and was consequently unable to work. The client successfully brought an action under negligence law for breach of duty of care, which was upheld at the Court of Appeal.

This example also illustrates the process of *how* a case of this kind is heard, when the courts may well be unfamiliar with the finer points of therapeutic practice. Under the *Bolam* test, adapted from medical negligence law, the therapist is judged according to the standard of care held by a body of competent professional opinion, as evidenced by expert witnesses. There was no expert who would support the therapist's practice in this instance. All the evidence pointed to a serious breach of professional norms in handling difficult transference relationships. The breach of duty of care was thus judged to have been instrumental in directly causing psychological and financial harm to the client.

In a second reported case, *Phelps v Hillingdon LBC*, a woman brought a successful case against her local authority, for the failure of an educational psychologist to diagnose dyslexia, as the probable cause of her substantial difficulties in school. This case shows how liability for negligence has shifted to include groups of professionals such as psychologists, and also social workers, who were previously considered immune from this kind of action. However, while this may raise anxieties amongst therapists about their apparently increasing vulnerability to litigation, in reality the problems facing clients who seek to bring such cases remain almost overwhelming. Briefly, these difficulties can include providing appropriate evidence, proving causation, satisfying criteria of psychiatric injury, obtaining and funding effective legal representation (Power, 2002).

These two cases illustrate another point about liability, which is important to underline. In the *Werner* case, the therapist was in private practice, and was therefore *personally* liable for his actions. In the *Phelps* case, however, the educational psychologist was employed by the local authority, which held vicarious liability, and was thus the defending party to the action. Therapists often confuse *professional and clinical responsibility* with their *legal liability*, as for example in the discussion over the contentious issue of the legal liability of supervisors. The concept of liability rests primarily on *employment* relationships. Hence freelance, or self-employed, therapists will carry personal liability for their practice, and employed therapists will be covered by their employer's vicarious liability. Employed therapists have a relative advantage of access to an employer's legal representation in these cases. Still, there is a strong argument for both employed and self-employed therapists to have their own legal representation, via a professional indemnity insurance policy, to ensure that the individual therapist's interests are fully represented in court and in any eventual settlement of the case (see fictional Clinical/legal scenario below).

Vignette I

Mr Ali Said brought a legal case against a well-known relationship-counselling agency for breach of duty of care, resulting in psychiatric injury and loss of earnings. He had been counselled by Sharon Jones, a trainee counsellor, on placement from a local university. He claimed that the counsellor was inadequately trained and supervised by the agency, and her constant 'reflect-ing of feelings' only succeeded in generating an increasingly incapacitating anxiety on his part. Due to confusion between agency and the university over their respective roles, the student had not received any supervision for the six-week period of the counselling. Mr Said had been signed off work for anxiety and depression immediately following the period of counselling, and had since lost his job because of absence due to ill-health.

The case was subsequently settled out of court without admission of liability by the agency, with an undisclosed payment being paid to Mr Said.

Litigation for negligence is a fast-changing field, where lawyers may be quick to take up new issues for clients seeking redress. The issue of informed consent to therapy is emerging as one of significance in the context of the NHS, and this may figure in future actions. The concept of informed consent derives from medical and psychiatric practice, but also applies to those using psychological therapies. Informed consent requires that the client has the legal capacity to make a choice between alternative options, based on an understand-ing of their relative advantages and disadvantages, and provides freely given and continuing permission for his or her participation in therapy. The client needs therefore to be informed about the possible risks to partners and family of undergoing changes via therapy, such as the client perhaps becoming much more assertive at work, or at home. Some clients need to be informed of the emotional risks of undergoing psychotherapy, if their sense of self is fragile and particularly vulnerable to challenge. (See Chapter 12 for a review of the potential adverse effects of therapy.) Another client might need to be informed about the relative advantages and disadvantages of using medication, rather than counselling, as a means of overcoming clinical depression.

The law may also be subject to change in another area, namely that of the therapist's 'duty to warn' other people put at risk by a client's behaviour, or by threats made towards them. In parts of the US, therapists are under a legal duty to warn those who are put at risk by a client who makes credible threats of harm against them. In England and Wales, the law is still unfolding on this issue. There is no clear legal obligation placed on therapists as yet to warn third parties, such as a client's partner at risk of domestic violence, unless this duty is already part of therapist's contract of employment. A therapist could pass on information about threats made by a client to the authorities, by acting in the public interest, namely to prevent a crime being committed, but this is not an easy or straightforward route to take. There is case law to suggest that the law in England and Wales could expand to adopt the concept of a duty to warn third parties, if the appropriate legal case came before the courts. The law is constantly changing, and therapists need to keep up to date with significant changes affecting their day-to-day practice with clients.

Contract law

A further aspect of civil law with direct relevance to many therapists is that of contract law. The idea of contracting with clients is current amongst many practitioners, as a necessary component of good professional practice. However, the legal concept of a contract is narrower and more specific that this broader professional expectation of setting out the characteristics of the therapy on offer to the client. A contract requires legal capacity of the persons involved, i.e. who are normally aged over 18. The process involves a firm offer and unequivocal acceptance, with a clear intention on both parties to create a legally binding agreement. Crucially, the contract needs to be supported by *consideration*, namely an exchange of goods, or services, for payment, or similar. These very specific criteria would seem to exclude many therapeutic agreements as legal contracts, where clients are not required to pay for the service on offer. The therapeutic contract in many cases might therefore be more accurately described as *a working agreement*, rather than a contract in a strict legal sense.

Where a legal contract does apply, for a therapist providing counselling to a client for payment, or a supervisor to a therapist on the same basis, or for an agency providing a service to an employer, then certain conditions will apply. The contract will include express terms, such as frequency of contact, duration and cost of sessions. Other terms may not be specified, but will be assumed, or implied, such as a duty to maintain confidentiality. It is also an implied term that the therapist exercise 'reasonable care and skill' in their practice, under the Supply of Goods and Services Act 1982. Either party may take legal action for a breach of contract through a simplified and relatively straightforward process in the Small Claims Court. Given the relative ease of this latter process, therapists may be much more likely to encounter claims for contractual issues, rather than full-blown litigation for negligence, if legal difficulties do arise.

Statute law

Therapists will be broadly familiar with the raft of legislation, which makes discrimination unlawful, codified in the Equality Act 2010. This covers employment and access to both private and public services in Great Britain. The Act prohibits discrimination on the 'protected grounds' of race, gender, sexual orientation, gender reassignment, age, religious beliefs, disability, marriage, civil partnership, pregnancy and maternity. In addition to this statute, a substantial body of case law has been built up over the last four decades, which addresses issues of sexual harassment, and discrimination on the basis of sexual orientation.

Mental health law

Therapists often need to have a good working knowledge of specific statute relating to particular client groups, such as those experiencing mental health problems. The provision of psychiatric care is governed by the Mental Health Act 1983, amended in 2007 and currently under review The 1983 Act endorsed the shift from hospital to community-based provision of services, and facilitated voluntary, rather than compulsory, forms of treatment. As with other major statutes, the detailed procedures of the Act are spelled out in a Code of Practice, which is periodically updated to take account of changes in law and practice (DoH, 2015). The Act sets out a series of safeguards for upholding the rights of patients, including procedures for application to a tribunal, with full legal representation.

'Mental disorder' includes any disorder or disability of the mind, as diagnosed by clinicians such as General Practitioners and Psychiatrists. Mental disorder provides the basis for compulsory detention under the Mental Health Act. The main principles of the Act include treatment for mental illness in the community, whenever possible, rather than via compulsory admission to psychiatric care. The grounds for compulsory treatment are set out below.

Main emergency provisions of the Mental Health Act 1983

Section 2: Admission for assessment: where a patient is assessed as in need of protection from causing harm to themself or to others, and they require detaining on the grounds of mental disorder, they can be admitted for 28 days on a compulsory basis. The 'section', as it is called, or being 'sectioned', needs to be applied for by the patient's 'nearest relative' (closely defined by the Act) or by an Approved Mental Health Professional (e.g. a social worker, or psychologist), and authorised by two doctors, such as a consultant psychiatrist and the GP.

Section 3: Admission for treatment: authorised on a similar basis to the above, it initially lasts six months, and is extendable for a further six months. It is thereafter renewable on an annual basis, subject to review by tribunal.

Section 4: Emergency admission for assessment: lasting 72 hours, this to be used only where it is not possible to obtain a Section 2 admission. Authorised usually by the patient's GP, the section can be applied for by the patient's 'nearest relative', or by an Approved Mental Health Professional.

Unless working within a statutory setting such as the NHS, therapists might have little direct contact with psychiatric services and with mental health law. However, it would be useful for therapists to have a working knowledge of how to refer a client for psychiatric treatment, or how to facilitate self-referral, if appropriate, for example, via the client's GP, or via contact with the local mental health services. Therapists may also work in the context of multi-disciplinary teams, providing counselling for clients with mental health issues, in the context of out-patient, community-based or after-care services, as under section117 of the Act. Familiarity with risk assessment protocols, the Care Programme Approach (CPA), and a willingness to work within an inclusive, team-based approach to client confidentiality are important aspects of therapeutic work in this kind of setting (see fictional Clinical/legal scenario below).

Vignette 2

Geraldine Sharp, a former social worker, was employed as a therapist in a primary care setting. She enjoyed a close working relationship with Paul Smith, a young man with a history of schizophrenia, who called in for counselling sessions on a regular, if infrequent, basis. Over a period of time, she became concerned at his deteriorating physical appearance, and his growing sense of isolation from his immediate family. Relationships with the latter had become increasingly strained, due to his verbally aggressive outbursts. Meanwhile, she was encouraged by her external supervisor to value the client's experience of hearing a number of different voices as a channel of communication, as an opportunity for therapeutic dialogue and as a productive arena for self-exploration by the client. In addition, Geraldine strongly valued the sense that Paul saw her as an important ally in an otherwise bleak and hostile world. Consequently, he trusted her with many of his innermost thoughts and fears, particularly about being 'taken over' by others. However, when she learned in one session that he had stopped taking his medication some time previously, she sought to persuade him to make an appointment with his GP. When he refused, on the grounds that he no longer needed medication, she informed him that she would contact the GP herself, as he was putting himself at risk by his action.

Law relating to children

Therapists will also be aware of the issues of child abuse and sexual exploitation, and the need for clear agency policies with regard to reporting suspected abuse to the authorities. The emphasis on reporting, and the vulnerability of young people to harm, can sometimes lead therapists to assume that there is a blanket legal responsibility for reporting in all situations. As discussed in Chapter 4, the responsibility for reporting abuse is more narrowly conceived as a *contractual* obligation arising from employment, rather than via a mandatory reporting duty on all citizens, or even on all healthcare professionals. The local authority has a duty to investigate where a child under the age of 18 is likely to suffer significant harm. Local Safeguarding Children Boards (LSCB) were set up on a statutory basis by the Children Act 2004, to coordinate and lead on protecting children from harm. Statutory bodies and voluntary agencies that have subscribed to LCSB procedures are then involved in exchanging information via a multi-disciplinary child protection conference. This is a meeting to plan action arising from initial reports or enquiries, such as making a child protection plan, or taking legal proceedings.

Therapists may have a primary interest in the child protection and safeguarding aspects of the law. The Children Act 1989 is much wider in its remit than this, however. It developed out of a lengthy and comprehensive review of the previous patchwork quilt of childcare law, and marked a major attempt at translating best principles of social work and court practice into law. The Act codified responsibilities of social workers with regard to children and families, based on a conception of *partnership*, rather than on intrusive monitoring. Resources, such as access to children's services, are targeted on specific groups, such as 'children in need', i.e. children who suffer disadvantage, those requiring services to avoid impaired development, and those who have a disability.

The Act contains a range of provision regarding children in need and at risk of harm, of which therapists may need to be aware, also set out in the key document on child protection, *Working Together* (DfE, 2015).

Main provisions of the Children Act 1989

> **Section 17:** duty of the local authority to safeguard and promote the welfare of children in need
> **Section 22:** duty to give due consideration to the child's wishes and feelings in making decisions
> **Section 26:** duty to provide a complaints system for children and families
> **Section 44:** power to remove and retain a child in their care, on application to the court (Emergency Protection Order)
> **Section 46:** police powers to remove and detain a child 'at risk' in police protection for 72 hours
> **Section 47:** duty of the local authority to investigate cases where a child is likely to suffer 'significant harm'

The Children Act 1989 brought together aspects of public law, which regulate the activities of public authorities, with private law, in the sphere of provision for children in family and divorce proceedings. Under s.8, courts can make child arrangement orders regarding a child's residence, or can authorise, or prevent, specific outcomes such as undergoing medical treatment, or attending a particular school. Crucially, the Act redefined parental rights in terms of *parental responsibility*, which can be assumed by key figures in a child's life, such as a grandparent, or shared with a local authority in the case of court proceedings. Overall, the Act is imbued with a highly participative approach towards children's rights. It acknowledges the right of young people to be actively involved in discussions about their own future with the professionals charged with looking after them. Therapists might work within the framework of the Act in any number of ways. Some may be employed, or contracted, by social services to provide therapeutic work for children and their families. Others will work with children in other settings, such as schools, where a keen awareness of child protection issues is expected.

There are several areas where the therapist's role and ethical responsibilities may come into conflict with their role, as defined by an agency working within the framework of the Act. One of these is where a young person may report alleged abuse, but may want this to be kept confidential. Under the *Gillick* principle, a young person under 16 has a right to confidential counselling, if judged to be of sufficient understanding. This represents potential conflict between the opposing principles of promoting the child's welfare or protection, and of respecting their wish for confidentiality. From an ethical perspective, there is clearly a need here for therapists to take into account the rights of the young person, together with the child's age, vulnerability and the perceived degree of risk, in reporting abuse.

A further area of difficulty in the past has related to the status of therapeutic work with children who are involved in pending criminal court proceedings. The message frequently (and incorrectly) conveyed to therapists is that *any* therapy will be seen to contaminate and undermine the effectiveness of the child's evidence in court, and should, therefore, be delayed until after the conclusion of any criminal proceedings. This can place therapists in a very difficult position, when the child desperately needs to work with their experiences of being abused, or to explore their feelings with a skilled practitioner, and moreover, one who is *not* directly involved with the process of abuse investigation. The position is clarified by *Practice Guidance*, which clearly states that the Crown Prosecution Service does not, in fact, hold a veto over pre-trial therapy for child witnesses, or for vulnerable and intimidated adult witnesses. Nevertheless, an accommodation between the therapy and the needs of the law must be carefully negotiated and respected by all parties, if the needs of the child or adult witness are to be properly met (CPS/DoH/HO, 2001, 2002).

Conclusion

Therapists inevitably work within some kind of legal context for their practice, although the exact nature of this will vary according to their work setting, client group and employment status. Broadly, therapists need to have an understanding of how civil law concepts such as contract, negligence and liability relate to their work with clients, in order to minimise the potential risk of hostile legal action against either themselves or, if relevant, their employer. The actual risk of litigation against therapists in the UK is sometimes exaggerated, as the system of peer defence against action for breach of duty of care has limited the numbers of successful reported cases to a handful. There may also be specific Acts of Parliament which are relevant to the therapist's role, such as the Children Acts of 1989 and 2004, or the Mental Health Acts of 1983 and 2007. This will depend upon the nature of the client group and the kinds of issues which impact on the therapeutic work being undertaken. Therapists accordingly need to maintain a basic working knowledge of the law as related to their work, in order to best protect their clients' interests and to promote their own competent and ethical practice.

Reflective questions

1. Which aspects of the law have the greatest potential or actual impact on your practice?
2. How do you access information on legal issues affecting your professional work?
3. To what extent does the 'legalisation of therapy' carry threats or opportunities to you as a therapist and your clients?
4. How might clients be better supported in bringing justifiable cases against therapists?

Note

1 Acts of Parliament and Statutory Instruments can be downloaded from www.legisla tion.gov.uk.

References

British Psychological Society. (2017) *Practice Guidelines*, 3rd edition. Leicester: BPS.
Crown Prosecution Service, Department of Health, Home Office. (2001) *Provision of Therapy for Child Witnesses Prior to a Criminal Trial: Practice Guidance*. London: CPS.
Crown Prosecution Service, Department of Health and Home Office. (2002) *Provision of Therapy for Vulnerable or Intimidated Witnesses Prior to a Criminal Trial: Practice Guidance*. London: Home Office Communications Directorate.
Department For Education. (2015) *Working Together to Safeguard Children: A Guide for Inter-Agency Working to Safeguard and Promote the Welfare of Children*. London: Stationery Office.
Department of Health. (2015) *Mental Health Act 1983: Code of Practice*. London: Stationery Office.
Jenkins, P. (2007) *Counselling, Psychotherapy and the Law*, 2nd edition. London: Sage.

Jenkins, P. (2010) Stress and the law. In A. Weinberg, V. Sutherland, & C. Cooper (Eds.). *Organizational Stress Management: A Strategic Approach*. Basingstoke: Palgrave Mac-Millan, pp. 37–52.

Jenkins, P. (2016) Chestnuts roasting on an open fire? Supervisor liability revisited. *Contemporary Psychotherapy*, 9(2). www.contemporarypsychotherapy.org/volume-8-no-2-winter-2016/chestnuts-roasting-on-an-open-fire-supervisor-liability-revisited/.

Newton, S. (2008) *Record Keeping: Guidance on Good Practice*. Leicester: Division of Clinical Psychology/British Psychological Society.

Power, I. (2002) Taking legal action against a therapist for professional negligence. In P. Jenkins (Ed.). *Legal Issues in Counselling and Psychotherapy*. London: Sage, pp. 34–44.

Legal references: cases

Bolam v Friern HMC [1957] 1 WLR 835, 2 All ER 118

Gaskin v UK [1990] 1 FLR 167

Gillick v West Norfolk AHA [1986] AC 112, [1985] 3 All ER 402, [1985] 3 WLR 830, [1986] 1 FLR 224

Phelps v Hillingdon LBC [1997] 3 FCR 621

Werner v Landau (1961) TLR 8/3/1961, 23/11/1961, Sol Jo (1961) 105, 1008

Legal References: statute[1]

Children Act 1989, 2004
Data Protection Act 2018
Equality Act 2010
Human Rights Act 1998
Mental Health Act 1983, 2007
Supply of Goods and Services Act 1982

Writing a report for use in Court and appearing in Court as a health professional and/or expert witness

Allan Winthrop

The decision to remove immunity for experts occurred as part of a Post Traumatic Stress Disorder (PTSD) claim involving a Psychiatrist and Clinical Psychologist (Jones (Appellant) v Kaney (Respondent) [2011] UKSC 13 on appeal from the High Court of Justice [2010] EWHC 61 QB. The loss of expert witness immunity means that experts are no longer 'immune' from civil action. Theoretically, if a person were to lose a case and believed that your report was instrumental to the loss, or thought you were negligent, they could pursue a claim for damages against you as expert. Experts should consider if they are providing the report as part of their employment, self-employment, a Limited Liability Partnership or Company. The legal standing and ramifications of each of these scenarios are different. The potential for legal claims mean that therapists must seek appropriate advice as to the best way to safeguard their personal and practice assets. Appropriate professional indemnity insurance must be in place.

Guidance about expert witness work is provided by The British Psychological Society (BPS) *Psychologists as Expert Witnesses: Guidelines and Procedure 4th Edition* (revised 2017). The document provides basic information on Lord Woolf's reforms to the way in which civil, criminal and family court disputes are handled within the Court system. As an expert, you need to sign a declaration stating you are aware of the procedural rules. The Procedural Rules provide information about the duties and obligations of an expert and also highlight how the expert can seek guidance from the court if needed. The content of these rules are covered in most expert witness training courses.

Who may request a report and what sort of report?

Requests for a report may include specialist rehabilitation or insurance companies, solicitors, government agencies, unions and disciplinary bodies. As a therapist, you may be asked to provide a professional report or an expert report.

Professional reports

In a professional report, the requesting agency is asking you to provide a report or disclose notes primarily because you are the treating therapist, as opposed to you being an independent expert who has never met the client before. Requests may include a Housing Agency asking you to comment on the person's mental health or domestic circumstances. Criminal Injuries Compensation Authority (CICA) may request information about a client's mental health if they have been the victim of a crime. A client's employer (occupational health) may ask that you summarise the client's current mental health status. In these cases, the client's consent for disclosure is needed unless you are required by a court order to release your notes, or unless there are defensible grounds for disclosure without the client's consent, i.e. child protection, or the prevention of terrorism. If the client does not want you to comply with a court order or you believe that to comply would be extremely destructive to the therapeutic relationship then legal advice should be sought and it is possible for the client or yourself as therapist to petition to have the court order set aside.

Expert witness reports

Here a therapist is known to have specialist knowledge or holds senior professional status relevant to the client's situation. The report is requested as part of a legal action, for example, to provide an opinion as to whether someone has suffered a personal injury. The term personal injury is used to mean a diagnosable psychiatric or psychological condition. It is important to note that the Courts will not compensate people for everyday stress and upset. There must be a positive recognisable condition present, e.g. Post Traumatic Stress Disorder or a driving phobia after an accident. Any diagnosis made should be confirmed by the *Diagnostic & Statistical Manual of Mental Disorder 5th Edition* (DSM-5) (APA 2013) or the *International classification of Diseases 10th Edition* (ICD-11) (WHO 1992). These are the current diagnostic manuals at the time of writing. A report may address a person's mental capacity to make a specific decision, disability and capacity for work, parenting skills, presence of malingering, forensic assessment of dangerousness, sexual offending risk and ability to comprehend charges and may include advice on 'fitness to plead.' An expert may also be involved in cases of asylum seeking, specialist assessment of child victims of sexual assault and those who assist the Court in family law child custody cases.

Instructions

'Instructions' should always fall within your area of expertise. It is wrong to agree to assist in a criminal case assessing for the presence of a specific disorder or the likelihood of reoffending if you do not have any experience or training in this field.

A professional report about a current client may be requested necessitating consideration of the impact upon the therapeutic relationship. Always remember that your duty of care is to the client, first and foremost. Then consider how the provision of a professional report may affect your duty of care. Explain to the client that if a report is requested for legal usage then your overriding duty in actually providing the report is to the Court and not to the client. If your professional opinion is at odds with the client's perception of the situation then this may rupture the therapeutic alliance. If you receive a court order or subpoena and the client does not wish you to release certain information, or doesn't want you to write a report, you should take legal advice. It may be in the best interests of your client to attempt to refuse a request. The therapist should always seek appropriately qualified legal advice in such situations.

When reports are requested it is always advisable to obtain the written consent of the client in a format that indicates they understand that the provision of the report is for the Court (or requesting agency). You may not need to obtain written consent in cases where you have been ordered by the court to assess the person without their agreement (e.g. forensic inpatient/prison settings). Therapists should consult their own professional regulator or association and ensure that they are acting within the guidance principles laid down for achieving consent. The Health & Care Professions Council (HCPC) alongside other professional bodies provides information on the seeking of consent for those it regulates.

Upon acceptance of a request to complete an expert report, be clear about the purpose of the report and what you are expected to ascertain. The initial outlining of the scope and purpose of the requested report is referred to as the 'instruction'. The 'instructions' that you receive from the requesting solicitor should always be in writing and be detailed enough as to ascertain the scope and role of the report. The 'letter of instruction' is a record of the request made and the areas to be investigated may include, to:

- Assess and provide a written report as to whether the person is suffering from a recognisable psychiatric or psychological disorder as a result of an accident or incident.
- Assess whether a person is fabricating or exaggerating symptoms of mental disorder.
- Assess whether a psychological condition could be used in mitigation of an offence (e.g. someone with Bulimia caught shop lifting a food item).
- Assess a person's capacity for work in their usual occupation.

Payment

It is standard practice for letters of instruction to agree 'to meet your reasonable fee' or to list the fee you have stated you will charge. It is good practice to document the payment timescale for clarity – e.g. fees 'are payable upon receipt of report by the instructing party' or 'following case settlement'. Agreeing to payment upon case settlement or cases involving legal aid may take over a year for you to receive payment.

There are no national fee scales agreed for psychological reports. Medico-legal agencies who use experts often set their own fees. Always ensure that the fee is commensurate to the work undertaken. If you are required to watch several hours of police interviews, surveillance tapes, CCTV footage and read significant documents then the fee should reflect that. If you are using complex psychometric assessments, then administration and scoring time must be factored in.

It is usual practice to receive copies of the client's medical notes and relevant reports other specialists have written. These are important in that they give a source of information as to previous health difficulties and can be indicative of the client's state of health immediately prior to the accident or incident. They can also help to identify pre-existing conditions and help isolate those conditions which are as a direct result of an accident or traumatic event, those which are not and those which may have been exacerbated by the event. It is preferable to receive the medical notes before interviewing the client where possible and certainly prior to writing the report. As part of the initial instructions, it is important to check whether there are any accompanying orders from the Court. These orders can stipulate a timescale for the preparation of a report. Acceptance of the instructions will usually bind you to these timescales.

When accepting to write a report for use in Court, your overriding duty is to the Court. It is your duty to provide a true and accurate opinion; this overrides your duty to those who instructed you. In order to help reduce legal costs and as a way of avoiding a 'plethora' of different experts being engaged by both sides of a dispute, it is now common practice to appoint one expert in the field under question. The importance of the independence and impartiality of the expert witness cannot be over stated. This independence and impartiality is often what makes the provision of a report on a current client to be extremely difficult. It is now common practice for a solicitor to request the curriculum vitae of three different experts and for both sides in a party to select and agree to the use of one of the experts. This is known as a Single Joint Expert (SJE) and helps to minimise the number of requested reports; the number of experts engaged and reduce the legal costs of obtaining expert involvement.

When conducting an assessment appointment always obtain written consent from the client as this is further assurance that the client knows why they are here. Giving an explanation to the client that your overriding duty is to the Court also emphasise your independence and that you cannot offer confidentiality or agree to keep relevant issues out of the report.

Format of the report

Most medico-legal reports follow a format. The most important aspect is to ensure that the report you write is directly addressing the questions asked in your instructions.

There are many suggested templates or 'example reports' available from a variety of expert witness associations. These templates can be useful to new expert witnesses. However, do not allow the report to appear generic and formulaic. Ensure it is individual to the client and focused upon the concerns being addressed.

It is useful to be aware of the different standards of proof that civil and criminal Courts will use. In a civil Court the standard of proof is '*on the balance of probabilities*', i.e. it is more likely than not. In the criminal Courts the standard of proof is '*beyond all reasonable doubt*'. In a civil suit, someone claiming social anxiety as a result of being bullied at work, would need to prove that on the balance of probabilities, the anxiety was more likely than not, caused by the workplace bullying.

Cover page	- Basic factual demographics
	- Pages/sections should be numbered
Introduction	- The writer of the report
	- Instructions received and from whom
	- Date and place of interview
	- Who was present
	- Any documents, medical notes, other professional's reports, which have been read
Interview	- Basic description of the client
	- Client's understanding of the purpose of the interview
	- Objective assessment of the client
	- The client's account of the issue under consideration and any subsequent developments
Personal history	- Birth to present date as relevant
Previous medical history	- Detailed by client
	- Detailed by medical notes
Psychometric test results	- If used
Discussion	
Opinion	- Diagnosis if applicable
	- Causation
	- Prognosis
Signed declaration / statement of truth	
Appendix	- listing qualifications and positions held by the writer

Figure 7.1 Suggested template for a medico-legal report

Information that should be present in each of the sections

Cover page

There should be an explicit initial statement at the top of the covering page which states, '*To the Judge, In the proposed action in the County Court*' or other Court as appropriate. Most experts simply type this in the top left hand of the page, underlined in bold. Addressing the report to the judge indicates that you are acknowledging your overriding duty to the Court.

The covering page is for basic administrative details, the client's name, address, date of birth, date of incident, date of interview, details of instructing solicitors or body, relevant case reference numbers. Include the date of the report and name of the report writer.

Introduction

This is an initial statement about the writer of the report and their professional status and field of expertise.

The writer

I am (insert name). I am a (insert profession). My specialist field is (for example, the psychological impact of trauma). Full details of my qualifications entitling me to give expert opinion and evidence are set out at the end of this report.

Instructions received

This includes information about what you have been asked to ascertain. It is important that when you see the client, you make sure that they are aware that the reasons for the meeting are for the purpose of preparing a medico-legal report, which will be seen by all parties involved. The normal therapeutic confidentiality agreement is not applicable as the report will be released to the solicitor and may be used in Court.

Allow adequate time for the assessment appointment – usually between one and two hours for fairly straightforward cases and considerably longer if complex psychometric assessments are being used.

The written statement of instruction should include what the Solicitor or instructing agency has asked you to do. You should provide a summary of your letter of instruction:

> Mr. C on a bus involved in a road traffic accident and as a result is experiencing severe psychological difficulties. I have been instructed by

Mr. Jones, Solicitor, to investigate for the Court whether Mr. Hirst has suffered any formal psychological/psychiatric condition as a result of this accident – and the effects and prognosis of this if applicable. I have been provided with copies of Mr. Hirst's general practice medical note and a copy of a report by Mr. Smith, Consultant in Emergency Medicine

Confirm whether or not some photographic proof of identity has been checked.

Interview

Provide an objective description of the client, for example 'Mr. Hirst presented as a smartly dressed man in his mid-sixties who was orientated to place and time' (if of course, he was so oriented). It may be relevant to specify ethnic origin if the case has any direct relevance to ethnic background (i.e. racially motivated crimes). It may also be pertinent to mention ethnicity if the client describes a history of ethnic or racially motivated bullying.

Include a statement to indicate whether there was any evidence of a formal thought disorder, psychosis or abnormal perception. Provide information as to whether the client appeared anxious, tearful, irritable entered the consulting room with the aid of a walking frame etc. Some experts use this section to provide a Mini-Mental State Examination (MMSE).

Client's account of the incident and subsequent events

This is the client's account of the incident (index event) and the difficulties that they believe to have occurred as a result. Use language that further indicates that this is the client's expression of the facts as they see them for example. 'The client stated that he hit the windscreen of the bus' or 'the client alleges that his partner hits him on regular occasions'. Following a statement of the incident, the course of any developing symptoms and the sequence of events should be documented. 'The client remembers being assisted by paramedics and taken to hospital by ambulance … '

The impact of the injury or incident should be documented as well as any period of time off work, GP consultations, prescribed drugs, physiotherapy, time in hospital, sleep disturbance due to pain or traumatic recollections, nightmares, loss of weight, whether any sports, hobbies or interests were affected, family, marital and any sexual difficulties. The aim is to give information about the impact of the event upon the client's life. The therapist will explore the chronological development of symptoms and psychological phenomena and question the client further to gain a clear and accurate overview of the situation from the client's perspective.

Personal history

The client's relevant life history and development from birth to the present day is detailed. Clients are asked about their birth and developmental milestones. As far as they are aware, were milestones within the expected times. What was the type and quality of education as well as parental and sibling relationships. Details of employment and relationship history. This information indicates the client's expected level of functioning in comparison to how they present at interview.

A comprehensive history can help in the identification of other traumatic life events that may be relevant to the issue being considered. It provides a general impression of the sort of person the client is and places their current difficulties in the wider context of the rest of their life.

Previous medical history

This section could be divided into two sub-sections. The first – medical history as presented by the client and second, medical history as delineated in the GP medical notes. The client should be asked about their general health and any serious conditions. They should also be specifically asked whether they have had any previous psychiatric or psychological problems and whether they have ever seen a psychiatrist/psychologist/therapist in the past. Similarly, it needs to be asked whether the client has received any treatment for the problem(s) with which they now present.

A client may give details of their previous history but upon checking the medical notes there is actually a much longer, more complex history. The dividing of the medical history into 'from client' and 'from medical notes' allows the more thorough documentation of medical history to be made. This is important in cases where a client is stating that the incident caused their current problems, when, in fact, the medical notes may show a lengthy previous history of consulting in respect of the same problem. It is then perhaps more the case that the incident may have exacerbated a pre-existing condition or that the client is trying to falsely claim compensation for an existing condition. Whilst it is important to document and draw attention to such discrepancies it is the role of the court to determine the facts of the case. It is preferable therefore to leave open the reasons for the discrepancies and simply report that the discrepancies are there. The court will determine the relevance it attaches to the discrepancy.

Psychometric test results

If you intend to administer lengthy psychometric tests you must allocate sufficient time to complete the test and interview. Ensure that the client knows beforehand how long the appointment will take and to bring spectacles and/or hearing aids if worn.

Test users should be fully qualified and competent in their administration and interpretation. You must state if anyone else administered or scored any tests on your behalf (Psychology Assistant/Trainee). If someone else was involved, then their name and qualifications must be given. You should present basic information about each test utilised and the client's result. In more complex cases tests of memory, personality, malingering and IQ may be needed. An indication should be given, as to whether the tests are being used to aid diagnosis or whether the tests are self-report symptom inventories. It is important to remember that many tests are not being used as a diagnostic tool, i.e. 'The Beck Depression inventory is a self-rating scale assessing severity of depression symptoms'. In itself, it does not diagnose depression. It is essential that the tests used are appropriate and relevant to the questions being asked and to the purpose of the report.

Discussion

This section is used to summarise all the information gathered and explain and expand upon it. The relationship between issues are discussed, consistencies/inconsistencies are explored. Information from the client and the consistency or otherwise with other test results is examined. Discrepancies are highlighted, and a discussion of potential diagnostic possibilities could occur. In straightforward cases this section is normally easy to write, whereas in more complex cases with several sources of information to draw upon, it may be a lengthy section of the report. The discussion is where your expertise as a therapist is used to make sense of multiple sources of information, which at times may be conflicting.

Opinion

In legal proceedings an expert is allowed to express their opinion based upon their findings. This section contains the writer's opinion after the relevant information has been considered. It may be helpful to include sub headings of diagnosis, causation and prognosis. The diagnosis should be supported by relevant information and it is often helpful to make reference to the claimant fulfilling the criteria of a specific diagnostic manual.

'Mrs. White would meet the criteria for a Specific Phobia (Driving) as defined by the Diagnostic and Statistical Manual of Mental Disorder 5th edition.'

An indication should be afforded as to the extent of the client's suffering and loss. Whether the clients report is reasonable and in line with others who suffer from this problem.

Causation

Your professional opinion as to the cause of the diagnosed condition and whether it is more likely than not (in a civil case) that the client's condition was caused by or has been materially contributed to by the incident under consideration.

Increasingly, many solicitors ask for a percentage allocation to be given in terms of causation and current distress. You may be assessing someone who presents with depression but has a series of depressive episodes in their history. The therapist may decide that a statement such as the index event being 70% causal and 30% causation being due to pre-disposing factors may be made. Any attempt to quantify psychological distress in such terms is difficult and will always be a complex task for therapists. If it is not clearly apparent, then it should be stated that it is just not possible to be so specific. It is of paramount importance that the therapist does not allow themselves to be pushed into stating more than can be professionally defended.

Prognosis

This section should address the likely course of the condition and whether you would predict resolution within, for example, a year without any treatment or six months with some psychological intervention. Would the situation worsen or deteriorate further without treatment?

Always stay within your area of expertise when making your opinions and comments about causation and prognosis. Your opinion needs to remain within the psychological field and you should not comment directly upon issues such as the extent of physical health problems, mobility loss due to physical injury or whether earlier medical treatment would have affected the outcome.

If you believe psychological treatment would help the client, then you should state the type of therapy and number of sessions suggested.

'I would expect Mr. Hirst to benefit from a course of Cognitive Behavioural Therapy of approximately 12 sessions. I would expect resolution of his difficulties within six months of commencing treatment.'

Declaration/statement of truth

Following the opinion section of the report, a declaration and Statement of Truth needs to be signed and dated by the author of the report. The solicitor's instructing letter normally includes the paragraph they would like you to use as a Statement of Truth, but the following factors are usually included:

A statement that shows – *you understand your duty to the Court and that you have complied with that duty.*

A statement that confirms *you are aware of the civil procedure rules (in civil cases).*

A statement that *you have formed your own opinion of the evidence that your fee is in no way dependent upon outcome of the case*

A statement of truth – *I believe that the facts stated within this report are true and that the opinions I have expressed are correct.*

The declaration and statement paragraphs provided by the instructing solicitors are usually more than adequate.

Signature and date at the end

Appendix

A brief narrative of your relevant professional experience. This should include a list of all your qualifications, professional, statutory registrations and any publications.

Upon receipt of the report, solicitors have 28 days in which to put to you written questions about the report. In practice due to work pressures and Court timescales, you may often receive questions outside of this timescale. These questions are usually to clarify aspects of the report. The civil/criminal procedure rules document further the procedure for dealing with questions relating to clarification of the report. The procedural rules also indicate how the expert can approach the Court for guidance if needed.

Appearing in Court

Appearance in Court as an expert witness is something that often induces anxiety in practitioners. (It may be helpful to observe a court case from a public gallery in order to familiarise yourself with Court protocol and procedures.) Since the introduction of the new procedural rules (civil and criminal), the written report of the expert is emphasised. The attendance at Court to give oral evidence (evidence in chief) is now less common in civil cases. It is fairly commonplace for the expert to be asked to testify in Criminal and Family Court matters where issues and the outcomes have severe, life changing consequences. When appearing in Court, you should present a professional and competent image. Clothing should be smart and appropriate. You should be prepared with your report and any notes used. You will be sworn in. This means you will be asked to take an oath based on your religious beliefs or to affirm your commitment to give an honest and truthful account. It is essential to remember that the Court is interested in your view as an independent expert and are usually very appreciative of the expert's contribution. Appearing as relaxed and confident as possible may add authority to your testimony. Before entering Court, seek clarification as to how the Judge should be addressed. This will depend upon the status of the Judge – 'Your Honour' in a County Court whereas 'My Lord' is used in a High Court.

Advice often given is to listen to the question being put to you and then turn towards the Judge to give your reply. The reply is addressed to the Court. Some experts prefer to stand '*side-on*' *to* the questioner and face the Judge. These tactics have been used to deal with *aggressive questioning* and to avoid face-to-face contact with the cross-examiner. Regardless of how you stand, it is important to remain calm and do not allow yourself to become obviously irritated if asked irrelevant or '*silly*' questions. Most importantly, do not allow yourself to be drawn into offering opinions on areas outside of your area of expertise, however tempting or leading any questioning may be. If you do stray from your area of expertise it will weaken your evidence and undermine your standing in the Court. You are present in Court as an expert in your particular field, your views and opinions on other things are irrelevant.

Therapist's levels of anxiety at testifying in Court are often tied up with fears over *saying the wrong thing* or being *made to look stupid*. It is important to remember that you are there to advise the Court, not to represent a client. Testifying in Court will be the same for you whether you have a current therapeutic relationship with the client or not. The difference will be in the impact your Court appearance has upon the therapeutic relationship with your client. The areas addressed in this chapter form a starting point from which to expand and develop thinking around the role of medico-legal work within the psychological and psychotherapeutic field.

Reflective questions

1.   Consider the issues that the use of diagnostic categories poses for psychological practitioners writing reports.
2.   What is the potential impact upon the therapeutic relationship of writing a report on a current client?
3.   How does the loss of immunity alter your willingness to be an expert witness?
4.   Should training to be an expert witness be essential within therapeutic training? Please consider reasons for your answer.

References

American Psychiatric Association (APA). (2013) Diagnostic *and Statistical Manual of Mental Disorders*, 5th edition. Arlington, VA: American Psychiatric Association.
British Psychological Society. (2017) *Psychologists as Expert Witnesses: Guidelines and Procedure*, 4thedition. (revised 2017), Leicester: BPS.

World Health Organisation. (1992) *The ICD-11 Classification of Mental and behavioural Disorders*, Geneva: WHO.

Useful websites

Academy of Experts: www.academy-experts.org/defaultin.htm
APIL: www.apil.org.uk Association of Personal Injury Lawyers
British Psychological Society: www.bps.org.uk
HCPC: www.hcpc.org Health Care Professions Council
Society of Expert Witnesses: www.sew.org.uk
The Academy of Expert Witnesses: www.academyofexperts.org
The Expert Witness Institute: www.ewi.org.uk
The Law Society: www.lawsociety.org.uk

Chapter 8

Regulation, learning from complaints

Brian Linfield

Sharing insight from complaints allows practitioners from whatever discipline they work in, an insight into peoples' experiences. Analysis of complaints can help practitioners understand the impact that service failures have on all those effected by such deficits. It can also help clients, patients or service users to know that their concerns have been heard. It is hoped that this chapter may enable all those involved in talking therapies to consider regulation and view the complaints procedures in a more positive light.

Having a complaint made against you

The hardest aspect of complaints for professionals to comprehend is the fact that their client/patient/service user, has not, in most cases, tried to resolve the complaint with them, before going to their Regulator. That said, complaints can be a powerful, positive tool and provide an opportunity for any professional to reflect on how they practise and how they deliver their professional services. Although, having a complaint made against you, may not feel like this, at least initially.

The 2013 Francis Inquiry highlighted the need to recognise the importance of patient complaints, and the need to create robust systems and cultures that are able to deal with and learn from them. In response the Government published *Hard Truths. The Journey to Putting Patients First* (2014) where the *Report of the Mid Staffordshire NHS Foundation Trust Public Inquiry* (2013), called for a '"fundamental culture change" across the health and social care system to put patients first at all times' (2013: 5). Robert Francis QC, the Inquiry Chair, called for action across six core themes: culture, compassionate care, leadership, standards, information, and openness, transparency and candour. The Government's initial response, Patients First and Foremost (Department of Health, 2013) response to the *Report of the Mid Staffordshire NHS Foundation Trust Public Inquiry*, sets out throughout the publication a radical plan to prioritise care, improve transparency and ensure that where poor care is detected, there is clear action and accountability.

Impact and triggers of complaints

A complaint for many Talking Therapy Professionals (TTP) whether they be counsellors, psychiatrists, psychologists, psychotherapists or social workers will come as a shock or surprise, especially if the complainant is still in therapy with them. The aim of all TTPs is to help and that involves building trust and a therapeutic relationship. Therefore, if a client or patient suddenly lodges a complaint it can be very distressing for the TTP. That said, I wonder after 30 years of dealing with complaints across many specialities and professions, why professionals feel it necessary to start their response to a complaint with a four-page curriculum vitae instead of dealing with the issues at hand, especially when their qualifications are not the subject of the complaint. Why not just answer the complaint? For example;

- Did you fall asleep during the therapy session?
- Did you disclose confidential information to a third party?
- Did you terminate therapy with immediate effect?
- Did you have an inappropriate sexual relationship with a client?

The majority of complaints should be capable of being resolved between the parties without the need of mediation or the professional Regulator. This can only happen though if dialogue is entered into in a non-confrontational way. Complaints can help practitioners improve the delivery of services to all future patients, clients or service users if reflected upon seriously and both parties have realistic expectations for the outcome of a complaint.

Responding to the NHS hospitals complaints system review 2013, Jane Cummings, The Chief Nursing Officer for England said in an NHS news release dated 29 October 2013:

> Our single most important purpose is to look after patients with compassionate care. That means delivering the best possible patient experience to every single patient, every single time. As part of this we must listen, take seriously and respond promptly, responsibly and openly to any complaint we receive. Poor complaints handling is unacceptable. We must learn from complaints and continue to work hard to ensure patients feel confident raising issues or concerns and that staff feel supported to respond.
> (www.england.nhs.uk/2013/10/comp-rev/)

Regulators produce advice for TTPs on what can trigger a complaint, some complaints can have more than one trigger, as identified in the United Kingdom Council for Psychotherapy (UKCP) Professional Conduct Committees or the Health and Care Professions Council Fitness to Practice annual reports. If practitioners are familiar with what the triggers are, they can often put protocols into place to prevent them happening.

Triggers for complaints

Breaches of confidentiality

If practitioners are required to write a report for use outside of health care, for example in a family court, what is the minimum amount of information needed to disclose and has permission been obtained to do so? New guidance on confidentiality from the General Medical Council (GMC) came into force on 25 April 2017. This document includes a detailed flowchart of the key questions that practitioners should ask themselves when presented with a situation involving confidentiality. While the underlying principles remain unchanged, the new document does provide clarification and the opportunity to look again at how confidentiality and the principles behind it affect healthcare practitioners and regulators. You can access the guidance at www.gmc-uk.org/guidance. There is also some useful information on the General Protection Data Regulations (2018).

Failure to maintain appropriate boundaries

Boundaries is a broad topic, and it is perhaps understandable that this is an issue that continues to arise in complaints. Dual relationships happen when someone is acting in two different roles that may conflict. Transient and unintentional dual relationships can occur naturally in the course of everyday life: for example, when you have or have had a professional relationship with the person serving you at the supermarket checkout. On one level, dual relationships blur the boundaries and create role confusion and, on the other, can verge on being or are actually harmful, this is why many complaints relate to this issue. Sexual exploitation is an obvious boundary violation, others, might include employing a service user or inviting them to a party in your home.

Knowledge is power and the knowledge that therapists have of their clients' internal and external worlds puts them in a unique and powerful position. Moving into a dual relationship could therefore potentially involve abuse of that power and the subsequent exploitation of the client. Such situations can to some degree, be pre-empted by including in the therapeutic contract, or as general information, a statement outlining how encounters that occur outside the therapy space will be managed, and setting clear expectations for communication between sessions.

Financial exploitation

Asking a client or patient to lend you money, encouraging clients or patients to employ you in their business, asking clients or patients to buy you computers or technology, allowing clients or patients to run up a substantive debt to you when you know they do not have the ability to pay, are examples of financial exploitation. These are all complaints that have been made to regulators in the fields of TTP's.

Failure to terminate therapy in an appropriate manner

Modality and other professional practices have to be considered here; however, codes of ethics specifically require you to act in the best interest of the client and practitioners need to ensure that the client/patient is not set adrift with no support. Only in exceptional circumstances, for example, the practitioner fearing for their own personal safety, should termination of therapy be immediate.

Look for the triggers in the following two scenarios and think about the questions posed. Although fictional, they are based on complaints received over the past five years.

Vignette I

'I consulted Mr Smith with the specific purpose of getting help for my son Adam following a difficult divorce. Over the course of four months Adam had weekly therapy with Mr Smith. I had agreed to pay for hour-long sessions but they only lasted 40 minutes; however, I didn't complain as the therapy was clearly helping Adam. Mr Smith was subsequently contacted by my ex-husband's solicitor following a court case ordering a report on my son for court proceedings initiated by him for contact with my son. At no time did Mr Smith contact me for permission to disclose this confidential information and I have signed no contract that allows disclosure. This is a clear breach of confidentiality that resulted in my ex-husband gaining access to my son.'

Therapist's response

'I am a family and child psychotherapist and family consultant. I am very well regarded within the therapeutic community. I am a supervisor, lecturer and trainer. I have never had a complaint made against me. Mrs A contacted me regarding her 12-year-old son Adam. It quickly became apparent that Adam was affected by his father's departure from the household. We managed to resolve this and Adam left therapy after about 16 weeks. Several months later I received a letter of instruction from solicitors acting for Adam's father quoting a court order and I supplied the requested report. There really is nothing more to say.'

Reflective questions

- Should the therapist have supplied the report requested?
- Would you have sought any further information from the solicitor, if so what?
- Did the therapist have consent to disclose the information or wasn't consent required?
- Would a contract with the client have helped here and if so, how?

Vignette 2

'I have been in therapy with Peter for some 15 years in respect of a severe childhood trauma. In 2010 I could no longer afford the fees due to financial difficulties and asked Peter to reduce his fee. Peter simply continued to see me (albeit less frequently) without asking me for any payment. In September 2017 Peter prepared a statement and asked me to sign documentation that would entitle him to his fees as part of my will once I pass away. I find this extraordinary and totally unprofessional. How can he allow £17,000 worth of fees to accumulate over seven years and expect it not to affect my life mentally or affect the power balance between us? How is this in my best interest to be in such a large amount of debt to someone? I will now have to inform my wife who doesn't know I'm still in therapy.'

Therapist's response

'This complaint comes after pressure from the wife of my client who he has had no emotional communication or involvement with for decades even though they live in the same house. She has no knowledge, interest or understanding of my client's emotional needs, as he keeps his life entirely separate from his wife. Apart from her financial support (withdrawal of which has caused this situation), he does not communicate with her. My client's childhood trauma resulted in an extreme and unusual dependency on therapeutic support, and very extraordinary attachment needs, not only to me over the last 15 years or so, but also to his previous therapists. My client has been paying a reduced rate for many years below my minimum fee. You will appreciate that he has been an extremely demanding client, and it would have been tempting and – from the perspective of my practice – convenient, at the point when he could no longer afford to pay, to just walk away, I believed it was in his best interest for me not to abandon him. My decision was influenced by the fact that a similar debt had accumulated some years earlier, when he could not work due to complications following a flawed operation. Once he could afford to, he had paid this off immediately and in full, without the slightest hesitation. So he and I have a good track record on this issue, and a basis for mutual trust and understanding around money. I am getting on in years and so need to get my affairs in order. The easiest way to secure payment, should anything happen to either of us, is to make me (or my executors) a beneficiary of his will. Should he die his wife will not settle his account!'

Is it ethical to allow a client to accumulate a large debt and then insist they have them lodged as a legacy in their will?

Was the debt accruing in the client's best interest?

Serious professional misconduct

My experience at the UKCP shows that the most serious allegations of misconduct, sexual assault, sexual relationship or fraud are either factually correct or vexatious. On occasions, there is overwhelming evidence to support an allegation of this type. In this technological age the evidence is usually all there in emails, texts and from social media screenshots. For the vexatious/transference complaints the evidence is often scant or contradictory. TTPs know the consequence of crossing over these ethical boundaries would most likely be erasure from their professional Register.

Vignette 3

'I saw Tom as my therapist from 2008–2010. I ended the therapy because we had started to have an intimate relationship during the allocated sessions at his house (which I was still paying for, the sessions not the house) and I wanted to have a legitimate relationship with him. I told Tom this and he agreed, and we started seeing each other. However, during this time my mental state deteriorated as I no longer had therapeutic support. I eventually started working with a different therapist; however, this upset Tom. Over time I realised I no longer wanted to have a sexual relationship with Tom, but hoped to continue a friendship. I tried to end the sexual relationship on several occasions, but it seemed as though Tom couldn't let go. I eventually had to ignore all of his communications. Before we started our relationship, Tom told me that he found me sexually attractive and that he had discussed it with his supervisor. This confused me as it seemed like his supervisor accepted his feelings and behaviour as normal.'

Therapist's response

'In one of our last sessions together, Patient A told me she had sexual fantasies about me. During our next session together, I told her that I also had sexual feelings toward her, that I found her sexually desirable and had been thinking about her since our last session. It was at this point that we embraced for the first time. At our next session I pleaded with Patient A to return to our normal psychotherapist/client relationship, but she said that was impossible. We ended the therapeutic relationship at this point. Although a relationship did technically start whilst she was still my client, we ended the therapy and did not have sexual intercourse until two weeks after this time. Although I regret that I was unable to be the therapist to help Patient A, I never resented her for seeing another therapist. I also refute Patient A's assertion that I refused to accept the end of our relationship – this suggests that I had a choice in it, which I didn't. When she decided to end the relationship that was that. I greatly regret breaching my ethical code and any harm and distress that I have caused Patient A. At the time this happened I discussed my actions with my supervisor and have entered into therapy to help prevent a reoccurrence of this behaviour.'

Regulation and sanctions for talking therapy practitioners (TTPs)

TTPs are experts when it comes to their own professions and are highly trained. However, only some TTPs get in-depth training in Regulation and the application of sanctions. Some professional bodies will offer some support, other TTPs will rely on their public liability insurance or professional indemnity to support them, for this is one source of getting the legal help they need, should a complaint be made against them.

For a Regulator to take a case forward, the case has to have a realistic prospect of succeeding. Can the Regulator prove that there has been a breach of the Code of Ethics? This means that, on the balance of probabilities, that it is more likely than not that the behaviour complained about did in fact occur. It is important to note that a TTP does not have to prove their innocence. Having decided the realistic prospect test, the regulator then has to determine if there is a current impairment to practise. If the realistic prospect test is passed and current impairment to practise is a possibility, then an independent Tribunal or Panel (TP) is convened to adjudicate on the matter.

If a case is found proved, the TP hearing the case then have to decide if a sanction is required to protect the public. The starting point is no sanction at all, there are many different sanctions in between, depending on the profession or regulator that would enable a professional to continue to practise albeit with conditions, culminating in the ultimate sanction of removal (erasure) from the professional register.

Not everyone who is removed from a professional register following a complaint is prevented from practising. This can be quite shocking for members of the public once they become aware of that fact. Generally, it is only the statutorily regulated professionals (psychiatrists, psychologists, social workers and nurses) that can be prevented from practising legally. In voluntary regulation (which applies to counsellors and psychotherapists), the ultimate sanction of removal from the register usually only prevents a former registrant from using the regulator's accreditation mark, the kite mark of excellent professional practise for the registrant. It is therefore of the upmost importance that a voluntary regulator informs the public if they have removed a TTP from their register. This is usually done by publishing the decision to erase on the Regulators website.

This was confirmed on an application for summary judgement in a judicial review application, against the United Kingdom Council for Psychotherapy's publication policy. His Honour Judge John Male QC (sitting as a Deputy High Court Judge) said he:

> did not find it obvious that it was not in the public interest to publish a determination that a psychotherapist has entered into an inappropriate sexual relationship with a client during treatment'. He went on to say 'The fact that this was a consensual relationship does not detract from the possible public interest in the matter. Other members of the public are entitled to know as this informs them on their choice of psychotherapist.
>
> (Raymond Bott-Holland v United Kingdom Council for
> Psychotherapy, 2017)

Complaints and the public interest test

This last year has been a busy time for the High Court when ruling on applications to them from both Regulators, Registrants and professional bodies. A particular theme being the protection of the public (public interest). In a highly unusual decision, the GMC brought a ruling from one of its own tribunals to the High Court to appeal its decision not to strike off a trainee doctor from its register. It is unusual because TPs are independent fact finding bodies and never before has a Regulator appealed a decision of their own Panel. In a controversial move the GMC appealed the ruling on the grounds that it was 'insufficient to protect the public'.

In 2017, the Medical Practitioners Tribunal Service (MPT) ruled Dr Bawa-Garba should not be removed from the medical register and went on to apply a sanction of two years suspension. It was this decision that the GMC appealed to the High Court. Lord Justice Goss, who sat with Mr Justice Ouseley described it as a tragic case. Mr Justice Ouseley said: 'I have come firmly to the conclusion that the decision of the Tribunal on sanction was wrong, that the GMC appeal must be allowed, and that this Court must substitute the sanction of erasure for the sanction of suspension'. An appeal from that decision was heard before The Lord Chief Justice of England and Wales The Master of The Rolls and Lady Justice Rafferty. Their approved judgement dated 13 August 2018 contained the following extracts:
Paragraph 76

> Secondly, there was a fundamental difference between the task and necessary approach of the jury, on the one hand, and that of the Tribunal, on

the other. The task of the jury was to decide on the guilt or absence of guilt of Dr Bawa-Garba having regard to her past conduct. The task of the Tribunal, looking to the future, was to decide what sanction would most appropriately meet the statutory objective of protecting the public pursuant to the over-arching objectives in section 1(1A) and 1(B) of Medical Act 1983, namely to protect, promote and maintain the health, safety and well-being of the public, to promote and maintain public confidence in the medical profession, and to promote and maintain proper professional standards and conduct for members of the profession: Bolton v Law Society [1994] 1 WLR 512, at 518F-H; Ziderman v General Dental Council [1976] 1 WLR 330 at 333; R (Redgrave) v Commissioner of Police of the Metropolis [2003] EWCA Civ 4, [2003] 1 WLR 1136 at [38]. As Laws LJ said in Raschid (at [18]) the Tribunal is concerned with the reputation or standing of the profession rather than the punishment of the doctor; so did Sales J in Yeong v General Medical Council [2009] EWHC 1923 (Admin), [2010] 1 WLR 548 at [19] and [21]. As Ms Fenella Morris QC put it elegantly in her skeleton argument for the Professional Standards Authority, the decisions of the Crown Court and the MPT are taken by different bodies, with different functions, addressing different questions and at different times.

Paragraph 87

Undoubtedly, there are some cases where the facts are such that the most severe sanction, erasure, is the only proper and reasonable sanction. This is not one of them. Once it is understood that it was permissible for the Tribunal to take into account the full context of Jack's death, including the range of persons bearing responsibility for that tragedy and the systemic failings of the Trust, as well as the other matters relied upon by Dr Bawa-Garba, and that the Tribunal plainly had in mind its overriding obligation to protect the public for the future, in the tri-partite sense stated in Section 1(1B) of MA 1983, it is impossible to say that the suspension sanction imposed by the Tribunal was not one properly open to it and that the only sanction properly and reasonably available was erasure.

The judgements conclusion at Paragraph 98 was that 'For those reasons we allow this appeal, set aside the decision of the Divisional Court, restore the decision of the Tribunal and remit the matter to the Medical Practitioners Tribunal Service for review of Dr Bawa-Garba's suspension'.

So why should TTPs be interested in this case and how does it impact on them? It is because this decision, confirms the test a Regulators Tribunal/Panel has to apply. Erasure is not always the inevitable outcome of even the most serious breaches of the ethical codes. Tribunals/Panels are confirmed as the experts in their field and after hearing all the evidence are still entitled to adjudicate that a TTP can continue to practice albeit with conditions or after a suspension, taking into account the individual facts of each case and how best to protect the public.

Protection of the public. What is the public interest test and how is it applied?

The public interest test is used by many to justify a wide range of actions and proposals. However, it is often unclear (even to those using the term) what they mean by this. There is no definitive definition. Many public bodies like the Crown Prosecution Service (CPS) and the Information Commissioner's Office (ICO) publish their own interpretations.

So how should we define the public interest test in the therapeutic arena? I would suggest as a starting point;

1. How serious is/are the alleged breach/breaches of the TTP's Ethical Code?
2. What is the level of culpability of the member/registrant?
3. What are the circumstances of and the harm caused to the client or others?
4. What is the potential impact on other clients or patients of the TTP?

Complaints and the future

The Government Consultation on Promoting professionalism, reforming regulation consultation October 2017 closed on 23 January 2018. The consultation document can be found on the following link: https://assets.publishing.service. gov.uk/government/uploads/system/uploads/attachment_data/file/655794/Regula tory_Reform_Consultation_Document.pdf

A variety of different organisations are dealing with complaints. As outlined on page two in the 2007 Government White Paper Trust, Assurance and Safety – The Regulation of Health Professionals in the 21st Century, the independence of the regulatory bodies is vital 'to sustain the confidence of both the public and the professions through demonstrable impartiality. Regulators need to be independent of government, the professionals themselves, employers, educators and all the other interest groups involved in healthcare'.

The British Association for Counselling and Psychotherapy (BACP), British Psychoanalytic Council (BPC) and the United Kingdom Council for Psychotherapy (UKCP) welcomed the consultation. They said:

> The consultation was an important opportunity to comment on the future of the regulatory environment and the fundamental issue of public protection. Currently, BACP, BPC and UKCP have registers accredited by the PSA and have in place robust professional conduct procedures. Through our responses to the Department of Health, we:

- Support regulators working more closely together.
- Agree that any regulatory changes should further the objective of improving standards and public protection.
- Urge the Department of Health to involve professional bodies in the regulatory reform work as we possess vital professional expertise.
- Support upstream prevention and proportionate responses to professional conduct issues.
- Will continue to progress our own work in defining standards for the profession alongside the work of the Department of Health.

Through our formal partnership, the Collaboration of Counselling and Psychotherapy Professions (CCPP) we are committed to continue to safeguard the public by effectively regulating the counselling and psychotherapy profession and we will continue to work together to ensure that we take an active part in responding to any regulatory developments.

Complaints – a developmental learning tool

Regulation allows for the collection of data that helps us understand why people are complaining and also helps us to pin point and learn from any trends in complaints. It is imperative that we continue to share this data with TTP's to enable then to review their practises and put in place protocols that will hopefully prevent misunderstandings from occurring. I would also suggest that an early engagement with the complainant and an apology though might lead into Alternative Dispute Resolution (such as mediation) that would be a chapter entirely of its own.

Conclusion

Sharing insight from complaints allows Regulators to share peoples' experiences s so that members understand the impact that failures have. A complaint can be an educational tool and positive tool that can help to improve the service your practise provides to clients/patients. If a complaint is made against you, engage with the process, reflect on what happened, look for any triggers and self-analyse if it would have been possible to avoid the complaint in the first place. Complaints are not usually an attack on an individual. They usually result where unrealistic expectations are not met or managed from the start.

Reflective questions

1. How would you deal with a complainant who was still in therapy/ treatment with you and could your therapeutic relationship continue? What factors would influence your decision-making?

2. Do you display or provide information on how to make a complaint, if not, why not?
3. Does protection of the public outweigh a practitioner's current fitness to practise?
4. When was the last time you read your code of conduct or ethical code?

References

Case No: CO/3036/2016, Between Claimant, and British Association for Counselling and Psychotherapy Defendant and United Kingdom Council for Psychotherapy – Interested Party. Available at: https://high-court-justice.vlex.co.uk/vid/co-3036-2016–655413309

Case No: CO/3089/2017 in the High Court of Justice Queens Bench Division Divisional Court Royal Courts of Justice Strand, London, WC2A 2LL Date: 25 January 2018, Before: LORD JUSTICE GROSS and MR JUSTICE OUSELEY Between: GENERAL MEDICAL COUNCIL Appellant and DR BAWA-GARBA Respondent. Accessed 17 May 2018.

Crown Prosecution Service. Public interest test online. Available at: www.cps.gov.uk/publication/full-code-test Accessed 1 June 2018.

Decision of the medical practitioners tribunal concluding on 13 June 2017 which heard the case of Dr Hadiza BAWA-GARBA. Online. Available at: www.mpts-uk.org/static/documents/content/Dr_Hadiza_BAWA-GARBA_13_June_2017_appealed.pdf

Department of Health. (2014) Hard Truths The Journey to Putting Patients First. Volume One of the Government Response to the Mid Staffordshire NHS Foundation Trust Public Inquiry. The Stationery Office: London. Available at: https://assets.publishing.service.gov.uk/government/uploads/system/uploads/attachment_data/file/270368/34658_Cm_8777_Vol_1_accessible.pdf

Department of Health. (2017) Promoting professionalism, reforming regulation. A paper for consultation. Crown Copyright 2016.

Department of Health. Patients First and Foremost. (2013) *The Initial Government Response to the Report of the Mid Staffordshire NHS Foundation Trust Public Inquiry.* London: The Stationery Office.

Francis, R. (2013) Report of the Mid Staffordshire NHS Foundation Trust Public Inquiry Executive Summary 2013. The Stationery Office.

General Medical Council. Confidentiality. Good practice in handling patient information. (2017) Available at: www.gmc-uk.org/guidance Accessed 25 May 2018.

General Protection Data Regulations. (2018) *Information Commissioner's Office(ICO) (2017) Overview of the General Data Protection Regulation.* Wilmslow: ICO. Available at: www.legislation.gov.uk/ukpga/2018/12/pdfs/ukpga_20180012_en.pdf

Information Commissioners Office. Public interest test. Online. Available at: https://ico.org.uk/.../documents/1183/the_public_interest_test.pdf Accessed 1 June 2018.

Neutral Citation Number: [2018] EWCA Civ 1879. Case No: C1/2018/0356 Gross LJ and Ouseley, J. [2018] EWHC 76 (Admin) Royal Courts of Justice Strand, London, WC2A 2LL. Date: 13/ 08/2018.

NHS England. News. 29 October 2013. NHS England Responds to NHS Complaint Review 2013. Online. Available at: www.england.nhs.uk/2013/10/comp-rev/Accessed 1 June 2018.

Professional Standards Authority: Response to government consultation – Promoting professionalism, reforming regulation January 2018. Available at: www.professionalstan dards.org.uk/publications/consultation-responses

Raymond Bott-Holland v United Kingdom Council for Psychotherapy: Oral Judgment of John Male QC (sitting as a Deputy High Court Judge) on summary judgment application 10.03.2017.

Secretary of State for Health: Government White Paper Trust, Assurance and Safety. Presented to Parliament. (2007) Available at: www.gov.uk/government/publications/trust-assurance-and-safety-the-regulation-of-health-professionals-in-the-21st-century Accessed 17 May 2018.

UKCP. (2018) Available at: www.psychotherapy.org.uk/news/response-department-healths-consultation-professional-regulation/Accessed 1 June 2018.

UKCP Annual Report. (2016.) Handling Complaints about Therapists. Report of the UKCP Professional Conduct Committee 1 January 2016 – 31 December 2016.

* Acts of Parliament and Statutory Instruments can be downloaded from www.legislation. gov.uk.

Part 3

Clinical considerations
and responsibilities

Chapter 9

Fitness to practise

Nicola Barden and Ruth Caleb

Introduction

Those whose work is to help others should be fit to perform their professional task. Whether the practitioner is a volunteer, in training or fully qualified with many years of experience they must be able to perform their role, so that those they support can have reasonable confidence in the 'treatment' they will receive. If a client has been offered help then they are entitled to assume that they will receive this; allowance is not made for personal difficulties in relation to the amount of care and skill that they can expect.

This creates challenges professions that place emphasis on the relational aspect of the work. Jung (1954) described psychotherapy as a 'dialectical procedure', the therapist as a 'fellow participant' in the process of individual development, with the implication that the whole being of the therapist is involved, over and above their skills and intellectual knowledge. While this is emphasised and theorised differently across the range of talking treatments, all therapeutic approaches require a degree of relationality between therapist and client, making the practitioner's emotional and physical health relevant to fitness to practise issues. The personal and professional are intertwined; as Bond (2010: 10) states, 'From the client's point of view, the personal ethics of the counsellor are inseparable from the standards and ethics of counselling because one is the foundation of the other'.

All of the major professional organisations recognise the fitness to practise requirement in some way and demonstrate it through their codes or frameworks of ethics, which are discussed below. There are difficult questions to answer: how does one recognise when one has become unfit? What are the suitable actions to take? Who is responsible for recognition and action? This chapter will consider first the major ethical codes relating to the subject of fitness to practise. It will then discuss the responsibilities of those involved, particularly the practitioner and their supervisor and workplace, if not in independent practice. Finally, it will consider what form appropriate action could take, and how decisions about it may be made.

Fitness to practise – ethical frameworks

All professional bodies have their own ethical codes or frameworks. Where there is no statutory requirement for regulation, the professional bodies will run their own complaints procedures to hear concerns about professional practice. Where there is a statutory requirement, the complaints procedure is run by a government body. Psychiatrists are required to be approved by the General Medical Council (GMC). Practitioner psychologists and social workers are subject to statutory regulation through the Health and Care Professions Council (HCPC), which has its own generic standards of conduct, performance and ethics (HCPC, 2012, 2016) as well as profession-specific standards of proficiency for training and ongoing development. Both the GMC and the HCPC are regulated by the government's Professional Standards Authority (PSA). Counsellors and psychotherapists are not regulated by statute (apart from arts therapists); however, many counselling and psychotherapy organisations have had their voluntary registers accredited by the PSA which publishes standards for the regulators and the organisations that hold voluntary registers (PSA, 2016a, 2016b).

If someone is removed from a statutory register they can no longer practise under that title; a psychiatrist could not continue to call themselves a psychiatrist. If they are struck off a voluntary register, they can no longer practise under the name of that professional body, but could still call themselves a counsellor/psychotherapist.

British Psychological Society (BPS)

The HCPC refers to fitness to practise for all practitioner psychologists in terms of conduct, health, up to date skills and knowledge, character and positive management of ' … the physical, psychological and emotional impact' of practice (HCPC, 2015: 8). While emphasising the importance of practitioners consulting with workplaces, colleagues, professional bodies, unions and training establishments in the process of resolving any dilemmas about meeting proper standards, they do this in the overall context of being expected to take responsibility for their own practice.

The BPS continues to be the major professional organisation for psychologists. It publishes its own advisory Code of Ethics and Conduct (BPS, 2018), which may be used as evidence of standards to which a psychologist would be expected to adhere. Taking personal responsibility for professional and ethical judgement is emphasised while the challenges of self-monitoring are recognised. This points towards the importance of consultation and discussion that is a necessary corollary to the independence of practice inherent in therapeutic work.

British Association of Social Workers (BASW)

While the professional body for social workers (BASW) covers all four home nations, the regulatory body is specific to each country, although the overarching message is deliberately similar. In England the HCPC (2017) includes in fitness to practise for social workers their personal health and well-being, managing the physical and emotional impact of their work and building professional resilience. Supervision is discussed as a tool to support and enhance practice. The Scottish Social Services Council (2016) emphasises the partnership between employer and social worker, expecting personal difficulties to be shared with the employer when they may impact on practice, and the employer to support the social worker appropriately. The Northern Ireland Social Care Council is specific about impaired fitness to practise potentially arising from 'serious and uncontrolled' mental health issues, alcohol and substance misuse, and any health condition that affects 'reasoned decision making, thinking and/or behaviour' (2016: 3). Social Care Wales (2017a, 2017b) picks out the importance of the practitioner's active participation in their own well-being and resilience. Throughout there is an expectation that practitioners should challenge poor conduct in others where they are aware of it.

BASW provides its own Code of Ethics (2014), which similarly urges critical evaluation of professional practice and self-referral to another professional where judged necessary. Employers are expected to provide supervision but the frequency of this is left open and, unlike counselling and psychotherapy, supervision can be provided by managers.

Royal College of Psychiatrists (RCPsych)

The College's code of ethics (RCPsych, 2014) makes clear that psychiatrists have a shared responsibility for each other's work and that they *must* report fitness to practise concerns to a colleague, a defence body or the GMC itself. Its good practice guidelines (RCPsych, 2009: 27) expand this into the responsibility to protect patient's from any 'risk of harm posed by another colleague's conduct, performance or health', and make clear that any health condition that could impact on performance should not only be discussed with a qualified colleague but must also 'follow their advice about investigations, treatments and changes to your practice that they consider necessary. You must not rely on your own assessment of the risk you pose to patients' (2009: 39). This makes very clear that the helper is not the best judge of their own fitness to practise. Because the GMC is also a body that supports doctors, it hosts the independent Medical Practitioners' Tribunals Service to hear cases against its members, separating investigation (is there a case to answer?) from adjudication (hearing and passing judgement on a case).

United Kingdom Council for Psychotherapy (UKCP)

UKCP undertakes the setting and monitoring of training standards, ethics and conduct for its members, under the approval of the PSA. It has 11 colleges representing significant therapeutic theoretical orientations or client contexts.

Each College and member organisation may have its own standards for education, training and practice that must be consistent with the UKCP central standards. The member organisations have their own complaints processes, which may subsequently be escalated to UKCP. All complaints against individual registrants are heard by UKCP itself, through the centralised Complaints and Conduct Process (UKCP, 2016).

UKCP has a central statement of Ethical Principles and Code of Professional Conduct which states, 'The psychotherapist accepts responsibility to ensure that they are competent and have sufficient supervisory arrangements and other necessary support to enable them to meet their psychotherapeutic obligations to any client' (2009: 6). It makes clear the therapist's responsibility to ensure that they are fit to practise in terms of their own physical and mental health or the impact of drugs/medication, and to take action if they are not. At the time of writing UKCP is engaged in a consultation over a new Code of Ethics which came into operation in 2019. A significant change in the draft is a vision for ethical practice under which sits the principles or foundation standards of such practice, and an elaboration of what that requires of practitioners.

British Association for Counselling and Psychotherapy (BACP)

BACP's register of practitioners is approved by the PSA. The Association's Ethical Framework (2018) specifically requires that clients should be 'put first' by practitioners 'making clients our primary concern while we are working with them' (BACP, 2018: 7). This is followed with a statement of the ethical values, principles and personal moral qualities that counsellors and psychotherapists are required to keep in mind. It closes with a more detailed section on the implications for practice. In terms of what is required for fitness to practise, it states that practitioners 'will maintain our own physical and psychological health at a level that enables us to work effectively with our clients' (British Association for Counselling and Psychotherapy (BACP), 2018: 19). This is underlined in a section on self-care that addresses the practitioner's responsibility to be physically and mentally able to meet the requirements of the work. It is specific about the role of supervision as essential throughout a practitioner's working life, sustaining their 'personal resourcefulness' (2018: 30). It also makes clear that where the therapist is qualified and/or experienced, despite the importance of supervision, the responsibility for meeting professional standards belongs finally to the therapist.

Fitness to practise – common factors

There is agreement across the different professional bodies that fitness to practise includes an emotional robustness and capacity to both contain and work with difficult emotional and cognitive states, and to be sensitive to the use of self within the work. It requires sufficient physical resilience in order for the client to experience a reliable and consistent presence in the therapist, and good cognitive functioning including the ability to reflect on what is being heard, make sense of it and consider how to use it for the client's benefit. The symptoms of physical or psychological conditions that need to be considered in terms of fitness to practise are those that affect this capacity to think, to feel, to be present and to communicate. The responsibility to recognise and address difficulties rests with the practitioner, the supervisor and their colleagues, not with the client.

Substance use

Alcohol has a depressive impact which overrides judgement and inhibition and should be avoided at times when it could affect practice. Even a small amount of alcohol can make a difference to perception and affect and the client may well recognise this even if the practitioner does not. There should therefore be no client contact when alcohol has been consumed, being mindful that it can have an impact for several hours after consumption. Being very clear on what response the client can expect out of hours is important here.

Clearly the use of mood altering and hallucinogenic non-prescribed drugs would be considered unethical, but prescribed drugs must also be considered as they too can have an impact on psychological awareness and mood. Practitioners must be able to monitor and account for any impact of their own medication, and crucial here could be openness in supervision and with medical and professional consultants.

Physical and mental health

Many illnesses are temporary and the effect on practice may be profound but short lived. Other conditions may be on-going or fluctuating. Mental ill health can include long-term, transitory and recurrent conditions that may or may not have an impact on therapeutic practice and should be discussed in clinical and managerial supervision. Some conditions may be recognised as a disability under the 2010 Equality Act and for employers in particular consideration of reasonable adjustments for the employee should be made, to facilitate a safe and helpful therapeutic service to clients. This can present particular challenges in supporting both the rights of the practitioner and the needs of the client.

Stress

Ongoing and severe stress can be similar to illness in terms of symptoms, causing headaches, addictive behaviours, appetite changes, disturbed sleep, poor concentration and tiredness. These may become noticeable to clients, but for the practitioner there may be denial of the stress itself and therefore of the symptoms. Identifying the source and impact of the pressure is the first step to managing and ameliorating it (Thurgood & Crampin, 2009). Support mechanisms, personal characteristics, resilience and use of stress management techniques all come in to play when considering fitness in this situation.

Life events

Life events might include problems that affect the practitioner through concern for a third party, such as the illness of a dependent; or they may be directly affected, for example redundancy or relationship breakup. Whether the problem is predictable or unpredictable, progressive or static, permanent or transient, all are considerations in the judgement of fitness to practise.

The question is not just *whether* someone is fit to practise, but also *what* they are fit to practise. Work context, client profile and theoretical orientation all affect decisions about what to do if fitness to practice is in question, whose responsibility it is to act and what ethical courses of action are open.

Fitness to practise – responsibilities

Alert and experienced practitioners who are aware that their practice is suffering will want to take steps to protect their clients. Agreed best practice is for concerns to be discussed with a supervisor and/or professional colleague or consultant who can bring an external view to bear, and with an employer who may well be able to support changes to working practices for a period of time.

While this is unarguable, there is a problem in that the person who is most subjectively involved at that point, namely the practitioner, is being asked to make the first move in recognising their own vulnerability. A client may feel very unconfident in judging whether their support worker is fit to practise, particularly if it their first experience of seeking help and there is little to compare it with. Indeed, their inclination may well be to assume that the practitioner is the expert and to assess their own experience in the light of this assumption.

Dale (2010) stated that in questioning fitness to practise there is a need for a clear and open conversation with the supervisor. However, there are barriers in honesty between supervisee and supervisor and the level of trust must be high for vulnerabilities to be disclosed (Webb & Wheeler, 1998), particularly where there is a managerial link. This is an argument that has been used against mixing the supportive and developmental with the monitoring functions of supervision. Barden (2001) argued that support and monitoring must be seen as a dual role of the supervisor as the monitoring function keeps the practitioner as well as the client safe, and it is false to create a division between the roles. Full monitoring is impossible in professions that work largely unobserved and depend on the honesty and awareness of practitioners. Indeed, if a practitioner is unable to be open about their vulnerability in supervision, it could be argued that they are unfit to practise.

When working for an organisation some supervisory/consultancy contracts give clear indications of accountability; others are less clear, and in some cases, there is no clinical contract, particularly where therapeutic practice is not the major function of the organisation. Supervisors may be expecting managers to assess someone's capacity to work adequately; managers may assume supervisors will tell them if they have concerns. With trainees there is the added dimension of whether the contract is between the placement, the trainee or the course – preferably a clear agreement between all three, but this does not always happen.

The BACP Ethical Framework underlines that supervisees must:

> be open and honest in supervision and … draw attention to any significant difficulties or challenges that they may be facing in their work with clients. Supervisors are responsible for providing opportunities for their supervisees to discuss any of their practice-related difficulties without blame or unjustified criticism and … support their supervisees in taking positive action to resolve difficulties.
>
> (2018: 31)

This recognises that it requires the joint effort of both parties to protect the client if there are concerns about poor practice. Other professionals such as experienced colleagues or line managers who are involved also carry responsibility. The unifying link is the protection of the client, which always comes first.

Notwithstanding all this, the primary monitor of fitness to practise remains likely to be the practitioner, with all the attendant complications. This raises issues for the training and selection of helping professionals and the importance of their personal qualities. There is a particular demand on private practitioners who may work largely in isolation and for whom ceasing to practise may have serious economic consequences. Practical steps like adequate insurance can be helpful here in making ethical decisions less distressing. Joining supportive practitioner groups and attendance at conferences and workshops can be essential sources of support and advice. The expectation that independent practitioners create a professional will outlining arrangements to care for the needs of clients in the case of their death, or accident/illness leading to incapacity to work, is now a requirement of registration with many professional bodies.

Fitness to practise – taking action

The most frequent recommendation made across all codes is that the practitioner should consider refraining from working when their fitness to practise is impaired. Yet this is not as simple as it might at first appear. As has been noted, helping professionals work in a variety of contexts, with a range of clients and from a number of theoretical orientations. Whether the work they are engaged in is long term or short term, in an agency where alternatives can be quickly offered or in a single person practice where onward referrals may be problematic, are all factors to be considered in deciding what is in the client's best interests.

Having recognised that each situation is different, there are several options to choose from. Practice can be stopped, restricted, reduced or adapted. Technology can provide solutions in some cases, providing alternatives to face-to-face contact. The balance sought is between what the practitioner can manage and what the client needs. These variables are examined through two vignettes.

Vignette 1 – serious illness

In a case recorded by Wheeler (1996) a trainee counsellor 'Jane' had a terminal illness that nevertheless allowed her to function well at the start of the training. The illness progressed more quickly than was anticipated and her therapist became concerned for the quality of Jane's work on her training placement. The therapist therefore was herself in an ethical dilemma, and pivotal was Jane's difficulty in confronting the possibility that her condition could be affecting practice. At a counselling session not long before her death:

She (Jane) was carried into the room. She was painfully thin, pallid and drawn. She had, however, been to her training session the previous evening and was fully intending to see her clients the following day. I confronted her with her responsibility to take care of herself and not see them while she was so ill, but she rejected that totally, saying 'My clients are my life'.

In a consideration of fitness to practise it is the client's needs, not the practitioner's, which come first. Jane had her life invested in her clients and could not admit to herself that she should not be seeing them. In not being able to process her own ending Jane was, at the very least, having to deny the possibility to the client of dealing with their ending too. This can be compared to Jeffries (2000) who, working in a university student affairs department, explored the management of her clients when she was diagnosed with cancer. Her treatment involved surgery, radiotherapy and periods of chemotherapy lasting two to four months, at unpredictable intervals depending on the progression of the illness. In explaining her absences and physical changes to her clients she encountered various reactions from distress and anxiety to guilt, anger and fear. How much she told each client depended on their reaction; it was done on a case-by-case basis rather than a single script, and always directly, as she felt emotionally strong enough to do this. Her strength was aided by a positive response from colleagues and strong personal support at home. Clients were given choices in how they wanted to go forward, for example changing counsellor, having an 'interim' counsellor, or waiting until the interruptions for treatment were over and then resuming sessions. Clients were naturally in different stages of neediness and dependency, and an individualised response respected this.

At the point at which she was cautioned by her oncologist that her life expectancy made it inadvisable to take on any long-term commitments, Jeffries restricted all new work to intake and short-term clients. The cancer remained a part of the work that required continuing attention.

> Although I have been well since my return to work … my prognosis has affected my practice in subtle ways. All the clients I have taken on this academic year are new to me and I have not felt that it has been appropriate or necessary to tell any of them that I have cancer. But I think I am working more actively, setting a faster pace, holding back from offering myself as available for as long as I am needed.
>
> (Jeffries, 2000: 481)

Jeffries' own robustness on the subject of her cancer made making these arrangements a different experience to the case of 'Jane'. However, it is worth reflecting that behind the scenes her decisions were unlikely to be reached without facing considerable amounts of ambivalence, fear and uncertainty in the process. Openness and ongoing support in supervision are essential parts of any such process; practitioners should not take a position as sole judge of their fitness to practise. Management support can also make a difference to the ease of decision-making, and managers should consider being proactive as well as sensitive in involving themselves in fitness to practice issues.

Vignette 2 – external demands

As Rosenberg attests,

> Upset children, a nagging headache, uncertain finances, an argument with a partner, indecision about the weekend's plans – these must somehow be held away during the session. That is the idea, at least, but the reality is that any number of these issues can and will push in, frustratingly.
>
> (2016: 11)

For most practitioners there will be times when the focus on a patient becomes compromised by their own problems or experiences. Take, for example, the case below.

Aki was a practitioner whose mother, who brought him up as the only child of a single parent, was showing signs of confusion and forgetfulness. She lived alone close by and became increasingly more demanding and absentminded. Aki was concerned that she was not caring for herself and may not be safe at home.

He had not discussed his family problems with his supervisor as he did not believe that his ability to care for his patients was compromised. However, his supervisor noticed that he seemed on edge during their supervision session, though he denied that there was a problem. During the next supervision session Aki received a phone call. He excused himself and left the room to take it. This was highly unusual behaviour as Aki had previously switched his phone off at the beginning of every supervision session. On his return his supervisor pointed this out and alerted him to her concerns in this and the previous session. Aki apologised profusely for accepting the phone call and explained that his mother had been ill, and he was worried about her condition. Their session continued as normal and there were no signs that the supervisor could pick up that his patients were not getting his full attention. The following session Aki arrived unusually late, looking exhausted. He acknowledged that he had been experiencing a hard time. He had had to cancel some sessions when his mother had a fall, and she had returned to live with him until she became mobile again. On returning to her own home she had become confused, and he was now waiting to take her to hospital to be assessed and hopefully to find some support for her condition. The supervisor sympathised with these difficult circumstances but felt that there may be patient issues that needed exploring. At first Aki seemed to be defensive and denied that his personal circumstances could possibly have any impact on his relationships or work with his patients. The supervisor gently persisted, and Aki agreed that it felt extremely challenging to try to care for his mother, take part in family life and be fully present for his patients. He had not been sleeping well and had only eaten sporadically.

With the supervisor's support Aki came to accept that his problems may be affecting his work and together they considered how he could deal with the issue including how he might support himself, and be supported by others, during this challenging time. They agreed to monitor this situation and discuss further help if or when required.

BACP describes supervisors as 'key allies working "upstream" … promoting an "ethics-aware" approach' (Jackson, 2018: 8). While a client's needs must take priority, care and concern for the practitioner must also be expressed. The supervisor's approach in this vignette was supportive rather than punitive, though it remained firm and focussed.

Conclusion

Larcombe pointed out that 'As practitioners, it is the "duty to self" that under-pins our duty of care to our clients and to the profession' (2008: 284). It will be clear that the concept of fitness to practise is not simple to define. Practitioners need to know that their work requires emotional robustness and a level of physical wellbeing. There is a need to be proactive in maintaining professional fitness, and reactive to situations that might compromise this. Having arrangements in place to support clients in the event of the latter may help to prepare for the unexpected.

Over the course of a long career it would be remarkable if life did not produce situations that challenged fitness to practise from time to time. Such challenges are not shameful but normal, and the simple guideline in facing them all is to make the first question, 'What is in the best interests of the client?' The ethical way forward will follow from that.

Reflective questions

1. How do you know if you are fit to practise?
2. How could you prepare for managing unexpected changes in your personal life that could impact on your practice?
3. What could interfere with your ability to make sound ethical decisions?
4. Who would you tell if you had concerns about your fitness to practise?

References

Barden, N. (2001) The responsibility of the supervisor in the British Association for Counselling and Psychotherapy's codes of ethics and practice. In S. Wheeler & D. King (Eds.). *Supervising Counsellors: Issues of Responsibility*, London: Sage, pp. 41–52.

Bond, T. (2010) *Standards and Ethics for Counselling in Action*, 3rd edition. London: Sage.

British Association for Counselling and Psychotherapy (BACP). (2018) *Ethical Framework for the Counselling Professions*. Lutterworth: BACP.

British Association of Social workers (BASW). (2014) Codes of ethics for social work. Available at: www.basw.co.uk/about-basw/code-ethics (Accessed 31 August 2018).

British Psychological Society (BPS). (2018b) *Code of Ethics and Conduct*. Leicester: BPS.

Dale, H. (2010) *Am I Fit to Practise as a Counsellor?* BACP Information Sheet P9. Lutterworth: BACP.

Health and Care Professions Council. (2012) *How to Raise a Concern*. London: HCPC.

Health and Care Professions Council. (2016) *Standards of Conduct, Performance and Ethics*. London: HCPC.
Health and Care Professions Council. (2017) *Standards of Proficiency: Social Workers in England*. London: HCPC.
Health and Care Professions Council (HCPC). (2015) *Standards of Proficiency: Practitioner Psychologistv*. London: HCPC.
Jackson, C. (2018) The only way is ethics. *BACP Therapy Journal*, 29(6), 8–11.
Jeffries, R. (2000) The disappearing counsellor. *Counselling Journal*, 11(8),478–481.
Jung, C.G. ([1935] 1954) Principles of practical psychotherapy, in The collected works of C.G. Jung, Vol. 16, *The Practice of Psychotherapy*. London: Routledge and Kegan Paul.
Larcombe, A. (2008) Self-care in counselling. In W. Dryden & A. Reeves (Eds.). *Key Issues for Counselling in Action*. London: Sage, pp. 284.
Northern Ireland Social Care Council (NISSC). (2016) Fitness to practice: What it means. Available at: https://niscc.info/storage/resources/20160525_ftp_whatitmeans.pdf Accessed 9 September 2018.
Professional Standards Authority. (2016a) *Standards of Good Regulation*. London: PSA.
Professional Standards Authority. (2016b) *Standards for Accredited Registers*. London: PSA.
Rosenberg, J. (2016) A therapist at sea. *BACP Therapy Journal*, 27(6), 11–13.
Royal College of Psychiatrists. (2009) *Good Psychiatric Practice*, 3rd edition. Available at: www.rcpsych.ac.uk/files/pdfversion/CR154.pdf Accessed 29 August 2018.
Royal College of Psychiatrists. (2014) Good psychiatric practice: Code of ethics. Available at: www.rcpsych.ac.uk/files/pdfversion/CR186.pdf Accessed 29 August 2018.
Scottish Social Services Council. (2016) *Codes of Practice for Social Service Workers and Employers*. Dundee: SSSC.
Social Care Wales. (2017a) *Code of Professional Practice for Social Care*. Cardiff: SCW.
Social Care Wales. (2017b) *The Social Worker: Practice Guidance*. Cardiff: SCW.
Thurgood, G. & Crampin, K. (2009) Assessing pressure in the workplace. *BACP Counselling at Work Journal*, 67,16–17.
United Kingdom Council for Psychotherapy. (2016) *The UKCP Complaints and Conduct Process: Making a Complaint*. London: UKCP.
United Kingdom Council for Psychotherapy (UKCP). (2009) *Ethical Principles and Code of Conduct*. London: UKCP.
Webb, A. & Wheeler, S. (1998) How honest do counsellors dare to be in the supervisory relationship? An exploratory study. *British Journal of Guidance and Counselling*, 26(4), 509–524.
Wheeler, S. (1996) Facing death with a client – confrontation or collusion, countertransference or compassion? *Psychodynamic Counselling Journal*, 2(2), 167–178.

Chapter 10

The role of social media in counselling and psychotherapy

Mary Creaner

I trained as a therapist in the pre-internet 1990s. Apparently, not having grown-up with digital technology I am considered a 'digital immigrant' rather than a 'digital native' (Prensky, 2001: 1) in contrast to the majority of the students, supervisees and clients with whom I work. Adapting to the virtual world and reflecting on its implications for professional practice has certainly caused me to consider my own biases and assumptions about social media and social networking, in particular. Informed by my theoretical orientation, which is essentially integrative with a humanistic core, dialogical questions have arisen in my reflections on the role of social media in my work context. These questions predominantly relate to the intersection of one's personal and professional life. The challenge is that of holding professional boundaries while seeking transparency and authenticity in the therapeutic relationship.

Although this consideration is not new in a traditional therapy setting and is continuous in reflective practice, social media use inherently challenges the personal and professional boundary in clinical practice and tests conventional perspectives on what constitutes the therapeutic space. However, at the heart of this dialogue is the commitment to maintaining ethical best practice, therapeutic integrity and ongoing reflection on Paul's (1969: 44) seminal question, 'what treatment by whom, is most effective for this individual with that specific problem and under which set of circumstances?' Hence, as a practitioner, multiple layers of complexity are presented when considering the role of social media in counselling and psychotherapy practice. This chapter sets out to discuss some of the opportunities and challenges that social media use presents in this context.

Internet technology in psychological therapy

Internet technology developments have become part of the fabric of our everyday lives. With the advent of the internet in the early 1990s, the last number of decades have seen rapid growth in the development of web-based therapy as evident in the growing body of literature in this area. What is also apparent is the increasing number of randomised controlled trials (e.g. Richards et al.,

2018) and meta-analyses (e.g. Andrews et al., 2018) being conducted to evaluate the efficacy and effectiveness of computer and internet-based intervention and through which an evidence base is being established. For example, in their meta-analysis of the effectiveness of web-based psychotherapy, Barak et al. (2008: 141) concluded that 'Internet-based therapy, on the average, is as effective, or nearly as efficacious, as face-to-face therapy'. They also reported that interactive web-based programmes had better outcomes in comparison to online programmes that did not require active user participation. However, only three treatment approaches (behavioural, cognitive behavioural therapy and psycho-education) were represented in the meta-analysis. Nonetheless, the findings may suggest that specific therapy approaches for particular symptoms may have better outcomes in online delivery. More recently, Andrews et al. (2018) concluded from their meta-analysis of 64 efficacy trials with adults, that computerized CBT (cCBT) and internet-delivered CBT (iCBT) were effective interventions for depression and anxiety and equivalent to face-to face CBT in terms of helpfulness. The authors note, however, that as there was variation in the content and method of delivery of the iCBT programmes in the studies meta-analysed, further investigation is warranted.

Among the reported advantages of web-based therapy are the convenience, ease of access, outreach to marginalised populations, and the relatively low cost involved (Callahan & Inckle, 2012). It may also have a destigmatizing and disinhibiting effect due to the relative anonymity associated with web based communication (Suler, 2004). Conversely, the disadvantages of online therapy, as summarised by Amichia-Hamburger et al. (2014) are associated with the lack of physical presence, the absence of verbal signals, the challenges of risk management, therapist and client technological competence and technological malfunctions. Other population specific concerns relate to young people's participation in websites that promote unhealthy behaviours (e.g. suicidal postings, Lehavot et al. 2012; extreme communities, Bell, 2007). Clients also present with issues that implicate the internet and social media use, for example; cyberbullying, online addiction (Giota & Kleftaras, 2014). Notwithstanding these disadvantages, online social networks offer a myriad of self-help and mutual support opportunities. The internet provides a wealth of readily accessible mental health information to the public and potential clients and the role of social media holds extraordinary potential for the wide dissemination of such information. For a comprehensive review of current applications of technology in mental health practice see Goss and colleagues (2016).

As potential and current clients increasingly seek mental health information online and frequently via social media sites, therapists need to be cognisant of the range and quality of such information as a resource for their clients (Bell, 2007). Alongside the internet's 'promise of the democratization of expertise' questions regarding the trustworthiness and professional standards of that expertise are raised (Harshman et al., 2005: 227). To that end many helping professions are concerned with the credibility of the information available to the public and how informed consent, professional boundaries, confidentiality and emergency protocols are adequately provided for in these situations (Santhiveeran, 2009).

Social media and social network developments

Within the landscape of technological developments, the innovation of social media platforms or Web 2.0-based technology (e.g. Facebook, YouTube, LinkedIn, Twitter, Second Life) has profoundly impacted upon global social communication. 'Ubiquitous' and 'proliferation' appear to be the most common words used to describe the exponential growth of social media usage, recently accelerated by mobile communication technologies (e.g. Smartphones). Web 2.0 technology is generally understood as a medium that facilitates user-generated content and promotes bi-directional and participatory communication rather than the passive observing of information as presented by Web 1.0 options (Anderson, 2007).

With reference to social media, Hansen, Shneiderman and Smith (2011: 12) offer the following broad definition and suggest that social media is;

> ... a catchall phrase intended to describe the many online sociotechnical systems that had emerged in recent years, including services like email, discussion forums, blogs, microblogs, texting, chat, social networking sites, wikis, photo and video sharing sites, reviews sites and multigaming communities.

Each social media platform has unique features within social network sites, facilitating users to create an online identity and develop a network of connections with other individuals with whom they interact to build communities or networks (Boyd & Ellison, 2007). The terms 'friend', 'fan' and 'follower' as used in social networks are interesting to consider in terms of social influence. In a study investigating the perceived trustworthiness of health information disseminated via a micro-blog (i.e. Twitter – a social media network that allows members to post short messages of 140 characters) the information was considered more reliable if it was sent by a professional who had many 'followers' (Lee & Sundar, 2013). The following vignette illustrates this point in a therapy setting.

Vignette 1

Hilary is an experienced therapist and maintains a popular stress management psycho-educational micro-blog. One of her 'followers' contacts Hilary via the social network to make a therapy appointment. At the first session, the client comments that considering the number of followers that Hilary has on the social network, she must be a 'brilliant therapist'. The client adds 'I really didn't think I'd be able to get an appointment with you so quickly ... I feel like I'm talking to a celebrity!'

Social media use in counselling and psychotherapy

Increasingly, practitioners are using social media in a professional capacity to participate in professional peer support networks and promote their clinical services on social network sites (Kolmes and Taube, 2016). Practitioners are embracing a variety of social media technology to deliver psycho-education (Giota & Kleftaras, 2014), provide and receive clinical supervision (Jencius & Baltrinic, 2015), and recruit research participants, especially with difficult to access populations (King et al., 2014).

However, it appears that many practitioners hold ethical concerns about providing therapeutic services or communicating with clients via social media sites due to the associated risks of compromising client confidentiality, privacy and professional boundaries (Giota & Kleftaras, 2014). For example, the issue of receiving a 'friend request' or 'out of office' contact request from a client via a social network highlights these risks and the acceptance or rejection of such requests requires critical reflection on the clinical, ethical and legal implications (Zur, 2015). From a technology perspective, the security risks inherent in many websites and communication systems compound these concerns (Kaplan et al., 2011).

Of further concern is how practitioners can keep their personal engagement in social networks separate from their professional role and if such a separation is realistic in the digital age (Lannin & Scott, 2013). Clients frequently search online for information about their therapist and whether or not the therapist maintains a deliberate social media presence; generally, much information is available in this public domain (Zur, 2008). In their survey of therapy clients ($N = 332$) who had sought personal information about a therapist online, Kolmes and Taube (2016) reported that 69.9% of their participants were successful in this attempt. The foremost domains of personal data discovered related to the therapist's age, education, home address, photographs, family and relationship information. Curiosity was cited as the main reason for conducting these searches and almost 75% of participants did not disclose the search to their therapist. In the context of therapist safety and client care, Zur (2008) recommends that therapists assume that their clients will read anything that they post online and advises that therapists should conduct an online search of their name to establish what information is readily accessible to clients.

Lannin and Scott (2013: 135) draw a useful comparison between social networking ethics and what they term 'small world ethics' pertaining to practitioners working in small rural communities and suggest that similar ethical issues can arise in both contexts. They recommend that practitioners remain mindful of the increased likelihood of encountering ethical challenges in the 'small world' of social networks. Different media sites warrant different levels of vigilance in assessing potential challenges to ethical practice. Whilst beyond the scope of this chapter to discuss the range of social media tools and virtual platforms, a number of ethical principles may be discussed as relevant to all such online communications. The key recurring themes in the literature refer to the establishment and maintenance of professional boundaries, privacy, confidentiality and informed consent.

Boundaries of professional practice: therapist self-disclosure

Associated with professional boundaries, therapist deliberate self-disclosure has been a widely debated concept in psychological therapy. Although individual differences exist among therapists and self-disclosure is frequently influenced by theoretical orientation (Ziv-Beiman, 2013), Henretty and Levitt (2010), recommend that therapists view self-disclosure as an empirically supported intervention, albeit one to be used judiciously, and provide practice guidelines to evaluate the therapeutic legitimacy of this intervention. They recommend that therapists deeply reflect on the reasons for the disclosure and assess its appropriateness for the individual client with due regard to cultural diversity. The authors further advise deliberation on the content, timing and manner by which the disclosure will be communicated. The nature of the therapist's disclosure is also of relevance evaluating this intervention. Ziv-Beiman (2013: 63) distinguishes between 'immediate' (in the moment reactions to the client or the therapeutic process or relationship) self-disclosure by the therapist and 'non-immediate' (disclosure relating to the therapist's personal life outside of the therapeutic frame) with appropriate immediate disclosure appearing to positively impact on therapy outcomes.

According to Zur et al. (2009), digital developments challenge our conceptions of therapist self-disclosure in contemporary clinical practice. The authors distinguish between appropriate disclosures that are clinically beneficial to the client and disclosures that are inappropriate and which may serve the needs of the therapist rather than those of the client. This is relatively clear within the boundaries of the therapy room but less so when considering the implications of therapists actively engaging with social media where self-disclosure is practically unavoidable, not necessarily immediate and frequently unintended (Zur, 2008). As suggested by Taylor et al. (2010: 157) 'online communications can also be more casual and spontaneous than other types of interactions, often leading people to disclose information online that they would have otherwise withheld'. The following example demonstrates a spontaneous disclosure with clear ethical and clinical implications, however inadvertently or perhaps naively made.

Vignette 2

Sarah is a trainee therapist and has recently commenced her first placement in a public health service setting. Sarah maintains an online presence via a social media site (e.g., Facebook). In a recent encounter with a client, Sarah was deeply moved by the session. Later she posted the following: 'My 3 o'clock today was SO inspirational!! This young lady has navigated the extremes of trauma. Much for me to learn.'

Subsequently, Sarah regretted the post and contacted her supervisor to discuss the situation.

Privacy, confidentiality and informed consent in social media use

Client privacy and confidentiality are fundamental to the ethical practice and integrity of psychological therapy and clear guidelines are presented in all professional codes of ethics to this effect. While there are limits to confidentiality in cases of risk every effort is made by practitioners to protect client privacy and confidentiality for legal as well as ethical and clinical reasons (Jenkins, 2017). As social media engagement is exercised in a public domain, the potential exists for any information generated in that environment to be permanently discoverable even after an account has been deleted (Giota & Kleftaras, 2014). Moreover, clients may not be aware of the public nature of the information they disclose or that contacting their therapist in a public forum may breach their own privacy and confidentiality (Zur, 2010). Vignette 3 illustrates client confidentiality and privacy being compromised in an online professional forum. Increasingly, listservs (mailing list server where mass emails are circulated to members) are being used for professional consultation and referral, although they may be vulnerable to unauthorised access (Collins, 2007).

Vignette 3

Daniel, an experienced therapist, has been working with Anya, who is now relocating to another part of the country. Anya asked Daniel if he could recommend a therapist in that area. Daniel agreed to seek a referral and posted the following message on his professional listserv; 'Seeking a Spanish speaking therapist in the Stevenage area with expertise in anxiety disorders for female client (mid 20's) who is relocating shortly'. Daniel did not disclose to Anya that he sought the referral online or discuss the implications of this.

Several authors have discussed therapists conducting online searches of their clients (see below) and such 'outside of office' information seeking is assessed by Zur (2010: 145) as 'uncharted clinical, ethical and legal territory'. In terms of ethical decision making in this regard, DiLillo and Gale (2011) recommend Clinton and colleagues' (2010) framework as a useful resource to determine the rationale for conducting such a search and to critically reflect on the clinical implications, issues of informed consent, decisions about sharing the information with the client and record keeping of the search.

In a study with graduate psychology students ($N = 854$) regarding their attitudes towards and their actual behaviour in relation to searching for client information online, DiLillo and Gale (2011) report that 97.8% of trainees searched for information pertaining to at least one client in the previous year and over 80% of the trainees reported that their clients were aware of the search. While such searches were conducted by most of the participants, 67%

of them believed it to be, in general, unacceptable to do so. The authors suggest that the variance between the participants declared online practices and their expressed attitudes may have been due in part to being asked to reflect on the acceptability of such practices.

In contrast, in Asay and Lal's (2014) study with trainees ($N = 407$) investigating their internet behaviours, 25% had searched online for information about their clients and almost 50% had sought online information about their supervisors. Interestingly, 74% of trainees reported that they modified information on their social network sites since commencing training and a large majority indicated apprehension about making ethical decisions concerning social media use. The authors noted that trainees seem aware of their online presence and the implications thereof and recommend that training programmes and supervisors facilitate intentional discussion on these issues with trainees.

Practising psychologists were the focus of a study conducted by Van Allen and Roberts (2011) who sought to identify critical incidents whereby client confidentiality or privacy was breached through the use of technology including social media. The incidents reported included examples of an email recipient inappropriately forwarding an email containing confidential client information to third parties and unauthorised access by hospital staff to a patient's file. Examples of clients compromising their own confidentiality were also reported and related to clients using an unsecured email address to contact their psychologist and sending a Facebook 'friend request'. To minimise the risk of ethical violations, Van Allen and Roberts (2011) recommend that agencies and practitioners have a secure client record management practice and note that this is particularly imperative when client information is accessed via mobile devices (e.g. smartphones) that do not have adequate security (e.g. encryption or passwords). Acknowledging that having a social media presence is a personal choice, the authors further recommend that practitioners maintain separate personal and professional profiles and pages on social networks and suggest that they develop a social media policy for their practice.

In a survey of social media practices among trainee and qualified child psychologists ($N = 246$) regarding their own activity and that of their child and adolescent clients, Tunick et al. (2011) reported that 65% of participants engaged in social networks with most respondents maintaining privacy settings on their profiles. However, 25% of those surveyed reported being 'friended' by clients and although most (87%) refused the request a small percentage (3%) accepted the invitation. On enquiring if respondents had read a client's social network profile, 32% affirmed that they had done so and declared their main motivations as 'curiosity', 'therapeutic concern' and 'request by the client or family member' (Tunick et al., 2011: 444). In these instances, in excess of 50% had requested the client's permission or had subsequently informed the client and approximately one third did so without the client's permission. 41% read a client profile with the client. Respondents who never reviewed a client's social network refrained from doing so because of boundary violation concerns. When working with adolescents and children, the authors advocate that guidance is given to this vulnerable population and to their parents or carers on the risks and benefits associated with social media engagement.

In their study on the experiences of mental health professionals (N = of 227) relating to seeking client information online, Kolmes and Taube (2014) reported that 48% of the respondents had deliberately done so without their client's permission. The types of information sought included ascertaining if the client was part of the practitioner's social network, criminal records, client relationships and so forth. Although a minority of the participants expressed distress at having sought this information and some considered it as a boundary issue, most of the participants reported that it had little or no effect on the treatment provided or on their therapeutic relationship. In addition, some participants considered the information as helpful, for example, to confirm client disclosures in therapy. However, as the authors note, in the absence of the client's perspective in this study, it is not possible to determine the actual impact on client outcomes.

Reflecting on the range of issues highlighted in the above studies, the recommendations provided to therapists by Tunick et al. (2011) are practical suggestions to minimise potential boundary breaches and maximise protection of client confidentiality, privacy and informed consent in the social media context. In summary, they suggest that practitioners;

- Continually reflect on their motivations to self-disclose.
- Maintain privacy settings on their social networking sites.
- Conduct an examination of the clinical and ethical risks and benefits when considering accessing client information online without their permission.
- Develop a social media use policy and discuss this with clients so they are fully aware and informed about social media use.

E-professionalism and resources

Professional codes of ethics speak to all professional activity whether off-line or online and recently regulatory bodies and professional organisations have begun to review the implications of social media use for practitioners. In addition, legal, ethical and professional questions arise for statutory and professional bodies in relation to their members jurisdiction of practice when technology facilitates the provision of global services (Kaplan et al., 2011).

The Health and Care Professions Council's (HCPC, 2017) document *Guidance on Social Media* acknowledges the benefits of social media for registrants apropos professional networking, development of the profession and informing the public and advocate that members seek advice if they are unsure about any aspect of social media use.

The British Association for Counselling and Psychotherapy (BACP, 2015) as part of their 'Good Practice in Action' Series offers a resource for counsellors using social media. Similarly, the British Psychological Society (BPS) Ethics Committee (2012a) have published supplementary guidelines for social media use and the BPS Division of Clinical Psychology have produced a document on 'E-professionalism' (BPS, 2012b), which provides guidelines for any online activity by its members.

Social media policies

In the interest of informed consent and as noted above, the use of a social media policy is advised for agencies, organisations and individual practitioners. This would form part of informed consent in the initial counselling contract discussion and help establish professional boundaries in this context. Kolmes (2010), who provides an example of a social media policy on her website, proposes that a social media policy would include explicit information on the therapist's use of social media, policies regarding online searches, how invitations to join a client's network are managed and how social media activity may impact the therapeutic relationship. Such a policy could also refer to record keeping, security procedures and provide explicit information on the risks associated with communicating on media networks. Similarly, in the context of supervision, Jencius and Baltrinic (2015) recommend discussion of social media use with supervisees and that a social media policy be integrated into informed consent contracts in supervision.

Conclusion

The use of technology in psychological therapy is not a new phenomenon and practitioners have adapted and integrated such innovations for decades. However, from a 'digital immigrant' position, the seemingly rapid development of social media may perhaps take time to accommodate. On the one hand, while the technology is new, ethical core principles remain constant. On the other hand, the innovation of social media technology presents many opportunities to develop new ways of delivering psychological therapy and may challenge us to re-consider Paul's (1969: 44) pre-internet question of 'what treatment by whom, is most effective for this individual with that specific problem and under which set of circumstances?', in the digital age. Whether or not social media will fundamentally influence psychotherapy theory development remains to be seen. There is much to be discovered and ongoing reflection and research are indicated to determine how social media may be optimally utilized in the best service of our clients.

Reflective questions

1. How might you respond if a current client 'liked' your social network page and added an emotion icon (*emoji*) of a smiling face?
2. What ethical issues arise in conducting an online search of an adolescent client without their permission?

3. How might you, as a supervisor, respond if you received a 'friend request' from a current supervisee?
4. Under what circumstances, if any, should client information that is sourced from a social network site be used in case conceptualisation and treatment planning?

References

Amichai-Hamburger, Y., Klomek, A.B., Friedman, D., Zuckerman, O., & Shani-Sherman, T. (2014) The future of online therapy. *Computers in Human Behavior*, 41, 288–294.

Anderson, P. (2007) What is Web 2.0? Ideas, technologies and implications for education: *Joint Information Systems Committee (JISC)*. Available at: www.jisc.ac.uk/media/docu ments/techwatch/tsw0701b.pdf

Andrews, G., Basu, A., Cuijpers, P., Craske, M., McEvoy, P., English, C. & Newby, J. (2018) Review: Computer therapy for the anxiety and depression disorders is effective, acceptable and practical health care: An updated meta-analysis. *Journal of Anxiety Disorders*. 10.1016/j.janxdis.2018.01.001.

Asay, P.A. & Lal, A. (2014) Who's Googled whom? Trainees' internet and online social networking experiences, behaviors, and attitudes with clients and supervisors. *Training and Education in Professional Psychology*, 8(2), 105–111.

BACP (British Association for Counselling and Psychotherapy). (2015) *Social Media (audio and video) and the Counselling Professions*. London: BACP.

Barak, A., Hen, L., Boniel-Nissim, M. & Shapira, N.A. (2008) Comprehensive review and a meta-analysis of the effectiveness of internet-based psychotherapeutic interventions. *Journal of Technology in Human Services*, 26, 109–160.

Bell, V. (2007) Online information, extreme communities and internet therapy: Is the internet good for our mental health? *Journal of Mental Health*, 16(4), 445–457.

Boyd, D.M. & Ellison, N.B. (2007) Social network sites: Definition, history, and scholarship. *Journal of Computer-Mediated Communication*, 13(1), 210–230.

BPS (British Psychological Society). (2012a) Supplementary guidance on the use of social media. Ethics Committee. Available at: www.bps.org.uk/sites/beta.bps.org.uk/ files/Policy%20-%20Files/Suplementary%20Guidance%20on%20the%20Use%20of% 20Social%20Media.pdf

BPS (British Psychological Society). (2012b) *E –Professionalism: Guidance on the use of social media by clinical psychologists*. London: BPS.

Callahan, A. & Inckle, K. (2012) Cybertherapy or psychobabble? A mixed methods study of online emotional support. *British Journal of Guidance and Counselling*, 40(3), 261–278.

Clinton, B.K., Silverman, B.C. & Brendel, D.H. (2010) Patient-targeted googling: The ethics of searching online for patient information. *Harvard Review of Psychiatry*, 18, 103–112.

Collins, L.H. (2007) Practicing safer listserv use: Ethical use of an invaluable resource. *Professional Psychology: Research and Practice*, 38(6), 690–698.

DiLillo, D. & Gale, E.B. (2011) To google or not to google: Graduate students' use of the internet to access personal information about clients. *Training and Education in Professional Psychology*, 5(3), 160–166.

Giota, K.G.A. & Kleftaras, G. (2014) Social media and counseling: Opportunities, risks and ethical considerations. *International Journal of Psychological and Behavioral Sciences*, 8(8), 2386–2388.

Goss, S., Anthony, K., Sykes Stretch, L. & Merz Nagel, D. (Eds.) (2016) *Technology in Mental Health: Applications in Practice, Supervision and Training*, 2nd edition. Springfield, IL: C. C. Thomas.

Hansen, D.L., Shneiderman, B. & Smith, M.A. (2011) *Analyzing Social Media Networks with Nodexl: Insights from a Connected World*. Boston, MA: Elsevier.

Harshman, E.M., Gilsinan, J.F., Fisher, J.E., & Yeager, F.C. (2005) Professional ethics in a virtual world: The impact of the internet on traditional notions of professionalism. *Journal of Business Ethics*, 58(1–3), 227–236.

Health and Care Professions Council. (2017) *Guidance on Social Media*. Available at: www.hcpc-uk.org/publications/brochures/index.asp?id=1394

Henretty, J., & Levitt, H.M. (2010) The role of therapist self-disclosure in psychotherapy: A qualitative review. *Clinical Psychology Review*, 30, 63–77.

Jencius, M.J. & Baltrinic, E. (2015) Training online supervisors. In T.G. Rousmaniere & E. Renfro-Michele (Eds.). *Using Technology for Counselor Supervision: A Practical Handbook*. Alexandria, VA: American Counseling Association, pp. 251–268.

Jenkins, P. (2017) *Professional Practice in Counselling and Psychotherapy: Ethics and the Law*. London: Sage.

Kaplan, D.M., Wade, M.E., Conteh, J.A., & Martz, E.T. (2011) Legal and ethical issues surrounding the use of social media in counseling. *Counseling and Human Development*, 43(8), 1–12.

King, D.B., O'Rourke, N. & DeLongis, A. (2014) Social media recruitment and online data collection: A beginner's guide and best practices for accessing low-prevalence and hard-to-reach populations. *Canadian Psychology/Psychologie canadienne*, 55(4), 240–249.

Kolmes, K. (2010) *Social media policy*. Available at: www.drkkolmes.com/docs/socmed.pdf

Kolmes, K. & Taube, D.O. (2014) Seeking and finding our clients on the Internet: Boundary considerations in cyberspace. *Professional Psychology: Research and Practice*, 45 (1), 3–10.

Kolmes, K. & Taube, D.O. (2016) Client discovery of psychotherapist personal information online. *Professional Psychology: Research and Practice*, 47(2), 147–154.

Lannin, D.G. & Scott, N.A. (2013) Social networking ethics: Developing best practices for the new small world. *Professional Psychology: Research and Practice*, 44(3), 135–141.

Lee, J.Y. & Sundar, S.S. (2013) To tweet or to retweet? That is the question for health professionals on Twitter. *Health Communication*, 28(5), 509–524.

Lehavot, K., Ben-Zeev, D. & Neville, R.E. (2012) Ethical considerations and social media: A case of suicidal postings on facebook. *Journal of Dual Diagnosis*, 8(4), 341–346.

Paul, G.L. (1969) Behavior modification research: Design and tactics. In C.M. Franks (Ed.). *Behavior Therapy: Appraisal and Status*. New York: McGraw-Hill, pp. 29–62.

Prensky, M. (2001) Digital natives, digital immigrants. *On the Horizon*, 9(5), 1–6.

Richards, D., Duffy, D., Blackburn, B., Earley, C., Enrique, A., Palacios, J., & Timulak, L. (2018) Digital IAPT: The effectiveness & cost-effectiveness of internet-delivered interventions for depression and anxiety disorders in the improving access to psychological therapies programme: Study protocol for a randomised control trial. *BMC Psychiatry*, 18(1), 59.

Santhiveeran, J. (2009) Compliance of social work e-therapy websites to the NASW code of ethics. *Social Work in Health Care*, 48(1), 1–13.

Suler, J. (2004) The online disinhibition effect. *CyberPsychology and Behavior*, 7, 321–326.

Taylor, L., McMinn, M.R., Bufford, R.K. & Chang, K.T. (2010) Psychologists' attitudes and ethical concerns regarding the use of social networking web sites. *Professional Psychology: Research and Practice*, 41(2), 153–159.

Tunick, R.A., Mednick, L. & Conroy, C. (2011) A snapshot of child psychologists' social media activity: Professional and ethical practice implications and recommendations. *Professional Psychology: Research and Practice*, 42(6), 440–447.

Van Allen, J. & Roberts, M.C. (2011) Critical incidents in the marriage of psychology and technology. *Professional Psychology: Research and Practice*, 42(6), 433–439.

Ziv-Beiman, S. (2013) Therapist self-disclosure as an integrative intervention. *Journal of Psychotherapy Integration*, 23(1), 59–74.

Zur, O. (2008) The Google factor: Therapists' self-disclosure in the age of the internet. *Independent Practitioner*, 28(2), 83–85.

Zur, O. (2010) To google or not to google ... our clients? When psychotherapists and other mental health care providers search their clients on the Web. *Independent Practitioner*, 30(3), 144–148.

Zur, O. (2015) *To Accept or Not to Accept? How to respond when clients send "Friend Request" to their psychotherapists or counselors on social networking sites.* Available at: www.zurinstitute.com/socialnetworking.html

Zur, O., Williams, M.H., Lehavot, K., & Knapp, S. (2009) Psychotherapist self-disclosure and transparency in the internet age. *Professional Psychology: Research and Practice*, 40(1), 22–30.

Chapter 11

Adverse effects of psychological therapies

Lorna Farquharson

Although there has been some recognition of the adverse effects of psychological therapies for over 40 years (Barlow, 2010), they have tended to be overlooked in the research literature. Unlike research involving medical interventions, investigations into the effectiveness of psychological therapies have not routinely documented adverse effects (Duggan et al., 2014; Jonsson et al., 2014; Vaughan et al., 2014). Instead, the emphasis has been on developing the evidence base for psychological therapies and promoting the benefits to increase access to a wider population (e.g. the Improving Access to Psychological Therapies programme in England). Within this, there has been an implicit assumption that talking therapies do not carry a risk of harm. However, it is increasingly being recognised that adverse effects occur on a frequent basis (Crawford et al., 2016; Mohr, 1995) and that the benefits of therapy need to be considered alongside any negative effects (Parry et al., 2016). There are calls for a shift in mindset so that explicit recognition of adverse effects is seen as a key part of being a competent and ethical practitioner (Linden, 2013; Wolpert, 2016). This chapter will discuss how adverse effects can be defined, identified and understood. It will also consider the strategies that can be used to address adverse effects and the implications for professional and ethical practice.

Vignette I

Kathyrn (a newly qualified therapist) was feeling upset and hopeless following her fourth session with Jess. She had found it hard to establish a good therapeutic relationship with Jess from the start. Jess had expressed a lot of anger and frustration at the length of time that she had been on the waiting list and seemed to expect Kathryn to 'fix' very complex and long-standing problems. In the session that had just ended, Jess had openly expressed her dissatisfaction with Kathryn and the lack of progress that had been made, resulting in her stating that she wanted to make a complaint. Kathryn knew that she should have discussed the difficulties that she was experiencing in supervision, but there were always so many other things to discuss. She had been given a large caseload due to the pressures on the service and she had also wanted to make a good impression as a new member of the team.

How would you respond if Kathryn was a colleague and shared this information with you?

Definitional issues relating to adverse effects of therapy

Multiple terms have been used in the literature to describe adverse effects, including negative therapeutic reaction, clinical deterioration, treatment failure, side effects, harm, adverse events, negative effects and negative outcome (Duggan et al., 2014; Parry et al., 2016). Some terms are very broad whereas others are more focused on either the outcome or experience of therapy. In some cases, the possible causes have been reflected in the definition with a distinction made between side effects that may result from therapy that has been competently provided and negative effects that may result from malpractice (Linden, 2013). However, there hasn't been consistent use of these terms and the plethora of terms, combined with a lack of agreed definitions, has presented some challenges when conducting reviews of the psychological literature.

It has recently been recommended that there should be greater standardisation of terminology and that the following three aspects of adverse effects need to be considered, recorded and reported in studies that are designed to evaluate psychological therapies (Parry et al., 2016).

1. Adverse events (e.g. mental health-related hospital admission, suicide) that occur during or shortly after therapy and are deemed to be related to or caused by therapy.
2. Clinically significant deterioration caused by therapy, which could also include the emergence of new difficulties. This may be observed by the practitioner or detected by completing standardised outcome measures.
3. Client-experienced harm, which may not be detected by just monitoring adverse events and using standardised outcome measures. This recognises that there are limitations to the other methods and that each client is an individual with their own potentially unique experiences of therapy, therefore it is also important to incorporate clients' own perspectives on any harmful aspects of therapy.

While the above recommendations provide a framework for considering different aspects of adverse effects and potential approaches to identifying them when conducting research, this is a hugely complex area and there are important questions for clinical practice that need to be considered. For example, there may be other factors (e.g. significant life events) that could explain an adverse event so how can we determine whether or not it might be related to or caused by the therapy? How can we distinguish increased levels of distress that might be temporary and an expected part of a therapeutic process from those that would be classified as harmful? What happens if a client and their therapist have very different perspectives on whether or not therapy has caused harm? Whose perspective is given greater priority? These questions will be returned to later in the chapter.

Prevalence of adverse effects

Although the problems with definitions and associated measurement need to be considered, there is some consistency in the research findings, which indicate that 5–10% of all clients experience adverse effects of therapy (Crawford et al., 2016; Hannan et al., 2005; Hatfield et al., 2010; Lambert, 2013). However, there can be considerable variability across therapists (Mohr, 1995; Saxon et al., 2017) and according to client characteristics (Crawford et al., 2016; Mohr, 1995; Saxon et al., 2017). Some of the therapist factors that have been associated with negative effects are lack of empathy, underestimation of the severity of difficulties, lack of clarity about the focus of therapy, negative emotional reactions to clients and unethical behaviour (Hardy et al., 2019; Mohr, 1995). For client characteristics, both clinical and demographic variables have been highlighted. For example, a recent large-scale survey of people receiving psychological therapy for anxiety and depression in England and Wales (Crawford et al., 2016) found that people from ethnic and sexual minority groups were more likely to report that they had experienced adverse effects of psychological therapies. To help explain these findings, it is important to consider the potential causes of adverse effects.

Understanding the possible causes of adverse effects

Understanding the reasons for adverse effects is complex as a key aspect of the intervention is the relationship between the therapist and client. It is also an under-researched area so there is limited evidence for causal mechanisms. However, there are several potential explanations. It may be a result of the intervention itself with some therapies having been listed as potentially harmful therapies (Lilienfeld, 2007). For example, critical incident stress debriefing has been listed as an intervention that has the potential to be harmful for at least some individuals following a traumatic event, perhaps because it interferes with natural coping and recovery. Another explanation for adverse effects is that there may be an inappropriate match between the intervention and the presenting difficulties (Duggan et al., 2014). There may be effective interventions indicated for the presenting difficulties, but a less effective or ineffective intervention has been selected. This may be due to several factors, including the therapist's preference for a particular way of working, gaps in knowledge in and of the evidence base, lack of fit with the service user's needs or preferences and service pressures. It is also important to acknowledge here that there are criticisms of evidence-based practice (see Chapter 17 for a full discussion of these) and the findings from randomised controlled trials, which are seen as the 'gold standard' of evidence, may not easily translate to an individual in a particular context. A further possibility is that a potentially appropriate intervention has been selected, but it has been inappropriately delivered and the adverse effects are therefore a result of the attributes of the therapist and their level of competence rather than the therapeutic approach itself (Duggan et al., 2014; Parry et al., 2016). For example, there may be unresolved difficulties in the therapeutic alliance, which could be due to a lack of therapist skill in noticing and repairing ruptures. There may also be a poor fit between the therapist and client, perhaps due to the nature of the presenting difficulties and the personal resonance for the therapist or differences in world views (Parry et al., 2016). Alternatively, it may be that the intervention seems to be appropriate, but there are client variables that result in adverse effects even when it is competently provided. That is, an intervention might be effective in general, but harmful for a minority (Duggan et al., 2014). In addition, there may be organisational factors that help to explain negative effects (Hardy et al., 2019; Parry et al., 2016). For example, limited information or choice provided by the service or high caseloads and pressure to work beyond the therapist's level of competence.

A recent large-scale mixed-methods investigation of risk factors for negative experiences of therapy (Hardy et al., 2019), which involved conducting surveys and interviews with both therapists and clients, produced a model of the different potential factors and how they inter-relate. This model highlighted that there may be an initial 'lack of fit' that could be due to service structures, therapist skills or patient needs. For example, there were frequent concerns about service and therapist inflexibility with some clients describing concerns about therapists' core clinical skills, a lack of understanding of their social context or being given very little information about the service, the therapy or their therapist. From the therapist perspective, there were also comments about service inflexibility and some accounts of working beyond their level of competence; sometimes only realising this later when reflecting on difficult experiences. Following on from any initial problems, there could be difficulties with safety and containment (e.g. a lack of structure or feeling ill equipped to deal with emotions or memories that had been brought to the surface) or difficulties with power and control (e.g. unable to raise important issues or being blamed for therapy not progressing). If left unresolved, these could lead to difficulties with trust, dreading sessions and pressure to perform with the ultimate consequences of feelings of failure, loss of confidence and loss of hope. These were frequently described from both therapist and client perspectives. Although this model has yet to be empirically tested, it provides a useful starting point for conceptualising different risk factors and indicates a range of ways of intervening to prevent or reduce the likelihood of adverse effects. Recommendations for identifying and addressing adverse effects will be discussed in the next part of the chapter, but it can be useful at this point to consider the following clinical vignette.

Vignette 2

Faisel is a builder who runs his own business. He lives with his wife and their three young children. He works long hours, but it is hard to make enough money to cover all of their bills due to the large debts that had built up in the past. Faisel frequently worries about their future and whether their house will be repossessed. These worries impact on his sleep and he has started to feel like a failure as a husband and a father. He initially presented to A & E with chest pains as he thought that he was having a heart attack, but he was told that there was no evidence of any problems with his heart. His GP then suggested that he try talking to a therapist. He was a bit sceptical of this idea but agreed to see if it might help. Although he tried to explain to the therapist the things that he was concerned about, she did not seem to understand his situation and said that she could not help with financial problems as it wasn't her role. He felt that he was just going around in circles talking about his problems and was starting to feel hopeless about the future.

Drawing on your knowledge and experience so far, how might you understand this scenario and what are your thoughts on an appropriate action to take?

Identifying adverse effects

As might be anticipated from the more limited attention to adverse effects of psychological therapies in the research literature, therapists may not have received specific training in identifying and responding to adverse effects (Bystedt et al., 2014; Castonguay et al., 2010). Furthermore, it has been found that therapists are very poor at identifying clients experiencing adverse effects, if they rely solely on their clinical judgment (Hannan et al., 2005; Hatfield et al., 2010). This is the case even when they are aware that adverse effects may occur. It has also been found that clients will often not spontaneously disclose negative effects (Hardy et al., 2019; Horigian et al., 2010). These findings indicate a need for therapists to be aware of the prevalence of adverse effects, to explicitly ask clients about potential adverse effects and to consider the use of additional methods to help identify them.

Routine outcome measurement completed on a session by session basis provides opportunities for therapists to closely monitor progress and become aware of when a client's presenting difficulties are getting worse rather than better. However, the outcome measures selected will determine the range of changes that can be detected, and this could be quite limited in scope. It is therefore important to also consider tools that have been specifically developed to assist with identifying and recording adverse effects (see Table. 11.1).

The Unwanted Event to Adverse Treatment Reaction checklist (UE-ATR: Linden, 2013) was developed with the main aim of assisting therapists to identify adverse effects in routine clinical practice. This is not to say that skilled clinicians may not pick up on these anyway, but it provides one way of systematically monitoring these. Linden (2013) also proposed that the UE-ATR could be used for training, supervision and research purposes. However, the psychometric properties have yet to be investigated. A recently developed

Table 11.1 Measures developed to identify and monitor adverse effects of psychological therapies

Measure	Description	Rating	Reliability/validity
Unwanted event to adverse treatment reaction (UE-ATR: Linden, 2013)	Clinician checklist, which includes a lack of progress, deterioration, emergence of new symptoms, difficulties in the therapeutic relationship and changes in the wider social context (e.g. strains in family or work relationships)	Each unwanted event is given a rating for the context in which it developed, the likely relationship to treatment and its severity	No published information on reliability or validity
Experiences of Therapy Questionnaire (ETQ: Parker et al., 2013)	63-item scale with five factors: negative therapist, preoccupying therapy, beneficial therapy, idealisation of therapist and passive therapist	Each item is rated on a five-point Likert scale	The five factors have good internal consistency and high test-retest reliability. There is also some evidence of construct validity
Negative Effects Questionnaire (NEQ: Rozental et al., 2016)	32-item scale with six factors: symptoms, quality, dependency, stigma, hopelessness, failure	Each item has a 'yes/ no' response, a severity rating and an indication of whether any negative experiences are likely to be related to therapy	Excellent internal consistency for the whole scale and acceptable to excellent internal consistency for the factors

measure that has included consideration of psychometric properties is the Experiences of Therapy Questionnaire (Parker et al., 2014, 2013). This is completed from a client perspective, but the focus has been on the use of this measure in clinical trials rather than routine clinical practice. Another recently developed measure completed from the client's perspective is the Negative Effects Questionnaire (NEQ: Rozental et al., 2016). Similar to the UE-ATR, it acknowledges that there may be other causes of adverse effects and considers the likely relationship to therapy, but this is explicitly from the client's perspective. The questionnaire has demonstrated internal reliability, is currently free to use and available in eleven different languages. It is therefore a potentially useful additional tool. However, the development and evaluation of the measure predominantly involved participants who had sought help for anxiety and used internet recruitment to the study. More research is therefore needed to demonstrate the applicability of this measure to other populations.

Reducing the likelihood of adverse effects in clinical practice

Given the potential role of organisational factors in understanding adverse effects (Crawford et al., 2016; Hardy et al., 2019), it is important to think about the wider service context and ways of intervening at an early stage in the client's journey. In addition, there is a need to provide clear information in advance, ensuring choice and shared decision-making. Shared decision-making requires a good therapeutic relationship and sharing of information with a focus on eliciting client preferences and views so that they can be considered during the decision-making process. Clients who have preferences that have been met have been found to be more likely to report that therapy has helped them with their problems (Williams et al., 2016). It is also important to have explicit contracting at the start of therapy and agreement about the number of sessions, as well as, how progress will be reviewed (Hardy et al., 2019). If we look at the following clinical vignette, we can see the importance of considering the context of the work, the expectations that Angelika had at the start of therapy, the initial information that her therapist provided, the strength of the therapeutic relationship, the extent to which there was shared decision-making, the way that the initial therapy sessions have been managed and any agreed plans for reviewing progress.

Vignette 3

Angelika is a young woman who has been experiencing problems with low mood and self-harm. She has attended three therapy sessions and is questioning whether it is worth continuing. Talking about events in the past has brought very distressing memories to the surface and she is increasingly on edge and finding it difficult to sleep at night. She has noticed herself being very short-tempered with her partner and distancing herself from friends. She is also self-harming on a more frequent basis. She thought that starting therapy would be a positive step to take and it had taken a lot of courage to ask for help, but it just seems to be making things worse.

Providing sufficient information about therapy can address prior expectations and provide greater understanding of the therapy process. Clients who feel that they have been given sufficient information about therapy before it started have been found to be less likely to report adverse effects (Crawford et al., 2016). It is recommended that the information provided should make clear that there can be negative, as well as positive effects and that this needs to be considered when obtaining initial consent. This is in line with the British Psychological Society (BPS) (2017) Professional Practice Guidelines and the Royal College of Psychiatrists (2014) Code of Ethics, which both emphasise that the consent process needs to include clear, accessible information about the benefits and risks of any interventions being proposed, any alternative options and the potential risks of not engaging. The British Association for Counselling and Psychotherapy (BACP) (2018) Ethical Framework for the Counselling Professions also makes explicit reference to known risks and being willing to discuss them with clients. Being clear about potential harm may encourage open discussions, provide opportunities to resolve difficulties and reduce the likelihood of therapists and clients feeling hopeless and blamed. However, there still seems to be important empirical questions to be answered about how best to discuss potential adverse effects at the start of therapy and the ways that this might influence initial engagement (Wolpert, 2016). There are also questions about the extent to which it is even possible to know in advance what many of the risks might be, given the multitude of factors that might contribute to the experience of adverse effects after commencing therapy.

Working with adverse effects of therapy

In addition to any initial discussions, it is recommended that there is an agreed process for considering both negative and positive effects during therapy. There is some evidence that alerting therapists to situations where a client has not improved as expected or where there seems to be a significant deterioration, as indicated by scores on standardised outcome measures, can prevent a negative outcome (Lambert, 2007), however, the reasons for this effect are not well understood. Therapists have reported that they would take a range of actions once they become aware that a client's presenting difficulties have worsened since starting therapy, including discussing the changes with the client, gathering more information, identifying precipitating events, consulting with peers, adapting the intervention, enhancing the therapeutic relationship and referring on to another clinician (Hatfield et al., 2010). Surprisingly, it has been noted that therapists may not use supervision to discuss lack of progress or deterioration (Hardy et al., 2019). This may be because of time constraints or lack of supervisor availability. However, it may also be because of the culture of the service and difficulties with openly discussing 'failures'.

It has been recommended that awareness and understanding of adverse effects is incorporated into core clinical training (Castonguay et al., 2010). Therapists need to be aware of the prevalence of adverse effects and that this is something that they need to attend to as part of their professional and ethical responsibilities. They also need to be aware that they are likely to have a positive bias when evaluating therapeutic progress such that adverse effects are not detected even when they may be aware that they could occur. Therapists therefore need to use specific tools to ensure that adverse effects are explicitly considered when reviewing progress and draw on their formulation skills to determine the appropriate action to take. In addition, it is important to make use of supervision to reflect on the factors that may have contributed to the adverse effects and the impact of identifying them.

Consideration of adverse effects in supervision

It is recommended that discussion of adverse effects is a regular part of supervision (Linden, 2013), which could help to embed it as a routine part of professional development and providing good quality care. However, supervisors will need to be sensitive to the fact that therapists may end up with feelings of hopelessness and failure. Attention needs to be given to the responsibilities of the supervisor in relation to the client and the supervisee, the quality of the supervisory relationship and the wider organisational culture. There needs to be an emphasis on promoting safe spaces for open discussions and a culture of learning rather than blame. This is in line with the statutory duty of candour that requires all health and social care providers to be open and transparent with people who use their services and to ensure that there is an organisational culture of openness, transparency and learning (Care Quality Commission, 2015).

Within supervision, it is important to have an awareness that there may be an accumulation of factors that need to be considered, including the wider social context. Close attention needs to be paid to the client's perspective, the quality of the therapeutic relationship and the ability of therapists to notice and repair ruptures in the therapeutic alliance. Identifying training and development needs in this area will require consideration of whether any difficulties in the therapeutic relationship occur across clients or whether they are more situation specific. This would help to determine whether there is a need to focus on the development of core clinical skills or whether it is about the fit between the therapy and the client or the therapist and the client. Consideration also needs to be given to the ways that difference and power are addressed in the therapeutic encounter. It is also important for supervisors to help their supervisees to recognise when cultural assumptions and biases may be impacting on the therapeutic relationship and to help identify ways of developing cultural competence (Bhui et al., 2015; Sue et al., 2009). Service factors, such as the options available and the pressure that therapists may feel to work beyond their level of competence, also need to be considered.

Conclusion

Adverse effects are sufficiently common that all therapists need to be aware of them and understand that there are a range of different strategies that can be used to address them in routine practice. These include providing sufficient information about therapy before it begins and ensuring that there are agreed systems for reviewing both positive and negative experiences of therapy, which take account of the wider social context. However, it is not just therapists' responsibility to attend to adverse effects. Adverse effects also need to be understood in an organisational context. Service and organisational factors will influence client experiences and the extent to which therapists are able to respond appropriately. Supervisors have a key role in ensuring that adverse effects are built into regular discussions in supervision and that there is consideration of the welfare of the client and supervisee training and support needs, as well as service developments that may be required. There also need to be developments in research to support clinical practice. Greater consideration of adverse effects in the evaluation of psychological therapies will help to inform discussions at the start of therapy and the formulation of adverse effects that may arise during therapy. Given the fact that a therapy may be effective overall, but harmful for a minority and that some groups are more likely to report adverse effects, it is essential that future research also helps to develop greater understanding of when and how adverse effects occur, not just the frequency of their occurrence. In addition, the effectiveness of strategies that can be used to try to prevent or reduce the likelihood of negative effects need to be investigated.

Reflective questions

1. What information do you provide in advance of starting therapy with a new client? Does this include any information about potential adverse effects?
2. How do you monitor and review therapeutic progress?
3. Have you previously been aware of any clients that have been adversely affected by therapy? If so, how did you become aware and respond? Would you do anything differently having read this chapter?
4. In what ways can you take potential adverse effects into account within your practice? (List at least three.)

References

Barlow, D.H. (2010) Negative effects from psychological treatments: A perspective. *American Psychologist*, 65, 13–20.

Bhui, K., Aslam, R.W., Palinski, A., McCabe, R., Johnson, M.R.D., Weich, S., Singh, S. P., Knapp, M., Ardino, V. & Szczepura, A. (2015) Interventions designed to improve therapeutic communications between black and minority ethnic people and professionals working in psychiatric services: A systematic review of the evidence for their effectiveness, systematic review. *British Journal of Psychiatry*, 207(2), 95–103.

British Association for Counselling and Psychotherapy. (2018) *Ethical Framework for the Counselling Professions*. Leicestershire: BACP.

British Psychological Society. (2017) *Professional Practice Guidelines*, 3rd edition. Leicester: BPS.

Bystedt, S., Rozental, A., Andersson, G., Boettcher, J. & Carlbring, P. (2014) Clinicians' perspectives on negative effects of psychological treatments. *Cognitive Behaviour Therapy*, 43 319–331.

Care Quality Commission. (2015) *Regulation 20: Duty of Candour*. Newcastle Upon Tyne: CQC.

Castonguay, L.G., Boswell, J.F., Constantino, M., Goldfried, M.R. & Hill, C.E. (2010) Training implications of harmful effects of psychological treatments. *American Psychologist*, 65, 34–49.

Crawford, M., Thana, L., Farquharson, L., Palmer, L., Hancock, E., Bassett, P., Clarke, J. & Parry, G. (2016) Patient experience of negative effects of psychological treatment: Results of a national survey. *British Journal of Psychiatry*, 208 260–265.

Duggan, C., Parry, G., McMurran, M., Davidson, K. & Dennis, J. (2014) The recording of adverse events from psychological treatments in clinical trials: Evidence from a review of NIHR-funded trials. *Trials*, 15, 335.

Hannan, C., Lambert, M.J., Harmon, C., Nielsen, S.L., Smart, D.W., Shimokawa, K. & Sutton, S.W. (2005) A lab test and algorithms for identifying clients at risk for treatment failure. *Journal of Clinical Psychology*, 61, 155–163.

Hardy, G.E., Bishop-Edwards, L., Chambers, E., Connell, J., Dent-Brown, K., Kothari, G., O'hara, R. & Parry, G.D. (2017) Risk factors for negative experiences during psychotherapy. *Psychotherapy Research*, 29 (3), 403–414.

Hatfield, D., McCullough, L., Frantz, S.H.B. & Krieger, K. (2010) Do we know when our clients get worse? an investigation of therapists' ability to detect negative client change. *Clinical Psychology & Psychotherapy*, 17, 25–32.

Horigian, V.E., Robbins, M.S., Dominguez, R., Ucha, J. & Rosa, C.L. (2010) Principles for defining adverse events in behavioral intervention research: Lessons from a family-focused adolescent drug abuse trial. *Clinical Trials*, 7, 58–68.

Jonsson, U., Alaie, I., Parling, T. & Arnberg, F.K. (2014) Reporting of harms in randomized controlled trials of psychological interventions for mental and behavioral disorders: A review of current practice. *Contemporary Clinical Trials*, 38, 1–8.

Lambert, M. (2007) Presidential address: What we have learned from a decade of research aimed at improving psychotherapy outcome in routine care. *Psychotherapy Research*, 17, 1–14.

Lambert, M.J. (2013). The efficacy and effectiveness of psychotherapy. In M.J. Lambert (Ed.), *Bergin and Garfield's Handbook of Psychotherapy and Behavior Change* (6th Edition). Hoboken, NJ: Wiley, pp. 169–218.

Lilienfeld, S.O. (2007) Psychological treatments that cause harm. *Perspectives on Psychological Science*, 2, 53–70.

Linden, M. (2013) How to define, find and classify side effects in psychotherapy: From unwanted events to adverse treatment reactions. *Clinical Psychology & Psychotherapy*, 20, 286–296.

Mohr, D.C. (1995) Negative outcome in psychotherapy: A critical review. *Clinical Psychology and Scientific Practice*, 2, 1–27.

Parker, G., Fletcher, K., Berk, M. & Paterson, A. (2013) Development of a measure quantifying adverse psychotherapeutic ingredients: The Experience of Therapy Questionnaire (ETQ). *Psychiatry Research*, 206, 293–301.

Parker, G., Paterson, A., Fletcher, K., McClure, G. & Berk, M. (2014) Construct validity of the Experience of Therapy Questionnaire (ETQ). *BMC Psychiatry*, 14, 369.

Parry, G.D., Crawford, M. & Duggan, C. (2016) Iatrogenic harm from psychological therapies – time to move on. *The British Journal of Psychiatry*, 208 210–212.

Royal College of Psychiatrists. (2014) *Good Psychiatric Practice: Code of Ethics*, London: RCPsych.

Rozental, A., Kottorp, A., Boettcher, J., Andersson, G. & Carlbring, P. (2016) Negative effects of psychological treatments: An exploratory factor analysis of the negative effects questionnaire for monitoring and reporting adverse and unwanted events. *PLoS ONE*, 11 (6): e0157503.

Saxon, D., Barkham, M., Foster, A. & Parry, G. (2017) The contribution of therapist effects to patient dropout and deterioration in the psychological therapies. *Clinical Psychology & Psychotherapy*, 24, 575–588.

Sue, S., Zane, N., Hall, G.C.N. & Berger, L.K. (2009) The case for cultural competency in psychotherapeutic interventions. *Annual Review of Psychology*, 60, 525–548.

Vaughan, B., Goldstein, H., Alikakos, M., Cohen, L.J. & Serby, M.J. (2014) Frequency of reporting of adverse events in randomized controlled trials of psychotherapy vs. psychopharmacotherapy. *Comprehensive Psychiatry*, 55, 849–855.

Williams, R., Farquharson, L., Palmer, L., Bassett, P., Clarke, J., Clark, D.M. & Crawford, M. (2016) Patient preference in psychological treatment and associations with self-reported outcome: National cross-sectional survey in England and Wales. *BMC Psychiatry*, 16(4), 1–8.

Wolpert, M. (2016) Failure is an option. *The Lancet Psychiatry*, 3, 510–512.

Part 4

Working with diversity
Professional practice and ethical considerations

Chapter 12

Ethical considerations when working with young people

Colman Noctor

Consent and involvement in decision-making

Working with young people, who are considered by legislation to be minors, can present professional and ethical challenges that are seldom experienced when working psychotherapeutically with an adult population. These challenges occur because young people have not yet reached the age of legal consent to mental health treatment, which in most countries is 18 years of age. Consent can differ from country to country, for example, in Ireland the legal age of consent for physical medical treatment is 16 years of age, whereas the legal age of consent for mental health treatment is 18 years of age (Daly, 2013). In the UK all young people aged 16 and over are presumed to have the capacity to consent to mental health treatment unless there is evidence to the contrary. If the child is deemed not legally competent, consent can be obtained from someone with parental responsibility, unless it is an emergency (British Medical Association, 2015).

These differentials can create anomalies which depend on each country's perspective on what constitutes a 'child'. Legislative particularities have a significant impact on professionals working with young people because those who are classed or categorised as 'children' or 'minors' do not share the same degree of autonomy over their decision-making that adults do. In this chapter, the term 'young people' will be used to refer to those who have yet to reach the legal age of consent to mental health treatment and/or are under 18 years of age. The term 'parent' will include any caregivers or assigned adults with the responsibility for the young person's care decisions.

The question of autonomy and protection is prominent in many debates concerning the rights of young people (Munro, 2008). These discussions often attempt to blend the rights of young people with their corresponding capacity to manage the responsibility associated with that right. This relationship between rights and responsibilities is at the heart of many of the contentious issues that arise when discussing the decision-making entitlements of young people. The rights of young people can include their right to participation, inclusion, protection and confidentiality (Graham et al., 2015). However, these rights also need to be aligned with the developmental level and decision-making capacity of the young person. This chapter explores some of these ethical dilemmas and provides guidance and considerations for the management of decision-making when working with young people with varying degrees of maturity in the therapeutic space.

Working with the young person, family triad and agencies

Children and young people represent a vulnerable population who are deemed to need special protection, and as a result they largely depend on the care and decisions of their parents or assigned adults (Koelch & Fegert, 2010). Several authors have discussed the ethical principles of working with young people in therapeutic settings (Belitz & Bailey, 2009; Sondheimer, 2008; Woodgate Tennent & Zurba, 2017) and raise the point that the central challenge is that the young person is part of a system that consists of parents, caregivers and other involved agencies who may all share an interest in the young person's care and treatment. Because of the multiple agencies involved, the integrity and autonomy of each member can be affected (Hart & O'Reilly, 2017). Mental health assessment is largely dependent on the data that is made available by the narrative of the storyteller (client). The interpretation of these narratives will then be influenced by the therapeutic lens and personal narrative of the clinical assessor (practitioner). This assessment is often made more complicated in Child and Adolescent Mental Health Services (CAMHS) because the compilation of narratives can involve multiple storytellers which include the accounts of the parents, the young person and perhaps schools and/or other agencies. In many cases, this can be very useful in gaining a comprehensive insight into the presenting difficulties from several perspectives; however, at times the experiences, impressions and desires of these storytellers are not always congruent. The ethical dilemma therefore exists for the practitioner on how much attention or credence is paid to the various sources of information. The merit apportioned to each storyteller may depend on one's therapeutic leaning or preference.

It is sometimes the case that young people engage in therapeutic work at the behest of their parents, carers or other parties, and therefore may begin therapy as reluctant volunteers in the therapy process (Brown, 2018). Therefore, the process of incorporating consent and negotiating the therapeutic engagement process can be considerably more complex. This is especially true when the young person and parent/s differ in their wishes and motivation for treatment. Consequently, factors such as confidentiality, protection and rights can also become contentious. To negotiate the conflicting ideologies of parents and young people, regarding autonomy and control, the practitioner needs to be able to integrate their knowledge of family systems, therapy and developmental psychology together with the usual clinical requirements to manage confidentiality, risk and therapeutic disclosures (Koocher, 2003). An example of this is highlighted in the following vignette:

Vignette 1

Brian is a 14-year-old with a diagnosis of ADHD who presents with behavioural problems at school and at home. Brian is convinced that his difficulties occur due to his anxiety in social situations. His parents however feel that his ADHD is at the root of his difficulties. Brian wants to work on feeling less anxious, whereas his parents want him to learn skills to attend better to his studies and the school environment.

• Which of these issues would you begin to address with Brian and his family?
• What is your rationale for this decision?

Confidentiality and competency

The classification of young people who range from 0–18 years of age as 'children', encompasses a period of development that involves an array of cognitive, emotional, physical and social change that occurs at a rapid pace. This variable developmental trajectory presents a range of different degrees of capacity for decision-making. In many instances, this not reflected in legislation that describe all young people under the age of 18 as children. Autonomy can be understood as someone's right to make his/her own choices and to act on their own beliefs/values (Koelch & Fegert, 2010). However, in accordance with the graduated maturational trajectory of childhood and adolescence, age can be an arbitrary guide when it comes to maturity. The period of adolescence occurs with a steep gradient of change and can often involve very different paces of physical, psychological, social and emotional development. For example, a 7-year-old will have a very different degree of autonomy in their decision-making compared to a 17-year-old, yet in some legislative directives these differentials are not considered. The mental health legislation in most countries states that anyone under 18 years of age is considered a 'child' and therefore these significant developmental distinctions are not recognised. It is therefore a 'grey area' when one considers the need to make allowances for maturity regarding a young person's confidentiality and preferences in the psychotherapeutic setting. This can also present a challenge when a young person has their 18th birthday while they are attending ongoing therapy. If traditionally up until this point the professional has communicated regularly with parents or carers about the young person's progress in therapy, the young person, can now instruct the professional to desist from doing this as they are now by law 'an adult'. This can be very difficult for parents, care givers and professionals whom up to that point have had an inclusive and open approach to keeping the parents and care-givers informed of their child's progress. This newly acquired autonomy can be a positive experience for the young person; however, the parents can now feel abruptly excluded from that process as the young person exercises their newly acquired autonomy. Therefore, it would seem optimal to have an individualised graduated allowance for autonomy that co-relates to these developments. Webb and Moynihan (2010) suggest using a flexible model with respect to adolescent autonomy, which depends on the severity of the decision being made and the wishes of the other family members. However, the challenge for implementing any such pro-forma graded age guideline is made difficult because the pace of maturity in childhood and adolescence is individual and therefore varies consid-erably from one young person to another, which makes age allocation of respon-sibilities arbitrary, complex and problematic.

When working therapeutically with young people, the ethical and respon-sible professional will obey the law and safeguard the best interests of the young person. According to the British Psychological Society's Code of Ethics (2018) the principles of Respect, Competence, Responsibility and Integrity should be at the heart of ethical decision-making. Therefore, ongoing ethical challenge in these incidences is to strike a balance between these elements by balancing the paternalistic elements of protection and beneficence versus the maleficence of obstructing the young person's right to autonomy (Koelch & Fegert, 2010). Koelch and Fegert (2010) point out that full autonomy may not help a young person who might be unable or too immature to utilise that autonomy effectively and therefore needs protection and guidance. Alterna-tively, over-protective paternalistic approaches can also limit a young person's rights when they are clearly competent to decide from themselves.

Confidentiality in the psychotherapeutic setting becomes especially import-ant when a conflict exists between the parents and the young person around an aspect of their narrative. The following vignette highlights an example of where this ideological conflict can occur.

Vignette 2

Elliott is a 15-year-old young person who declares they are transgender and suggests that they want to socially transition from female to male. They have asked that you, as their professional, refer to them using the male pronoun of their preferred gender. Their parents clearly oppose this request to socially transition and feel it is just a phase that must not be encouraged and have instructed you not to use the male pronoun. In this vignette the practi-tioner is faced with the dilemma of using the preferred pronoun as requested in the therapeutic setting, thereby validating Elliott's feelings and desires or risk creating a conflict with the parents, which may result in the young person being withdrawn from the psychotherapeutic process.

* What might you do in this situation?

This vignette highlights the importance of working agreements being discussed and made explicit at the outset of a therapeutic relationship, which outline what may occur as and when issues might arise between the young person and their parents. These ethical dilemmas can often create a demand for the therapist to 'pick a side'. In such instances, if the professional affords a degree of autonomy and protects the confidentiality of the young person in the therapeutic space, this can be interpreted as disloyalty to the parents, because this information is being withheld from them. Conversely, if the practitioner insists on adhering to the legislative guidelines that direct them to inform the parents/carers of all the young person's disclosures, then this can be interpreted as a disloyalty by the young person and negatively impact on the trust they have in the therapeutic relationship, which is crucial to its effectiveness.

These ethical decisions are further complicated by the fact that in the case of some presentations, such as Anorexia Nervosa, Conduct Disorder, Psychosis or Emotionally Unstable Personality Disorder, sufferers may lack a degree of insight into the nature of the disorder and have a reduced capacity for decision-making as part of the disorder itself (Koelch & Fegert, 2010).

Vignette 3

Sophie is a young person presenting with Anorexia Nervosa. She has disclosed to you that she is currently getting up at night and replacing her nutritional supplement drinks with water and taking laxatives, unbeknown to her parents. She is currently losing weight rapidly and her family are at a loss as to why this is happening.

* In this situation, can you uphold Sophie's request not to inform her parents of her weight reduction strategies?

Creating confidentiality agreements

Frequently, issues concerning confidentiality are addressed through a discussion with all the participants involved in the treatment, and the degree of autonomy afforded to the young person is negotiated on an individual basis from the outset (Koocher & Keith-Spiegal, 2008). However, this can be a challenging process, which demands the professional holds a great deal of tension and uncertainty for all the people involved. Under the UN Convention of the Rights of the Child (1989) the will of the child must be respected with allowance for their development, where the right of autonomy needs to be balanced in each case by weighing the aspects of maturity, the level of impairment caused by the disorder and the adequacy of the intervention. It is the professional's responsibility to understand the legal obligations of their own governance framework and apply this to their treatment of each young person. Where a degree of risk is involved that is not overt and does not apply to the governance guidelines of each discipline, it will often come down to the professional's clinical experience and their capacity to exercise discretion according to their individual knowledge of the family. The use of regular clinical supervision can be an important component to this decision-making process whereby practitioners can reflect on and think about their professional and ethical clinical decisions in a safe and supportive environment.

Disclosure and reporting of risk – safeguarding

The issue of breaking therapeutic confidentiality is clearer when it comes to obvious issues of personal safety. Where there is a clear concern over the ongoing risk to self or others, there is a clear need to break the confidentiality agreement between the young person and the professional and inform the parents and other authorities to protect the safety of all involved. This is also applicable to situations where there is a suspicion of physical, sexual or emotional abuse. Often when these revelations are disclosed in the psychotherapeutic setting, they require an assessment of the potential imminence of the ongoing risk and an evaluation of the severity and authenticity of the claims being made. The following vignette illustrates a scenario where the circumstances are less clear and where an ethical decision is required

Vignette 4

Mary is a young person who reveals that some time ago her father 'lost his cool' with her and 'pushed' her in a period of heightened stress. Mary indicates that this incident occurred two years ago, and nothing has happened since and therefore she does not experience any ongoing fear of her father. She currently reports a very positive relationship with her father and she is confident no such incident would happen again.

- What would you consider to be an appropriate response to this disclosure?
- What are the potential ramifications of reporting or not reporting this incident?

The ethical question in this scenario is how much of this disclosure needs to be escalated to appropriately protect the rights and welfare of the young person, considering the potential negative impact this may have on the current positive relationship that they have with their parent and the professional. To initiate official child protection proceedings in this instance would perhaps be interpreted as excessive and a potentially damaging response to this disclosure, which would potentially hamper the current positive relationship between the professional, the young person and their family. However, if this disclosure is not reported, the professional runs the risk of being seen to be negligent if there is another, more serious incident of violence in the future. To not report the disclosure of the earlier incident may be negatively viewed by authorities who can accuse the practitioner of withholding this information and not allowing the child protection authorities an opportunity to fully investigate any potential further risk.

These disclosures present ethical dilemmas, which are a central feature of working therapeutically with young people and their families. Suspected incidences are usually managed by instituting one's clinical judgement, while holding the uncertainty and tension for a period of clarification. This judgement call is usually informed by the professional's knowledge of the case and their insight into the dynamics of the various relationships in the family and their professional experience. However, inevitably these decisions involve a degree of personal and professional judgement which may carry a personal and professional risk of which there is no adequate legislative guidance or provision. The legal requirement to mandatorily report all cases of suspected abuse, does not consider the subtleties and important nuances of each complex set of family circumstances. In the event of no clear policies around these incidents, this can result in a considerable amount of responsibility falling to discretion and the decision-making capacity of the professional and/or the treating team.

It is important to add that legislation regarding mandatory reporting may be different from country to country and discipline to discipline, so it is wise to consult one's own legislative guidelines when it comes to reporting disclosures of abuse that emerge in therapeutic sessions.

As mentioned previously, the triad dynamic of working with families can result in the professional being asked to align themselves with the parents or the young person, with regards to confidentiality. The variations in the stance can be indicative of numerous dynamics that can be at play with each client, family and context, all of which can influence and impact on the practitioner's role and ethical decision-making process. Therefore, while each situation is unique, it is essential to pay attention to the interpersonal and intrapersonal psychodynamics in psychotherapeutic relationships with young people and their families, and therefore engage in adequate clinical supervision, which is a crucial component to ethical practice. Legislation and child protection guidelines can offer a broad stroke negotiation of this terrain; however, it is important to acknowledge how the intrapersonal dynamics within the professional can often influence the clinical choices and outcomes. Given the emotional dynamics that occur in these relationships there is an obligation on the therapist to tune into the 'self' and engage in clinical supervision to limit the influence of biases or emotive vulnerabilities on their ethical decisions.

Social media and young people

There is little doubt that internet technologies have led to dramatic changes in our culture in terms of online identities and connectivity, which has also impacted on the world of therapy (Balick, 2014). Although use of the internet is applicable to all age groups, the literature identifies the pervasive use of online technologies playing a more prominent role in the lives of younger people (Singleton, Abeles & Smith, 2016). This evolution has also impacted on the practitioners who work with children and adolescents.

Core transitional challenges for young people, such as identity formation, experimental risk-taking and anti-social behaviour are now being articulated, enacted and observed in online activities as well as their offline lives (Singleton et al., 2016). Given the ubiquity and pervasiveness of technology in young people's lives, what are the considerations for therapists when working with young people in this space? First, it is important to state that internet law is continually evolving, and as a result there are many unknowns when it comes to the specific legalities of some online behaviours (Aiken, 2017). This creates uncertainties for therapists when it comes to reporting areas of concern that emerge in therapeutic conversations. The challenge is that the internet is a largely unregulated space where access and age verification is easily manipulated (Aiken, 2017). This results in young people being able to access content in a way that is very difficult to supervise.

The regulation of online content is an evolving picture, as soon as regulators feel they have made some progress in regulating content, another similar site may appear within minutes. This calls for users to exercise 'self-regulation', which young people may find challenging as they may have not developed this ability yet.

Young people will often see the internet as the 'first port of call' when it comes to information seeking and therefore the availability of unregulated content becomes a concern as it may provide inaccurate or unhelpful content to the inquisitive young person (Singleton et al., 2016). When considering the legal, ethical and moral guides to online activity, the rule of thumb is that whatever is considered illegal in the offline world is also illegal in the online world. This involves accessing underage pornography, purchasing off-label medicines, extortion, harassment and stealing, etc. However, the surveillance of these activities is much more difficult in the online space, therefore people may be engaging in these activities undetected for some time (Aiken, 2017). In terms of this information emerging in therapeutic conversations, it is imperative that the therapists consider the legality of the reported online activities and seek the guidance of an expert in online law enforcement and internet law.

This is especially unclear when it comes to the sharing of images without consent and cyberbullying or cyber-exclusion.

Another issue regarding negotiating the online landscape for young people is that many of the sites that they visit may not be age appropriate and as a result the young person may be reluctant to raise these concerns in therapy, for fear that the therapist will inform their parents. This is a contentious issue, as if it does emerge that inappropriate content is being reported, it may well be necessary to inform their parents. Confidentiality can therefore not be guaranteed, but the professional should encourage open disclosure and explain that they will manage this information as sensitively as possible.

Cyberbullying

Unfortunately, bullying and exclusion behaviours can be observed on online social media platforms (Singleton et al., 2016). Some young people may report such incidences in the therapeutic setting and it is important that the therapist is knowledgeable enough to respond (Balick, 2014). Bullying and harassment is the same whether it occurs in an online of offline setting. Therefore, these incidences need to be managed by approaching the school or police to inform them of the events. Young people are encouraged to keep an electronic record of these exchanges when necessary so that they can be produced as evidence (Aiken, 2017). The issue of social media exclusion is harder to address as it can be difficult to prove. Approaching the school may be recommended but again this is not straight forward. The issue of jurisdiction is a contentious issue in cyber-based interactions, as many schools and sports organisations may explain that they cannot be responsible for interactions that occur outside of their hours of responsibility and buildings. This makes addressing cyber based interactions difficult.

The area of technological communication can throw up many challenges and there is a notable absence of clear solutions or responses. As a therapeutic professional, one must weigh up the degree of risk that is involved in reporting incidents and they must consider the legal, moral and ethical implications of these events. The response may be a legal one, but it may not be. There is a need to educate young people to become critical consumers of technological communication. This involves informing them of their rights and supporting them to engage in a healthy way with technology. This involves not over-investing in the importance of social media feedback, questioning the authenticity of online information, being able to self-regulate their usage and allowing them to prioritise meaning and importance. This is an ongoing challenge and one that the therapeutic field needs to continue to develop practitioners' understanding of the dynamics of the online space (Balick, 2014).

Conclusion

Issues concerning young people's rights and responsibilities require practitioners to have a good understanding of child and adolescent developmental trajectories and at the same time demands the practitioner to hold a great deal of tension and uncertainty for all the people involved with the young person's well-being. The advent of technology and social media has brought with it many contemporary challenges to young people growing up, which can also emerge in the therapeutic setting. It is important that practitioners attempt to learn more about the online space and have an understanding as to the role it can play in the contemporary lives of young people as well as the legal and safety issues that can arise as a result of online behaviour.

Reflective questions

1. What are the main ethical differences of working therapeutically with young people compared to adults in a therapeutic setting?
2. What are the ethical challenges for you as a practitioner in reporting historical cases of minor physical abuse in young people's mental health settings and how do you manage them?
3. What ethical challenges have you encountered due to the advent of technology and computer-mediated-communication and how do you work with these challenges?
4. What ethical challenges have you encountered concerning disclosures from young people regarding behaviours relating to their online safety and how have you addressed such challenges?

References

Aiken, M. (2017) *The Cyber Effect: A Pioneering Cyberpsychologist Explains How Human Behavior Changes Online*. New York: Spiegel & Grau.
Balick, A. (2014) *The Psychodynamics of Social Networking: Connected-up Instantaneous Culture and the Self*. London England: Karnac Books.
Belitz, J. & Bailey, R.A. (2009) Clinical ethics for the treatment of children and adolescents: a guide for general psychiatrists. *Psychiatric Clinics*, 32(2), 243–257.
BMA (British Medical Association). (2015) Assessment of mental capacity. *The Law Society*. London.
BPS (British Psychological Society). (2018) Code of ethics. Available at: https://www.bps.org.uk/news-and-policy/bps-code-ethics-and-conduct. Accessed 8 January 2020.
Brown, J., (2018) Parents' experiences of their adolescent's mental health treatment: Helplessness or agency-based hope. *Clinical Child Psychology and Psychiatry*, 23(4), 644–662.

Daly, M. (2013) Children and Minors: Issues relating to consent and confidentiality. Available at: https://www.icgp.ie/speck/properties/asset/asset.cfm?type-LibraryAsset% id-5369878C-9660-2170-1986D6711F9EC569&property=asset&revision-tipdisposi tion-attachment&app-icgp&filename-Children_and_Minors_-_Issues_Relating_to_Con sent_Confidentiality.pdf. Accessed 8 January 2020.

Graham, A., Powell, M.A. & Taylor, N. (2015) Ethical research involving children: Encouraging reflexive engagement in research with children and young people. *Children & Society*, 29(5), 331–343.

Hart, T. & O'Reilly, M., (2017) The challenge of exchanging and sharing information between CAMHS and education: Multi-agency communication implications. First published: 06 October 2017. 10.1111/camh.12245 Accessed 10 July 2018.

Koelch, M. & Fegert, J.M. (2010) Ethics in child and adolescent psychiatric care: An international perspective. *International Review of Psychiatry*, 22(3), 258–266.

Koocher, G.P. (2003) Ethical issues in psychotherapy with adolescents. *Journal of Clinical Psychology*, 59(11), 1247–1256.

Koocher, G.P. & Keith-Spiegal, P. (2008) *Ethics in Psychology and the Mental Health Professions: Standards and Cases*. New York: Oxford University Press.

Munro, E. (2008) *Effective Child Protection*. London, UK: Sage Publications.

Nations, U. (1989) Convention on the rights of the child 20 November. *Annual Review of Popular Law*, 16(95), 485–501.

Singleton, A., Abeles, P. & Smith, I.C. (2016) Online social networking and psychological experiences: The perceptions of young people with mental health difficulties. *Computers in Human Behavior*, 61, 394–403.

Sondheimer, A. (2008) Ethics and risk management in administrative child and adolescent psychiatry. *Child & Adolescent Psychiatry Clinics of North America*, 19(1), 115–129.

Webb, E. & Moynihan, S. (2010) An ethical approach to resolving value conflicts in child protection. *Archives of Disease in Childhood*, 95(1), 55–58.

Woodgate, R.L., Tennent, P. & Zurba, M. (2017) Navigating ethical challenges in qualitative research with children and youth through sustaining mindful presence. *International Journal of Qualitative Methods*, 16(1), 1–11F.

Chapter 13

Professional and ethical issues in working with older adults

Afreen Huq, Maureen McIntosh and Rachel Tribe

In Britain, older adults are defined as people aged 65 years and over, though definitions will vary across countries. The issues of ageism, stigma service usage and age discrimination will also be discussed. The Royal College of Psychiatrists noted that 'Age discrimination is now more pronounced in mental health services than in other areas of healthcare. … the principles of age-appropriate, non-discriminatory services still appear to be misunderstood by services and commissioners, in particular, the issues of indirect discrimination and age appropriateness' (Anderson, 2011: 1). Most professional organisations within the 'psy' professions (psychology, psychiatry, psychotherapy) all stipulate the clinicians need to be skilled at working with people across the age range including older adults, though in reality this does not always occur. This chapter discusses the professional and ethical issues that may arise when undertaking therapeutic work with older adults.

Current statistics

The number of people in the UK aged 65 and over is increasing. In 2017 this was 18%, with 2.4% aged 85 and over (Office for National Statistics, 2017). Globally, the picture is similar. By 2050, the proportion of the world's population over 60 years will nearly double, from 12% to 22%. Therefore clinicians need to be adequately prepared to work with this group of people.

The World Health Organisation (WHO) (2017) states that in relation to older adults that:

- More than 20% of adults over 60 years of age suffer from a neurological or mental disorder. 6.6% of all disability adjusted life years (DALYS) are caused by this.
- Depression and dementia are the most common disorders.
- Anxiety disorders affect 3:75 % of older adults.
- Substance abuse is common among nearly 1% of the world's population of older adults.
- Approximately 15% of adults aged 60 and over suffer from a mental disorder.

There has been an assumption among some clinicians that older adults will not benefit from talking therapies (Pettit et al., 2017), although evidence shows this is not correct. For example, NHS England (2018) in a review noted that 'Psychological therapies are as effective for older people as for those of working age'. NHS Health Education (2018) states that one in five over-65s living in the community are affected by depression but, despite Improving Access to Psychological Therapies (IAPT) services being open to all adults, older people are underrepresented amongst those accessing services (Boddington, 2011). Further information about psychotherapy with older adults is detailed by Orbach (1996). Barriers for older adults may come from both clinicians and service users. As stated earlier, clinicians may hold negative stereotyping and ageist ideas and service users may feel that services are not appropriate for their needs, sensory and mobility issues can also make accessing services harder. Age UK (2014) notes that people aged 65 and over were contributing £61 billion to the economy through employment, caring and volunteering. This amount was six times more than the money that was spent on social care by local authorities in England at that time (Department of Communities and Local Government, 2014). Professional and ethical practice should ensure that commissioners and service planners account for these issues when planning services.

A useful resource relating to information about mental health and older adults was launched in 2018 by NHS Health Education England, it can be used by older adults, their families and clinicians. While NHS England and NHS Improvement (2017) published a report on mental health in older people titled 'A practice primer for practitioners', although the target audience are GPs and Clinical Commissioning Groups, there is much that may be of interest to any clinician. The Royal College of Psychiatrists' College Centre for Quality Improvement (CCQI, 2018) recently published a report on depression in older people admitted to acute hospitals which shows that depression is currently under-detected in older adults. While in 2017, the World Health Assembly endorsed a Global action plan on the public health response to dementia for the period 2017–2025. The provides a detailed plan which it hopes will improve the experiences of people living with dementia, as well as their carers and families. It also hopes to reduce the impact of dementia on individuals, communities and countries. They have also developed an observatory, for both policy-makers and researchers to facilitate monitoring and the sharing of information and data on related policies, service delivery, epidemiological patterns and research in relation to dementia.

Working with the older person

The work of clinicians is based on the fundamental acknowledgement that all people have the same human value and the right to be unique individuals, who will treat all people, both clients and colleagues, with dignity and respect and will work with them collaboratively as partners towards the achievement of mutually agreed goals. The attitude that the clinician brings to working with older adults is fundamental in delivering person-centred care, whereby the older person is treated as an individual, rather than based on stereotypes and/or assumptions. Clinicians need to be aware of this and actively reflect upon their own attitudes to older adults. Clinicians also need to be aware that ageing may be culturally and socially defined (Gawande, 2014). Therefore best practice would require service users' views and requirements being taken into account throughout the clinical work. A key professional and ethical principle is that assumptions about how ageing is viewed by an individual, their family or their carer should not be taken for granted.

Older adults with intellectual/learning difficulties may require specialist help and additional professional and ethical issues may require consideration (Oladosu and Kydd-Williams, 2017). Emerson and Heslop (2010) predict that by 2030 the number of adults aged over 70 with intellectual disabilities who require health and social care services will more than double. Therefore future planning for this population is vital, if services are to be available and appropriate, this also has workforce planning implications. Clinicians are therefore highly likely to encounter this group in their work and may need to ensure that they have undertaken the relevant training or obtained best practice knowledge. In addition, lesbian, bisexual, gay, transgender or intersex (LBGTi) older adults have reported a range of issues relating to professional and ethical practice, these have included an assumed heteronormativity (Varney, 2012) and discrimination (Broadway-Horner, 2017; Hughes et al., 2011).

Clinicians need to be aware of the need to adhere to and also be guided by professional, codes, legislation and organisational requirements combined, as stated earlier, with ongoing consideration of the wishes of older adult service users.

Certain characteristics associated with ageing such as the high prevalence of medical illness, cognitive impairment or disorder, frailty and health needs deserve special consideration. It is the co-morbidities that increase the risk of vulnerability in older people. Differentiate ageing occurs, which means that people age at slightly different rates. Positive or 'successful' ageing (Reichstadt et al., 2010) and due consideration of the resilience and coping strategies that many older adults have used throughout their lives needs to form part of any therapeutic encounter and requires as much attention as the difficulties which they may be presenting with (Lane, 2017). Research suggests that resilience will not decline with age and older adults are just as resilient as younger people (Gooding et al., 2012). Older adults are all individuals who have successfully negotiated their lives with all the challenges they may have encountered. Clinicians need to be mindful of this.

Managing confidentiality and boundary issues in the multidisciplinary team and with the service user and their family or carer should be considered. Some older adults may have carers and others will be carers. Almost 1.3 million people aged 65 or over are carers (Carers UK, 2014) and some will require therapeutic help. The 2011 census conducted in Britain found that 92% of carers described caring as having a detrimental effect on their mental health including depression and stress related illnesses. The important role of carers is recognised in legislation (Care Act, 2014), which came into force in April, 2015 and details how local authorities are obliged to conduct carer's assessments. Finally, attitudes towards working with older adults will be addressed as part of the reflective and reflexive practitioner process together with some discussion on risk issues and safeguarding procedures to protect the service user.

Guidelines and competencies

The National Service Framework in the UK (2001b) was developed to make certain that older people are able to access the services that they need, although there is some acknowledgement that inequalities in how resources are distributed for older people is still problematic. For example, there is recognition that too often there remains a lack of recognition of the mental health needs of older people (Age Concern, 2006; Royal College of Psychiatrists, 2018). Age UK (2016) published a report entitled *Hidden in Plain Sight: The unmet mental health needs of older people*. There key recommendations were:

> Implementation of Mental Health Taskforce recommendations should include a work stream dedicated to meeting older people's mental health needs. This should include ensuring wide use of the new Commissioning for Quality and Innovation (CQUIN) **system** for depression in older patients. (The CQUIN system makes part of NHS healthcare providers' income conditional on demonstrating improvements in quality and innovation in specified areas of care).

> * Local health and care commissioners should fully understand the prevalence of common mental health conditions among the over 65s in their areas.
> * Each clinical commissioning group and local authority should consider appointing 'older people's mental health champions'.
> * All services should be appropriately funded and equipped to deliver."
>
> Age UK, (2016:6)

Clinicians who specialise in other areas of health and social care can expect to interact with an older person regularly in their clinical practice. Therefore, it is essential that those who work with older people have the clinical skills necessary to deliver an appropriate service. Age UK (2019) makes freely accessible a range of information on the older population for free, including policy position statements on dementia and on health and wellbeing.

Ageism

'Ageism is discrimination or unfair treatment based on a person's age' (Age UK, 2020a, Royal College of Psychiatrists' position statement, 2009). The World Health Organisation (2019) notes that ageism marginalises and excludes older people in their communities and can be detrimental to health and wellbeing. Age discrimination is still the most common type of prejudice experienced by people aged 55 and over. Ageist attitudes are embedded in some cultures, often reinforced by the media through negative images of older adults. Ageism threatens the dignity of older adults and it implies that they are somehow deficient relative to other age groups. Such a negative view permeates society and contributes to people internalising negative ideas about older people, as well as affecting professionals within organisations, service provision and access to services. For example, Pettit et al. (2017) demonstrated the low referral rate to IAPT services for older adults. The following fictitious case vignette illustrates how Bill's physical health problems reverberate in every area of his life, regarding how he experiences others and how ageist assumptions marginalise him further.

Vignette I

To relate these issues to clinical practice, imagine for a moment that your client Bill tells you that throughout his lifetime he has worked hard to care for his family and contributed to society and he was looking forward to enjoying his retirement. Aged 67, Bill suffered a stroke, which left him partially paralysed on one side; this affected his mobility, meaning that he now needs a walking stick and his speech is slurred and quite slow. Bill's lived experience now is that he is treated differently because of his day-to-day challenges, and every moment he is in company, he is made to feel excluded, invisible and it is assumed that he will not understand enough to participate in a dialogue. For example, Bill comes into contact with services a great deal and whenever he attends with a younger carer, he has found that in clinical meetings professionals can make plans about his care in his presence, but without collaborating with him and then he is given the care plan.

• How do you think Bill experiences this style of interaction and how would you facilitate Bill's ability to reconnect with his personhood?

Bill is aged 85 and he was born in the UK. He worked until he was 78 years old in a small family-owned tailors until he had a fall at work and broke his hip. After his hip operation Bill developed a urinary tract infection and subsequent delirium. Shortly after he was discharged from hospital his wife informed him that she has coronary heart disease. Due to his poor mobility Bill found it very difficult to adjust to his changed life and he became despondent. His wife's health deteriorated and 12 months later she passed away. Kind neighbours would check in on Bill daily. Bill found it increasingly difficult to cope on his own and he became more isolated, declining offers from friends to go out. One morning Bill decided that he did not want to live anymore and he took an overdose of his pain medication. He was found by a neighbour and an ambulance was called. While in hospital he was referred for psychological therapy.

Reflective questions

1. What kinds of questions would you ask during the assessment to get a sense of their personhood?
2. How would you develop a shared understanding of the meaning for Bill of these major of the life events and re-formulate to build on his strengths?
3. What other services would be useful to involve helping with Bill's recovery?

A developmental perspective

There are a number of different theories about lifespan development, for example, Erikson (1982). Disengagement theory was developed in the 1950s and 1960s, which suggested that older people needed to withdraw from their social roles in order for them to respond to their 'natural' biological decline to enable younger people opportunities. Active ageing theory (Knight & Ricciardelli, 2003) focuses on the productive potential of older people and the need to maintain health and social activities and to live independently, although this has been subject to criticism (Stenner et al., 2011; Van Dyk et al., 2013). These authors argue that active ageing is part of a moral narrative and political strategy to individualise responsibility and to re-invent the meaning of ageing in society, and, to re-consider questions relating to the rights and duties of older adults. However, different 'theories of ageing' rarely include older people as researchers or in developing new 'models of ageing' (Knight & Ricciardelli, 2003). So as clinicians and researchers it is important to think about the ways that current narratives lead to theories being developed about older people and inform our own attitudes as well as considering how contemporary theories inform clinical thinking, practice and services.

Elder abuse

This is a serious professional and ethical issue that is often hidden but which clinicians need to be alert to. Abuse can take many forms ranging from involuntary institutionalisation, neglect in the home by others, not feeding or providing drinks for older people who are unable to feed themselves, financial abuse, bullying, physical violence, over-medication, sexual assault, and emotional/psychological abuse causing confusion and isolation (Hardin, 2005).

The WHO (2018) reports that

- Rates of elder abuse are high in institutions such as nursing homes and long-term care facilities, with two in three staff reporting that they have committed abuse in the past year.
- Elder abuse can lead to serious physical injuries and long-term psychological consequences.
- Elder abuse is predicted to increase as many countries are experiencing rapidly ageing populations.
- The global population of people aged 60 years and older will more than double, from 900 million in 2015 to about 2 billion in 2050.

Clinicians need to follow the local government safeguarding procedures to raise an alert in case of the risk of any form of abuse of an older adult. The steps taken to protect older people may also involve liaison with health and social care organisations and the police while addressing the need for on-going support for the older person.

Engagement and the therapeutic relationship

Engaging with our clients in order to develop a therapeutic relationship is central to the work no matter which modality the clinician adopts. Ultimately, it is about how the clinician connects with the older person and how they experience the response and service. Ageing can be a challenging process for many people and some older adults report the realisation 'of a changed self' (McIntosh & Sykes, 2016). Older adults may have concerns about whether young clinicians will understand them and their life experiences and vice versa (Lane, 2017). Both parties may have concerns about whether therapeutic engagement may result in a dependent relationship (Martindale, 1989), while clinicians may have anxieties about their own mortality or ageing. In addition, loneliness and isolation has a debilitating impact on the psychological health of older adults (Age UK, 2020b). The Joe Cox Loneliness Commission in England called for a National Strategy for loneliness across all ages to tackle what is described as an urgent crisis. In 2018, the British government appointed a minister for loneliness.

When considering cultural issues and the therapy relationship, it is widely known that black and ethnic minorities are often under-represented within therapy and counselling (Bhui et al., 2013), as are older adults with intellectual disabilities (Oladosu & Kydd-Williams, 2017). In order to provide a culturally appropriate service it is important that there is an understanding about how age, 'race', ethnicity, or intellectual ability, and mental health status may interact and intersectionality (Crenshaw, 1989) occurs; this is where the different types of discrimination intersect. Clinicians need to be aware of this and consider this in their work. Older adults from different ethnic groups in the UK are under-represented in research studies and there is a need for services to incorporate culturally appropriate and accessible services that meet the needs of this client group (Oomen, Bashford & Shah, 2009). Staff may lack training or understanding of the importance of culture and mental health or how to provide culturally competent or sensitive services (Bhui et al., 2013; Livingston, et al, 2003). Individual clinicians, managers, service providers and commissioners need to ensure that regular audits of the ethnic profile of their geographical area are undertaken and consider this when establishing or updating services and ensure that relevant training is available.

Additionally, the complexity of this type of work can bring up issues for the therapist, for instance, anxiety about their own mortality or ageing. When working with older clients the clinician needs to be mindful that there may be other factors that can interrupt the engagement process. For instance, there are times when a client is referred for therapy and due to the person's physical ill-health getting started can be delayed due to hospitalisation or other factors that may mean they are not well enough to begin therapy. Flexibility in managing some of these dilemmas is important, as this can help when dealing with the complexity of the work, and also when unexpected situations arise.

Confidentiality

Blurring of boundaries can dis-empower older people and leads to subjugation of their wishes to those of others, for example when professionals more readily form alliances with younger family members or carers (Tribe & Lane, 2017). Also consider the earlier example of Bill's experiences. Family members may feel that the clinician's role is to implement their wishes. Clinicians working with older adults often need to work with multiple systems, including carers and other family members. Sometimes the referral is for family work, where the whole family including the older person are the clients. The skill of the clinician in negotiating how the work will take place and how to manage confidentiality is essential in order to keep the family engaged in the process. There are occasions when family members who are not the identified clients may enquire about the older person, often their enquiry is motivated by worry about how their relative is progressing or the older person could be in crisis and perhaps has demonstrated behaviour that the family may not understand. Again, the skill to empathically listen and contain the anxieties of the family, while maintaining client confidentiality is important.

Although managing confidentiality when working within a multidisciplinary team can be challenging, it can provide an opportunity to inform and educate through consultation, teaching/training and supervision. Older adults are not one homogenous group and therefore the importance of multidisciplinary team working to help support the individual to retain their independence is a key characteristic of teamwork (Webster, 2002). Each member of the multi-disciplinary team brings specific knowledge and skills which can be used in the service of the older adult. For example, clinicians working in community mental health teams may have the knowledge and skills to share psychological case formulations, which can support other disciplines to think psychologically and this can contribute to ethical decision making, ensuring that the person is at all times kept involved in his/her care. Formulation and formulation summaries integrate a range of bio-psychosocial causal factors. These are based around the meaning-making and and understanding of the psychological experiences of the service user and are developed in active collaboration and consultation between the clinician and the service user. The multi-disciplinary team may also input into the formulation if deemed appropriate and helpful. constructed collaboratively with service users and teams. Dexter-Smith et al. (2010) have developed 'The Roseberry Park CBT formulation framework' that routinely uses CBT psychological formulation in older people's mental health services. They assert that by using formulation in teams it pulls together 'the narrative of a person's life' and this helps the team take a holistic view of the individuals' problems.

The reflective and reflexive practitioner

The nature of the work with older adults can bring up issues for clinicians and trainees that they need to make sense of, and seek support when required. Being a reflexive practitioner is a process whereby clinicians can explore their own beliefs, frames of reference, the language that is used, that carries its own meaning and how this informs their own clinical work. Reflecting upon one's own practice involves professional and personal consideration and analysis that requires the practitioner to think about how their interaction with their clients impacts on them, and also how the client may have experienced that encounter. Reflection is a learning opportunity and psychologists and therapists use this process routinely in their clinical work.

Tribe and Lane, (2017) argue that the multifaceted nature of the work may raise ethical and moral issues, but through reflection there are opportunities to convey feelings, express frustration about aspects of the work and talk about what is going well. For example, the fictitious vignette below can be a typical complex case that clinicians working with older people face. The issues presented here can have an impact on the clinician because respecting the client's end of life request may contradict their own personal and professional beliefs about sustaining life. Bringing issues of this type to supervision or staff reflective practice groups can be a supportive forum to work through these aspects of the work.

Vignette 2

Claire is an 81-year-old woman with long-standing history of depression and suicidal ideation. Recently, she has been diagnosed with lung cancer in the end stage. Claire has refused any invasive treatment or procedures and she continues to struggle to live her life. Claire is unsteady on her feet, with giddy spells, and she copes by using a trolley for support. If the weather is too windy she does not go out to the local shop to buy her newspapers, fearing that she might fall. Claire enjoys doing crosswords and when she cannot go out she becomes more isolated and housebound. She is frustrated that she has to rely on dial-a-ride to take her shopping because it takes away her independence and her spontaneity. Another complication is that she needs to move home and face the dilemmas about needing more supported care and maintaining her choice and independence. She fears losing control over decisions about her care, in the context of adverse stories in the media highlighting poor ethical and moral practices in some of the Care Homes.

Throughout history marginalised groups have experienced oppression and discrimination, which is promoted in society through legislation, stigma, politics and stereotypical assumptions. Clinicians are not immune from the many years of social conditioning, as it is embedded within society and perpetuated by the media and discourses that take place, between people, among groups of people, within communities and nations worldwide. Phillips et al. (2010) argue that 'Old age is viewed as having low status and little respect, older adults generally are at risk for poor treatment to resources. The burden of each status (i.e.: age, race/ethnicity, gender and/or social class) builds from numerous social experiences'.

Conclusion

The needs of older adults need to be taken seriously. There are challenges and opportunities in relation to the future of mental health care for older people, given the global picture of ageing; this may impact upon service provision within mental health as well as all aspects of therapeutic or mental health intervention. Clinicians need to be aware of their own values and views about older adults and how these may influence their perception and expectations relating to older adults. The importance of actively involving service users in the design, auditing and evaluation of services is being increasingly recognised as not only a professional and ethical requirement but also as a positive addition to ensuring that services are appropriate, accessible and meaningful.

Additional champions to advocate for the rights of older adults at every level, within organisations, commissioning groups, health and social care services and within communities, to influence strategy and policy and to challenge stereotypes about older people has been suggested. This would enable older people's voices to be heard more clearly and lead to older adults being valued, treated fairly and also to receive the right type of support that meets their needs.

Reflective questions

1. What beliefs do you bring into the consulting room about ageing and the older adult and how have they helped or hindered the therapeutic process?
2. What is your perception of the psychological impact of social isolation and loneliness on the quality of life of the older adult?
3. How would you prepare yourself when your client who is frail, with poor vision, shares his experience of hearing voices telling him he needs to die, because he is old and of no more use? How can you avoid reinforcing those ageist views?
4. How would you prepare yourself to undertake an assessment with a client with visual, hearing or memory difficulties and complicated medical difficulties?

References

Age Concern. (2006) UK inquiry into mental health and well-being in later life. Coordinated by Age Concern. Available at: www.ageconcern.org.uk Accessed 10 October 2018.

Age UK. (2014) Chief economist report. Spring 2014. Available at: www.ageuk.org.uk/Documents/EN-GB/For-professionals/Research/Age_UK_chief_economist_report_spring_2014.pdf?dtrk=true Accessed 8 February 2019.

Age UK. (2016) Available at: www.ageuk.org.uk/brandpartnerglobal/wiganboroughvpp/hidden_in_plain_sight_older_peoples_mental_health.pdf Accessed 20 January 2019.

Age UK (2019) Available at: www.ageuk.org.uk/professional-resources-home/knowledge-hub-evidence-statistics Accessed 24 January 2019.

Age UK. (2020a) Available at: https://www.ageuk.org.uk/northern-ireland/information-advice/work-learning/discrimination-rights/

Anderson, D. (2011) Editorial: Age discrimination in mental health services needs to be understood. *BJP Bulletin*, 35 (1), 1–4.

Bhui, K., Stansfeld S., Hull S., Priebe S., Mole F. & Feder G. (2013) Ethnic variations in pathways to and use of specialist mental health services in the UK: Systematic review. *British Journal of Psychiatry*, 182, 105–106.

Boddington, S. (2011) Age equality overviews: Where are all the older people? Equality of access to IAPT services. *PSIGE Newsletter*, 113, 11–14.

Broadway-Horner, M. (2017) Ageing, sexual orientation and mental health: Lesbian, gay, bisexual, transgendered and intersex older people. In P. Lane & R. Tribe (Eds.). (2017) *Anti-Discriminatory Practice in Mental Health for Older People*. London & Philadelphia: Jessica Kingsley, pp. 232–257.

Care Act. (2014) Available at: www.gov.uk/government/publications/care-act-statutory-guidance/care-and-support-statutory-guidance Accessed 9 February 2019.

Carers UK. (2014) Available at: www.carersuk.org Accessed 10 February 2019.

Crenshaw, K. (1989) Mapping the margins: Intersectionality, identity politics and violence against women of color. *Stanford Law Review*, 43(6), 1241–1299.

Department of Communities and Local Government. (2014) Local Government Financial Statistics No 242014. Available at: www.gov.uk/government/uploads/system/uploads/attachment_data/file/316772/LGFS24_web_edition.pdf Accessed 8 February 2019.

Dexter-Smith, S., Hopper, S. & Sharpe, P. (2010) Integrating psychological formulations into older people's services-three years on (Part 2): Evaluation of the formulation training. *PSIGE Newsletter*, 112, 12–15.

Emerson, E. & Heslop, P. (2010) *A Working Definition of Learning Disabilities*. Manchester: Learning Disabilities Observatory.

Erikson, E. (1982) *The Life Cycle Completed: A Review*. New York: Norton.

Gawande, A. (2014) *Being Mortal: Medicine and What Matters in the End*. London: Wellcome.

Gooding, P.A., Hurst, A., Johnson, J. & Tarrier, N. (2012) Psychological Resilience in young and older adults. *International Journal of Geriatric Psychiatry*, 27(3), 262–270.

Hardin, E. (2005) Elder abuse – "society's dilemma". *Journal of the National Medical Association*, 97(1), 91–94.

Hughes, A.K., Harold, R.D. & Boyer, J.M. (2011) Awareness of LGBT ageing issues among aging services network providers. *Journal of Gerontological Social Work*, 54, 659–677.

Improving Access to Psychological Therapies. Guidance for Commissioning IAPT Training (2012/13) Available at: www.iapt.nhs.uk.

Knight, T. & Ricciardelli, L. (2003) Successful aging: Perceptions of adults aged between 70 and 101 years. *International Journal of Aging Human Development*, 56(3), 223–245.

Lane, P. (2017) Conceptualising ageing and anti-discriminatory practice. In P. Lane & R. Tribe (Eds.). *Anti-discriminatory Practice in Mental Health for Older People*. London & Philadelphia: Jessica Kingsley, pp. 19–47.

Livingston, G. & Sembhi, S. (2003) Mental health of the ageing immigrant population. *Advances in Psychiatric Treatment*, 9, 31–37.

Martindale, B. (1989) Becoming dependent again: The fears of some elderly persons and their younger therapists. *Psychoanalytic Psychotherapy*, 4(1), 67–75.

McIntosh, M. & Sykes, C. (2016) Older adults' experience of psychological therapy. *Counselling Psychology Review*, 31(1), 20–30.

National Service framework in the UK (2001b) Available at: www.gov.uk/government/publications/quality-standards-for-care-services-for-older-people   Accessed 24 January 2019.

NHS England. (2017) Available at: www.england.nhs.uk/wp-content/uploads/2017/09/practice-primer.pdf Accessed 10 February 2019.

NHS Health Education. (2018) Available at: https://mindedforfamilies.org.uk/older-people Accessed 10 February 2019.

Office for National Statistics (2017) Available at: www.ons.gov.uk/peoplepopulationand community/.../overviewoftheukpopulation/ Accessed 9 February 2019.

Oladosu, M. & Kydd-Williams, R. (2017) Ageing and mental health issues for people with learning disabilities. In P. Lane & R. Tribe (Eds.). *Anti-discriminatory Practice in Mental Health for Older People*. London & Philadelphia: Jessica Kingsley, pp. 205–231.

Oomen, G., Bashford, J. & Shah, A. (2009) Ageing, ethnicity and psychiatric services. *Psychiatric Bulletin*, 33, 30–34.

Orbach, A. (1996) *Not too Late: Psychotherapy and Ageing*. London: Jessica Kingsley.

Pettit, S., Qureshi, A., Lee, W., Stirzaker, A., Gibson, A., Henley, W. & Byng, R. (2017) Variation in referral and access to new psychological therapy services by age: an empirical quantitative study. *British Journal of General Practice*, 67(660), 453–459.

Phillips, J., Ajrouch, K. & Hillcoat-Nalletamby, S. (2010) *Key Concepts in Social Gerontology*. London: Sage Publications.

Reichstadt, J., Sengupta, G., Depp, C.A., Palinkas, L.A. & Jeste, D.V. (2010) Older adults' perspectives on successful aging: Qualitative interviews. *American Journal of Geriatric Psychiatry*, 18(7), 567–575.

Royal College of Psychiatrists. (2018) Depression in older people admitted to acute hospitals. Available at: www.rcpsych.ac.uk/pdf/Depression%20Survey%20Report% 202018.pdf.

Royal College of Psychiatrists' College Centre for Quality Improvement (2018) https:// www.rcpsych.ac.uk/improving-care/ccqi/national-clinical-audits/national-clinical-audit-of-anxiety-and-depression/what-is-ncaad.

Royal College of Psychiatrists' position statement. (2009) Age discrimination in mental health services: making equality a reality. PS2/2009.

Stenner, P., McFarquhar, T. & Bowling, A. (2011) Older people and 'active ageing': Subjective aspects of ageing actively. *Journal of Health Psychology*, 16(3), 467–477.

Tribe, R., & Lane, P. (2017) Caring for carers in. In P. Lane & R. Tribe. (Eds.). *Anti-discriminatory Practice When Working in Mental Health with Older People*. London & Philadelphia: Jessica Kingsley, pp. 147–174.

Van Dyk, S., Lessenich, S., Denninger, T. & Richter, A. (2013) The many meanings of "active ageing": Confronting public discourse with older people's stories. *Recherches sociologiques et anthropologiques*, 44, 1, 97–115.

Varney, J. (2012) *Minorities within minorities – the evidence base relating to minority groups within the LGB&T community*. London: GLADD. Public Health England.

Webster, J. (2002) Teamwork: understanding multi-professional working. *Nursing Older People*, 14(3), 14–19.

World Health Organisation. (2017) Available at: www.who.int/news-room/fact-sheets/ detail/mental-health-of-older-adults Accessed 21 January 2019.

World Health Organisation. (2018) Available at: www.who.int/news-room/fact-sheets/ detail/elder-abuse Accessed 21 January 2019.

World Health Organisation. (2019) Available at: www.who.int/ageing/ageism/en/ Accessed 9 February 2019.

Chapter 14

Working with lesbian, gay, bisexual and transgender people

Neil Rees

This chapter sets out to acknowledge the diversity of the sexual and gender minority while drawing the reader's attention to the common experiences of discrimination and marginalisation that LGBT people face and the impact of these on psychological well-being. It also looks at ethical approaches to working with LGBT people, starting with the practitioner's own stance in relation to this work. You may think it unnecessary to say it, but first and foremost lesbian, gay, bisexual and trans (LGBT) people are people. So all the skills available to the practitioner are relevant here. Commonly used language may suggest otherwise, however. The current habit of using the term 'the gays' suggests an all-consuming identity that ignores other characteristics, even the fact that gay men are (hu)men. Lesbians have had to endure this for some time of course. Along with this reductionism can come assumed homogeneity; as if a book chapter like this can assume total relevance to all sexual and gender minority people. There is as much variation in this population as there is in the heterosexual population. The most commonly used model of sexual identity formation (Cass, 1979, 1996) suggests a final phase of identity synthesis when lesbian, gay and bisexual (LGB) people acknowledge sexuality to be merely one aspect of who they are. Diversity also extends to the range of identities and expressions of sexuality and gender within the sexual minority and so the term LGBT will not fully reflect the makeup of this population. Trans agendas have become aligned with those of the LGB communities because of common experiences of marginalisation and discrimination, but not without some disagreement (BPS, 2012), and this again warns us against assuming homogeneity. A 'queer' identity has been adopted by those who wish to move beyond simplistic dichotomies of sexuality and gender and this position is supported by queer theory (Seidman, 1996). Similarly, there are a range of gender minority identities, which fall under the umbrella term of trans and include for instance identities of gender queerness, androgyny and the third sex (BPS, 2012). However, despite these important caveats there are ethical considerations specific to these populations that require attention, especially if we remember that Psychology and Psychiatry have a long history of pathologising LGBT people (BPS, 2012).

Presence in services

If we acknowledge that same-sex attraction is a normal variant of human sexuality (BPS, 2012) then therapists will encounter sexual minority people in their practice. More recent surveys have found lesser numbers of LGB people in the population than the often reported 10% from the early Kinsey surveys in the US (Kinsey et al., 1948, 1953). Survey methods in this area are fraught with difficulties, of course, and it is probably safe to assume that numbers represent an under-estimation due to reluctance to disclose or differences in self-identity and labels used. The Observer British sex survey of 2014, which ensured anonymity via online data collection, found that 8% of people described themselves as homosexual or bisexual. However, 21% of those aged 16–24 defined themselves as homosexual or bisexual. At present, there is no official estimate of the trans population. The Gender Identity Research & Education Society (GIRES) estimated in 2011 that about 1% of the UK population experience some degree of gender variance.

Psychological distress

Whatever the true figures, it is unarguable that LGBT people are regular users of psychological services, and the numbers of LGBT service-users are increasing. There has been a rapid rise in referrals to gender identity clinics nationally, with some clinics' referrals rising by several 100% (The Guardian, 2016). This is provoking much discussion and does not simply suggest an increase in psychological distress related to gender identity alone. Many have wondered if shifts in acceptance and a move towards non-binary perspectives, accelerated through media coverage and social media presence are playing a role (Transgender Trend, 2017).

There are many indications that LGBT people are at increased risk for psychological distress but it is important to stress that this is not related per se to their sexual or gender identity but to experiences of discrimination, rejection and stigma that results from societal systems' positioning of the sexual minority. Stonewall's 2018 survey of over 800 trans people reveals the impact that discrimination and exclusion are having on trans people's quality of life. Two in five trans people had to deal with a hate crime or incident in the last 12 months. More than a quarter had experienced domestic violence, and one in four had experienced homelessness at some point. The National Institute for Mental Health in England (2007) systematic review of the mental health of LGB people found that rates of attempted suicide more than double for lesbian, gay and bisexual people and they are one and a half times more likely to experience depression. Meyer (1995) introduced the concept of 'minority stress', which is a way of understanding the impact of being part of a group less valued by society, which can lead to internalised negativity and expectations of rejection and discrimination.

These difficulties can be exacerbated by the actual experience of accessing services which are frequently discriminatory themselves (PACE, 1998). Stonewell conducted research in Wales which found that 39% of sexual minority people entering services experienced homophobia (Central and North West London NHS Foundation Trust, 2012). Although many trans people do not opt for medical interventions, those who do are required to undergo psychological assessment in order to pursue gender reassignment. Many trans people, as it is with many LGB people, will come to services with difficulties not related to their gender or sexual identity, yet it may be difficult for trans people to access non-specialist services (BPS, 2012). If they do access them the experience can be very disappointing. For instance, two in five trans people said that healthcare staff lacked understanding of specific trans health needs when accessing general healthcare services in the last year (Stonewall, 2018). The reader can increase their familiarity with the fight for LGBT equality by referring to the timeline presented on Stonewall's website (www.stonewall.org.uk/about-us/key-dates-lesbian-gay-bi-and-trans-equality).

Diversity within the LGBT population

The focus in the literature on the differences between the sexual/gender majority and the sexual/gender minority has created an impression of homogeneity in the lives and experiences of LGBT people and the diversity of these lives can be lost.

> Whilst there are reasons why non-heterosexual communities may present a relatively unified or internally positive front, in reality such unity is often not the case, with differences amongst members as salient and powerful as those between non-heterosexual communities and other community groups.
>
> (Riggs & Das Nair, 2012: 13–14)

This suggests that practitioners need to add complexity to their understanding when working with these populations as reducing the issues faced by LGBT people to only those related to sexuality and/or gender will fail to address all of the issues they face in their lives. Riggs and Das Nair (2012) go on to caution against addressing complexity by adding more identities and treating them as discrete identities as this misses the interactions between them. These interactions have been described as intersectionality, a term first coined by Crenshaw in 1991.

The interactions can increase the experiences of marginalisation that LGBT people face. Sexual and gender identities may intersect with many characteristics, including socio-economic status, age, disability and health (including HIV related health issues) and even geographic location with experiences differing greatly between rural and urban environments. Of course, forms of discrimination based on various aspects of minority identity can interact in the same way. When minority identities intersect, a person may face discrimination on multiple levels. For instance, Butler (2010) points out that when people with disabilities express sexual needs they can be positioned as deviant, especially if these needs are of the same-sex variety. This is further illustrated by the intersectionality between sexual/gender identity and ethnic/cultural identity. Butler et al. (2010) stress that much of the literature relating to the sexual/ gender minority has been written in an 'ethnicity vacuum', failing to take account of how sexual and gender identities interact with racial, ethnic and cultural identities. Das Nair and Thomas (2012) focus on the coming out process to illustrate this, reminding us that beginning to share your sexual identity with others is widely acknowledged to be an ultimately positive process, although they go on to highlight that the process for BME sexual minority people in coming out is often less positive. There is sometimes a pressure to come out in order to avoid being judged inauthentic but for ethnic minority LGBT people this process can be complicated by having to manage minority sexual identities that can be in opposition to cultural and religious beliefs. This has been described as facing identity barriers on many fronts simultaneously (Fontaine & Hammond, 1996). Social networks that support the development of LGBT identities are understood to be crucial. The task of finding networks that support numerous minority identities can be a difficult one. People may feel forced to choose between contexts that foreground sexual and gender identities and those that foreground ethnic and cultural identities. Although stressful for many, it is possible to move between contexts of course, and people do. Das Nair and Thomas (2012) conclude that 'we need to be careful not to indiscriminately *prescribe* it [coming out] as a rite of passage for all non-heterosexuals' (p. 70). It is also important to remember that the process of coming out is not a one-off event but something that is repeated throughout life as LGBT people encounter novel situations and circumstances, as illustrated in the following scenario.

Vignette 1

Grace, a 45-year-old woman arrived in the UK two years ago from Angola. She described persecution in Angola because of her gender identity as she describes herself as androgynous. She is sexually attracted to women and has visited lesbian venues. She feels unable to connect with lesbian women in the UK who she thinks see her as exotic and she has not come across another lesbian woman from Angola. She has made good connections, however, with a local community organisation that supports people from central Africa. She feels more understood in this context, but has not told them of her sexual or gender identities. She fears being cut off from other Angolan people if she discloses this information.

LGBT people across the lifespan

Age also offers an important pivot for intersectionality. The experiences (including coming out) of older LGBT people often differ to their younger counterparts in a number of ways, which relate not only to developmental issues but also to positive changes in societal attitudes towards the sexual and gender minority, some of which have now been enshrined in law. For instance, many older adults have lived in a time when their sexuality was a criminal offence (until 1967 in England, 1980 in Scotland and 1982 in Northern Ireland) and a 'mental illness' (until 1973). The Gender Recognition Act 2004 still considers being trans as a mental illness (Stonewall, 2018). Long lives lived experiencing institutionalised discrimination and a dearth of positive role models may have had a detrimental effect on the development of their sexual and gender identities. There are currently no specialist housing options for older LGBT people in the UK (although Manchester City Council have announced plans to create one) and there is very real fear of homophobic abuse in services and residential settings (DOH, 2007). Older LGBT people may have a greater need for health and social care services because, compared with their heterosexual contemporaries, they are two and a half times as likely to live alone and four and a half times as likely to have no children to provide support (Knocker, 2006). It seems important to keep in mind that because of the experiences described above it may be difficult for older LGBT people to trust in the professionals they are working with.

Recent changes in law and some indications of positive changes in societal attitudes toward LGBT people may suggest that life is easier for sexual and gender minority people. The first same sex marriages took place in the UK in March 2014 and in 2015, the Republic of Ireland became the first country to legalise same sex marriage by public vote. Young people are certainly developing minority sexual identities at earlier ages (Ryan, 2001) but associations between minority sexuality and mental health problems sadly remain elevated. Through the coming out process young people still often face rejection, abuse and homelessness. LGBT youth have increased vulnerability for homelessness. The Albert Kennedy Trust (2015) found that young LGBT people comprise up to 24% of the youth homeless population, with 69% citing family rejection as a reason for their homelessness. It is important to remember that institutionalised discrimination begins in the educational system and homophobic bullying is endemic in British schools. In their report Stonewall (2012) reported that 55% of young LGB people have experienced homophobic bullying and almost all (99%) of young LGB people hear the phrase 'that's so gay' in school. Secondary school teachers say that homophobic bullying is the most frequent form of bullying after bullying because of weight and body shape. More than a third of trans university students in higher education have experienced negative comments or behaviour from staff in the last year (Stonewall, 2018).

The practitioner's stance

Before starting to work with LGBT people it is essential that practitioners explore their own attitudes, beliefs and feelings about sexuality and gender, and sexual and gender minorities in particular. This applies to LGBT as well as heterosexual practitioners as both may hold prejudices and misinformation, but also assume knowledge about their clients or similarity to their clients. This can begin with exposure to the realities of the lives of LGBT people and experiential exercises can be useful tools for beginning this process. Experiential exercises that reverse the majority–minority continuum can be particularly illuminating as they give a sense of the lived experience of people in a minority group as well as the emotional impact of these experiences. The Heterosexual Questionnaire (Rochlin, 1992) asks questions of heterosexual people that are often asked of LGBT people and the person answering can gain a sense of how it feels to be questioned in this way and a sense of the assumptions being made that underpin the questions, a sample of which follows:

- What do you think caused your heterosexuality?
- When and how did you decide that you were heterosexual?
- To whom have you disclosed your heterosexuality? How did they react?
- If you've never slept with a person of the same sex, how do you know you wouldn't prefer that?
- Why do you insist on being so obvious and making a public spectacle of your heterosexuality? Can't you just be what you are and keep quiet?

Rochlin (1992: 203–204)

Butler (2004) in a successful attempt to achieve a similar goal has written a vivid story named 'Homoworld', which gives an account of a day in the life of a heterosexual person living in an inverted world where LGBT people make up the majority. This gives the reader insight to the day to day experiences of invisibility and discrimination that sexual minority people face. 'Homoworld' has also been made into a short film by the Professional Doctorate in Clinical Psychology at the University of East London and this is freely available online (www.youtube.com/watch?v=HJXw8PthD0M). Scenes from the film include television and advertising being saturated with images of LGBT people, a heterosexual couple being jeered at in the street for holding hands, and the character's mother hoping that her heterosexuality is just a phase.

Staying with self-awareness, it is important for the practitioner to reflect on their own sexual and gender identity, particularly when they are considering whether to disclose this identity to their clients. Careful consideration is essential and especially when working with LGBT youth, not least because adolescents often test the boundaries of the therapeutic relationship and seek disclosure. They may ask directly about the sexuality of the practitioner. If they are part of the sexual or gender minority, and the client is aware of this, there are opportunities for the LGBT person to relate to a positive role model and to see that a future LGBT life is not necessarily a bleak one. Consideration needs to be given at least to the possible effects that knowing the therapist's sexual identity will have on the client. Practitioners must be fully aware of the requirements of the Health and Care Professions Council Standards of Conduct, Performance and Ethics (HCPC, 2016). The BPS (2012) advises practitioners considering disclosing their own sexual orientation to clients to exercise appropriate caution by ensuring that they examine carefully their own motives and also consider the possibility that the client could potentially misconstrue their reasons for making such disclosure, as illustrated below.

Vignette 2

Simon is a 15-year-old boy who is described in the referral as identifying as bisexual. He presents with low mood and some deliberate self-harming behaviour through cutting his arms. After the first few sessions with the therapist he describes himself as gay. He says that he can never let his family know this and he looks forward to leaving home so that he can be himself. He is convinced that his family will disown him if he comes out. In the fifth session he asks the therapist directly if they are gay/lesbian. If choosing to answer this question, the therapist needs to make a judgement about whether there are any risks in sharing their sexual identity with Simon and they need to examine their own motives for doing so.

Approaches to therapy and the therapeutic encounter

The full range of approaches to therapy are relevant to sexual and gender minority people and the same considerations about what would be best for a client and/or their presenting problems should still apply. It is important to recognise, however, that some approaches have historically been discriminatory towards LGBT people, such as traditional psychoanalysis (Mohr, 2010) or perhaps have not attended sufficiently to all aspects of sexuality and gender. For instance, Beckian cognitive behavioural therapy ignores sexuality in its theorising (Butler, 2010). There are unique clinical issues that need to be considered in developing formulations and interventions when working with LGBT people. There have been some attempts to focus the commonly used therapy approaches onto issues of minority sexuality. For example, from a cognitive perspective, exposure to negative attitudes about same-sex attractions can result in the development of negative core beliefs about the self (Safran & Rodgers, 2001). Narrative therapies may be particularly helpful in co-ordinating stories of identity with the cultural and religious stories held by the systems that LGBT people inhabit (e.g. Fredman, 2002). These approaches are recognised for offering interventions that are culturally sensitive and acknowledge the role of power and privilege in the construction of stories about what it means to be LGBT in particular societies (Saltzburg, 2007).

Some approaches have been developed specifically to respond to the lives of sexual minority people, such as sexually affirmative therapies (Gabriel & Davies, 2000). Butler (2012) stresses that these are not novel therapy approaches but form an adjunct to existing approaches which take the stance of affirming a sexual minority identity as equally acceptable and as positive as a heterosexual one. She summarises the basic principles of these approaches (which fit with any therapeutic model) as the therapist needing to be comfortable with their own sexuality and respectful of the sexuality of others, and needing to show an awareness of the pervasiveness of homophobia and the socio-political history of sexual minorities. Stone Fish and Harvey (2005) have developed a 'nurturing queer youth' approach to family therapy. By making use of queer theory, they describe its therapeutic tasks as creating a refuge to validate the unique pressures faced by LGBT youth, lessening isolation and promoting a sense of uniqueness while improving the family context so that it can emotionally contain all of its members. The authors describe as pivotal the creation of a safe space, within the therapy context, where family members can step away from heterocentric norms and fully get to know each other and learn about multiple sexual identities, including minority sexual identities. The approach aims to help families through the transition from being a family of heterosexuals to having multiple sexual identities in the same household.

Regardless of the specific approach taken, all work with LGBT clients should be affirming of that identity. This starts at the very first contact when the language used and the questions asked of clients can give very clear messages of affirmation or rejection. Being asked questions that assume the gender of a partner indicates the heteronormative assumptions being made. Simply asking someone if they have a partner can give a powerful message, as does asking more directly if they form sexual and romantic relationships with men, women or either. LGBT clients are likely to be on the lookout for such signs in order to judge the safety and potential efficacy of this contact. This can also include judgements made about the level of comfort apparent in the therapist when discussing sexuality and gender, even down to the identity labels used. Best practice is to adopt the language of the client. This necessitates getting used to the language used.

> People have to get over it, get used to it, if they are to convey an ease when in conversation with gay people … to affirm the person's sexual orientation identity in a positive way which again is much easier if you are not stumbling or hesitating over the key words.
>
> (CNWL, 2012: 8)

Therapies aimed at changing sexual orientation, so-called conversion therapies, are no longer routinely practised in the UK, and certainly not in the NHS, although they are still used in the USA. Reparative therapy (Nicolosi, 1991) is a particular form of conversion therapy based on the premise that homosexuality is an unsatisfactory resolution of sexual development. The American Psychiatric Association (1998) has published a clear position statement on conversion therapies, which stresses that any therapy based on the principle that homosexuality is a disorder is unethical.

If we remember that it is the systems around LGBT people that primarily create the difficulties they face, then we must accept that direct therapeutic work with LGBT people tends to be limited to helping them cope with these toxic systems, and does not include achieving change within the systems themselves. Practitioners need to work directly with these systems if change is to be achieved and these may include families as mentioned, as well as schools, residential services, communities and third sector organisations. This may include direct therapeutic contacts as well as approaches to early intervention including providing training and education, supervision and consultation, and influencing policy making.

British psychological society guidelines

The BPS (2012) has produced practice guidelines for psychologists working therapeutically with sexual and gender minority clients. The document sets out a series of guideline statements with overarching themes so they are not bound to any one model of therapy and represent general affirmative good practice. It also presents an extended, evidence-based text. Some of the headline statements are reproduced here with the kind permission of the BPS as they serve as a useful summary of the material covered in this chapter:

Psychologists are encouraged to:

- Remember that sexual and gender minority identities and practices are not in themselves indicative of a mental disorder.
- Recognise that attitudes towards sexuality and gender are located in a changing socio-political context, and to reflect on their own understanding of these concepts.
- Reflect on the limits to their practice when working with sexual and gender minority clients and to consider appropriate referral and training when indicated.
- Understand the ways in which social stigmatisation (e.g. prejudice, discrimination and violence) pose risks to gender and sexual minority clients.
- Be knowledgeable of the diversity of sexual and gender minority identities and practices.
- Be mindful of the intersections between sexual and gender minority and sociocultural/economic status.
- Recognise the needs and issues of young people from gender and sexual minorities, and their particular vulnerabilities and risks.

- Seek training in sexual and gender minority issues, how to work in an affirmative manner, and be encouraged to reflect on their own beliefs around these issues.
- Avoid attempting to change gender or sexual minorities on the basis that they can be 'cured' or because of stigmatising theory, personal, religious and/or sociocultural beliefs.

Conclusion

While this chapter has recognised and stressed the vulnerability of LGBT people, it seems important to end on a reminder that mental health problems are not associated with minority sexual and gender identities per se. The majority of LGBT people live happy and fulfilled lives. For instance, recent research is calling into question the often ascribed pathologised positions of LGBT youth (e.g. Talburt et al., 2004). 'Unencumbered with this knowledge about how they are supposed to feel, act, and believe, millions of teens with same-sex attractions continue to live their daily life with as much happiness and angst as any other teenager' (Savin-Williams, 2005: 49). However, the systems around LGBT people often, and, in fact, usually provide negative and stigmatising contexts for LGBT identity formation. Consequently, LGBT people manage to develop minority sexual and gender identities in spite of these systems promoting the heterosexual and gender-dichotomous norm and so the resilience of this population should be acknowledged and celebrated.

Reflective questions

1. What is your own sexual or gender identity? Is it always the same in all situations?
2. How should professional training programmes prepare trainees to address LGBT issues in practice?
3. How might the experience of LGBT people be shaped by other aspects of themselves; their ethnic and cultural identities for instance?
4. Who do you picture in your mind when a referral states someone's sexual or gender identity? How do you put this to one side?

References

American Psychiatric Association (APA). (1998) *Reparative Therapy*, [Position statement] Washington, DC: APA.
British Psychological Society (BPS). (2012) *Guidelines and Literature Review for Psychologists Working Therapeutically with Sexual and Gender Minority Clients*, Leicester: British Psychological Society.

Butler, C. (2004) An awareness-raising tool addressing lesbian and gay lives. *Clinical Psychology*, 36, 15–17.

Butler, C. (2010) Sexual and gender minorities: Considerations for therapy and training. In C. Butler, A. O'Donovan, & E. Shaw (Eds.). *Sex, Sexuality and Therapeutic Practice*. London: Routledge, pp. 85–128.

Butler, C. (2012) Disability. In R. Das Nair, & C. Butler (Eds.). *Intersectionality, Sexuality and Psychological Therapies: Working with Lesbian, Gay and Bisexual Diversity*, Chichester: John Wiley & Sons, pp. 213–238.

Butler, C., Das Nair, R., & Thomas, S. (2010) The colour of queer. In L. Moon (Ed.). *Counselling Ideologies: Queer Challenges to Heteronormativity*. Surrey: Ashgate, pp. 105–122.

Cass, V.C. (1979) Homosexual identity formation: A theoretical model. *Journal of Homosexuality*, 4, 210–235.

Cass, V.C. (1996) Sexual orientation identity formation: A Western phenomenon. In R. Gabaj, & T. Stein (Eds.). *Textbook of Homosexuality and Mental Health*. Washington DC: American Psychiatric Press, pp. 227–252.

Central and North West London NHS Foundation Trust (CNWL) (2012) *"You can't ask about that (... or can you?)"*. London: CNWL.

Crenshaw, K. (1991) Mapping the margins: Intersectionality, identity politics, and violence against women of colour. *Stanford Law Review*, 43(6), 1241–1299.

Das Nair, R., & Thomas, S. (2012) Race and ethnicity. In R. Das Nair & C. Butler (Eds.). *Intersectionality, Sexuality and Psychological Therapies: Working with Lesbian, Gay and Bisexual Diversity*, Chichester: John Wiley & Sons, pp. 59–87.

Department of Health. (2007) *Older Lesbian, Gay and Bisexual (LGB) People: Briefings for Health and Social Care Staff*. London: Department of Health.

Fontaine, J.H., & Hammond, N.L. (1996) Counselling issues with gay and lesbian adolescents. *Adolescence*, 31(124), 817–830.

Fredman, G. (2002) Co-ordinating cultural and religious stories of identity. *Clinical Psychology*, 17, 29–32.

Gabriel, L., & Davies, D. (2000) The management of ethical dilemmas associated with dual relationships. In C. Neal, & D. Davies (Eds.). *Pink Therapy 3: Issues in Therapy with Lesbians, Gay, Bisexual and Trans Clients*. Buckingham: Open University Press, pp. 35–54.

Gires. (2011) The number of gender variant people in the UK – Update 2011. Available at: www.gires.org.uk/wp-content/uploads/2014/10/Prevalence2011.pdf (Accessed 30 May 2018).

Health and Care Professions Council. (2016) *Standards of Conduct, Performance and Ethics*. London: HCPC.

Kinsey, A.C., Pomeroy, W.B., & Martin, A.C. (1948) *Sexual Behaviour in the Human Male*. Philadelphia: W.B. Saunders.

Kinsey, A.C., Pomeroy, W.B., & Martin, A.C. (1953) *Sexual Behaviour in the Human Female*. Philadelphia: W.B. Saunders.

Knocker, S. (2006) *The Whole of Me: Meeting the Needs of Older Lesbians, Gay Men and Bisexuals Living in Care Homes and Extra Care Housing*. London: Age Concern.

Meyer, I. (1995) Minority stress and mental health in gay men. *Journal of Health and Social Behaviour*, 36, 38–56.

Mohr, J.A. (2010) Oppression by scientific method: The use of science to "other" sexual minorities. *Journal of Hate Studies*, 77(22), 21–45.

National Institute for Mental Health in England. (2007) *Mental Disorders, Suicide and Deliberate Self-Harm in Lesbian, Gay and Bisexual People*. London: NIMHE.

Nicolosi, J. (1991) *Reparative Therapy of Male Homosexuality: A New Clinical Approach*, Northvale, NJ: Jason Aronson Inc.

PACE (Project for Advice, Counseling and Education). (1998) Diagnosis: Homophobic. In *The experience of Lesbians, Gay Men and Bisexuals in Mental Health Services*. PACE: London, 4–7.

Riggs, D.W., & Das Nair, R. (2012) Intersecting identities. In R. Das Nair, & C. Butler (Eds.). *Intersectionality, Sexuality and Psychological Therapies: Working with Lesbian, Gay and Bisexual Diversity*. Chichester: John Wiley & Sons, pp. 9–30.

Rochlin, M. (1992) Heterosexual questionnaire. In W.J. Blumenfeld (Ed.). *Homophobia: How we all Pay the Price*. Boston: Beacon Press, pp. 203–204.

Ryan, C. (2001) Counselling lesbian, gay and bisexual youths. In A.R. D'Augelli, & C. J. Patterson (Eds.). *Lesbian, Gay and Bisexual Identities and Youth: Psychological perspectives*. New York: Oxford University Press, pp. 224–250.

Safran, A.S., & Rodgers, T. (2001) Cognitive-behavioural therapy with gay, lesbian and bisexual clients. *JCLP/In Session: Psychotherapy in Practice*, 57(5), 629–643.

Saltzburg, S. (2007) Narrative therapy pathways for re-authoring with parents of adolescents coming-out as lesbian, gay, and bisexual. *Contemporary Family Therapy*, 29 (1–2), 57–69.

Savin-Williams, R.C. (2005) *The New Gay Teenager*. Cambridge: Harvard University Press.

Seidman, S. (1996) *Queer Theory/Sociology*. Oxford: Blackwell.

Stone Fish, L., & Harvey, R.G. (2005) *Nurturing Queer Youth: Family Therapy Transformed*. New York: W.W. Norton.

Stonewall. (2012) *The School Report: The Experiences of Gay Young People in Britain's Schools in 2012*. London: Stonewall.

Stonewall. (2018) LGBT in Britain: Trans report. Available at: www.stonewall.org.uk/comeoutforLGBT/lgbt-britain-trans-report Accessed 30 May 2018.

Talburt, S., Rofes, E., & Rasmussen, M.L. (2004) Transforming discourses of queer youth and educational practices surrounding gender, sexuality, and youth. In M. L. Rasmussen, E. Rofes, & S. Talburt (Eds.). *Youth and Sexualities: Pleasure, Subversion in and out of Schools*, New York and Basingstoke: Palgrave MacMillan, pp. 1–13.

The Albert Kennedy Trust. (2015) LGBT youth homelessness: A UK national scoping of cause, prevalence, response and outcome. Available at: www.akt.org.uk/Handlers/Download.ashx?IDMF=c0f29272-512a-45e8-9f9b-0b76e477baf1 Accessed 30 May 2018.

The Guardian. (2016) Gender identity clinic services under strain as referral rates soar. Available at: www.theguardian.com/society/2016/jul/10/transgender-clinic-waiting-times-patient-numbers-soar-gender-identity-services Accessed 30 May 2018.

The Observer. (2014) British sex survey. Available at: www.theguardian.com/lifeandstyle/2014/sep/28/british-sex-survey-2014-nation-lost-sexual-swagger Accessed 30 May 2018.

Transgender Trend: Parents Questioning the Trans Narrative. (2017) Is it surprising that referrals of children to the Tavistock clinic continue to soar? Available at: www.transgendertrend.com/surprising-referrals-childrentavistock-clinic-continue-soar? Accessed 30 May 2018.

Chapter 15

Professional and ethical practice in a multicultural and multiethnic society

Julio Torales and Israel González-Urbieta

Introduction

As globalization becomes more widespread around the world and with the increasing movement of people across national borders, clinicians, including psychologists, psychiatrists and therapists are more likely than ever to encounter people with different backgrounds, ethnicity, 'race', orientations, values and beliefs in their practice (Schouler-Ocak et al., 2015). In a survey by the American Psychological Association, 86% of their members reported providing services to racial and ethnic minority patients/service users. This inevitably means that patients/service users will present to the mental health services with different worldviews, and varied ways of experiencing problems and situations which may be different or similar to those held by the clinician who is working with them.

One approach to this issue is to reduce the gap in representation. In this regard, the British Psychological Society (BPS) has taken different measures to achieve this goal, including; the development of a revised Equality, Diversity and Inclusion Policy, initiating a Social Justice and Inclusion group to promote good practice within the Society, and promoting initiatives such as the Division of Clinical Psychology Inclusivity Conference (Bullen & Hacker Hughes, 2016). It also supported two conferences on the topic of Action not Words which were concerned with developing knowledge around culture and black and ethnic minority experiences for those involved in all aspects of applied psychology, as well as in shaping psychological services for adults, children and young people.

In the US, the National Council of Schools and Programs of Professional Psychology states that they are 'committed to diversity', although this in itself will not bring about change, and they are developing programs to attract a more diverse group of people to the profession (DeAngelis, 2006). However, representation is not necessarily the only way to address this issue, or the most effective. Both the European Psychiatry Association (EPA) and the APA have developed guidelines and programs to foster what we call culture competence. Although this term has been criticized as not paying due attention to issues of power amongst other things (Beagan, 2018).

What is culture?

In order to achieve cultural competence, we need to reach an agreement on what we call culture. While there are many definitions of this term (which is in itself a testament to the complexity of the subject), in this chapter we try to reach a definition that is usable for clinicians in clinical practice and research, but also for program directors looking for ways to integrate cultural competence into their curriculum.

Culture is a set of norms, beliefs, values and customs that are shared by a group of individuals. It is not fixed or static, but it evolves with its members as they adapt to new situations and different challenges. Factors such as a proximity, education, gender, age and sexual preference can also shape culture. While there will be overarching cultural features, culture is dynamic and individual, and is influenced by a range of variables which include but are not limited to individual, familial and community meaning-making (Tribe & Tunariu, 2018). The term culture refers to the meaning that its members assign to words, symbols and experiences, thus shaping the way in which they make sense of the world. Culture has both a subjective component: the ideas and meaning shared by its members; and an objective one: their observable behaviour. Finally, culture is learned and, therefore, it can be taught and understood (Ton & Lim, 2006).

Culture partly determines what we consider normal, and it shapes the way in which individuals express their symptoms. In the relationship between the physician and the patient, three cultures collide: the culture of the physician, the culture of the patient and the culture of therapy or treatment itself (Betancourt et al., 2018). The culture of the clinician consists of their individual style, their personal beliefs and their professional knowledge. Psychiatrists and other mental health professionals have their own expectations – or biases – about the behaviour and the needs of patients from different backgrounds which affect the way they approach the therapeutic relationship with a patient from a different group to the one they identify with. The mental health provider should try to be aware of their own biases in order to be in a better position to address them appropriately. Psychiatric and therapeutic interventions, both in research and in clinical settings, can frequently feel insulated from the social context, unless conscious efforts are made to align the methods and goals of the therapy with those of the patients.

Each of these aforementioned cultures (clinician, service user and therapy or treatment) brings their own views and their own interpretation of the problem or the symptoms, and they can suggest the way the issue will be approached. Cultural competence is the ability of the clinician to navigate this situation in order to provide the highest standard of care to the patient, regardless of their background, race or ethnicity.

Vignette I

Juana is a 40-year-old undocumented immigrant woman from Venezuela now living in Paraguay. She is referred to the psychiatrist's office by her GP because she refuses to take medications for her depression. Since she couldn't speak English fluently, the hospital provided a Spanish interpreter for the interview. For the last three weeks she has been feeling sick, she is experiencing weight loss, fatigue, headaches, with occasional palpitations and dizziness. On further questioning, she admits frequent episodes of unmotivated crying, pain and muscle tension, difficulty sleeping and nightmares. She stopped working and following her daily routine. 'I knew it was a mistake to go to the hospital', she protests, 'I already know what I have but no one wants to believe me, that doctor completely dismissed my explanations and treated me like I'm crazy or something'. She states that what she is experiencing is called *paje*,[1] and that it must be the work of someone who doesn't want her to be happy. 'I really wish I could go back to my country where they understand what's going on with me and where they can fix it, but if I leave, I won't be able to come back here.'

In this example, it appears that the culture of the patient has clashed with that of physicians before. As clinicians, it's important that we remember that psychiatric illnesses existed long before diagnostic criteria and treatment guidelines were developed. Therefore, people from different cultures often have different names and different explanations for their symptoms. Psychiatrists also need to have an integral view of the patient, and consider not only their symptoms, and how the patient understands them, but also their socio-economic context, which can be an additional source of stress, especially in the case of people deemed to be vulnerable or who are living in very difficult circumstances.

Defining cultural competence

Cultural competence can be defined as a set of behaviours, attitudes and policies that enable individuals to work effectively in cross-cultural situations (Manoleas, 2011). While the term can be misinterpreted as a calling to be aware and sensitive only to the differences in culture, it also pushes an awareness of the similarities between individuals, and the process of discerning the path between similarity and difference from the perspective of the patient or service user (Newland et al., 2015). The term can also be misconstrued to mean that the psychiatrist or clinician must have an exhaustive understanding of the cultural background of the different patients that they see. While gaining a basic knowledge of the culture of the patients that we work with can be useful, it is unreasonable to expect that clinicians will be able to acquire all that knowledge, and even then, it is important to remember that just knowing the characteristics of every culture is not enough to become culturally competent. Cultural competence is a requisite for the practice of modern clinicians, including those who practice in relatively homogenous societies, considering that differences will exist even when the cultural background of the patient is not radically dissimilar from that of the clinician. By this definitions, every encounter can be considered to be transcultural (Comas-Díaz, 1988).

The qualities of the culturally competent clinician

Clinicians are first exposed to the concept and basic principles of cultural competence during their years of training, but they continue developing their cultural skills and qualities throughout their entire career, gaining more experience and insight with every interaction with their patients.

Tseng and Streltzer (2004) have compiled a list of basic qualities that clinicians need to attain. These qualities are listed and briefly explained in Table 15.1.

These qualities are essential for the practice of therapy. They can be learned, and trainees need to gain them through their inclusion in the curricula and through supervised interaction with patients from different backgrounds. Senior clinicians should monitor and assess the progress of young clinicians in treating patients from different backgrounds during their learning journey. Values such as empathy, curiosity and respect, can guide the clinician in the process of becoming culturally competent (Carrillo et al., 1999).

Table 15.1 The qualities of the culturally competent therapist. Adapted from Tseng and Streltzer (2004)

Cultural sensitivity	Recognition and unbiased appreciation of the diversity of viewpoints, attitudes, and lifestyles among human beings.
Cultural knowledge	Acquiring basic anthropological knowledge regarding the variation in the habits, beliefs, value systems and illness behaviour of different groups.
Cultural empathy	The ability to understand the patient's own cultural perspective on an emotional level.
Culturally relevant relations and interactions	The ability to recognize and address ethnic- or race-related transference and countertransference, considering the history of discrimination and imbalance of power between members of majority and minority groups.
Cultural guidance	The assessment of the extent to which and the ways in which cultural factors are relevant to the patient's problems.

The patient-based approach

Based on concepts from medical anthropology, and sociology, as well as medical interviewing, Carrillo et al. (1999) developed a framework to allow clinicians to use every encounter to learn about patients' social and cultural factors that affect the way they perceive and experience their problems and situations, and to propose strategies to work together with the patients to achieve the best possible outcome. We consider that these strategies are equally applicable for psychiatrists, psychologists and other mental health care providers. In Table 15.2 we present the main components of this approach.

Table 15.2 Components of the patient-based approach. Adapted from Carrillo et al. (1999)

Assess core sociocultural issues	The Toronto consensus found that 54% of patients do not share their complaints with their therapists, and up to 50% of patients stated that their therapists did not address their main complaint (Díaz Méndez & Latorre Postigo, 2014). Furthermore, some patients may present with idioms of distress (unexplained bodily symptoms); it is important that psychiatrists recognize when these physical symptoms may be signs of psychological distress (Desai & Chaturvedi, 2017).
	These misunderstandings can often be attributed to differences in cultural values and expectations.
	Instead of requiring therapists to develop in-depth knowledge of the details of every culture, they should recognize a set of issues that are common in cross-cultural encounters. The most common issues to take into account are the styles of communication; mistrust and prejudice; decision-making and family dynamics; traditions, customs and spirituality; and sexual and gender issues.
Explore the meaning of illness	Therapists should make an effort to understand the patient's view about the cause of their symptoms, their concern about their illness and their expectations about the treatment.
Determine the patient's social context	Socioeconomic conditions can have a great impact in the problems that the patients bring to the clinician's office (Pincus et al., 1998). Learning about the patient's environment, their level of literacy, their ability to control their environment and gather support can give the therapist an idea of the risk factors and the resources that the patient can gather to overcome their problem.
Engage in negotiation	Negotiating does not mean that the therapist should convince the patient to accept a specific treatment. It means involving the patient in an agreement that respects their values and beliefs, and that is beneficial for their issue. Clinicians should understand the patient's beliefs and try to accommodate their offers in order to build a therapeutic

(Continued)

Table 15.2 (Cont.)

relation that promotes adherence and achieves better outcomes.

While patients under involuntary treatment regimes may be compelled to receive certain types of treatment, providers need to make sure that this approach is only used in exceptional circumstances, and always with the goal of returning full autonomy to the patient (Bhugra et al., 2017).

Current guidelines

Both the APA and the EPA have developed guidelines for cultural competence that span the range of clinical activity, including assessments, formulations and interventions, research activities, service design and delivery. They provide direction on areas in which psychiatrists can improve in their efforts to offer professional and ethical therapeutic services in a multicultural society. These guidelines are not meant to be used as checkboxes to fill, but instead as a guide in the process of becoming more culturally competent.

APA guidelines

The best practice guidelines published by the APA can help psychiatrists to understand the background and culture of the patient in order to provide the best quality of care for minority and diverse populations (American Psychiatric Association, 2018). These guidelines are specific for each group and they emphasize paying attention to the distinct cultural characteristics of each BME group. They stress the idea that psychiatrists must make an effort to address their own bias and be willing to try to understand the problem of the patients in their social context. The complete documents and explanatory videos can be accessed at the APA website.

EPA guidelines

The European Psychiatric Association also provides a comprehensive set of guidelines to promote cultural competency not only for psychiatrists, but also for policy makers and organizations (Schouler-Ocak et al., 2015). In their recommendations, they remind the health care provider that multicultural encounters can happen even when treating patients from the same country or race as the psychiatrist, since there are many variations in attitudes, knowledge and behaviour.

The following recommendations are given for psychiatrists to achieve cultural competence:

- Training in cultural competence should be mandatory.
- Quality standards for providing court opinions for minority groups should be available and employed when appropriate.
- Psychiatrists need to learn about culture-specific issues in the area where they practice.
- Information should be made available to minority groups in their preferred language.
- Cultural psychiatry should be included in the curriculum for undergraduates and residents.
- Research aimed at understanding and addressing the needs of minority groups should be encouraged and appropriately funded.
- Psychiatrists need to try to be aware of their own cultural biases and learn to communicate with patients through an interpreter.
- Psychiatrists must also be knowledgeable about the relationship between culture and health and illness.

Racism in the clinician–patient relationship

The clinician and the patient bring to the relationship their own historical, political and cultural experiences of privilege, disadvantage and discrimination (Newland et al., 2015). We know that ethnic and racial differences between the patient and the clinician can have an effect on therapy outcomes (Karlsson, 2005; Sue et al., 1991). In a survey of more than 650 psychologists who were members of the American Psychology Association with experience in cross-cultural therapy, most of the psychologists surveyed, reported having discussions about race or ethnicity (Maxie et al., 2006). Although a large number of patients don't feel able to express their concerns with the clinician for fear of making them uncomfortable, which can lead to negative feelings, withdrawal or early termination (Chang & Berk, 2009).

In the setting of cross-cultural therapy, racism can arise from both sides of the relation (Sue et al., 2007). Sometimes in the form of microaggressions and, less often, in the form of overt racist commentaries. There are no official guidelines regarding the response that clinicians should have to these expressions of racism, but most authors agree that being open about issues of race and discrimination from the beginning can alleviate some of the concerns of the patients or clinicians regarding these subjects.

From the clinician's perspective, cultural competence requires being aware of one's own biases and working with the patients to learn about their perspective on the issue. It also means being humble and learning from one's inevitable mistakes.

> **Vignette 2**
>
> Michael is a 27-year-old black male admitted to the inpatient unit of a psychiatric ward with the diagnosis of schizophreniform disorder. He was brought by the police after his next-door neighbour called complaining of someone yelling in his apartment. In his notes explaining the admission, the attending psychiatrist wrote 'patient looks distrustful, his attitude is hostile and aggressive, does not accept being admitted to the psychiatric ward, possible paranoid schizophrenia'. When being interviewed the next day by Dr Jeffords, a black doctor, Michael was calm and forthcoming. He told Dr Jeffords that he has been feeling 'down in the dumps' for the last couple of months after he was fired from his job for making many mistakes: 'I just couldn't concentrate, I think it was because I couldn't sleep well anymore, I kept waking up in the middle of the night'. In the last couple of days, he started hearing a voice that told him that he was a failure: 'I was yelling because I couldn't get rid of the voice, I thought I was going crazy'. Michael said he was glad that Dr Jeffords was on call that day: 'Finally someone who actually listens to me'. He was switched from a schedule of intramuscular antipsychotics to an oral schedule, and an antidepressant was added.

Conclusion

For the modern clinician, cultural competence is a necessary and highly important asset. Patients are particularly sensitive to cultural incompetence acts (Meyer & Zane, 2013): or racism such as stereotyping (Meyer & Zane, 2013) microaggressions, and generally failing to listen to and learn from the patients' experiences to reach better assessments and provide interventions that are tailored to their needs. There are now countless books, articles and guidelines that can help the clinician to become skilled in this area, but they do not replace the experience of learning from patients, especially in a supervised setting.

Since clinicians are likely to differ from their patients in at least one area (e.g. race, education, socioeconomic status, religion), all encounters can be considered cross-cultural. It is important that clinicians recognize this reality and that they approach every encounter with humbleness, introspection and curiosity and at the same striving to treat every patient as an individual, respectfully and humanely.

> **Reflective questions**
>
> 1. How would you start a conversation about race with a patient/ service user from a different ethnic group to your own?
> 2. If a patient/service user refuses to be seen by you because of your race or gender, what would you do and what would influenced this?

3. How might you deal with racist comments made by a colleague or a supervisor?
4. What would you do if a patient/service user refuses a psychiatric intervention or treatment because of their religious beliefs?

Note

1 *Paje* is an example of a Hispanic culture-bound syndrome listed in the Latin-American Guide for the Psychiatric Diagnosis, Text Revision (GLADP-VR, for its initials in Spanish). The affected individuals can present with gastrointestinal changes, accompanied by affective symptoms and other non-specific somatic symptoms (Asociación Psiquiátrica de América Latina, 2012; Brítez Cantero, 1998).

References

American Psychiatric Association. (2018) Best Practice Highlights for Treating Diverse Patient Populations. Available at: www.psychiatry.org/psychiatrists/cultural-compe tency/treating-diverse-patient-populations Accessed 2 October 2019.

Asociación Psiquiátrica de América Latina (2012) *Guía Latinoamericana de Diagnóstico Psiquiátrico - Versión Revisada.* (Á. Otero, J. E. Saavedra, J. E. Mezzich, & I. M. Salloum, Eds.), 1st edition. Lima: Asociación Psiquiátrica de América Latina.

Beagan, B.L. (2018) Cultural competence in applied psychology:Assumptions, limitations, and alternatives in frisby. In L. Craig & W.T. O' Donohue (Eds.). *Cultural Competence in Applied Psychology An evaluation of current status and future directions.* New York: Springer, pp. 123–138.

Betancourt, J.R., Green, A.R., & Carrillo, J.E. (2018) Cross-cultural care and communication. En J. A. Melin (Ed.), UpToDate, Waltham, MA Accessed 7 March 2019.

Bhugra, D., Tasman, A., Pathare, S., Priebe, S., Smith, S., Torous, J., & Ventriglio, A. (2017) The WPA-Lancet Psychiatry Commission on the Future of Psychiatry. *The Lancet Psychiatry*, 4(10), 775–818.

Brítez Cantero, J. (1998) *Paje: Síndrome Cultural del Paraguay,* 1st edition. Asunción: Editorial de la Facultad de Ciencias Médicas (EFACIM). Asunción.

Bullen, K., & Hacker Hughes, J. (2016). Achieving Representation in Psychology: A BPS Response. Available at: https://thepsychologist.bps.org.uk/volume-29/april/representa tiveness-psychologists-bps-response Accessed 29 October 2018.

Carrillo, J.E., Green, A.R. & Betancourt, J.R. (1999) Cross-cultural primary care: A patient-based approach. *Annals of Internal Medicine*, 130(22), 829–834. doi:10.7326/0003-4819-130-10-199905180-00017.

Chang, D.F., & Berk, A. (2009) Making cross-racial therapy work: A phenomenological study of clients' experiences of cross-racial therapy. *Journal of Counseling Psychology*, 56(4), 521–536.

Comas-Díaz, L. (1988) Cross-cultural mental health treatment. In L. Comas-Díaz & E. E. H. Griffith (Eds.). *Clinical Guidelines in Cross-Cultural Mental Health.* Oxford, England: John Wiley & Sons.

DeAngelis, T. (2006) A culture of inclusion. [Internet]. Monitor on Psychology. Available at: www.apa.org/monitor/may06/inclusion Accessed 7 March 2019.

Desai, G., & Chaturvedi, S.K. (2017) Idioms of distress. *Journal of Neurosciences in Rural Practice*, 8(Suppl 1), S94–S97.

Díaz Méndez, D., & Latorre Postigo, J.M. (2014) Psicología médica. Elsevier Health Sciences Spain - T.

Karlsson, R. (2005) Ethnic matching between therapist and patient in psychotherapy: An overview of findings, together with methodological and conceptual issues. *Cultural Diversity and Ethnic Minority Psychology*, 11(2), 113–129.

Manoleas, P. (2011) *The Cross-Cultural Practice of Clinical Case Management in Mental Health*. London & New York: Routledge.

Maxie, A.C., Arnold, D.H., & Stephenson, M. (2006) Do the rapists address ethnic and racial differences in cross-cultural psychotherapy? *Psychotherapy*. 43(1), 85–98.

Meyer, O.L., & Zane, N. (2013) The influence of race and ethnicity in clients' experience of mental health treatment. *Journal of Community Psychology*, 41(7), 884–901.

Newland, J., Patel, N., & Senapati, M. (2015) Professional and ethical practice in multi-cultural and multiethnic society. In R. Tribe & J. Morrisey (Eds.). *Handbook of Professional and Ethical Practice for Psychologists, Counsellors and Psychotherapists*, 2nd edition. East Sussex: Routledge, pp. 173–183.

Pincus, T., Esther, R., DeWalt, D.A., & Callahan, L.F. (1998) Social conditions and self-management are more powerful determinants of health than access to care. *Annals of Internal Medicine*, 129(5), 406–411.

Schouler-Ocak, M., Graef-Calliess, I.T., Tarricone, I., Qureshi, A., Kastrup, M.C., & Bhugra, D. (2015) EPA guidance on cultural competence training. *European Psychiatry*, 30(3), 431–440.

Sue, D.W., Capodilupo, C.M., Torino, G.C., Bucceri, J.M., Holder, A.M.B., Nadal, K.L., & Esquilin, M. (2007) Racial microaggressions in everyday life: Implications for clinical practice. *American Psychologist*, 62(4), 271–286.

Sue, S., Fujino, D.C., Hu, L.T., Takeuchi, D.T., & Zane, N.W. (1991) Community mental health services for ethnic minority groups: a test of the cultural responsiveness hypothesis. *Journal of Consulting and Clinical Psychology*, 59(4), 533–540.

Ton, H., & Lim, R.F. (2006) The Assessment of culturally diverse individuals. In R. F. Lim (Ed.). *Clinical Manual of Cultural Psychiatry*, 1st edition. Arlington: American Psychiatric Publishing, p. 314.

Tribe, R., & Tunariu, A.D. (2018) Psychological interventions and assessments. In D. Bhugra & K. Bhui *The Textbook of Cultural Psychiatry*. Cambridge: Cambridge University Press. pp. 458–471.

Tseng, W.-S., & Streltzer, J. (2004) Culture and psychiatry. In W.-S. Tseng & J. Streltzer (Eds.). *Cultural Competence in Clinical Psychiatry*, 1st edition. Arlington: American Psychiatric Publishing, pp. 1–20.

Part 5

Research, supervision and training

Chapter 16

Research in therapeutic practice settings

Ethical considerations

Trishna Patel

The reciprocal relationship between research and practice is strongly emphasised in professional psychology and therapy training, particularly in courses where the scientist-practitioner model prevails. Yet, research and clinical practice skills are frequently addressed as if they are distinct. Research is typically viewed as important but as a hindrance in, therapeutic settings. Consequently, research skills are commonly seen by trainees and clinicians as an additional requirement, instead of a core skill. Post-qualification, political and service pressures often result in a de-emphasis on research activities, which can discourage research and narrowly define what is permissible, required, or deemed desirable. While research in services can improve overall performance and practices (Mckeon et al., 2013), clinically relevant research is increasingly viewed as only research that informs evidence-based practice (EBP). EBP is a contested area, including questions relating to what data is collected and how it is analysed and unsurprisingly, many clinicians hold negative views (Baker et al., 2008; Spring, 2007), as well as questioning how EBP can limit service user (SU) and clinician choice (Kerridge, 2010). See Chapter 17 for further discussion on EBP.

In this chapter, it is argued that research in therapeutic settings is essential and useful in generating relevant data to inform clinical practice, service development and health-related policy. Researchers do not need access to numerous resources, employ complex methodology or recruit large sample sizes to conduct meaningful, high quality research with 'real' and immediate clinical implications. There are a range of avenues to conduct research in services and each pose their own practical, methodological and ethical challenges, some of which are addressed here before outlining an approach to ethical decision-making.

Defining research in therapeutic settings

Several activities in services involve information collection and it is important to distinguish whether data gathered falls under the umbrella of research, audit or service evaluation. The differences lie in the purpose and methods of data collection and the processes followed. Clinical records constitute data collection, but often are not anonymised and are subject to data protection. Intake information may be collated and the data anonymised – but this data may be for monitoring service activities, demographics, etc. Where data is gathered specifically for reviewing a particular aspect of the service, it may be considered an audit, or service evaluation. Where data is collected for addressing a particular question about the service, or a practice, or interventions used, this can be considered data for research.

The key characteristic of research is that procedures followed are in addition to, or different from, routine care; for example, random allocation or interviews with SUs. Research will therefore involve administration of a Participant Information Sheet (PIS) outlining study details and consent-seeking procedures. Audit or service evaluation examines existing data collected as part of routine care, though it may also involve questionnaire administration or interviews. Interviews can be controversial; one could propose that if the focus is on the experience of the care received then this could be framed as service evaluation. A clear articulation of the goals of the activity planned and proposed methods is crucial to ensure that ethical concerns are systematically addressed, preventing unethical data use.

Research in therapeutic settings often involves asking questions driven by the needs and goals of service users and providers, to identify areas for change in the type and frequency of care offered. Once research questions are generated, the research design best suited to answer those questions will require selection. Good practice (see Table 16.1) includes ensuring the research questions inform methodology rather than which type of evidence is viewed as most valid or rigorous. The multiple roles of the researcher and potentially conflicting agendas require careful consideration in terms of how participants are recruited, who collects data and possible adverse impacts on participants. Inclusion criteria should reflect the diversity of SUs referred to services and not be bound by linguistic barriers. In order to address the needs and goals of

Table 16.1 Summary: good practice in research in therapeutic settings

- Form research questions based on service user and provider needs.
- Select the most appropriate design for the research question.
- Address the role of practice-based evidence.
- Recruit realistic sample sizes.
- Consider dual roles of the researcher and participants.
- Acknowledge and make transparent competing agendas (of the service, clinicians, researchers, SUs).
- Consult and collaborate with SUs in deciding what and how data is collected.
- Ensure the inclusion criteria do not unfairly exclude particular groups.
- Work in partnership with interpreters, where needed in research.

all SUs (including those from minority ethnic backgrounds and those whose first language may not be English) as closely as possible, SUs should be consulted, and the research may require interpreters and/or SUs. This can be a complex process; the challenge is to ensure that researchers work in partnership with SUs and/or interpreters (see Morrow et al., 2010; Patel, 2003).

Ethical considerations: where do they begin?

Within the context of research, ethics have been described as 'moral principles specifically needed to guide scientific investigation' (Thompson & Russo, 2012: 33). Yet ethical issues are pervasive and multifaceted; they are not always predictable nor can they be 'tackled' using universal protocols and general guiding principles. Profession-specific guidelines and the process of seeking ethical approval have led to an overly sanitised approach to research which disregards the numerous challenges and unique ethical considerations specific to who the research is with and where the research is conducted. While useful, guidelines can be mistakenly treated as checklists, beyond which unique features of a clinical setting or research study are neglected. Further, the process of identifying and detailing the management of ethical issues, as if solely for the ethical approval process, can mask unexpected or unknown dilemmas that might arise. This also discourages and/or minimises the need for ongoing reflection and discussion of ethical considerations.

Traditionally, ethical concerns focus on the treatment of participants, researcher safety and the handling of data. However, there are a plethora of ethical challenges that require numerous, sometimes repeated and complex decision-making processes. Ethical considerations begin much earlier than procedural aspects of the study; they can start at the point of choosing or

Table 16.2 Choosing a research topic: ethical considerations

- Is the topic an over-researched area?
- Who are the participants and their backgrounds (e.g. ethnicity, class) in the majority of those studies?
- Who or which research teams dominate in their contributions to the literature? How are they funded, by who and what are their research agendas?
- What topic areas/population groups are under-researched? Why might that be?
- How could your study contribute to this (or not)? Why design a study in this area?
- Who is asking for this study to be conducted? What are their priorities and why?
- What aspects of privilege and power would the proposed study potentially reinforce? How might a study be designed to offer an alternative perspective?
- Whose voice and agendas will be served by the findings? How might the findings be used/misinterpreted, by who and with what possible impact and on whom?

considering an area to be researched and the formulation of the research question. The researcher should ask a range of questions to determine what, why and the implications of designing a study in a particular area (Table 16.2).

Differing agendas of funders, services and researchers can create challenges. For instance, service commissioners might place an emphasis on certain outcomes and favour specific outcome measures, which clinicians or SUs might object or assign less weight to (e.g. symptom reduction versus SU goals). It is therefore vital that the researcher is able to acknowledge why the study is being conducted and form meaningful and relevant questions that do not simply satisfy particular stakeholders or generate data to support a set of predetermined outcomes. Ultimately, the questions should fit as closely as possible to the objectives of the service and SU experience.

The research question is commonly viewed as the driver that informs all other decision-making processes in a linear fashion, though there is an important relationship between the research question and epistemology.[1] Specifically, the researcher's epistemological position informs the framing of the research question, while the research question is informed by the way a topic is researched and conceptualised in the field, dominated by a particular epistemological stance (e.g. positivist research seeking to establish specific relationships between certain symptoms or diagnoses and other factors). As the research question is a visible marker of the ethical positioning of the study, it demands careful construction and ethical scrutiny. The framing of a research question inevitably embeds particular assumptions and the researcher should be aware of implicit assumptions to ensure consistency and coherency in subsequent stages. This includes examining the framework used to interrogate the literature; epistemological and ontological[2] positioning; methods employed; and data analysis. Ethics is a connecting strand, from selecting the topic area to how findings are used and should not be viewed simply as an attempt to satisfy reviewing bodies.

Task 1: Review the research question 'Has racism increased in healthcare settings in the United Kingdom following Brexit?'

Consider the following:

- What assumptions are implicitly present? Does their presence matter and why?
- What needs to be made clear about the constructs used?
- How might racism be measured? Is it possible to measure? What does measurement imply?
- How might the question be reframed to avoid unwanted assumptions or implications of quantifying racism?

Research designs in the therapeutic context

A number of designs can be employed in the clinical context: small-N, which can include both quantitative and qualitative data; pure qualitative approaches; large-N designs, which rely on group comparisons. Each has advantages and disadvantages but importantly, all raise ethical questions.

Small-N

Narrative case studies, single-case and case-series experimental designs combine research and practice in an organic way. Ethically, these idiographic approaches are less problematic as the participant serves as their own control (i.e. an intervention does not need to be withheld from a control group). Instead of comparing data between participants, data is compared at different phases for the same participant – mapping individual change. Consequently, change does not need to be solely defined by service protocols or clinician expertise, but can be generated by the SU. Unlike tightly controlled large-N studies where exclusion criteria strip away the complexity and diversity of those referred to services, small-N approaches can be participant-focused and -led. Nonetheless, small-N studies are seen as more prone to bias and are less valued as evidence, in comparison to meta-analyses for example, where its purported value increases the likelihood of funding and publication, thereby perpetuating the privileging of more studies using these methods. Researchers have a responsibility to question how they can engage with research to shift this restrictive exertion of scientific power, embedded in the hierarchy of evidence, which has been criticised, for example, on its failure to serve the needs and realities of public policy (Parkhurst & Abeysinghe, 2016). Research designed and carried out by clinicians in *real* therapeutic settings is likely more valuable and relevant to SUs, professionals and services. Small-N designs link more closely to the clinical needs of the individual rather than epidemiological factors that form the basis of larger studies; and they allow practice-based evidence as one way of using a bottom-up approach to inform policy.

The publication of small-N studies is on the rise, perhaps a result of attempts to increase credibility with the introduction of randomisation (Kratochwill & Levin, 2010) and the employment of various statistical analyses, including effect size. Despite an increase in statistical options, results can differ based on the technique used (Parker & Brossart, 2003), and so caution is advised and a clear rationale should be provided for the chosen analysis (e.g. avoid selecting techniques that simply support research questions). Ethical dilemmas continue to emerge at the analysis stage, for example, as significant findings are more likely to be published, non-significant findings are generally dismissed; however, both could lead to new questions and lines of enquiry.

Many criticisms are directed at traditional case studies, but in an attempt to reduce researcher bias, increase external validity and link change to therapy, there is a drive for systematic approaches that collect quantitative data and

Table 16.3 Ethical considerations in small-N designs

* How can the influence of the research agenda of the clinician/researcher be reduced?
* What issues arise with using data retrospectively once the intervention 'success' is known?
* Is it always unethical to disseminate/publish data from small-N studies without SU consent? When might consent not be an issue?
* Can removing personally identifiable information always ensure confidentiality?
* What issues might arise as a result of excessively removing identifying information?
* How could the misuse of power by the clinician/researcher be monitored?
* How can ethical considerations be addressed in reporting (e.g. conferences) or publishing findings from small-N studies?

include multiple assessment points and cases (Elliott, 2002). This may create problems for studies using therapies with less emphasis on observable phenomena and where using quantitative measurement to map onto constructs of interest is not possible. Unfortunately, in order for small-N designs to be regarded as credible and rigorous they have increasingly adopted qualities of designs more common to cohort studies and RCTs.

Ethical considerations in small-N designs are complex (see Table 16.3). For example, with respect to informed consent and confidentiality, using data for research purposes without the SU's permission could be seen as unethical. Others might advocate that clinicians are continually formulating and testing hypotheses during their clinical work, thus recording data does not interfere with this process, and consequently does not require SU consent. Small-N approaches involve more identifiable information due to the nature and amount of data gathered and it can be easier to identify services – making it imperative to consider how to ensure informed consent and confidentiality, and monitor researcher bias, which can influence the research agenda.

Qualitative studies

Similar to small-N, qualitative studies which are smaller in scale might be better placed to address service user and provider issues (Harper & Warner, 1993). The focus on context, meaning and experience may allow SU concerns and goals to emerge more readily, requiring the researcher to articulate questions which elicit information that do not simply support existing frameworks or ideas, and to genuinely listen to participants. However, qualitative methods should not be chosen based on the misconception that they are ethically superior. Hammersley (1999: 18) argues that qualitative 'ethicism' is problematic as it may lead to a lack of engagement with complex moral dilemmas regardless of the methodology adopted. In fact, due to the increased amount and type of interaction between researcher and participant in qualitative methods, some researchers argue that these approaches raise additional ethical issues (Brinkmann & Kvale, 2008). Researcher reflexivity and attention to the researcher's own personal values, social position and background (and biases) are essential to ethical considerations; though this could be said of all research designs. The impact of questioning participants from the researcher's own position requires reflection and the focus should not be restricted to differences between researcher and participant, but also on the consequences of assuming sameness.

Large-N

Large-N studies are more resource-intensive and in therapeutic settings typically involve assessing the effectiveness of an intervention. The way in which an intervention is evaluated has implications for its applicability to those accessing services. Randomised control trials (RCTs) positioned at the higher end of the hierarchy of evidence, assess the ability to produce the desired outcome under tightly controlled, stable circumstances. In contrast, effectiveness trials assess the effect under 'real world' service settings. RCTs are viewed as the gold standard of EBP regardless of significant criticism in terms of their design and usefulness. Cartwright (2007) questions whether it is possible to have a universal 'best method' and concludes that it is not, and instead selection should be study dependent. The endeavour of RCTs to achieve high internal validity has come at a cost to external validity (Cartwright, 2010) and their promotion has led to a divide between research and practice (Carey et al., 2017). Hence, conducting RCTs requires careful consideration to ensure that findings are meaningful at multiple levels (e.g. SU, clinician and service).

Overall, RCTs assume causality based on statistical associations, but do not answer questions regarding mechanisms of change. Therapeutic interventions involve numerous interrelated technical and relational variables and accordingly, Elliott (2010) argues that 'true' EBP should involve multiple lines of change process evidence (how and why change occurs). EBP reliant on RCTs has been critiqued for prioritising the needs and values of funders and service providers, while limiting SU choice (Kerridge, 2010). RCTs determine the nature and frequency of care offered by services, and SUs who do not match subsequent guideline expectations are viewed as drop-outs or non-engagers (Carey, 2018). Researchers need to ask themselves how research can continue to be viewed as rigorous and valuable *and* be led by SU perspectives. Outcome measures typically used in these studies focus on symptom reduction and neglect other forms of change, which are potentially problematic as SUs may continue to score within clinical ranges but report improved quality of life, thereby missing the perspective of the SU. Participatory Action Research aims for equal involvement from both researchers and participants using an iterative process and offers a compelling alternative. As an approach it acknowledges that participants are not passive in the research process and actively involves them (Baum et al., 2006). However, it is not a panacea and does not *fit* all epistemological positions and methodologies.

Practically, RCTs are costly and time-consuming and they cannot easily be integrated into a clinician's daily work, which brings into question who carries out these studies, who funds them and with what agenda. There is an assumption that treatment effects will be the same across different contexts and despite issues with external validity the findings of RCTs continue to inform policy. For example, as intervention components individually and combined largely remain unstudied, there is a lack of clarity about how these factors interact with context (Bonell et al., 2012) and therefore, how they can be replicated. Bonell et al. (2012) argue that a more meaningful question than the traditional 'what works for whom' is asking *what works for whom and under what circumstances?* This highlights the need for further effectiveness studies, which can be more readily carried out within services and anchored in terms of geographical location and demographic characteristics of the local population.

Data collection: challenges to ethical practice

Data collection in services usually takes the form of self-report, ranging from structured questionnaires to unstructured interviews. An unavoidable ethical tension for clinicians conducting research in such settings is the duality of roles (clinician–researcher). Juggling too many roles can impact upon the ability to make ethical decisions (Seider et al., 2007) and competing agendas and participant expectations can lead to role conflict (Yanos & Ziedonis, 2006). For clinician–researchers conducting research in their own service, organisational and clinical agendas or responsibilities may compete with the research agenda. If the participant is a SU (SU–participant), they may struggle to distinguish between the roles and expect clinical input (Holloway & Wheeler, 1995). Furthermore, what one might do in therapy is not what is expected as a researcher; the roles are governed by different obligations. The goal of a clinician is to provide client-centred care and ensure wellbeing – there is flexibility in terms of how this may be achieved. Within research, the rights, safety and wellbeing of participants are given a significant platform, but the researcher has to adhere to specific and often standardised procedures to ensure 'quality' of data. It is, therefore, key that the clinician–researcher makes clear their role within each interaction and clarifies the parameters of how information communicated by the SU can be responded to. It is recommended that researchers who have an existing therapeutic relationship with a participant avoid direct contact, such as recruiting or interviewing (Sales & Folkman, 2000). Nevertheless, even the association of a clinician name with a study has implications, as SUs' trust in clinicians can increase the likelihood of them opting into research (Kaminsky et al., 2003).

A systematic review of clinician–researcher dual role experiences in health research highlighted the vital role of supervision (Hay-Smith et al., 2016).

Others have argued for an integration of roles to form a 'coherent moral identity' as a way to minimise unethical practices and protect participants (Miller et al., 1998). In fact, some suggest the aim should be to develop internal models driven by underlying principles which direct one's work, to enable clinician–researchers to learn how to prioritise and resolve conflicts (Yanos & Ziedonis, 2006). Additionally, professional training courses need to dedicate reflective spaces to explore these ethical tensions.

Interviews

Interviews with SUs, carers or professionals may take the form of individual interviews and/or focus groups. Interviews allow participants to direct the conversation to some extent, with less of a researcher framework imposed than structured methods. Clinical skills in being curious, listening actively and empathically are advantageous here, although clinician–researchers may unknowingly misuse these skills, for example, where participants communicate information that they may not wish to share (Brinkmann & Kvale, 2008).

Depending on the topic area and sample, considerations should be given to where interviews are conducted and by whom (e.g. gender, ethnicity, role). The researcher should be aware of their own position and the values that they bring to the interaction, in addition to the power differential between researcher and participant. Interviews can be emotive, and the participant should not feel obliged to continue (e.g. for fear of upsetting the researcher/clinician, fear of withdrawal of service, etc.). Unexpected content may emerge during the interview and consent to use in the research should be revisited at the end of the interview. Similar to small-N approaches, the nature of data collection may lead to participants being more identifiable, and extra precautions need to be used, such as, the use of pseudonyms, changing or removing names and/or places. Confidentiality and anonymity require particular attention when conducting focus groups; there needs to be an agreement that members do not discuss information following the group or share information with others. This can be more difficult to guarantee, which points to the need to justify why relevant data can only be obtained in group interaction.

Questionnaires

Questionnaire data can be collected face-to-face (subject to the aforementioned ethical dilemmas) or electronically. The latter may reduce some of the issues raised, but questions emerge regarding how to: ensure valid consent; assess and manage the emotional impact of participation; sufficiency of online debriefing (British Psychological Society, 2017). In terms of data security, it is paramount that secure platforms are used to collect data and that storage is on organisation, password protected, computer files rather than cloud services.

Task 2: How might a clinician–researcher explain their role and the parameters of their responsibilities to a SU–participant?

- Will this be a one-off explanation?
- Which aspects require emphasis?
- How might one ensure that different interactions do not become confusing for the SU–participant?
- How can the clinician–researcher remain clear about their role within a given interaction?

Ethical questioning and decision-making throughout the research process

Through a series of illustrative, not exhaustive questions (see Table 16.4) this section addresses aspects commonly scrutinised by ethics committees, and more subtle dilemmas frequently overlooked. However, it is not possible to predict all possible ethical dilemmas a study may pose and unexpected issues will undoubtedly arise.

Ethical decision-making can be more straightforward for certain aspects due to legal frameworks, such as the General Data Protection Regulation (GDPR; Data Protection Act 2018, c. 12). This new stringent European legislation is likely to ensure increased accountability, particularly the collection, handling and storage of identifiable data, essentially to reduce data breaches. Nevertheless, all decision-making processes should be viewed as equally important in terms of ethical practice, despite less obvious or explicit penalties. Furthermore, even when there are legal obligations as with the GDPR, the practical implications are debatable and will require ongoing discussion by all researchers.

Conclusion

A focus on EBP has led to a misconception that research in therapeutic settings should take the form of large, tightly controlled, comparison studies. In reality, there are a range of clinically relevant questions that demand a range of methodologies, based on questions and priorities of SUs and services. Conducting research in services can be challenging and generate a minefield of ethical issues, due to political and professional pressures, multiple roles and agendas, the diversity of SUs accessing services and the operation of power (in research frameworks, service-level systems and in the SU/participant/researcher/clinician relationships). To carry out research that is as closely aligned to the concerns and experiences of SUs, and appropriately generalisable, research in the therapeutic context should involve working in partnership

Table 16.4 Ethical considerations for research in therapeutic settings

Stage	Questions to ask
Advertisement	How are participants made aware of the study (e.g. posters/leaflets in waiting areas, staff circulating PIS – direct requests can exert pressure on SUs)? Whose name is associated with the project (clinician trust can influence decisions to participate)? How is the study 'sold' (e.g. will help other SUs, quicker access to help, etc. – implications of such statements)?
Recruitment	Are staff involved in the SU's care inviting participants? How do staff decide who to invite and what are their assumptions, expectations and biases? Is an external researcher involved in recruitment? What challenges might this overcome and/or raise? Has it been made clear that a decision not to participate will not affect care the SU continues to receive from the service? Has a time pressure to opt-in been communicated? What other options are available? Has the SU's motivation for participation been explored?
Inclusion/exclusion criteria	Are the selected criteria all necessary? Will the criteria exclude particular groups – who is explicitly, and implicitly excluded and why? What are the implications for the study and findings? How might this (e.g. those who do not speak English as a first language) be overcome? Does the criteria sufficiently represent those referred to the service or the target group? Will the criteria lead to particular findings being supported (i.e. reinforce existing outcomes)?
Information sheet	Are there opportunities to access the information via other means (e.g. brail, audio, languages other than English, etc.)? Will deception be used? Is this necessary? Have the consequences been considered? Has information regarding supporting agencies been provided in case of withdrawal?
Consent	Does 'capacity' need attending to? In what way? Is parental/guardian consent required? Will consent be revisited as an ongoing process?
Demographic information	Is unnecessary information being collected (i.e. not relevant to answer the research question/s)? How is information being collected? What are the implications (e.g. closed categories such as, male or female, what might be participants' perception of an 'other' option, could a free text box be used, what challenges might it pose)?

(Continued)

Table 16.4 (Cont.)

Stage	Questions to ask
Data collection	Who is collecting data? What agendas do they bring? How is data being collected (e.g. interpreters) and where? Is only necessary information being collected? If electronic data collection, are secure platforms being used?
Right to withdraw	Has it been made clear that participants are free to withdraw at any time (even after an interview) without the need to provide a reason and with no negative repercussions? How could the obligation to continue in fear of disappointing the referring clinician/researcher be reduced?
Data storage and security	Has all identifying information been removed? Has identifying information that needs to be kept been stored separately to data and contact details? How long will data be kept for (i.e. data should not be kept for longer than necessary, typically three to five years)? Has identifying information been shared with anyone outside the research team? Where and how has data been stored (e.g. appropriately encrypted, password protected files, separate networks that are not shared, not on cloud services)? If in locked cabinets, who has access? What issues might arise related to location of data storage with online questionnaires (i.e. UK versus USA-based)?
Withdrawal of data post-participation	Is there an option to withdraw data post-participation? How will this be managed? What if participation was anonymous?
Debriefing	If deception was involved, has the necessary information been communicated and the impact of withholding this information assessed? Have participants been appropriately signposted to supporting agencies?
Compensation	Are financial incentives being provided? If yes, in what form, why and with what implications?
Dissemination	It can be viewed unethical not to disseminate – who would benefit from learning about the study (other than academic/professional audiences)? Who has been involved and at what stage (e.g. interpreters, SUs, management)? Has their input been acknowledged? How? Is SU involvement tokenistic or genuinely ensures co-production (e.g. co-authorship)? Will findings be shared with participants? If not, why? Has the impact of seeing/hearing the results been considered? How can the misuse of findings be prevented?

with SUs – it cannot be solely steered by policy makers, funders and service providers. Numerous systemic and economic barriers will need to be navigated to conduct ethical research, which requires ongoing questioning, discussion and supervision.

Reflective questions

1. How might a researcher design a study led by SU perspectives while managing conflicting agendas?
2. In what circumstances might a researcher choose to conduct a study where findings could be used to support ethically questionable agendas?
3. How might a researcher reduce the power differential in the researcher-participant relationship?
4. What should a researcher do if a participant discloses information that has negative implications in relation to their clinical care?

Notes

1 Epistemology = the nature of knowledge, what claims can be made.
2 Ontological = the nature of 'reality'/being, what is there to know.

References

Baker, T.B., McFall, R.M., & Shoham, V. (2008) Current status and future prospects of clinical psychology: Toward a scientifically principled approach to mental and behavioral health care. *Psychological Science in the Public Interest*, 9(2), 67–103.

Baum, F., MacDougall, C., & Smith, D. (2006) Participatory action research. *Journal of Epidemiology and Community Health*, 60(10), 854–857.

Bonell, C., Fletcher, A., Morton, M., Lorenc, T., & Moore, L. (2012) Realist randomised controlled trials: A new approach to evaluating complex public health interventions. *Social Science and Medicine*, 75(12), 2299–2306.

Brinkmann, S., & Kvale, S. (2008). Ethics in qualitative psychological research. In C. Willig, & W. Stainton-Rogers (Eds.). *The Sage Handbook of Qualitative Research in Psychology*. London: Sage, pp. 263–279.

British Psychological Society. (2017). *Ethics Guidelines for Internet-Mediated Research*. Leicester: British Psychological Society.

Carey, T. (2018) *Patient-Perspective Care: A New Paradigm for Health Systems and Services*. New York: Routledge.

Carey, T.A., Tai, S.J., Mansell, W., Huddy, V., Griffiths, R., & Marken, R.S. (2017) Improving professional psychological practice through an increased repertoire of research methodologies: Illustrated by the development of MOL. *Professional Psychology: Research and Practice*, 48(3), 175–182.

Cartwright, N. (2007) Are RCTs the gold standard? *BioSocieties*, 2(1), 11–20.

Cartwright, N. (2010) What are randomised controlled trials good for? *Philosophical Studies*, 147(1), 59–70.

Data Protection Act 2018. (c. 12) Retrieved from www.legislation.gov.uk/ukpga/2018/12/contents/enacted. Accessed 18th July 2018.

Elliott, R. (2002) Hermeneutic single-case efficacy design. *Psychotherapy Research*, 12(1), 1–21.

Elliott, R. (2010) Psychotherapy change process research: Realizing the promise. *Psychotherapy Research*, 20(2), 123–135.

Hammersley, M. (1999) Some reflections on the current state of qualitative research. *Research Intelligence*, 70, 16–18.

Harper, D. & Warner, S. (1993) Discourse, social constructionism and clinical psychology. *Changes: An International Journal of Psychology and Psychotherapy*, 11 (1), 72–79.

Hay-Smith, E.J.C., Brown, M., Anderson, L., & Treharne, G.J. (2016) Once a clinician, always a clinician: A systematic review to develop a typology of clinician-researcher dual-role experiences in health research with patient-participants. *BMC Medical Research and Methodology*, 16(95).

Holloway, I., & Wheeler, S. (1995) Ethical issues in qualitative nursing research. *Nursing Ethics*, 2(3), 223–232.

Kaminsky, A., Roberts, L.W., & Brody, J.L. (2003) Influences upon willingness to participate in schizophrenia research: An analysis of narrative data from 63 people with schizophrenia. *Ethics and Behavior*, 13(3), 279–302.

Kerridge, I. (2010) Ethics and EBM: Acknowledging bias, accepting difference and embracing politics. *Journal of Evaluation in Clinical Practice*, 16(2), 365–373.

Kratochwill, T.R., & Levin, J.R. (2010) Enhancing the scientific credibility of single-case intervention research: Randomization to the rescue. *Psychological Methods*, 15(2), 122–144.

Mckeon, S., Alexander, E., Brodaty, H., Ferris, B., Frazer, I., & Little, M. (2013) *Strategic Review of Health and Medical Research: Better Health Through Research*. Canberra: ACT: Department of Health and Ageing.

Miller, F.G., Rosenstein, D.L., & DeRenzo, E.G. (1998) Professional integrity in clinical research. *JAMA*, 280(16), 1449–1454.

Morrow, E., Ross, F., Grocott, P., & Bennett, J. (2010) A model and measure for quality service user involvement in health research. *International Journal of Consumer Studies*, 34(5), 532–539.

Parker, R.I., & Brossart, D.F. (2003) Evaluating single-case research data: A comparison of seven statistical methods. *Behavior Therapy*, 34(2), 189–211.

Parkhurst, J.O., & Abeysinghe, S. (2016) What constitutes "good" evidence for public health and social policy-making? From hierarchies to appropriateness. *Social Epistemology*, 30(5-6), 665–679.

Patel, N. (2003). Speaking with the silent: Addressing issues of disempowerment when working with refugee people. In R. Tribe, & H. Raval (Eds.). *Working with Interpreters in Mental Health*. Hove: Brunner-Routledge, pp. 219–237.

Sales, B.D., & Folkman, S. (2000) *Ethics in Research with Human Participants*. Washington: American Psychological Association.

Seider, S., Davis, K., & Gardner, H. (2007) Good work in psychology. *The Psychologist*, 20(11), 672–676.

Spring, B. (2007) Evidence-based practice in clinical psychology: What it is, why it matters; what you need to know. *Journal of Clinical Psychology*, 63(7), 611–631.
Thompson, A., & Russo, K. (2012) Ethical dilemmas for clinical psychologists in conducting qualitative research. *Qualitative Research in Psychology*, 9(1), 32–46.
Yanos, P.T., & Ziedonis, D.M. (2006) The patient-oriented clinician-researcher: Advantages and challenges of being a double agent. *Psychiatric Services*, 57(2), 249–253.

Chapter 17

Evidence-based practice
The ethical dimension

Kenneth Gannon

Evidence-based practice is an approach to the evaluation and application of research evidence to clinical practice. While it is difficult to identify a specific point of origin, most authors locate it in the work of the British epidemiologist Archie Cochrane. Cochrane (1972) proposed that healthcare resources should be used to deliver interventions and services that well-designed evaluations had shown to be effective. A group of epidemiologists, biostatisticians and experts in medical informatics at McMaster University restated these principles (Evidence Based Medicine working group, 1992) and called it Evidence-Based Medicine (EBM). Since then it has been adopted by most healthcare professions, hence the term 'Evidence-based Practice' (EBP). The term and its relatively recent appearance begs the question 'What was the basis for medical practice before EBM?' Howick (2011) has suggested that three approaches supported claims for treatments; one argued for observation of the effects of treatment based on group comparisons, one held that underlying causes of disease must be understood and targeted and the third was grounded in expert opinion. Although EBM was touted as a 'paradigm shift' (Evidence-Based Medicine Working Group, 1992) at its base it represents an elaboration and formalisation of the first of these. The success of the concept is such that its influence has been felt beyond healthcare and the term Evidence-Based Policy Making (EBPM) is now frequently employed (e.g. Cartwright & Hardie, 2012; Solesbury, 2001). A recent example of this development is the UK government's decision to establish four centres that will 'produce and disseminate research to local decision-makers, supporting them in investing in services that deliver the best outcomes for citizens and value for money for taxpayers' (Cabinet Office, 2013). I will use the acronym EBP for simplicity and relevance throughout this chapter.

The pervasiveness and the degree of influence enjoyed by EBM/EBP/EBPM indicates the importance of understanding how the approach is conceptualised and examining the ethical issues that have been raised in relation to it. The aim of this chapter is to examine some of the complexities, challenges and indeed contradictions inherent in the approach and to explore some of the implications for the ethical practice of healthcare.

What is evidence based practice?

A useful place to start is with the definition of EBM put forward by Sackett et al. (1996), whose book on EBM (Sackett et al., 1997) is arguably one of the most influential texts in the area.

> Evidence-based medicine is the conscientious, explicit, and judicious use of current best evidence in making decisions about the care of individual patients. The practice of evidence-based medicine means integrating individual clinical expertise with the best available clinical evidence from systematic research.
>
> (Sackett et al., 1996: 71)

These authors subsequently developed this in a way that appears to give greater weight to the views of the patient:

> Evidence-based medicine requires the integration of best research evidence with our clinical expertise and our patient's unique values and circumstances.
>
> (Straus et al., 2011: 1)

Greenhalgh (2010: 1) defined the approach in a manner that emphasises the formal, quantitative aspects:

> the use of mathematical estimates of the risk of benefit and harm, derived from high-quality research on population samples, to inform clinical decision-making in the diagnosis, investigation or management of individual patients.

There are several elements in these definitions that warrant attention, but it has probably been the identification of 'current best evidence' or, more precisely, 'mathematical estimates of the risk of benefit and harm' as the starting point of the process that has been especially influential on the development of thinking and practice in this area. Attempts to operationalise precisely what is meant by the phrase have led to the development of various hierarchies of evidence. Although these are somewhat different from each other in their details, they have largely converged upon the same approach to ranking evidence. The logic underpinning all of them is that the best evidence is garnered from approaches to data generation and evaluation that conform most closely to the standard hypothesis-testing approach of the natural sciences. This entails establishing a situation analogous to a controlled experiment in which the researcher manipulates one variable and determines its effect on another variable while holding constant or controlling for all other variables that might also affect the outcome. This has resulted in the Randomised Controlled Trial (RCT) being placed at or near the top of the hierarchy, only being supplanted by meta-analyses in which the data from several such trials is combined and analysed or by systematic reviews in which evidence on a particular issue is searched for across a range of sources and evaluated according to strict criteria. An example of such a hierarchy is that proposed by Guyatt et al. (1995)

1. Systematic reviews and meta-analyses
2. Randomised controlled trials (RCT) with definitive results (confidence intervals that do not overlap the threshold clinically significant effect)
3. Randomised controlled trials with non-definitive results (a point estimate that suggests a clinically significant effect but with confidence intervals overlapping the threshold for this effect)
4. Cohort studies
5. Case-control studies
6. Cross sectional surveys
7. Case reports.

Here we can see the standard model of ranking based on the premises of EBP in which RCTs and material based on them are at the top and data derived from other approaches is ranked lower. For many authors the RCT is the gold standard for acquiring reliable information and for offering us the best guidance of how to make decisions about treatment allocation (what treatment for which condition) and funding (which treatment(s) from a range of options should be paid for by states or insurance companies). For example, a report for the UK Government (Cabinet Office Behavioural Insights Team, 2012) states

> Randomised controlled trials (RCTs) are the best way of determining whether a policy is working. They have been used for over 60 years to compare the effectiveness of new medicines.
>
> (p. 6)

However, the whole enterprise of EBM, and consequently of the central role in it granted to the RCT has been subject to vehement criticism. Miles (2009) has argued that the practice of holistic care is incompatible with EBM and has stated that:

> Practising holistic medicine will necessarily involve the abandonment of the core tenets of EBM.
>
> (p. 947)

It might seem strange that an approach that is explicitly committed to identifying and using the best available evidence of what works best for treating particular health problems has been subjected to criticism of any sort, let alone criticism that strikes at the very heart of the whole enterprise. It may seem odd that people can hold such diametrically opposed views about the approach and it may seem axiomatic that the only ethical course for practitioners is to offer their patients, clients and service users treatment for which there is good evidence that it will both help cure them and expose them to no or minimal risk or at least provide a favourable benefit: harm ratio. After all, who would want to receive a treatment for which the only available evidence that it worked was based on precedent, authority or anecdote and which could be as likely to hurt as help them? In other words, why even ask the question of whether EBP, particularly the central place accorded to RCTs within the approach, raises ethical issues? Surely it would be unethical to practice in any other way? Indeed, one of Cochrane's (1972) primary concerns was that too often medical care was based on interventions for which the evidence was poor with a consequent risk of harm at both the individual and population level. He wanted to ensure that there should be equitable access to treatment for which there was good evidence.

In order to understand why it is even possible to speak of ethical concerns in relation to EBP it is necessary to understand the underlying assumptions of EBP, the procedures involved in generating the inputs to EBP and their limitations, the implicit values underpinning EBP and the ways in which particular sorts of evidence are given priority.

Epistemology, values and competing interests in EBP

Epistemology is the branch of philosophy that is concerned with the nature of knowledge and the basis upon which we are entitled to make claims about truth. Philosophers have advanced a variety of accounts of how we come to know and what, precisely, we can claim knowledge of. Some have emphasised the role of experiences while others have focused on the role of social processes. EBP is grounded in an empiricist, realist epistemology, which proposes that we can come to have knowledge of entities and objects that exist independently of us through a process of observation and manipulation of variables to isolate cause-effect relationships. For many a great merit of this approach is that it produces unambiguous, robust evidence that enables informed decision-making, and which avoids the influence of social and political factors (e.g. Catwell & Sheikh, 2009). For critics this is precisely the problem. The implicit claim that evidence is neutral and does not entail a commitment to moral values of any sort is, in their view, fundamentally mistaken. Kelly et al. (2015), for example, have argued that values intrude at all stages of EBP, starting with decisions about which questions to ask, while largely ignoring the value systems of patients and clinicians. EBP, in this view, makes strong epistemic claims while setting aside values. Furthermore, in claiming that a particular course of action leads to a particular outcome there is an implicit assumption that the outcome in question is desirable. This is inherently a moral claim and is the reason that Kerridge (2010) stated 'Evidence-based medicine ... has and confers both epistemic and moral authority' (p. 365).

Of course, there are certain outcomes, such as removing or shrinking cancerous tumours, that very few people would probably want to claim were undesirable. The effectiveness of interventions intended to produce such outcomes can also be straightforwardly assessed within an empirical framework, so here there is consonance between the epistemological and (implicit) value claims. However, not all 'problems' are as relatively straightforward as cancer. Consider, for example, the appearance and disappearance of disorders from the Diagnostic and Statistical Manual (DSM) of the American Psychiatric Association. Homosexuality was removed from the second edition of the DSM in 1972, but up to then it would have been perfectly legitimate to develop evidence-based guidelines for the treatment of homosexuality while 'infantile autism' was first listed in DSM-III in 1980.

In addition to the implicit valorisation of certain domains of concern and particular sorts of outcomes within EBP the hierarchy of evidence that underpins it assigns varying degrees of importance to the values and concerns of different groups. Marks (2009) has argued that 'In medicine and health care there is a large and increasing gap between what gets measured and what matters most to clients and patients' (p. 476). Focusing on the centrality of RCTs and their derivatives, Cornish and Gillespie (2009) have written:

RCTs are particularly suitable for determining which of a limited number of interventions is most effective at producing a pre-determined health outcome within a specific stable context. They answer to scientific interests in comparing the effects of different pharmacological treatments, or other clearly defined interventions, and to health professionals' interests in choosing between treatments. RCTs are excellent means of achieving these particular ends, but these are not the only ends that may be served by health research. Indeed, to place RCTs at the top of the hierarchy may be to prioritize certain interests, and thus, an exercise of power, rather than a reflection of an objective hierarchy among methods.

(p. 803)

The interests served by placing RCTs and their products at the top of the hierarchy are arguably those of the people whose job it is to prioritise and fund health treatments. Even a well-designed and definitive RCT will only show that on average a particular treatment does better than no treatment, an alternative or a placebo but it will not allow determination of whether a particular treatment will work for a particular patient in a particular setting. Indeed, this is why some authors prefer to speak of 'epidemiology-based practice'.

As Kerridge (2010), among others, has pointed out, a hierarchy that prioritises the needs and values of providers and funders can be used to justify restriction of expenditure and patient choice and to restrict the options open to clinicians, thus limiting the autonomy of both groups. This is a potential concern both in systems in which healthcare is funded from the public purse, as in the UK, and in which healthcare is largely paid for through insurance schemes, as in the USA. In the UK the National Institute for Health and Care Excellence (NICE) was established in 1999 to reduce variation in the availability and quality of NHS treatments and care. (NICE (a), 2013). Their approach to doing this is described by NICE in these terms:

NICE guidance supports healthcare professionals and others to make sure that the care they provide is of the best possible quality and offers the best value for money.

(NICE (b), 2013)

In relation to developing clinical guidelines the process is initiated by means of a referral from the Department of Health. A guideline development group is then established, which assesses the available evidence and makes recommendations. It is worth noting here that the initiative comes from a branch of government and part of the agenda is to identify interventions that offer the best value for money. There is nothing inherently wrong with wanting value for money, indeed taxpayers (and those contributing to insurance schemes) would probably demand it. Nevertheless, the requirement that value for money be an important consideration in making recommendations regarding treatment creates a tension from the outset between what might be best for the individual (and would be preferred by them and by those treating them) and what the state or insurance company is willing to fund. Indeed, there have been a number of cases in the UK in which individuals and groups have challenged NICE guidance that denied them treatment that they or their clinicians preferred. For example, there have been challenges to restrictions on cholinesterase inhibitor treatment for Alzheimer's dementia (Sellars & Easey, 2008) and an (unsuccessful) challenge to the guidelines for Chronic Fatigue Syndrome (Dyer, 2009).

Another problem with prioritising particular interests above others is that an exclusive focus on the scientific understanding and treatment of a disease can lead 'directly to the assumption that what is right for the disease is automatically right for the patient, representing a fundamental misunderstanding of the relationship between the partial nature of the disease and the totality of the person' (Miles, 2009: 944).

Greenhalgh et al. (2015) identified a number of 'biases' against patients and carers in EBM. Among these was the lack of patient input in published research, the devaluation of the individual patient experience and the role of power imbalances, which can suppress the voice of the patient. These three 'biases' are closely associated with the evidence hierarchy in EBP and together with the issues already discussed arguably constitute a form of injustice in relation to decisions related to the types of evidence that are prioritised. Fricker (2007) has identified a particular type of injustice that she has termed Epistemic Injustice. The essence of her argument is that a person can be wronged in terms of how they present or possess knowledge. Fricker identified two types of injustice,

Epistemic and Hermeneutic but it is the former which she defined as 'A wrong done to someone specifically in their capacity as knower' (Fricker, 2007: 1) that is applicable here. Carel and Kidd (2014) have applied Fricker's insights to the context of healthcare and have argued that while health professionals and ill persons are epistemically privileged in different ways the knowledge of the professional takes precedence. This sidelining of the individual patient perspective can be viewed as a consequence of the utilitarian perspective that is implicit in EBP and the hierarchy of evidence. The focus on outcomes that are beneficial at a population level ignores other approaches to framing moral choices. Alternatives, such as deontological and virtue-based approaches place greater emphasis on what the individual is entitled to receive or what is best for them. While definitions of EBM acknowledge the need to incorporate the views of patients the centrality of 'best evidence' and the ways in which this is operationalised inevitably result in a utilitarianism.

How applicable is the evidence in EBP?

A central assumption underpinning EBP is that evidence of what has proven to be effective in well-conducted studies conducted elsewhere can be sensibly and meaningfully applied to similar problems encountered by the evidence-base practitioner wherever they happen to be working. This transferability of findings is normally assumed to be guaranteed by the methodological architecture of RCTs, that is random selection and allocation of participants, control of confounding variables, use of control groups, double- or triple-blinding etc. These procedures enable the researcher to claim that the observed effect (the reduction in tumour size, the reduction in pain scores, the reduction in depression scores, etc.) is due to the 'cause' embodied in the particular intervention being evaluated (perhaps a new cancer drug, a physiotherapy intervention or cognitive behavioural therapy).

Cartwright and Hardie (2012) provide an extensive and detailed analysis and critique of the assumptions underpinning and the processes involved in the move from (in their terminology) 'It worked there' to 'It will work here'. Essentially, they are concerned with what warrants the claim for such transferability and this relates to the distinction between efficacy and effectiveness. Efficacy is what is demonstrated in a standard RCT in which there is a positive outcome, i.e. the intervention was successful in some sense. Effectiveness is whether the intervention will work in the world outside the constraints of the RCT. As Cartwright and Hardie (2012) put it 'No matter how much gold standard evidence you have that "it worked there", you cannot pave the road from there to here with gold bricks' (p. 8). Now this may not appear to be an ethical issue *per se, but* given the implicit ethical injunction entailed in EBP it is certainly important to examine the basis upon which the claims underpinning it are made. Cartwright and Hardie (2012) argue that in order to have confidence that an intervention or policy will work in a particular context we must find evidence that gives us reason to believe that the intervention played a causal role in the situation in which it was tested (the RCT), we must be able to identify the support factors that enabled its success and we need evidence that these support factors actually apply in our particular context. Essentially, support factors are factors that must be present in the environment in which the trial was conducted and without which the intervention will not work. They give the example of a study designed to test the impact of homework on reading test scores. In order for this intervention to work it needs the support of a host of other factors, including student motivation, student ability, supportive family, study space, consistent lessons and work feedback. Without these it would not work and if we wish to use it as an intervention in our setting we must have good reason to believe that these factors will be present here too. This may seem obvious, but it is easy to ignore it and Cartwright and Hardie give examples of interventions that worked well in one context failing in others because such factors were not attended to. It takes a lot of work to move from having evidence that something worked in one place to being confident that it will work somewhere else.

The question of the relevance of findings obtained in one setting or context to different ones goes deeper than the issue of the presence or absence of the necessary support factors. There is growing concern among clinicians and researchers about the consequences of the stringent inclusion and exclusion criteria that are employed in RCTs. Such criteria are required in order to rule out potentially confounding factors (i.e. variables that influence the relationship between the independent and dependant variable). For example, in studies of drugs for the treatment of cancer it is common to exclude people with comorbidities of various kinds. Chao et al. (2010) examined the eligibility criteria for trials of chemotherapy for prostate cancer over the period 2004 to 2008 and identified a range of exclusion criterial including psychiatric illness, obstructive pulmonary disease and cardiac disease. They then applied the criteria to a population of men treated for prostate cancer in the Veterans Affairs system in Connecticut and determined that 45% of this population would have been excluded from RCTs. They highlighted the challenges that this poses to transposing and applying the findings of RCTs to routine clinical practice. In relation to the concerns of the present chapter, it also suggests that stringent exclusion criteria have serious implications for the ability of patients with comorbidities to make informed choices concerning treatment options.

How complete and unbiased is the evidence base?

There is a growing concern with the way in which the involvement of commercial interests in researching interventions can systematically distort the evidence base. A particular concern is the involvement of multi-national pharmaceutical companies in the development, testing and marketing of new drugs. Such companies usually carry out the initial development of new drugs themselves, but they fund academic and clinical researchers to conduct the all-important clinical trials. A number of recent authors (e.g. Goldacre, 2013; Moncrieff, 2013) have expressed concern about the way in which this close involvement of commercial interests in clinical evaluations can distort the findings of trials in a manner favourable to the companies and their products. Particular concerns arise in relation to industry-sponsored trials, where the sponsors (drug companies) often own the data and the academics who ostensibly conducted the trial, analysed the data and whose names appear on the paper have limited access to the raw data from the trial (Lundh et al., 2011).

Some authors (e.g. Tannock et al., 2016) have argued that the challenges in generalising from RCTs to typical clinical populations identified above are due in part to the vested interest of commercial sponsors of research in obtaining positive results that demonstrate a benefit of their treatment. Another problem in many such trials is the use of surrogate end points that do not relate directly to patient-relevant outcomes such as duration of survival or quality of life. Prasad et al. (2015) conducted a systematic review of the relationship between surrogate end points and survival in cancer trials and found a low correlation between them. Furthermore, many oncology drug trials do not include quality of life measures, in spite of the fact that both cancer and the side effects of treatment can have a very substantial impact on this (e.g. Tannock et al., 2016). This latter point highlights again the failure to adequately represent the voice of the patient in EBP.

A further concern related to the role of commercial interests is identification of new types of disorder by pharmaceutical companies in order to create a new market for their products. A fairly recent example of this is the case of female sexual dysfunction. Following the success of Viagra in treating erectile dysfunction in men, companies sought to extend the market to women by identifying a disorder that could be treated with Viagra. This depended on collaboration between the industry and academic researchers that aimed to normalize certain patterns of female sexual arousal and performance and, in the process, pathologise others (Tiefer, 2006).

Conclusion

The intention here has not been to demonize EBP, RCTs, hierarchies of evidence and the people advocating these approaches. Nor has it been to construct a 'straw person' in respect of the enterprise of EBP. Indeed, practitioners of EBP have been quick to respond to criticism of the approach and modify and adapt it accordingly. Rather the aim has been to identify and explore some of the frequently unexamined moral and ethical assumptions that lie at the heart of EBP and which are inextricable from the ways in which evidence and the evidence hierarchy are conceptualised. Adopting an EBP approach gives rise to complex challenges in squaring the need to make the best use of scarce resources, avoid useless or dangerous interventions and deliver optimal care while not losing site of the complex needs of individuals. Healthcare practitioners need to draw on moral philosophy and ethical principles as well as research expertise when making decisions regarding interventions. While EBP acknowledges the importance of attending to unique values and circumstances of individuals ways of making this more central to the practice of EBP need to be identified and developed.

Reflective questions

1. Is it possible to take patient/service user perspectives into account when making decisions regarding the provision of healthcare services? How might this be done?
2. Is it ethical to ration the provision of services based on cost? What ethical principles are relevant to such decisions?
3. If we accept that cost-based rationing is inevitable, how can we take account of the values and priorities of those using the services?
4. In what circumstances, if ever, would it be ethically justifiable to use an intervention for which the evidence base was weak or absent?

References

Cabinet Office. (2013) What *Works: Evidence Centres for Social Policy.* London: Stationary Office.

Cabinet Office Behavioural Insights Team. (2012) Test, *Learn, Adapt: Developing Public Policy with Randomised Controlled Trials.* London: Stationary Office.

Carel, H. & Kidd, I.J. (2014) Epistemic injustice in healthcare: A philosophical analysis. *Medicine, Healthcare and Philosophy,* 17(4), 529–540.

Cartwright, N., & Hardie, J. (2012) Evidence-*Based Policy: A Practical Guide to Doing It Better.* New York: Oxford University Press.

Catwell, L., & Sheikh, A. (2009) Evaluating eHealth interventions: The need for continuous systemic evaluation. *PLOS Medicine,* 6(8), e1000126.

Chao, H.H., Mayer, T., Concato, J., Rose, M.G., Uchio, E., & Kelly, W.K. (2010) Prostate cancer, comorbidity, and participation in randomized controlled trials of therapy. *Journal of Investigative Medicine,* 58, 566–568.

Cochrane, A.L. (1972) *Effectiveness and Efficiency. Random Reflections on Health Services.* London: Nuffield Provincial Hospitals Trust.

Cornish, F., & Gillespie, A. (2009) A pragmatist approach to the problem of knowledge in health psychology. *Journal of Health Psychology,* 14(6), 800–809.

Dyer, C. (2009) High court rejects challenge to NICE guidelines on chronic fatigue syndrome. *British Medical Journal,* 338, b1110.

Evidence-Based Medicine Working Group. (1992) Evidence-based medicine. A new approach to teaching the practice of medicine. *Journal of the American Medical Association,* 268(17), 1187–1192.

Fricker, M. (2007) Epistemic *Injustice: Power and the Politics of Knowing.* Oxford: Oxford University Press.

Goldacre, B. (2013) *Bad Pharma: How Medicine is Broken, and How We Can Fix It.* London: Fourth Estate.

Greenhalgh, T. (2010) *How To Read a Paper: The Basics of Evidence-Based Medicine*, 4th edition. London: Wiley-Blackwell.

Greenhalgh, T., Snow, R., Ryan, S., Rees, S., & Salisbury, H. (2015) Six 'biases' against patients and carers in evidence-based medicine. *BMC Medicine*, 13, 200.

Guyatt, G.H., Sackett, D.L., Sinclair, J.C., Hayward, R., Cook, D.J., & Cook, R.J. (1995) Users' guides to the medical literature. IX. A method for grading health care recommendations. *Journal of the American Medical Association*, 274, 1800–1804.

Howick, J. (2011) *The Philosophy of Evidence-Based Medicine.* Oxford: John Wiley & Sons Ltd.

Kelly, M., Heath, I., Greenhalgh, T., & Howick, J. (2015) The importance of values in evidence-based medicine. *BMC Medical Ethics*, 16(1), 69.

Kerridge, I. (2010) Ethics and EBM: Acknowledging bias, accepting difference and embracing politics. *Journal of Evaluation in Clinical Practice*, 16, 365–373.

Lundh, A., Krogsbøll, L.T., & Gøtzsche, P.C. (2011) Access to data in industry-sponsored trials. *The Lancet*, 378(9808), 1995–1996. Original Text.

Marks, D.F. (2009) How should psychology interventions be reported? *Journal of Health Psychology*, 44, 475–489.

Miles, A. (2009) On a medicine of the whole person: Away from scientific reductionism and towards the embrace of the complex in clinical practice. *Journal of Evaluation in Clinical Practice*, 15, 941–949.

Moncrieff, J. (2013) Psychiatric medication. In J. Cromby, D. Harper, & P. Reavey (Eds.). *Psychology, Mental Health and Distress.* London: Palgrave Macmillan, pp. 158–172.

NICE (a). www.nice.org.uk/aboutnice/whoweare/who_we_are.jsp Accessed 5 December.

NICE (b). www.nice.org.uk/aboutnice/about_nice.jsp Accessed 5 December 2013.

Prasad, V., Kim, C., Burotto, M., & Vandross, A. (2015) The strength of association between surrogate end points and survival in oncology. A systematic review of trial-level meta-analyses. *JAMA Internal Medicine*, 175, 1389–1398.

Sackett, D.L., Richardson, W.S., Rosenberg, W., & Haynes, R.B. (1997) *Evidence-Based Medicine: How to Practice and Teach EBM.* London: Churchill Livingstone.

Sackett, D.L., Rosenberg, W.M., Gray, J.A., Haynes, R.B., & Richardson, W.S. (1996) Evidence based medicine: What it is and what it isn't. *British Medical Journal*, 312 (7023), 71–72.

Sellars, C. & Easey, A. (2008) First successful legal challenge to NICE guidance. *Journal of Intellectual Property Law & Practice*, 3(11), 692–694.

Solesbury, W. (2001) Evidence based policy: Whence it came and where it's going. *ESRC UK Centre for Evidence Based Policy and Practice*: Working Paper 1.

Straus, S.E., Glasziou, P., Richardson, W.S. & Haynes, R.B. (2011) *Evidence-Based Medicine: How to Practice and Teach It*, 4th edition. Edinburgh: Churchill Livingstone.

Tannock, I.F., Amir, E., Booth, C.M., Niraula, S., Ocana, O., Seruga, B., Templeton, A.J., Vera-Badillo, F. (2016) Relevance of randomised controlled trials in oncology. *Lancet Oncology*, 359, e560–e567.

Tiefer, L. (2006) Female sexual dysfunction: A case study of disease mongering and activist resistance. *PLoS Medicine*, 3(4), e178. doi: 10.1371/journal.pmed.0030178.

Chapter 18

Teaching ethics for professional practice

Maria Castro Romero

A professional discipline's ethical code is meant to reflect the profession's values and purposes, and it is the individual's responsibility to know, understand and professionally abide by the standards for the professional group of which they are a member. However, teaching ethics cannot be a mere communication of professional codes. The chapter will begin by briefly commenting on ethical codes in the UK and those of other countries to exemplify how professional ethical codes are borne out of particular contexts. This will be followed by thinking about the link between the personal and professional, ways in which we can harness trainees' development as ethical professionals and then measuring teaching and practice/placement outcomes in relation to ethics. The aim of this chapter is to be of use to trainers and trainees in any of the diverse professional training courses available for psychologists, counsellors and psychotherapists and other health and social care professionals, such as social workers, psychiatrists or occupational therapists.

Professional ethics codes

There are several professional bodies in the UK regulating psychologists, counsellors and psychotherapists. The British Psychological Society (BPS), the British Association of Counsellors and Psychotherapists (BACP), Health and Care Professions Council (HCPC) and the United Kingdom Council for Psychotherapy (UKCP), all have their professional standards described in their individual codes, which members are expected to follow. Other countries' professional societies also subscribe to codes of conduct and ethical practice, for example, our neighbours in France, the Société Française de Psychologie (SFP), Italy, the Consiglio Nazionale Ordine Psicologi (CNOP) and Spain, the Colegio Oficial de Psicólogos (COP) or, further afield, the American Psychological Association (APA) and the Australian Psychological Society (APS).

All ethical codes have similar purposes, such as the protection of the public, promotion of sound professional practice and regulation of what is appropriate and what is inappropriate behaviour. They also contain details about the authority to scrutinise and discipline members to protect the integrity and interests of the profession. Nevertheless, professional societies differ in their approach to advising members of their particular professional standards. For example, the British Psychological Society (BPS) Code of Ethics and Conduct (2018) states that 'No code can replace the need for Psychologists to use their professional and ethical judgement' (p. 2); the Spanish code highlights explicit and implicit social norms (i.e. the importance of community), and what is thought of as suitable and unsuitable in any place and moment in time, as aspects to take into consideration (COP, 2014); and the French Psychology Society points out that 'the complexity of psychological situations opposes the automatic application of rules' (SFP, 2012: 1), calling for respect towards the code in the form of ethical reflection, rather than an obligation to follow the principles.[1]

Reconstructing ethics

This variation in ethical codes within one continent must maintain our curiosity about the range of positions taken when we include countries in other continents. Notwithstanding the fact that there are European (European Federation of Psychologists' Associations, 2005) and global codes (International Union of Psychological Science, 2008), more widely embracing codes may be impossible to incorporate locally, depending on each country's code (Stevens, 2010) and the levels of conflict with legal frameworks (Fisher, 2008).

The deontological[2] direction of ethics in our profession is Western, rather than multicultural or international and, hence, implies a privilege of particular views, which (no matter how well intended) can be perceived by some of the peoples or communities with whom we work as dissonant at best, and oppressive at worst. Some of these issues will be discussed further with regard to particular client population, see section 4 of this book.

It is, therefore, important to think critically about ethical codes, as arising contextually; in the UK, as holding Anglo-centric values, or an admittedly 'British eclectic tradition' (BPS, 2009: 4). Additionally, while the emphasis to 'Promote and protect the interests of service users and carers' (Standard 1, HCPC, 2016a: 5) would not be debated by anyone, we should deconstruct and in doing so highlight differing opinions, possibly opposing outcomes – what this statement means, for example:

- Who is involved in defining, and how are 'interests' defined?
- Who decides what are service users' interests?
- What happens if these are in conflict with carers' interest?
- Whose voice/s is/are stronger?
- What professional/personal ideas affect the decision-making process?

To answer these and other questions, in addition to the wider context of ethical codes, given that the personal and professional is inextricably linked, it is important to be aware of the ethics we bring into the profession as a result of our heritage and personal journeys.

The personal and professional

Since awareness and inquiry into one's own personal ethics are necessary to practise ethically, we must harness reflexivity and reflection as professionals. Freire (1998: 56) reminds us that 'our awareness of our unfinishedness makes us responsible beings, hence the notion of our presence in the world as ethical … it is only because we are ethical that we can also be unethical'. To be constantly mindful of this caution, I think of being ethical not as a state to which we aspire and can reach through appropriate training but as an action, as something we achieve by what we do, in what we do, upon which (as 'responsible beings') we need to be reflecting. In acknowledging the link between the personal and professional both our integrity and accountability are enhanced (Tomm, 1993), thus, also our being in the world ethically.

Perhaps because thinking about and discussing ethics is not generally part of most people's day-to-day life in our social context, it is possible for people to grow up and attend formal education without having much of a sense of their ethical principles – this is not to say that people will be unethical or without ethics, but that they may not have made explicit the values by which they live. However, by the time people access professional training, as well as having obtained background in the profession (academically and clinically), a degree of reflexivity and self-awareness has to be demonstrated to be offered a place for training. Although it is assumed that most trainees will have a good idea of their value base as a starting point, we need to move beyond becoming aware and making explicit our principles, to examining their history, consequences and contingencies, including:

- Where do these ethics come from?
- Which discourses and practices are they privileging and which are they undermining?
- What do these ethics do to how we position ourselves in the world and how we relate to others?
- What do these ethics do to how we position others (particularly people seeking our help) and how does this positioning influence their relating to us and to themselves?

The following vignette can facilitate reflection on these questions in relation to ethical dilemmas raised by situations practitioners could encounter in their work:

Vignette 1

Two male and one female white British, middle class psychologists, on ending their training, go to Zimbabwe to work for six months in a Trauma Service set up to provide Cognitive Behavioural Therapy (CBT) for Post-Traumatic Stress Disorder (PTSD). The Service was set up by UK psychologists because CBT is recommended by the National Institute for Health and Clinical Excellence (NICE) guidelines for the treatment of PTSD in the UK; the service is now led by a local psychiatrist and other local professionals. On their return to the UK, the three recently qualified psychologists recruit students in their final year of training to go to Zimbabwe to provide clinical supervision in the Trauma Service and training and teaching on local Counselling and Counselling Psychology courses.

Are the recently qualified psychologists:

1. Acting in a manner that demonstrates awareness of their gendered, ethnic and class-related identity, assumptions, beliefs and values?
2. Showing an awareness of the historical context of colonialism and oppression, and how this may influence what they bring to the Trauma Service and their relationships with the other professionals and people accessing the service?
3. Demonstrating a critical appraisal of PTSD and sensitivity to cultural differences in the application of NICE guidelines and CBT?
4. Respecting the ability of the psychiatrist and the other professionals in managing the Trauma Service, providing supervision and training?
5. Making decisions indicative of professional and ethical awareness and their level of competence and the level of competence of pre-qualifying colleagues?

Given the above, it is important for courses to begin training with a central engagement with ethics, for example, the Tree of Life methodology (Ncube, 2006) can be used to consider personal values and history as a welcome and getting to know each other exercise. Throughout the training, different pedagogical processes will also need to be utilised to aid the development of trainees as ethical professionals.

Teaching ethics

Ethics teaching, as the matter of ethics, is complex and multidimensional, and it involves the person as a whole (Pasmanik & Winkler, 2009); teaching is itself an ethical act, of co-involvement, co-researching and jointly venturing

(Freire, 1972, 1998), and is ultimately transformative for the educator and educands.[3] It is important to first contextualise where this teaching of ethics occurs, i.e. the ideas influencing our teaching, and my ethical base. I trained at the UEL Professional Doctorate in Clinical Psychology, which has historically favoured critical thinking – the relevance of this for teaching ethics is discussed below – and a social constructionist epistemology.[4] In addition to these ideas, the Narrative Framework (e.g. White & Epston, 1990), critical pedagogy (Freire, 1972, 1974, 1998; Hooks, 1994) and Liberation Psychology, in particular, the idea of doing psychology as doing ethics (Martín Baró, 1994), guide my thinking and teaching.

Ethical guidance and standards for professional training

In the UK, the UKCP Standards of Education and Training in Psychotherapy with Adults (2017) has one basic requirement:

> Training courses shall publish the Code of Ethics and Practice to which they adhere. This must include the UKCP ethical code. It may also include others such as the code(s) of the relevant UKCP college, the training organisation itself and/or another body.

> (p. 4)

There are further standards around the integration of ethics in all aspects of training and dedicated time for ethical reflection (p. 7), and an additional standard in Child Psychotherapy around 'knowledge base and practical competence' in 'Legal and Ethical Issues' (UKCP 2008: 4).

The BPS sets standards for the accreditation of professional doctorates in clinical psychology; ethics are the focus of the second of these standards (Table 18.1).

In recent years, the BPS has published guidance for teaching and assessing 'ethical competence' at all levels of psychology education (BPS, 2015a), in support of the BPS Code of Ethics and Conduct (2018) and revised Standards for the accreditation of Doctoral programmes in clinical psychology (2015b). Although it is a welcome development that the BPS is giving serious consideration to the teaching and assessment of ethics, this is centred around Rest's (1982) Four Component Model, which is just one model out of many and, in focussing on only one of these, there is a risk of limiting the options for thinking and teaching in relation to ethics. Furthermore, statements such as 'students usually know that they need to seek the client's valid and informed consent to an intervention' (British Psychological Society, 2015a: 17) obscure the complexity and uncertainty of therapeutic processes, or contexts such as involuntary hospitalisation or forensic settings, where engaging with care programmes is necessary to gain temporary leave and, eventually, discharge.

Table 18.1 Programme standard 2: working ethically

The programme must include teaching on the British Psychological *Society's Code of Ethics and Conduct*, and evaluation of students' understanding of working ethically, as appropriate to the level of study.

- The inclusion of this standard reflects the particular importance of ethics and ethical practice to psychologists.
- The *Society's Code of Ethics and Conduct* and supplementary ethical guidelines provide clear ethical principles, values and standards to guide and support psychologists' decisions in the difficult and challenging situations they may face. Further information can be found at www.bps.org.uk/ethics.
- The Society's Ethics Committee has produced Guidance on teaching and assessment of ethical competence in psychology education (2015a), available at www. bps.org.uk/ethics, which outlines ethical competencies, and how these may be taught and assessed at different levels of study. Programmes are encouraged to make use of the guidance as appropriate to their provision.
- In addition to providing teaching on the Society's Code of Ethics and Conduct and relevant supplementary ethical guidelines, Masters and Doctoral programmes are also expected to make students aware of the Health and Care Professions Council's Guidance on Conduct and Ethics for Students.
- All accredited programmes are expected to include formal teaching on ethics, and should be able to demonstrate how working ethically is integral to all aspects of their provision, including research (as outlined below), and placement activities (where applicable).
- Students need to understand the ethical frameworks that apply to their research, and how to engage with these, as well as understanding the ethical implications of the research that they encounter and working with people more generally.
- Programmes should also seek to foster appropriate understanding of and competencies in ethical decision-making and practice, both at the general level and specific to the sorts of situations and contexts that applied psychologists face in their work, at the appropriate level.
- In evaluating students' understanding of working ethically, education providers should have in place mechanisms for identifying and dealing with academic and professional misconduct, as appropriate to the programme(s) offered. The programme should consider the ways in which these mechanisms are publicised to students.

Source: Standards for the accreditation of Doctoral programmes in clinical psychology (British Psychological Society, 2015b: 40)

Ethics in the curriculum

It is unclear to what extent graduates will be conversant with ethics codes prior to commencing professional training; nonetheless, research shows that knowledge of ethical codes is not enough, as their guidance is not unproblematic. This is due to several reasons, such as conflict with legal parameters (Fisher, 2008; Knapp et al., 2007), psychologists agreeing with principles but not following these in clinical practice (Smith et al., 1991), not always consulting or steering themselves by ethics codes (Alvear et al., 2008) or feeling safer to follow their own judgment when they are experienced (Clemente et al., 2011), perhaps departing from ethical codes in relying on previous resolutions of ethical conflicts and related outcomes.

While, as stated above, there are different models for teaching ethics, such as Rest's (1982) or the Acculturation Model (Handelsman et al., 2005), ethics teaching requires the development of critical thinking, i.e. critical reflexivity and reflection. Teaching post-structuralist theories (e.g. Foucault, Gergen) introduces a useful frame of reference from the very beginning of training because 'critical reflection involves making explicit any ethical, political or social issues' (Smith, 2011: 217) and their effects. Hence, it makes sense for ethics teaching to be integral to all components of the programme, with teaching explicitly focusing on critical and ethical reflection. This is generally new to trainees and gets them questioning their previous knowledge. Unsurprisingly, trainees often report at the beginning of training that they feel 'de-skilled' or have lost their confidence. This resonates with the first of Taylor's (1987) four stages in the transformative process of learning to think critically: disorientation, exploration, reorientation and equilibrium. Although stages models over-simplify the learning process and any process for that matter – we could say that we try to help trainees onto the last stage of Taylor's model but this may not happen until, post-qualified when people reorient themselves to their work context and find their equilibrium in their particular setting. To assist development in a stimulating, perhaps challenging but supportive manner, various building blocks can be employed in teaching ethics, as illustrated below.

Video recording and public reflecting

As Freeman and Combs (1996: 285) explains 'there is nothing as effective as public reflection in training therapists to think and talk in respectful, non-pathologising terms about the people they work with.' Within clinical skills (which includes confidentiality, boundaries, note taking/keeping, etc.), video recordings can be used to, for example, practice introductions to persons referred for therapy regarding being a trainee (in accordance with HCPC, 2016b) or the limits of confidentiality. Working in small groups, each trainee can take turns in playing the different roles (e.g. therapist, person seeking help, family member). Through the review of the visual material with a programme team member, trainees can be facilitated and supported to reflect on their interactions from an observer position.

Other practices to enhance learning can include actors experienced in presenting clinical scenarios. Also, there can be small group sessions throughout the training programme in which trainees take their turn to present examples of their current practice so the group can help the trainee in unpacking assumptions, making links between the theory taught on the course and the work they are doing on placement and so on.

Experts by experience

While reflecting with a group of peers and tutors goes some distance in promoting ethical ways of thinking and talking about their work, it is key to involve people who access mental health services and their families in teaching; who are possibly the one audience to which we should be most accountable, because when people are 'othered' they are made more vulnerable to misconduct on the part of professionals. Further, breaking the them–us divide is not only a way to transparently hold ourselves accountable but an act of being ethical. Experts by experience are involved in teaching on every component on our programme, which includes planning (e.g. deciding on content) and conducting teaching, and setting exam questions to evaluate this. They are also involved in research, not in the usual capacity as participants but as consultants or co-researchers. Additionally, people who are/have accessed services and carers form the People's Committee, an expert panel with variable and open membership, to examine and influence selection, curriculum and placement review, in order to maintain ethics at the centre of the academic, research and practice aspects of the programme.

Personal and professional skills development (PPSD)

PPSD runs through the three years of training, using a range of structures to facilitate ethical personal and professional development of trainees. Teaching sessions in the style of workshops are aimed at providing trainees with a space to critically reflect on the profession, their professional identity and their place within the profession and wider contexts. These workshops are followed by small group sessions to provide a space, facilitated by the same tutor throughout training, to develop greater self-awareness and reflexivity.

In year two and three of the programme, in addition to the small PPSD groups, there are whole-cohort group sessions led by an external facilitator. It is intended that through PPSD trainees will be:

1. Familiar with general issues, such as registration, legal issues, codes of conduct, (e.g. the HPCP's *Standards of Conduct, Performance & Ethics*) etc., and the extent to which these might conflict with the interests of the people with whom we work
2. Able to identify and monitor their own level of self-awareness and ongoing development needs in this area; adopting an appropriately critical approach to reflective and reflexive practices; and understanding of their own gendered, ethnic, class-related, etc., history, identity, assumptions, beliefs, values and behaviour and their relevance to clinical practice

3. Understanding of how inequalities have evolved and been maintained in service provision within the NHS and of innovative services developed to be accessible and empowering to the people with whom we work
4. Aware of the socio-political and ethical contexts of clinical work and of the impact this may have on aspects of theory and practise, and able to evaluate and challenge discriminatory practices within clinical psychology in a constructive and professional manner

Vignette 2 illustrates how these outcomes could become directly relevant to challenges presented throughout the working life of psychotherapists, counsellors and psychologists.

Vignette 2

A psychotherapist has been away for a month from the unit in which she is based. On her return she meets Rose, a 70-year-old woman who was admitted the day after she left. She learns that Rose has spent the whole month nearly mute, looking at the floor, sat on a chair when out of her bed, and often crying. When her daughter visits, Rose asks her to take her home to care for her husband, who is housebound. Rose is kept in the unit although she is not under a section of the Mental Health Act and no Capacity Act Assessment has been carried out. The psychiatrist thinks Rose may have dementia and will need to go into residential care but there is no firm diagnosis. The psychotherapist engages with Rose, and with her daughter when she visits, and Rose becomes more communicative and active in the unit, helping other inpatients. The psychotherapist will soon leave the service but joins the Occupational Therapist in a home assessment, which goes very well and leads to plan a discharge home. After a few sessions preparing for endings, the psychotherapist says goodbye to Rose who requests a contact number from the psychotherapist for when she is in need when she is back home, as she feels the psychotherapist was the only person that truly helped her.

1. How might professional codes of conduct conflict with the interests of Rose?
2. How might this conflict be negotiated?
3. What may be the consequences of respecting this request and what may be the consequences of disregarding it both for Rose and for the psychotherapist?
4. Is it legal or ethical to keep Rose in the unit when she is asking to be home?
5. Should the psychotherapist have challenged this discriminatory practice of the unit and how might she have done this in a constructive and professional manner?

Although assessing the outcomes of ethics teaching is not unproblematic and runs the risk of simplifying something that in a way is not possible to formalise (Smith, 2011), there is a trimodal approach to evaluation.

Evaluating outcomes of ethics teaching

This is possibly a more difficult task than evaluating other teaching outcomes, because it is not a matter of mechanically following a set of generalised, guiding ethical principles but centring ethical practice as something of personal responsibility. The clinician-to-be should see each therapeutic conversation as a unique ethical encounter. This does not mean that we should do away with ethical codes, but there needs to be a critical engagement with these and, as well as the specificity of the person, family, group, organisation or community with whom we are working at any particular time, ethical responsibility needs to be central to ethical practice. Evidence of ethical personal and professional development should be found in various forms of formal programme assessment.

Academic work

In our programme, there are one essay and three practical reports, three exams, a service related research and a thesis project to complete throughout the training programme; for all of these, the marking criteria includes 'ethical and professional aspects' (see Table 18.2). In addition, each year there are essay titles specifically requiring a deep engagement with ethical issues, for example:

• If social inequalities are a main source of psychological problems what can clinical psychology contribute to this and how?
• '... psychologists have tried be to enter into the social process by way of the powers that be. The attempt at scientific purity has meant in practice taking the perspective of those in power.' (Martín-Baró, 1994: 29). How can we as clinical psychologists place ourselves in this process not alongside the dominator but alongside the dominated?

In answering these kinds of questions, and in the practical reports, trainees are encouraged to write in first person, to embody their ideas, which makes these able to be critically explored (Fook, 2002).

Clinical work

Learning in professional practice is evaluated by the placement supervisor and reviewed formally with one member of the programme team at midpoint, through a Mid-Placement Review meeting; the same tutor will follow the development of each trainee through the three years of training.

Table 18.2 Marking criteria for professional and ethical issues

Score 0–1	2–3	4–5	6–7	8–9	10
No consideration of ethical or professional issues.	Little evidence of awareness of ethical issues or professional issues.	Acknowledges ethical and professional issues; but with limited appreciation of import.	Sound ethical reasoning. Focuses on professional issues and perspectives.	Subtle ethical reasoning demonstrated. Shows good comprehension of professional issues.	Excellent appreciation of ethical issues. Evidence of independent thought on professional dilemmas.

At the end of each of the six placements there is a formal assessment of all aspects of learning on placement, the End of Placement Assessment, with qualitative and quantitative feedback on a range of competencies, including ethical professional development – each aspect is rated from 0 (not evident) to 3 (established); Table 18.3 contains examples on two domains.

Table 18.3 End of Placement Assessment

Personal and professional skills	*Understands ethical issues* and can *apply* to complex clinical contexts
	Appreciates the inherent power imbalance between practitioners and clients and *how abuse can be minimized*
	Exercises *personal responsibility* and largely autonomous initiative in complex and unpredictable situations in professional practice, *aware of limits of own competence and accepts accountability*
	Carries out work reliably, has good time keeping and *professional conduct*
	Works collaboratively with fellow psychologists, colleagues, service users and *respects diverse view points*
Transferable skills	Demonstrates *self-awareness* and working as reflective practitioner, including the *impact of one's own value base* upon clinical practice
	Able to think *critically, reflectively and evaluatively*

(italics added)

Critically reflecting on ethics teaching

One problem in setting and evaluating target outcomes is that this sits in the broader educational context of the competency framework, extensively critiqued, for example, for lack of validity and contextualisation, being reductionist, technical/mechanical and static (e.g. Akhurst et al., 2016; Collins, 1987; Dzjidic et al., 2013), which make it a poor framework for thinking about ethics, teaching and assessment.

In addition, it is important for teaching itself to be evaluated. We do this through asking trainees to reflect on the different aspects of the teaching, their practice and learning, and through our own reflection. Since teaching is an ethical act, the educator must live and teach with coherence to be an example of integrity – of being ethical. Our commitment to critical reflection needs to start from our practice, and it is only by continuing to scrutinise our work that we can own our position, rather than impose our assumptions on others. Freeman and Combs (1996) gathered some narrative practices that help this process:

- Situating ourselves (i.e. transparency)
- Listening and asking questions (i.e. not making assumptions)
- Accountability practices (e.g. counter-practices)
- Externalising conversations (i.e. collaborative relationships)
- Reflecting practices (e.g. outsider witness practice)
- Acknowledging the effects of relationships on us (i.e. catharsis).

Critical reflection of our values and how these link to our knowledge, including, of course, psychological knowledge, facilitates the building of relationships in which we are not omnipotent teachers or experts but 'fallible human beings' (Freeman & Combs, 1996: 275), to some extent redressing the power imbalance in teaching relationships so trainees can contextualise the teaching and critically engage with us as actors in their learning, i.e. 'educands'.

Conclusion

Developing as an ethical professional is interlinked with developing critical thinking, including a reflection on context and what one brings (reflexivity). Therefore, I began the chapter by, first, problematising ethics as universal and reconstructing ethics codes as contextual; they privilege a particular story of a specific time and place. Ethics codes should not be viewed as prescriptions to follow, but understood as principles with which to critically engage in developing a practice of being ethical. Second, linking the personal and professional; when we export our assumptions, including psychological concepts/models, we are imposing certain ethical underpinnings, communicating that what we know is right – which implicitly sets up the dichotomy 'what others know is wrong' or, at best, not quite as good. I presented ethics teaching as a collaborative endeavour set within particular programme structures. Perhaps one way of thinking about our approach to ethics teaching could be – turning the critical gaze inwards: through reflexiveness, reflecting and 'ethicalising' psychology, i.e. thinking of the ethics implicit in psychological knowledge and models and their practical application. The ideas and practices presented here are just one possibility that fits with our programme ethos; the close of this chapter is not a coming to an end but adding to the continued reflection on ethics and ethics teaching. As Freire (1998: 54–55) explains 'I cannot perceive myself as a presence in the world and at the same time explain it as a result of forces completely alien to me. If I do so, I simply renounce my historical, ethical, social and political responsibility for my own evolution …'

Reflective questions

1. Why is critical thinking important in developing as an ethical professional?
2. How can ethics teaching be part of the curriculum in professional training?
3. What teaching methods would work best for you in developing as a critical and ethical professional?
4. What difference might developing as a critical and ethical professional make in terms of your thinking and practice?

Notes

1 "La complexité des situations psychologiques s'oppose à l'application automatique de règles. Le respect des règles du présent Code de Déontologie repose sur une réflexion éthique et une capacité de discernement, dans l'observance des grands principes suivants."
2 Meaning 'duty-based'
3 Freire's (1972) term 'educands' reflects the active role or agency of students in their learning.
4 Situating knowledge claims in context instead of holding modernist assumptions about absolute truth.

References

Akhurst, J., Kagan, C., Lawthom, R., & Richards, M. (2016) Community psychology practice competencies: Some perspectives from the UK. *Global Journal of Community Psychology Practice*, 7(4), 1–15. www.gjcpp.org/pdfs/6Akhurst-etal.pdf.

Alvear, K., Pasmanik, D., Winkler, M.I., & Olivares, B. (2008) ¿Códigos en la postmo-dernidad? Opiniones de psicólogos/as acerca del Código de Ética Profesional del Cole-gio de Psicólogos de Chile A.G. *Terapia Psicológica*, 26, 215–228.

British Psychological Society.(2009) *Code of Ethics and Conduct. Guidance published by the Ethics Committee of the British Psychological Society*. Leicester: British Psycho-logical Society.

British Psychological Society. (2015a) *Guidance on Teaching and Assessment of Ethical Competence in Psychology Education*. Leicester: British Psychological Society.

British Psychological Society (BPS). (2015b) *Standards for the Accreditation of Doctoral Programmes in Clinical Psychology*. Leicester: British Psychological Society.

British Psychological Society (BPS). (2018) *Code of Ethics and Conduct. Guidance pub-lished by the Ethics Committee of the British Psychological Society*. Leicester: British Psychological Society.

Clemente, M., Espinosa, P., & Urra, J. (2011) Ethical issues is psychologists' professional practice: Agreement over problematic professional behaviours among Spanish psych-ologists. *Ethics & Behaviour*, 21(1), 13–34.

Colegio Oficial de Psicólogos (COP). (2014). Código Deontológico. www.cop.es/pdf/CodigoDeontologicoPsicologo-Modif-AprobadaJGral13-12-14.pdf

Collins, M. (1987) *Competence in Adult Education: A New Perspective*. Lanham: Univer-sity Press of America.

Dzjidic, P., Breen, L.J., & Bishop, B.J. (2013) Are our competencies revealing our weak-nesses? A critique of community psychology practice competencies. *Global Journal of Community Psychology Practice*, 4(4), 1–10.

European Federation of Psychologists' Associations. (2005) Meta-code of ethics. http://ethics.efpa.eu/metaand-model-code/meta-code/

Fisher, M.A. (2008) Protecting confidentiality rights: The need for an ethical practice model. *American Psychologist*, 63(1), 1–13.

Fook, J. (2002) *Critical Theory and Practice*. London: Sage.

Freeman, J., & Combs, G. (1996) *Narrative Therapy: The Social Construction of Pre-ferred Realities*. London: Norton.

Freire, P. (1972) *Pedagogy of the Oppressed*. Harmondsworth: Penguin.

Freire, P. (1974) *Education for Critical Consciousness*. New York: Continuum.

Freire, P. (1998) *Pedagogy of Freedom. Ethics, Democracy, and Civic Courage*. Lanham: Rowman & Littlefield.

Handelsman, M.M., Gottlieb, M.C., & Knapp, S. (2005) Training ethical psychologists: An acculturation model. *Professional Psychology: Research and Practice*, 36, 59–65.

Health and Care Professions Council. (2016a) *Guidance on Conduct and Ethics for Stu-dents*. www.hcpc-uk.org/assets/documents/10002C16Guidanceonconductandethicsforstudents.pdf

Health and Care Professions Council (HCPC). (2016b) Standards of conduct, perform-ance and ethics. www.hcpc-uk.org/assets/documents/10004EDFStandardsofconduct,performanceandethics.pdf

Hooks, B. (1994) *Teaching to Transgress. Education as the Practice of Freedom*. New York: Routledge.

International Union of Psychological Science. (2008) *Universal Declaration of Ethical Principles for Psychologists*. www.iupsys.net/about/governance/universal-declaration-of-ethical-principles-for-psychologists.html

Knapp, S., Gottlieb, M., Berman, J., & Handelsman, M.M. (2007) When laws and ethics collide: What should psychologists do? *Professional Psychology: Research and Practice*, 38(1), 54–59.

Martín-Baró, I. (1994) *Writings for a Liberation Psychology*. Harvard: Harvard University Press.

Ncube, N. (2006) The tree of life project: Using narrative ideas in work with vulnerable children in Southern Africa. *The International Journal of Narrative Therapy and Community Work*, 1, 3–16.

Pasmanik, D., & Winkler, M.I. (2009) Searching for orientation: Guidelines for teaching professional ethics in psychology in a context with a post-modern emphasis. *Psykhe*, 18(2), 37–49.

Rest, J. (1982). A psychologist looks at the teaching of ethics. The Hastings Center Report, 12(1), 29–36.

Smith, E. (2011) Teaching critical self-reflection. *Teaching in Higher Education*, 16(2), 211–223.

Smith, T.S., McGuire, J.M., Abbott, D.W., & Blau, B.I. (1991) Clinical ethical decision-making: An investigation of the rationales used to justify doing less than one believes one should. Professional Psychology. *Research and Practice*, 22, 235–239.

Société Française de Psychologie. (2012). Code de déontologie des psychologues. www.codededeontologiedespsychologues.fr/LE-CODE.html

Stevens, M.J. (2010) Etic and emic in contemporary psychological ethics. *Europe's Journal of Psychology*, 4, 1–7.

Taylor, M. (1987) Self-directed learning: More than meets the observer's eye. In D. Boud, & V. Griffin (Eds.). *Appreciating Adults Learning: From the Learner's Perspective*. London: Kogan Page, pp. 179–196.

Tomm, K. (1993) The ethics of dual relationships. *Dulwich Centre Newsletter, 3 & 4*, 2–9.

UK Council for Psychotherapy. (2008) *Standards of Education and Training. Guidelines for Sections for the Development of Training Standards in Child Psychotherapy: Full Training*. London: UKCP.

UK Council for Psychotherapy. (2017) *Standards of Education and Training. The Minimum Core Criteria Psychotherapy with Adults*. London: UKCP.

White, M., & Epston, D. (1990) *Narrative Means to Therapeutic Ends*. London: Norton.

Chapter 19

Training supervision
Professional and ethical considerations

Jean Morrissey

Clinical supervision plays an integral role in the process of becoming a counsellor, psychologist, psychotherapist or psychiatrist and is a recommended contributory element of continuing professional development for many mental health practitioners. The knowledge, skills and modelling that a supervisor conveys are important aspects of helping the supervisee to assist their client by offering support, a reflexive safe space to explore successes and difficulties, an opportunity to learn, as well as promote best practice in both the therapeutic and supervisory relationships. However, the nature of clinical supervision and in particular, training supervision engenders several important professional and ethical considerations for both participants of the supervisory dyad. Such considerations therefore require serious attention in terms of their impact on the welfare of the client and the process of learning. This chapter examines some of these issues and their potential to influence the supervisory experience. Although the chapter focuses on training supervision, ideas and application will also be of relevance to qualified practitioners either in their role of supervisor, supervisee or both. The term supervision will refer to clinical supervision throughout the chapter.

Understanding supervision

From the outset, it is important to clarify what is meant by supervision; essentially supervision is an experiential learning process whereby a 'psychotherapeutic practitioner (or trainee) presents their client work to a designated supervisor as a way of enhancing their practice through careful reflection and reflexive practice on the process' (UKCP, 2018: 3). Supervision is a process within a formal working relationship with an explicit purpose that is to promote and protect the ongoing welfare of the client and the development of the supervisee (Carroll, 1996, 2014). This dualistic role incorporates many functions of supervision including educating, supporting and monitoring the supervisee's professional and clinical development, and where supervision is part of a training it has the additional function of assessing and evaluating the supervisee's professional learning and development. It is important to note that supervision is not personal therapy nor is it a form of, or substitute for, line management or appropriate training.

Although there is no legal requirement for supervision, all the major professional bodies regulating counsellors, psychologists and psychotherapists such as, the British Association of Counsellors and Psychotherapists (BACP) (2018), the British Psychological Society (BPS) (2017, 2018), Health and Care Professions Council (HCPC) (2016) and the United Kingdom Council for Psychotherapy (UKCP) (2018) acknowledge and support the role of supervision as a core element of professional training. Supervision can take place in facilitated groups, peer groups, on a one-to-one basis, by telephone or by use of digital media. Appropriate modes of supervision will need to be determined by the circumstances and use of different methods (BACP, 2018; BPS, 2017; UKCP, 2018). Guidance about the frequency of supervision and the specified number of supervision sessions for trainees, qualifications of the supervisor and format, i.e. individual or group supervision vary across the different therapeutic approaches, training organisations and accrediting professional bodies (BACP, 2018; BPS, 2018; UKCP, 2018). For example, the current requirement for a BACP accredited course is 1: 8 ratio of supervision to client work, the frequency of which should be not less than fortnightly and include a combination of individual and group supervision (BACP, 2018). The specified number of supervision sessions for trainees, for example, for their Chartered status varies across different sub-disciplines of psychology (BPS, 2017). Supervision, however, does not end post training; the BACP, clinical and counselling psychology divisions of the BPS and many sections of the UKCP all consider supervision as a basic ethical and professional expectation in order to support effective practice. All members, therefore, are expected to engage in regular supervision for their client work from a suitably appropriate person throughout their working career. Recognising that quantity itself cannot ensure either the quality of the supervision received or meet the needs of all supervisees, specific number of supervision hours are not stated for registered BACP members. Instead, it is the responsibility of each supervisee to have supervision at a frequency and duration that allows discussion of all aspects of the person's work in all contexts, and considers the demands or complexities of each supervisee's caseload, level of experience and training, development needs and aims along with any specific issues and difficulties. Similarly, the BACP requires all practicing supervisors to have regular ongoing supervision for their supervised work.

The mandatory nature of regular ongoing supervision post training has raised debates; one argument that challenges the role of mandatory supervision is the paucity of empirical evidence about its impact on the outcome of clinical practice. Notwithstanding the ample anecdotal evidence about the efficacy of supervision, the lack of empirical data about how or whether supervision works raises questions for all stakeholders, including client change, which Ellis and Ladany (1997) identifies as the gold standard of supervision outcome. For further coverage of discussion concerning supervision measures see Beinart and Clohessy (2017) and Watkins and Milne (2014, part 4).

Supervision – consultative and training

Supervision is invariably described as either consultative or training supervision. 'Consultative supervision refers to the process whereby an experienced and qualified practitioner seeks consultation with a peer or a more experienced therapist concerning their clinical work, whereas training supervision describes the process of supervision for therapists during training' (Gilbert & Evans, 2000: 3). For the supervisor, the latter involves a position of authority and power, and almost invariably a responsibility to assess formally the trainee's ongoing professional development and competence. Although the supervisor's responsibility will differ considerably between the two types of supervision, the responsibility to ensure ethical standards are maintained throughout the therapeutic process applies to both.

Formats of supervision

There are many different formats of supervision; individual supervision is the most frequently used modality and group supervision is a close second. While training organisations commonly use both, each format presents different learning opportunities and challenges that are often interchangeable and context dependent (Carroll, 1996). Exposure to both can provide a good learning opportunity for supervisees – whereby they can experience both the intensive attention of individual supervision and the opportunity to contribute to and learn with others in a group. This can help supervisees to identify which format might best meet their learning needs at the different stages of their professional development. Similarly, it is important for supervisors to be aware of their preferred format and areas of development. In practice, however, constraints of time, finance or expertise often dictate the supervision format for both supervisees and supervisors, which in turn can influence the quality of the supervisory experience. Ideally, the best use of group or individual supervision should start from a positive choice for all participants, yet compromises are likely to be a reality. Supervisees may express a preference for individual supervision, which is often considered a more traditional format; however, limited evidence exists that either format takes precedence in terms of their training outcomes, albeit from a small literature base (Mastroas & Andrews, 2011).

Supervision models

Over the last 50 years, numerous supervision-specific models have emerged concerning different components of supervision, for example:

- Developmental Models (Stoltenberg et al., 1998)
- Functions model (Inskipp & Proctor, 1995a and 1995b)
- System's Approach (Holloway, 1995)
- Tasks Model (Carroll, 1996); (Scaife, 2019)
- Cyclical Model (Page & Wosket, 2015)
- Seven-Eyed (Process) Model (Hawkins & Shohet, 2012)
- Supervisory relationship (Beinart, 2012)

All of these supervision-specific models inform and guide how supervision is currently understood and applied in practice. Not surprisingly, there are differences as to how the generally agreed aims of supervision might be best applied and achieved. Such differences can sometimes lead to misunderstandings and misconceptions about the meaning of supervision and more importantly its application in practice. Establishing a shared understanding and agreement between all participants involved in the supervision contract about its purpose and practice is essential from the outset. Issues related to contracting will be addressed later in the chapter.

> **Reflective questions**
>
> Take a few minutes to reflect on and answer the following questions
>
> - What words would you use to describe supervision?
> - What is your preferred format of supervision and why?
> - What model of supervision are you familiar with as a supervisee and/or supervisor?
> - What do you expect from supervision?

Learning to be a supervisee

Carroll (1996) believes that it is the supervisor's responsibility to educate the trainee about the role of supervision and how to prepare for it; in contrast, Inskipp and Proctor (1995a) argue that this responsibility lies with the training organisation. Reflecting on my own experience as a supervisor – while most trainees increasingly receive some preparation about the use of supervision, the extent of the preparation can and does vary between different training organisations. However varied the preparation, the supervisor needs to establish the supervisee's prior understanding and experience of supervision from the outset and facilitate their learning accordingly. It is important that supervisees and particularly those who have minimal experience of supervision are prepared so that they can make the best use of supervision either as individuals or in a group, as illustrated in the fictitious vignette below. The latter is also important when working with novice trainees who understandably may find it difficult to distinguish the boundaries between supervision and therapy, particular as both share situational and behavioural similarities. For example, both are helping processes, comprise an authority – dependency relationship and use albeit differently similar skills (Page & Wosket, 2015). However, they are not the same, each is a separate activity with different aims; 'the aim of supervision is to help supervisees become better therapeutic workers whereas the aim in counselling stresses becoming a better person' (Carroll, 1996: 59), nonetheless, the centrality of the working alliance is essential for both.

> **Vignette I**
>
> Borgen is a trainee therapist on a three-year degree programme in integrative counselling/psychotherapy. She has just completed her second year and is about to commence her clinical placement whereby she will take on a small case load of two clients. Her course tutor has provided a list of supervisors and discussed the role of supervision and how to prepare for it. As part of her course requirements, she is required to attend individual supervision fortnightly. Knowing that you have much experience of supervision, Borgen seeks your advice about choosing a supervisor and asks the following questions. How would you respond to her questions?
>
> - What questions should I ask when contacting/meeting a supervisor?
> - What is considered a good supervisor?
> - How do I prepare for supervision?
> - What factors do you think are the most important for trainees new to supervision when choosing a supervisor and why?
> - What would you recommend that I do to get most from supervision?

The supervisory relationship

Whether it comprises a dyad or a group, the supervisory relationship plays a crucial role in the learning and acquisition of knowledge and skills. Central to this process of learning is the quality of the supervisory relationship (Beinart & Clohessy, 2017; Creaner, 2014). Supervising trainees is a complex interpersonal process and usually involves a number of potentially conflicting relationships and interrelationships. These comprise the client, the supervisee's placement/agency, personal therapist and training organisation, together with the anxieties and particular learning needs of the trainee, and the requirement of a formal assessment. The supervisor must consider all issues especially in terms of their effect upon the learning alliance. Codes of ethics can and do provide boundaries and determine some aspects of the supervisory relationship however, they cannot determine how the relationship is translated into practice or indeed its quality. Furthermore, codes on their own cannot cover all supervisory eventualities or the contexts in which they occur – each supervisory situation is different and therefore requires individual professional judgement, which at times can be both complex and challenging.

Supervision and boundaries

Similarly to the therapeutic relationship, supervision is characterised by certain codes of practice and boundaries. As Bond (2015) points out, it is equally important to have a sound ethical foundation within the supervisory relationship as it is for the client in the therapeutic relationship. In training supervision, however, one of the most fundamental challenges is whether it is possible, and if so how, to provide safety and containment that encourages risk taking and non-defensive behaviour while simultaneously having an assessment role. Undoubtedly, occupying and managing the dual relationship of supervisor and assessor presents several professional and ethical challenges for both participants of the supervisory dyad, particularly given the power differential that exists between the supervisor and supervisee (Murphy & Wright, 2005). These issues will be discussed further in this chapter.

Dual relationships of any sort can be problematic. For example, if a supervisor is a supervisor as well as manager, this is potentially problematic, as it may include the loss of objectivity due to conflict of interest, different objectives, a compromising of confidentiality, and as a result can interfere with the supervisor's capacity to carry out their role effectively. Supervisors therefore have a responsibility to establish and maintain appropriate boundaries that are clearly distinguished from other significant relationships, such as a spouse, business partner or other relationships with whom would cause a potential conflict of interest. Sexual relationships between the supervisor and supervisee are prohibited by all professional codes of conduct and ethics and the general expectation is that the supervisory relationship will be kept clearly separate from any managerial role, although in reality this does not always happen.

Establishing the supervision contracting: bilateral agreement

Contracting in supervision as in therapy plays a vital function in underpinning the entire supervisory process and relationship, that is to contain, support and direct the agreed working alliance and goals for supervision. In creating the working agreement both parties clarify and negotiate the boundaries, expectations, learning styles, roles, responsibilities, and the purpose and tasks of supervision, which then guides and outlines the agreed working alliance and goals for supervision (Beinart & Clohessy, 2017; Morrissey, 1998; Page & Wosket, 2015). In training supervision, negotiation of the contract should also include information and discussion about the assessment process, procedures and requirements. Although the contracting process usually takes places at the outset, it is an ongoing process, subject to regular reviews and re-contracting as and when the supervisee's learning needs change. The way in which the supervisor conducts the negotiation process will vary depending on the supervisor's theoretical orientation, style of facilitation and experience as a supervisor. The formality with which such agreements are made may also vary from formal and written to informal and unrecorded.

The contracting process itself also helps supervisees to begin to think about their learning needs, preferred learning styles as well as how they might make the best use of their supervision time. However, for many novices and even some experienced supervisees, expressing their learning needs and goals to a person in a position of authority and power, i.e. the supervisor, and where supervision comprises a group other supervisees or peers, can often be an unfamiliar and anxiety-provoking experience. Acknowledging and encouraging openness from the outset while at the same time ensuring that the needs of the supervisee and client can best be met, can also help reduce supervisees' anxieties and fear of disclosure. This, of course, is dependent on the supervisor's judgement and skill in knowing how best to assist each supervisee engage in the contracting process. Nevertheless, it is essentially the supervisees' responsibility to make use, or at least begin to, the opportunities made available to them.

Contracting – multilateral agreement

Supervising trainees may also involve the same person in a series of many different interrelated contracts; for example, the supervisor may also be employed by the training organisation or placement agency in the role of a trainer or consultant. Alternatively, the supervisor may work independently and have no direct relationship with either of the above, other than through the supervisee. Working with and within such complexity highlights the importance of a shared understanding and agreement between all parties, particularly about clinical responsibility and confidentiality issues. This then raises the question of responsibility for establishing a clear working agreement between the placement agency, training organisation or the supervisor. As part of good practice for the management of clinical placements, training courses may initiate the supervisory agreement however, this is not always the case or should be relied upon. The BACP (2018: 23) states that 'Careful consideration will be given to the undertaking of key responsibilities for clients and how these responsibilities are allocated between the supervisor, supervisee and any line manager or others with responsibilities for the service provided'. Such arrangements also need to be reviewed at least once a year, or more frequently if required. Failure to do so may result in each assuming that the other is clinically responsible for the work undertaken by the trainee or alternatively the supervisor may find themselves in a situation where they may be left carrying the responsibility, without knowing this. Both place the client, trainee and supervisor in a vulnerable position. Best practice requires that there should be an explicit working agreement between all parties – supervisor, training organisation and placement agency and at best prior to the trainee commencing clinical practice. Failure to do so increases the possibility for misunderstanding and miscommunication both within and beyond that of the bilateral agreement. Details of each contract will vary; however, clarification and agreement of the requirements, expectations and responsibilities will always need to include the following as outlined below by Izzard (2001: 89). See Scaife (2019) for greater coverage of the contracting process in supervision.

- expected caseload for a trainee
- need for suitable clients to be allocated
- lines of accountability for the trainee's clinical work
- the complaints procedure that should be followed by clients
- lines of communication for routine feedback and in case of concern
- evaluation process, including criteria of assessment
- code of ethics and practice within which each party practices.

Vicarious responsibility

From a legal perspective, lines of accountability for clinical practice differ between America and Britain. In the US, supervisors have been legally held accountable for the work of their supervisees see the Tarasoff case established in US law (Tarasoff v. Regents of the University of California, 1974). In Britain, the position is somewhat different in that there is no line of responsibility between the client and supervisor, although case law remains to be tested. The BACP (2018: 23) states 'when supervising qualified and/or experienced practitioners, the weight of responsibility for ensuring that the supervisee's work meets professional standards will primarily rest with the supervisee'. Nonetheless, supervisors cannot abdicate responsibility and 'supervisors will conscientiously consider the application of the law concerning supervision to their role and responsibilities'. Clearly, several issues would need to be examined before the supervisor could be held responsible for any harm caused by the supervisee's actions. However, if the supervisor was aware of or anticipated a potential problem between the supervisee and client and failed to act promptly and appropriately, the supervisor could to some degree be held responsible for any harm caused to the client. Trainee supervision will require the supervisor to collaborate with training and placement providers in order to ensure that the trainee's work with clients satisfies professional standards. The arrangements for collaboration will usually be agreed and discussed with the trainee in advance of working with clients (BACP, 2018: 23). The fiduciary role of the supervisor, that is, an obligation of one party to act in the best interest of another, concerns the *obligation* of the supervisor to act in the best interest of both the supervisee and client therefore not only carries a responsibility for taking an ethical approach to conducting supervision but also the responsibility to ensure that the supervisee's practice is both safe and ethical (Scaife, 2009). As such, having access to legal representation via professional indemnity insurance is essential for both supervisors and supervisees. This is in addition to any insurance that may be provided by a placement, employer or training institution.

Confidentiality

The duty of confidentiality in supervision is twofold – it applies to both clients and supervisees. Legally and ethically the emphasis is on protecting all personal identifiable information, including client details. Best practice therefore requires all case material in supervision to be anonymous. For supervisees, it is essential to inform clients that confidential communication will be shared with the supervisor and to obtain their consent. Clients also need to be informed of the limits of confidentiality where supervision comprises a group. Similarly, supervisees need to be informed of the parameters of confidentiality such as, where information is shared with the supervisor's own supervisor and whether information (if any) is shared with the training organisation or clinical placement, as well as how this might affect the use of supervision. Maintaining confidentiality requires the supervisor to be mindful of any potential situations whereby the supervisee might unknowingly be at risk of breaching confidentiality and to take appropriate action. Essentially, the supervisory relationship must be confidential, yet given the different circumstances of each case it is difficult, if not impossible to provide absolutes. Clearly any breach of confidentiality by the supervisor is never an easy decision and requires careful consideration about the needs of the client and supervisee, although fundamentally the client's welfare must take precedence. For, example the supervisor may have to inform the trainee's training organisation that the trainee is not fit to practice at that time. Such decisions also require collegial and supervisory support and discussion about the presenting professional, ethical and legal issues of the client case, along with the consequences of taking action (or not) rather than simply responding to a code of ethics. See Chapters 5 and 14 for further discussion on confidentiality issues concerning *confidentiality in social media use*.

Dual-role relationships within supervision

As previously mentioned, the nature of training supervision often involves the supervisor occupying a dual role – supervisor and assessor – suitable to enhancing the trainee's learning and professional development. These roles are integrated into the tasks of supervision and include the role of educator with that of providing support, monitoring and in most situations assessing and evaluating the trainee's professional and clinical competence. Managing these roles can be challenging since the expectations and responsibilities can appear to contradict or compete with each other and as a result may compromise the role of the supervisor as well as the quality of the supervisory relationship. For example, whereby the supervisor facilitates the learning process by offering support, encouragement and guidance and yet at the same time has a responsibility to monitor, challenge and evaluate the trainee's professional learning and competence. These roles are further compounded by the unequal relationship inherent in training supervision. This raises the question whether the role of the supervisor and assessor should be kept clearly separate. Even if such roles were separate, Barden (2001) argues that supporting and monitoring must be viewed as a dual role of the supervisor, as the monitoring functions aims to keep the counsellor and the client safe and therefore the 'complete absence of a monitoring role is neither possible or desirable' (p. 53). Besides, failure to provide evaluative feedback raises serious ethical concern because the supervisor fails to provide one of the most essential tasks of supervision. For the supervisor, being able to effectively handle these roles is of critical importance to ensure the welfare of the client and that the tasks of supervision are carried out to the highest possible standard. Notwithstanding this, in practice this is sometimes easier said than done.

Supervisors have a responsibility for monitoring and assessing supervisees' performance consistently, carefully and constructively. As previously mentioned, issues concerning the process and procedure of the assessment should be discussed at the outset of the supervisory relationship. In order to make a judgement about the trainee's performance; the supervisor must have sufficient knowledge about the trainee's professional and clinical competence, particularly when acting in the role of gatekeeper to the profession (Scaife, 2019). The responsibility to evaluate the trainee can be anxiety provoking for both members of the supervisory dyad. No matter what efforts are made to minimise it, both are aware that the supervisor's judgement may affect the supervisory relationship and in some instances the trainee's professional career. Occasionally supervisors will encounter a trainee who is either unwilling or unable to learn the skills necessary for effective therapy, or who might be considered 'unfit' to practice. In such instances, the supervisor has a responsibility to fail the trainee or recommend that the supervisee temporarily withdraw from clinical practice. Such actions are never an easy task and are only carried out after much consideration and discussion with the trainee, training organisation and having explored and implemented various remedial strategies to assist the trainee in their difficulties. As always, such actions are guided by the supervisor's primary responsibility to the client, public and profession.

Disclosure and supervision

In supervision, disclosure of case information as well as the supervisee's (trainee's) thoughts feelings and behaviours are considered important given that the supervisor depends on this information to improve understanding of the client and possibly enhance the supervisee's professional and therapeutic development (Bernard & Goodyear, 2014). However, evidence suggests that when confronted with professional and/or ethical dilemmas, trainees may with-hold important information either consciously or unconsciously (Hess et al., 2008; Mehr et al., 2010), which, may contribute to reduced clinical effectiveness and missed learning opportunities (Gray et al., 2001). Non-disclosure of relevant material may also lead to increased exposure to risk for the client, supervisee, colleagues and supervisor (Pearson, 2000). The reasons in supervision for non-disclosure are numerous. Supervision can be a threatening experience often involving the trainee feeling under scrutiny and experiencing uncomfortable feelings of *shame* or not being *good enough* and as a result they may find it difficult to disclose particular difficulties or mistakes to the supervisor (Singh-Pilay & Cartwright, 2018; Yourman, 2003). Therefore, not unlike the therapeutic relationship, change can be both desired and simultaneously feared, and in seeking help the trainee may therefore defend their ways in which they has previously learned. Clearly such responses will vary with each trainee and depend on their prior experience of supervision, level of professional and personal development as well as the nature of the supervisory relationship. In addition, the responses of both the supervisee and supervisor are likely to be laden with transferential reactions, which are bound to influence the supervisory relationship and the process of learning. The presence of other factors both within and outside the supervisory context are also likely to influence the extent of the supervisee's level of disclosure in supervision, however, the quality of the supervisory relationship plays a significant influencing role. Essential to this experience is the supervisor's ability to assist the supervisee to overcome his/her fears by creating and maintaining a safe and supportive learning environment whereby the supervisee may feel safe to openly share difficult issues while at the same time provide constructive feedback to enhance the supervisee's personal and professional development as a practitioner. This, of course, cannot be prescribed and like everything else in the supervisory experience is context dependent and grounded in supervisory skill and judgement rather than being a product of chronology.

Reflective questions

- What material/issues have you not disclosed, when and for what reasons?
- Thinking about this now, what have you learnt from this non-disclosure

---

The supportive role in supervision

The supportive role involves offering supervisees a forum to reflect on their personal reactions arising from working with clients, or indeed with supervisors. This function includes the use of counselling skills although in supervision the central task is to focus on the work between supervisee and client. Based upon the arguments of dual relationships, the supervisor should not become, intentionally or unintentionally, the supervisee's therapist yet sometimes there may be instances where it is difficult or unethical not to be. As with many ethical dilemmas, determining the boundaries between counselling as personal therapy and counselling as a role within supervision is rarely clear-cut, as illustrated in the following fictitious vignette.

Vignette 2

Niamh is a trainee counselling psychologist working in an Adult Mental Health Centre. She has been attending supervision with Louise for about eight months, on a fortnightly basis. During one meeting, Louise, noticed that Niamh was unusually unfocussed and distant when presenting her work, and commented on this. At this point Niamh began to cry uncontrollably. After a while she told her supervisor that her marriage of ten years had ended and she didn't know how to tell her two young sons. Louise asked Niamh if she wished to use the remaining time to talk about this further or to continue with her clinical work. She chose to use her supervision time primarily to talk about her feelings of loss. Louise listened empathetically and explored Niamh's support structures. In this situation the supervisor used counselling to understand how Niamh's personal problems was affecting her performance while at the same time giving her the responsibility to find ways to help her during this difficult time.

Conclusion

Supervision clearly plays a central role in promoting and maintaining best practice within the therapeutic profession. However, the demand for a shared understanding and agreement of the tasks and responsibilities by all participants is essential if safe ethical practice and learning is to take place. The supervisory relationship is central to determining the quality of the learning alliance and as such the supervisor is required to conduct the various complex tasks professionally and ethically. The role of supervision carries a responsibility to address/consider the needs of the client, supervisee and public as well as the profession. Given the complexity of such relationships and responsibilities as well as the power differential involved, many ethical dilemmas can arise, including issues of confidentiality, competency, dual relationships and clinical accountability. As with all ethical dilemmas there are often no absolutes and therefore each situation must be given careful professional thought and judgement to ensure best practice. While professional codes and guidelines provide some guidance and support, they are by no means conclusive or intended to be prescriptive. This being the case, supervisors must have the capacity to be ethically minded in undertaking their challenging but important role.

Reflective questions

1. How does supervision differ from therapy?
2. In what way has your experience of clinical supervision enhanced your professional learning and competence? Give examples.
3. What issues relating to your clinical work have you withheld or been tempted to withhold from your supervisor and for what reasons?
4. What aspects of the supervisory experience have helped or hindered your professional learning and development? Give examples

---

References

Barden, N. (2001) The responsibility of the supervisor in the British Association for Counselling and Psychotherapy's Codes of Ethics and Practice. In S. Wheeler, & D. King (Eds.). *Supervising Counsellors: Issues of Responsibility*. London: Sage, pp. 41–58.

Beinart, H. (2012) Models of supervision and the supervisory relationship. In I. Fleming, & L. Steen (Eds.). *Supervision and Clinical Psychology: Theory Practice and Perspectives*. Hove, UK: Brunner–Routledge, pp. 36–50.

Beinart, H., & Clohessy, S. (2017) *Effective Supervisory Relationships Best Evidence and Practice*. Chichester, UK: Wiley Blackwell.

Bernard, J.M., & Goodyear, R. (2014) *Fundamentals of Clinical Supervision*, 5th edition. Harlow, UK: Pearson.

Bond, T. (2015) *Standard and Ethics for Counselling in Action*, 4th edition. London: Sage.

British Association for Counselling and Psychotherapy. (2018) *Ethical Framework for the Counselling Professions*. Leicestershire: BACP.

British Psychological Society. (2017) *Professional Practice Guidelines: Third Edition*. Leicester: BPS.

British Psychological Society. (2018) Code of ethics and conduct. www.bps.org.uk/news-and-policy/bps-code-ethics-and-conduct accessed 1.5.18.

Carroll, M. (1996) *Counselling Supervision Theory, Skills and Practice*. London: Cassell.

Carroll, M. (2014) *Effective Supervision for the Helping Professions*, 2nd edition. London: Sage.

Creaner, M. (2014) *Getting the Best Out of Supervision in Counselling and Psychotherapy*. London: Sage.

Ellis, M.V., & Ladany, N. (1997) Inferences concerning supervisees and clients in clinical supervision: An integrative review. In C.E. Watkins (Ed.). (2014) *Handbook of Psychotherapy Supervision*. Hoboken, NJ: Wiley, pp. 447–507.

Gilbert, M., & Evans, K. (2000) *Psychotherapy Supervision an Integrative Relational Approach to Psychotherapy Supervision*. Buckingham: Open University Press.

Gray, L.A., Ladany, N., Walker, J.A., & Ancis, J.R. (2001) Psychotherapy trainees' experience of counterproductive events in supervision training and education in professional psychology. *Training and Education in Professional Psychology*, 6(4), 229–237.

Hawkins, P., & Shohet, R. (2012) *Supervision in the Helping Professions*, 4th edition. Glasgow: Bell & Bain Ltd.

Health and Care Professions Council (2016) *Guidance on conduct and ethics for students*. http://www.hcpc-uk.org/assets/documents/10002C16Guidanceonconductandethicsforstudents.pdf

Hess, A.K., Hess, K.D., & Hess, T.H. (Eds.) (2008) *Psychotherapy Supervision: Theory, Research, and Practice*, 2nd edition. Hoboken, NJ: Wiley.

Holloway, E.L. (1995) *Clinical Supervision: A Systems Approach*. Thousand Oaks, CA: Sage.

Inskipp, F., & Proctor, B. (1995a) *Becoming a Supervisor*. Twickenham: Cascade Publications.

Inskipp, F., & Proctor, B. (1995b) *Making the Most of Supervision*. Twickenham, UK: Cascade.

Izzard, S. (2001) The responsibility of the supervisor supervising trainees. In S. Wheeler, & D. King (Eds.). *Supervising Counsellors' Issues of Responsibility*. London: Sage, pp. 75–82.

Mastroas, S.M., & Andrews, J.J. (2011) The supervisee experience of group supervision: Implications for research and practice. *Training and Education in Professional Psychology*, 5(2), 102–111.

Mehr, K.E., Ladany, N., & Caskie, G.I.L. (2010) Trainee disclosure in supervision: What are they not telling you? *Counselling & Psychotherapy Research*, 10(2), 103–113.

Morrissey, J. (1998) Contracting and supervision. *Counselling Psychology Review*, 13(1), 13–17.

Murphy, M.J., & Wright, D.W. (2005) Supervisees' perspectives of power use in supervision. *Journal of Marital and Family Therapy*, 31(3), 283–295.

Page, S., & Wosket, V. (2015) *Supervising the Counsellor and Psychotherapist: A Cyclical Approach*, 3rd edition. London: Routledge.

Pearson, Q.M. (2000) Opportunities and challenges in the supervisory relationship: Implications for counsellor supervision. *Journal of Mental Health Counseling*, 22, 283–294.

Scaife, J. (2009) *Supervision in Clinical Practice A Practitioner's Guide*, 2nd edition. London: Routledge.

Scaife, J. (2019) *Supervision in Clinical Practice A Practitioner's Guide*, 3rd edition. London: Routledge.

Singh-Pilay, N., & Cartwright, D. (2018) The unsaid: In-depth accounts of non-disclosures in supervision from the trainees' perspective. *Counselling Psychotherapy Research*, 19, 83–92.

Stoltenberg, C.D., McNeill, B.W., & Delworth, U. (1998) *IDM Supervision: An Integrated Developmental Model for Supervising Counselors and Therapists*. San Francisco: Jossey-Bass.

Tarasoff v. Regents of the University of California. (1974) 118 Cal Rptr.129, 529 P.2d 533.

UK Council for Psychotherapy. (2018) *Supervision Standards of Education and Training*. London: UKCP.

Watkins, C.E., & Milne, D. (Eds.) (2014) *The Wiley International Handbook of Clinical Supervision*. Chichester, UK: Wiley Blackwell.

Yourman, D.B. (2003) Trainee disclosure in psychotherapy supervision: The impact of shame. *Journal of Clinical Psychology/In Session*, 59(5), 601–609.

Chapter 20

Trainee perspectives on professional, ethical and research practice

Rachel Tribe

This chapter details the findings from a survey undertaken with a range of trainee therapists, counselling, clinical and community psychologists and counsellors over 12 years. In total, 96 trainees participated in the survey from a number of British training institutions and courses. Trainees were asked a number of open-ended questions and focus groups were held. This chapter discusses the issues these trainees identified as important to their own development or were areas of concern for them. Issues relating to social media are not covered here, as Chapter 10 discusses these. This chapter does not attempt to be conclusive or to determine which areas are most important. It discusses the issues that this group of trainees viewed as important. Scenarios or reflective questions are interspersed throughout the text to assist consideration of ethical, professional and research dilemmas. Quotes given by the trainees (set as displayed text) are used as illustrations throughout to identify a theme that was raised by a significant majority of trainees. In total, 93% of trainees reported that professional, ethical and research codes, combined with related teaching, provided containment, support and helped the trainees uphold standards and professionalism for all parties, thus drawing attention to potential pitfalls or dilemmas in clinical practice and when conducting research.

> To ensure we are fit to practice in a safe, contained manner and adhere to policies and procedures to ensure the safeguarding of ourselves and clients. Protecting research participants.
> Ethics are important as they ensure clients are able to be supported fairly, equally, safely and competently.

Being a trainee

> Some ethical and professional dilemmas impact upon the therapeutic process and these may cause a lot of anxiety and effect your confidence about your work, however they are important aspects of the learning process and personal and professional development and if dealt with appropriately and discussed in seminars and supervision can have a positive impact on therapeutic process.

Trainees reported that professional and ethical dilemmas may be further compli-cated by the fact that they are trainees; in that clients may project anxieties or concerns relating to being allocated someone 'not yet fully qualified'. Trainees also frequently have anxieties about their level of competence, and may feel they 'should know more'. This may prevent trainees from seeking help, particularly when their line manager or clinical supervisor appears unavailable or very busy, or, if the trainee has particular issues about asking for help. This is a complex issue and therefore this chapter considers only some of the key findings.

> Clients may project their unwillingness to take responsibility for therapy onto the counsellor being a trainee.
>
> As a trainee counselling psychologist, I am into my seventh year of train-ing in psychology but when clients read that I am a counselling psychologist in training, they may believe I have had very little training and wish to see a more experienced practitioner.

Reflective question

How would you deal with a query from a service user who was engaged in therapy about your level of training and competence to practice?

Length and scope of training

The content and duration of training that different therapeutic professionals receive varies considerably. This may have implications for trainees' perspec-tives. Psychiatrists, psychologists, social workers and nurses in the UK have compulsory regulation, while counsellors and psychotherapists currently do not, although The Department of Health (2017) recently completed their Con-sultation on the Regulation of Health Professionals.

The BPS, BACP and the UKCP have launched new ethical guidelines during 2017/2018. It is clear that the major professional organisations are com-mitted to ensuring their members comply with rigorous ethical and practice guidelines, although as one trainee noted there are some practitioners who do not belong to any of these organisations or do not hold the requisite qualifica-tions to enable them to do this.

> I've come across counsellors who have attained certificates or diplomas in counselling without doing supervised client work and with no personal therapy at all, I think such qualifications should be differently labelled.

Different countries use the terms psychologist, psychotherapist or social worker differently or interchangeably and have diverse requirements relating to who is able to offer psychological services, as well as a range of regulatory practices and ethical frameworks (Tribe et al, 2014).

Bond (2015) helpfully describes an ethical framework as being like meta-phorical scaffolding, which enables work to safely take place on the building supported by the scaffolding. Trainees expressed a variety of opinions in relation to ethical frameworks with some showing ambivalence about the role of professional and ethical frameworks in training as detailed below.

Teaching professional and ethical issues

Professional and ethical issues in therapeutic and research practice have some-times been seen by trainees as 'boring', 'common-sense', 'legalistic' or 'scary'. Trainers and supervisors may need to be innovative in the way they teach these issues to show their importance, particularly at the beginning of training, where trainees may have little experience of clinical work or conduct-ing research and may be anxious about both of these.

> Some of the issues are surrounding decision-making and not being confi-dent in our decisions without a lot of reassurance. … To me, this has applied to my research practice such as asking my supervisor constantly if I am doing something right or if they would do something differently.
>
> Whilst ethics provides some structure and security for trainee practi-tioners, it strikes me that as a subject/topic it is the least interesting, which I see as a 'brake' on our work.… As an analogy it is a bit like studying safety issues/learning about equipment before being allowed to go flying/mountaineering/sailing etc. I can see the need, but it is really legalistic.

Anxieties about litigation or complaints

In total, 78% of trainees reported how litigation and complaints appeared to be increasing and that this was a cause of worry for them. Details of the UKCP report (2016) on Handling Complaints about Therapists provides useful infor-mation. The Health and Care Professions Council is responsible for the statu-tory regulation of practitioner psychologists, social workers and several other professions in the UK, and also provides detailed information. The BACP, BPS, HCPC and UKCP all run workshops around complaints. Khele et al. (2008) in an initial analysis of complaints made to the BACP found that the largest percentage of complaints made are from people also working in the counselling field and more complaints are made against male practitioners. Bond (2015) stated that it is difficult to obtain accurate information about com-plaints made against counsellors, as some may be made at the organisational or agency level rather than at national level. Most professional organisations now publish this information, although this process is not without its critics.

Besides ensuring teaching is relevant to the trainee's level of training and experience is clear, it may also be important to acknowledge that there may be ambivalence towards learning about ethical, professional and research practice issues. Tribe and Morrissey (2005) cautions against assuming that ethics will be learned just through modelling or osmosis/passive observation. Carroll and Shaw (2016) write about developing ethical maturity. (The author has found that the use of imaginary dilemmas and trying as a group to think about writing an ethical code can help in bringing professional and ethical issues into training.) Experience would suggest that trainees in the early part of training often want to be told what to do in any given circumstance without realising the subtle differences within the therapeutic process, agency context and other relevant variables. The desire for a containing frame or set of 'perfect' guidelines in a new and complex field is quite understandable. While ambivalence may exist, ethical and practice guidelines may also be attributed by some trainees to have a totally prescriptive value and almost talismanic significance. This is reflected by the following comments.

> Awareness that there are different courses of action can be disabling, this can lead to overly rigid adherence to 'rules' to avoid dilemmas and 'get it right'.
> Professional and ethical guidelines provide some guidance on what is accepted and their role in training and working. In a world and profession that is fast becoming "very unsafe" in regards of the risk of being sued or suspended etc. The professional and ethical guidelines can be a "safe haven" to work under.
> Certain important issues may not be researched as people think the ethical and professional issues are so great, nothing is done, what are the ethics of that?

Reflective question

What is your worst fear about professional, ethical and research practice issues? If you found yourself confronted with a dilemma, what would you do? Who would you consult?

In total, 68% of trainees reported finding it hard to ask for advice and help at the beginning of their training/placements, particularly when they felt that there might be an element of judgement involved. This applied to clinical and research issues.

> At times it makes you feel inadequate, not knowing where to go, what to do, who to talk to. We think we 'should' know it all, prevents us from

asking. In a busy part of the NHS where I am based, everyone seems to be working so hard and have so little time.

The risk the research findings will pose for the organisation. I am researching – i.e. it will put a bad light on them – thinking about the wider issues – which are true – but there is a reluctance for them to be explored and acknowledged.

These findings offer challenges to the way professional, ethical and research considerations are presented to trainees and integrated into all aspects of the training in a way that is digestible, lively and relevant. Codes of ethics will require refinement and development due to societal changes. For example see Chapter 10 on the role of social media which was not a major issue ten years ago.

Reflective question

If you were asked to consider designing professional and ethical guidelines, what principles might motivate or guide you? These might be personal, societal, familial, philosophical or other.

What are ethical dilemmas?

'Ethical dilemmas exist whenever there are "good" but contradictory reasons to take conflicting and incompatible courses of action' (Kitchener, 1984: 43). Guidelines cannot cover all eventualities and cannot therefore be prescriptive. Every instance is different, and complex situations may require independent professional judgement and discussion with supervisors or managers. Guidelines are structured to provide a framework against which dilemmas can be considered, and by their very nature must evolve as society changes (Tribe et al, 2014). Several ethical dilemmas presented by trainees are given below to illustrate this complexity.

I had a patient whose son (nine years of age) was witnessing his partner's violent and abusive behaviour. I was in a dilemma whether to report the matter as the son could have been in danger. I took it to supervision and sought "hypothetical" advice from the local mental health crisis team. I also advised the patient of our initial contract and suggested she took action to end this relationship (she had already planned to do this), as I would have to report the situation. I would behave in the same way in the future.

I had a client tell me they were feeling like they were falling in love with me. I reported this to my supervisor and had a discussion with the client on boundaries and how this is not possible.

A client told me they were being very rough, possibly physically abusive to their child – by the time I had checked this out any trust/rapport between myself and my client was lost and therapy ended prematurely.

Reflective question

What would you do in these situations, with particular reference to safe guarding?

Ethical, practice and research issues are frequently imprecise, they may be challenging and necessitate considerable thought, reflection and discussion.

A patient had an addiction to sex – he would expose himself to women in public – my dilemma was, do I contain this or do I report him or do I refer him to our forensic team? I have contained his behaviour and he does not expose himself any longer but he is still is addicted to extra-marital affairs – we are working on this now.

In relation to research to constantly feel that as a researcher, I'm only 'getting' from my participants and not giving anything back to them.

Reflective question

What do you think you would do in these situations? What would guide your thinking? Who might you consult? How might your personal views/beliefs have influenced you?

As trainees progressed through their professional training, they appeared to perceive the value of professional, ethical and research guidelines somewhat differently. They noted that the guidelines provided containment and that they helped integrate and reinforce other areas of their learning as opposed to being viewed as restrictive, as they had felt when they started their training.

In my first year of training I found it really helpful to be able to say that I could not do certain things, such as requests to continue the therapy on a private basis after finishing the NHS contract because the agency guidelines did not allow this. I now feel able to say this myself for therapeutic reasons.

In relation to research – deciding on a topic which will direct my future career.

Major themes raised by trainees

In total, 90% of trainees stressed the importance of good clinical supervision and 68% highlighted personal therapy.

> I have learnt so much from being in therapy and to a lesser degree in clinical supervision, I was not sure at the beginning; it was expensive and time-consuming, and I rather resented it. But I think these provide, and continue to provide, some of the best training experiences there are, for me anyway.
> Both supervision and therapy were essential parts of my professional development.

The importance of these two cornerstones is recognised by most training organisations, although there is some variation among training institutions, professional bodies and therapeutic models as to their importance. While the empirical evidence on the importance of personal therapy is not unequivocal, and a range of views about its relevance are held by practitioners, the author's views it as having a key role in equipping trainees to work as therapists and of contributing to professional and ethical practice. The interested reader is referred to Halewood and Tribe (2003).

Personal therapy

The different strands of training often provide overlapping experiences, which inform and reinforce one another. In addition to the strands of university or institution-based teaching, and supervision, trainees' experiences of personal therapy before and during training has also proved to be a fertile training ground for experiences of bad and good professional, ethical and research practice.

Trainees reported some examples of unethical practice with therapists. However, before starting their own preparation for training, trainees may have little experience of finding a therapist, and often select on the basis of geographical proximity or cost. Nevertheless, the trainees in general found personal therapy an invaluable source of learning about professional and ethical practice, apart from its other important functions.

> My therapist told me they were cutting back on their hours and would no longer be able to see me, although they would be keeping some people on. This made me feel unimportant and discarded. We had been working on my self-esteem!
> My therapist kept leaving the room to check on their baby, I didn't feel able to say that I thought this inappropriate, so I just left after a couple of sessions.

Having negotiated a fee before starting counselling, the counsellor informed me that he had decided to raise the fee, there appeared to be no room for negotiation and I felt trapped.

Reflective question

If you believed your therapist was engaging in unethical professional practice what would you do? What factors might influence your decision-making?

Personal values

The issue of personal belief systems in how professional and ethical issues are viewed, was mentioned by some trainees (44%). Trainees reported that although they were aware of a theoretical/academic perspective of various issues or beliefs which they viewed as having personal significance and which a proportion had discussed in their own therapy, they were still surprised at how their own views and material sometimes mediated in their clinical work. Trainees gave a number of examples but one is used below to illustrate this point.

When I was working with a woman who suffered from domestic violence, I was struggling with my role as a therapist and woman who needed to protect the client. I struggle to work with clients who have strong views against women, although such clients are referred to me.

I was not convinced a client was not at risk, I knew this situation, but I had to concede in supervision, they held the power.

How far can/should psychologists cascade techniques/strategies to non-psychologists for use in other settings? E.g. teachers to use in schools? What are the ethical and professional issues relating to this? Are they always considered adequately?

Issues of power and trust in work with clients and in personal therapy were raised as challenging by many trainees. This is an issue, which may have particular resonance when issues of difference and diversity form part of the work. These issues need to be regularly considered and integrated into training and practice if high professional and ethical standards are to be maintained.

Gifts

Being given gifts by service users was mentioned as a difficult issue by a high percentage of trainees (37%) and caused much concern about 'doing the right thing' and maintaining professional and ethical practice and 'manners'. Kent (2017) refers to this issue in a practice guideline for the BACP. This issue seems to become increasingly complex when cultural norms and context are considered. The author of this chapter holds the view that gifts should not be accepted by therapists, and that if they are offered in therapy, the issue needs to be dealt with in the therapeutic process. There is not scope to discuss this complex issue at length here but it is clearly one that merits reflection and discussion. The issue of different cultures, belief systems and explanatory health beliefs has been discussed by a number of writers including Welfel (2013; 2014) and Tribe et al. (2014). Welfel (2013) and Fernando and Moodley (2018) discuss this issue and other boundary issues while also privileging culturally norms and appropriateness. The following quotes show how two trainees described their dilemmas.

> In my culture, it would be extremely bad manners not to accept a gift. It is a mark of respect, and one would almost expect it.
>
> A patient gave me a present in the middle of a therapeutic process, I didn't know what to do, I refused the gift, but the client insisted on me taking it. The client thought I was rude to refuse it and later became rather 'distant' in sessions. ... Now I would deal with it differently, probably would use the gift to explore what made the client bring it, and use this gift as a metaphor within the therapeutic process.

Reflective question

What would you do if a client brought you a present of some sweets/ cakes that they said they had 'baked especially for you' to mark a cultural/religious festival in session four of therapy? What factors would influence your thinking? Would you feel differently if the gift were an expensive one?

Whistle blowing

The issue of whistle blowing has received increasing attention in recent years (The Health and Social Care Act 2008 {Regulated Activities} Regulations 2014 duty of candour {regulation 20} and the Freedom to speak up Report, 2015). It appears that as society becomes increasingly litigious everyone feels more anxious about the possibility of being sued or of having complaints proceedings taken against them. Apart from ensuring that their own practice was ethical, the issue of whistleblowing or of believing that colleagues were guilty of unethical practice was mentioned by a number of trainees. The Freedom to Speak report grew out of concern about the difficulties associated with whistleblowing in the NHS, and the treatment of staff who had done this. The report details 20 principles and arrangements for implementation by NHS healthcare organisations.

The establishment of Freedom to Speak Up Guardians in organisations was suggested as well as the requisite psychological support for those who whistle blow. Walshe and Shortell (2004) reviewed major healthcare failures in several countries and found that a culture of secrecy, professional protectionism, defensiveness and deference to authority were core to these failures. Whilst Dixon-Woods et al. (2014) note that focussing too much on specific goals or targets can lead to a distorted view about what is important, they also noted that taking a purely managerial view can be out of synch with professional values. Clinicians, supervisors and managers may need to ensure that trainees are familiar with professional guidelines and know where they can locate support.

As trainees stated,

> I believed a colleague was 'over familiar' with clients, this raised real issues for me, I was only a trainee and there appeared to be a culture of collusion which accepted this person's 'foibles'.
>
> How far is it ethical for psychologists cascade techniques/strategies to non-psychologists for use in other settings? As a trainee can I question this without getting labelled.

Reflective question

If you believed a colleague might be engaged in unethical clinical or research practice, what would you do? Who might you raise the issue with? Are you familiar with your organisation's code of practice and any guidelines on this issue?

In total, 85% of trainees reported in relation to a fictitious scenario that they would raise this with management, with 15% saying they would raise it with the individual.

Levels of competence

Being asked to work at the edge or beyond their felt professional competence was a theme mentioned by trainees. Tangential to this was the importance of being honest about one's level of difficulties and concerns about not being seen in a negative light by trainees' supervisor or placement manager. Universities and training institutions/placements also have responsibilities to monitor and consider such instances in a coherent manner.

> Assistant psychologists are under pressure to maximise their own experience, possibly beyond their expertise, while services are under press to use cheaper workers. Where are service users' needs in all this?!

Inappropriate referrals was another issue raised by trainees. Trainees reported feeling they were fortunate to have been given the placement, (which are increasingly competitive and difficult to find) and this may have further complicated matters. These issues may be exacerbated when the trainee's supervisor is also their line manager.

> At times it is difficult to know who we can talk to and trust, as trainees we feel vulnerable if we open too much or contradict our managers/supervisors.
>
> Once I took a client who I would describe as 'difficult' and beyond my competence, but the same client was on 'top of the waiting list' and my line manager told me I should work with her. I wasn't sure if I should continue working with this client or if we terminate – would that impact on the client.
>
> Anxiety about these issues can damage the patient/therapist relationship but not dealing with these issues properly can leave the clients vulnerable and open to abuse…Clients may decide to withhold information (about their violent tendencies for example) which would really block the therapy.

Dual roles/relationships

Dilemmas associated with dual roles and relationships were raised by a number of trainees. (Dual roles and relationships refer to having other roles/relationships with a service user, for example, being involved in counselling and then being asked to write a report that would be used in legal proceedings, or being asked to sort out housing or welfare issues, key working or undertaking advocate duties). Whenever possible, dual roles should be avoided, but there may be occasions when they are unavoidable (Bond, 2015). Herlihy and Corey (1992), offer a useful decision-making model for considering and managing dual relationships. Different organisations have different polices on this. It is important to realise that if a legal report is to be written (frequently associated with access to resources or compensation), this is likely to affect the dynamics of the therapy and the decision to engage with legal report writing needs to be considered from the start.

> I found myself doing a case report for court with my clients consent but of course the client became less disclosing of their underlying issues as their children who are in care are being considered for return, if I was asked again I think I would refuse the task, it confused the boundaries for both of us.
>
> My experience of being asked to undertake a so called dual role was that my client decided to opt out of therapy … It may affect other patients so much that they would not return to therapy.

Where there are criminal, domestic violence or child welfare issues, a service user may present for therapy as they believe that this will reflect well on them in legal proceedings but with no intention of fully engaging in the therapeutic process. How people position ourselves in relation to dual roles is likely to be determined by the therapeutic model we practice, agency tasks and policies, personality and personal belief systems. The more thought that is put into considering these issues in advance the better.

Reflective question

You have been seeing Mr S for therapy for two months in a clinic that specialises in addiction issues. Although he has attended regularly, you feel that he has not really engaged in the therapeutic process, but is merely 'going through the motions'. Your manager tells you to write a report for Ms V's forthcoming court case where his addiction issues/ mitigating circumstances may be relevant.

What are your initial thoughts about the issues that dual roles/relationships might precipitate? How do these relate to your therapeutic model, the agency employing you, personal issues or belief systems? Do you think your decision-making might be different if you were working in private practice? If so, for what reasons?

Boundaries, confidentiality and issues of disclosure

Confidentiality, boundaries and issues of disclosure are issues that many trainees reported struggling with. Dilemmas associated with working in a multidisciplinary team was another; – trainees reported instances of clients being discussed informally by members of the multi-disciplinary team, by which they meant client information being talked about over coffee or in staff rooms. They also expressed concerns (particularly in primary care contexts) about the security of notes and clinical information. Several trainees reported finding what appeared to be 'fuzzy' boundaries, extremely un-containing in this environment. Although other trainees reported excellent practice in multidisciplinary teams with clear and open communication channels and where everyone considered the best interests of the client.

> I'm aware that supervisors are sometimes faced with the dilemma of whether information divulged in supervision should be passed on to the manager. For example, a counsellor struggling because of a bereavement. As a counsellor (and trainee supervisor) I learnt the importance of having an explicit contract and checking the boundaries if I were unsure.

Self-disclosure was also mentioned. There were varying views about this, probably reflecting different theoretical positions. Trainees at the start of their training found it harder to deal with being asked to self-disclose than more experienced practitioners.

> My client asked me directly if I had a family, as the material we were working with related to difficulties my client was experiencing with her children. I really struggled to deal with this; lots of different thoughts went through my mind about how to answer. I don't think I dealt with it very well, but think I will be better prepared should this happen again.

Reflective question

What are your thoughts about therapist self-disclosure? What factors do you think influenced your answer? What kind of information do you keep in your clinical notes? Are they purely factual, or do they contain clinical opinion or are they interpretative or a combination of the three? Are you ensuring that you are not in breach of any data protection legislation? You have been seeing a client for three months and they demand to see their notes – what would you do?

Conclusion

This chapter has reflected upon a selection of trainee views on professional, ethical and research practice issues. The chapter does not attempt to be definitive, but to share the views of trainees from a range of institutions and courses who participated through completing questionnaires or taking part in focus groups or seminars. It is hoped that the issues raised will assist the reader in thinking about some of the professional and ethical dilemmas that can arise in training and beyond. The chapter made some suggestions about how some of these issues may be integrated into training and offered reflective questions in relation to a number of the issues raised. If you are a trainee or inexperienced practitioner you may find it helpful after reading this chapter to make a list of the ethical and professional practice dilemmas you are worried about encountering and discuss them with a colleague or seminar group. You might also wish to consider what guidelines, policies or legislation are appropriate to your work? How do you ensure you are informed about updates? The codes of ethics are available to assist you and regular or specific updates will be issued, these are generally available from your professional organisation or via their web-site.

Reflective questions

1. How do you ensure that you uphold and monitor your own professional and ethical standards?
2. You know that your clinical supervisor had a recent bereavement and seems to be unavailable to you in supervision sessions. What would you do?
3. A client tells you she committed a serious crime but was never caught for it. What would you do?
4. A colleague tells you 'in strictest confidence' that she is now dating an ex-client.

The author would like to thank the many trainees who gave so generously of their time in either completing questionnaires or through participating in focus groups at various institutions in several countries.

References

Bond, T. (2015) *Standard and Ethics for Counselling in Action*, 4th edition. London: Sage.

Carroll, M., & Shaw, E. (2016) Towards ethical maturity in Counselling Psychology. In B. Douglas, R. Woolfe, S. Strawbridge, E. Kasket, & Galbraith (Eds.). *The Handbook of Counselling Psychology*. London: Sage, pp. 244–258.

Department of Health. (2017) Consultation on the Regulation of Health Professionals, entitled Promoting professionalism and reforming regulation. Available at: https:// assets.publishing.service.gov.uk/government/uploads/system/uploads/attachment_data/ file/655794/Regulatory_Reform_Consultation_Document.pdf Accessed 1 March 2018.

Dixon-Woods, M., Baker, R., Charles, K., Dawson, J., Jerzembek, G., Martin, G., McCarthy, I., McKee, L., Minion, J., Ozieranski, P., Willars, J., Wilkie, P., & West, M. (2014) Culture and behaviour in the English National Health Service: Overview of lessons from a large multimethod study. *BMJ Quality and Safety*, 23(2), 106–115.

Halewood, A., & Tribe, R. (2003) What is the prevalence of narcissistic injury among trainee counselling psychologists? *British Journal of Medical Psychology*, 76, 87–102.

Herlihy, B., & Corey, G. (1992) *Dual Relationships, American Association for Counselling and Development*, Alexandria: VA.

Kent, R. (2017) BACP Information sheet no 4 (2017) What do counsellors and psychotherapists mean by 'professional boundaries'. Available at: www.bacp.co.uk/media/2638/bacp-what-therapists-mean-by-professional-boundaries-c4.pdf Accessed 16 December 2018.

Khele, S., Symons, C., & Wheeler, S. (2008) An analysis of complaints to the British Association for Counselling and Psychotherapy, 1996–2006. *Counselling and Psychotherapy Research*, 8(2), 124–132.

Kitchener, K. S. (1984). Intuition, critical evaluation and ethical principles: The foundation for ethical decisions in counseling psychology. *Counseling Psychologist*, 12, 43–55.

Tribe, R., & Morrissey, S. (2005) Teaching Ethics for Professional Practice. In Tribe, R. & Morrissey, J. (Eds.). *The Handbook of Professional and Ethical Practice for Psychologists, Psychotherapists & Counsellors*. London: Brunner-Routledge, pp. 291–302.

Tribe, R., Weerasinghe, D., & Parameswaran, S. (2014) Increasing mental health capacity in a post conflict country through effective professional volunteer partnerships: a series of case studies with government agencies, local NGOs and the diaspora. *International Review of Psychiatry*, 26(5), 558–565.

United Kingdom Council for Psychotherapy (UKCP). Available at: www.psychotherapy. org.uk/wp-content/uploads/2016/08/UKCP-PCC-Annual-Report-WEB-USE.pdf Accessed 13 December 2018.

Walshe, K., & Shortell, S. (2004) When things go wrong: How health care organisations deal with major failures. *Health Affairs*, 23(3), 103–111.

Welfel, E. R. (2013) *Ethics in Counseling & Psychotherapy 5th edn*. California: Cengage Learning.

Chapter 21

Continuing Professional Development (CPD)

Professional and ethical considerations

Lucia Berdondini and Thomas Elton

Introduction

Continued or Continuing Professional Development (CPD) is recognised as an essential requirement for many professions, including teachers, health professionals (doctors, nurses, psychologists, psychotherapists and counsellors), social workers and managers (Earley & Porritt, 2008). Professional bodies in different areas have established methods of monitoring and reviewing CPD of individuals and employers as a way of ensuring that professionals keep updating their knowledge and skills, in a visible and evidenced manner (Friedman & Tinner, 2016). This chapter will explore several dimensions related to CPD in the fields of Psychology, Psychotherapy and Counselling, including how to measure CPD and its outcomes, the current resources available in this field, the challenges and limitations and what is the likely future of CPD in these professions.

Understanding CPD

The definitions of CPD vary, some examples are presented. The Training and Development Agency for Schools (TDA), defines CPD as:

> Continuing professional development consists of reflective activity designed to improve an individual's attributes, knowledge, understanding and skills. It supports individual needs and improves professional practice.
> (TDA, 2007, and www.gov.uk/government/organisations/
> training-and-development-agency-for-schools)

The Nursery and Midwifery Council (2015: 22) claims that CPD is fundamental for nurses and midwives as it 'maintain safe and effective practice, improve practice or develop new skills'.

The Professional Association Research Network, defines CPD as 'any process or activity that provides added value to the capability of the professional through the increase in knowledge, skills and personal qualities necessary for the appropriate execution of professional and technical duties, often termed competence' (Professional Associations Research Network, www.parn.com).

Finally, The Health and Care Professions Council (HCPC) define CPD as 'a range of learning activities through which health professionals maintain and develop throughout their career to ensure that they retain their capacity to practise safely, effectively and legally within their evolving scope of practice' (Health and Care Professions Council: www.hcpc-uk.org/cpd).

In the fields of psychology, psychotherapy and counselling, within the UK, professional bodies such as the British Psychological Society (BPS), the British Association for Counselling and Psychotherapy (BACP) and the United Kingdom Council for Psychotherapy (UKCP) have clear policies and guidance about the expected CPD for their accredited members. Examples of general activities that can be undertaken by professionals in these areas as forms of CPD go from reading and attending conferences and seminars (including online), to taking new qualifications and awards, attending training courses (including e-learning), undertaking research, teaching and training students in these fields and expanding personal development for example through personal therapy.

The Royal College of Psychiatrists (RCPsych) requires professionals to attend a minimum of 50 hours every year of CPD with at least 30 hours defined by the RCPsych as being within the clinical domain. Half of the annual required hours (25) can be carried out through CPD online (www.psy chiatrycpd.co.uk/) that is an interactive website offered by the RCPsych with more than 200 Modules of CPD. All Modules are peer reviewed and cover clinical, academic and professional areas. Psychiatrists need to be part of CPD peer groups that have responsibility to support individual professionals to identify areas for their specific professional development and to explore the effectiveness of these activities on their clinical and professional practice. The peer groups can be of any size and are considered a crucial element of the CPD process.

Finally, the British Association of Social Workers (BASW) is the Professional Membership Organization for Social Workers in UK. Social workers have to register to one of the four UK councils, which are: the Health and Care Professions Council (HCPC) in England, Care Council for Wales, Northern Ireland Social Care Council (NISCC) and Scottish Social Services Council (SSSC). Each of these councils has different requirements and criteria. However, CPD is a fundamental requirement across all the councils. For example, HCPC doesn't require a specific minimum number of hours of CPD as long as the learning activities chosen cover at least three areas of the core competences expected from Social Workers. Every year HCPC randomly selects 2.5% of social workers for audit and in that case the professional selected has to provide evidence of the activities undertaken.

A crucial point highlighted by all professional bodies mentioned so far is the reflective aspect of the process to identify specific CPD activities that inform the individual's practice at that specific stage. In the field of psychology and counselling, for example, professional bodies like BACP, BPS and UKCP stress the importance of professional engaging with CPD identifying, first of all, areas that in their personal and professional development need more learning and consequently, making a plan, taking action and evaluating again the outcome, rather than just 'ticking boxes' collecting random CPD activities (Golding & Gray, 2006). The commitment to CPD is part of the ethical integrity of the professional, where the choice of specific topics and the forms of learning, derives from a reflective and meaningful process, with the specific intention of monitoring, fostering and guaranteeing their own safety to practice. This process is commonly known as the 'The CPD Cycle' (see Figure 21.1).

For the *individual professional* in the field of Psychology, Psychotherapy and Counselling, then, CPD is important on a number of levels. For example it:

- Allows practitioners to fill gaps in knowledge and skills to become more productive and efficient.
- Builds confidence and credibility to develop appropriate competencies and helps to clarify what specific contribution the practitioner can offer to the whole professional body.

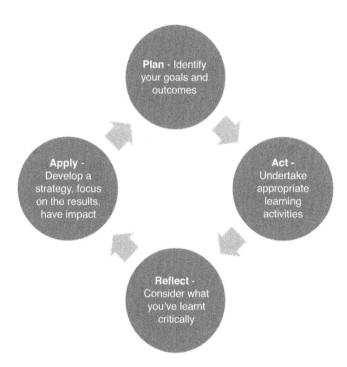

Figure 21.1 The CPD cycle (The British Psychological Society, 2018)

- Achieves career goals.
- Increases self-awareness, reflectivity and reflexivity.
- Helps engaging with networks of colleagues and communities.

It is then not just an individual development, but it has an impact on the wider world of professionals, in terms of colleagues and peers, beneficiaries and communities. This implies that CPD is important and essential also for workplaces and professional systems, as it guarantees a better quality of services for the public that uses these services (Association for Project Management, 2017).

For the employer and service user CPD can be seen particularly useful as it:

- Enhances service user confidence.
- Increases employee competency, resulting in greater efficiency in the workplace.
- Boosts morale and motivation in the workforce.

CPD cycle and professional bodies regulations

As mentioned above, the CPD cycle is a process that is recommended for individuals to follow continuously, allowing professional development to have a tangible and meaningful impact. The ability to be able to measure impact and reflect on learning is imperative to the perceived success and benefits.

HCPC as the regulator and BPS/BACP use an outcome/output model where self-reflection and the impact of professional development is undertaken. Reflection is a key component of the CPD cycle, where by individuals should consider what they have learnt. Evaluation learning can be considered by reflecting upon how the learning has impacted on your own practice, service users and employers. The approach to this should not only be considered immediately after engagement in professional development activities, but also in the months that follow in order to provide a measure of the impact. The BPS provides a range of professional development activities for practitioners both centrally, through member networks and external providers 'approved' through the BPS Professional Development Centre. These interactions are planned and delivered taking into consideration what is important to practitioners for their career development and knowledge and skills. Professional development activity organised internally is mostly delivered by members, allowing the sharing of research and good practice by peers.

To deliver professional development through the BPS there are a number of formal processes in place to ensure what is being delivered is of a high standard, which includes peer reviewing of submitted proposals.

HCPC as the regulator for practitioner psychologists operates independently from the BPS. As CPD is linked to HCPC Registration, practitioner psychologists must meet a number of standards for Continuing Professional Development to maintain registration.

1. Maintain a continuous, up-to-date and accurate record of their CPD activities
2. Demonstrate that their CPD activities are a mixture of learning activities relevant to current or future practice
3. Seek to ensure that their CPD has contributed to the quality of their practice and service delivery
4. Seek to ensure that their CPD benefits the service user
5. Upon request, present a written profile (which must be their own work and supported by evidence) explaining how they have met the Standards for CPD.

HCPC is not prescriptive on the type and length of professional development engagements, and offers guidance on activities that can be undertaken. These fall under the following categories:

1. Work-based learning
    Activities include:

    *   Learning by doing, on the job;
    *   Case studies;
    *   Peer reviewing;
    *   In service training;
    *   Active representation on committees;
    *   Work shadowing;
    *   Supervising staff or students;
    *   Project work

2. Professional activities
    Activities include:

    *   Involvement in a professional body, special interest group;
    *   Mentoring;
    *   Being an expert witness;
    *   Presenting at conferences;
    *   Being a national assessor

3. Formal and educational
    Activities include:

    *   Courses/workshops;
    *   Further education;

- Research;
- Attending conferences;
- Distance or online learning;
- Writing articles or papers;
- Delivering a professional development course

4. Self-directed learning
   Activities include:

- Reading journals/articles;
- Reviewing books/articles;
- Keeping a file of your progress

5. Other

- Relevant public service or voluntary work
  (HCPC, 2018)

It is important for the practitioner to retain materials related to any professional development undertaken, either in handouts and notes either electronically or paper based, and materials showing the practitioner has reflected and evaluated the impact of the activities as this can be required as evidence in case of an audit by the HCPC.

Renewal of HCPC registration takes place every two years, and it's where HCPC conduct their CPD audit. Currently HCPC randomly selects 2.5% of registrants to audit their CPD. It is at this stage where registrants, if selected, have three months to submit their CPD profile. The profile will need to include a list of activities from the last two years, a summary of recent work, an explanation of how the HCPC CPD standards have been met, and supporting evidence of each example used. Non completion of CPD activities could lead to the removal from the Registry.

The BPS aims to complement this approach by HCPC, by offering a range of opportunities to engage in professional development and with full access to MyCPD, a tool for members to record and reflect on their CPD engagements (www.bps.org.uk/psychologists/professional-development/mycpd).

BACP requires every registered member to annually confirm, while renewing their registration, that they are undertaking and recording CPD. The minimum required by BACP is 30 hours every year in a different combination of activities. The activities accepted are those already mentioned within areas of possible personal and professional development initiatives. Registered members are required to keep a record of these activities with evidence of having clearly reflected, planned, acted and evaluated each activity, as suggested by the CPD cycle. If required (for example if selected for audit by the professional body) the individual member is expected to submit this record. Usually BACP is facilitative towards the validation and acceptance of CPD activities but in case of non-conformity or failure to present an adequate evidence of CPD activities, this can result in the removal from the register (www.bacp.co.uk/media/1475/bacp-registered-member-cpd-guide.pdf). Practitioner members of UKCP need to renew their accreditation every five years. This professional body requires 250 hours CPD over a five-year period as the minimum requirement for continued UKCP registration. In any one year a minimum of 20 hours CPD including supervision is required. Activities that may be regarded as relevant, in addition to supervision, are: attendance at conferences, seminars or workshops; giving lectures, seminars and workshops; writing original articles, reviews, case studies or similar; teaching or training received; experience as teacher or trainer; journal clubs; committee and organisational work; relevant personal development activities. A minimum of 16 hours a year of the total CPD hours must be specifically in the field of Sexual and Relationship Psychotherapy. Similarly to the other professional bodies, UKCP requires psychotherapists to submit evidence of the activities undertaken.

Facilitating and promoting CPD in the UK

The BPS offers a regular variety of opportunities for psychologists (including supervisors) to expand and deepen their professional knowledge and competence. Most of these activities are delivered through workshops, e-learning, conferences and events. BPS has a CPD Approval Scheme that assesses and approves programmes and events in accordance to its standards for professional development. On the BPS website (www.bps.org.uk/cpd) practitioners can access a list of updated approved CPD events.

On the same website, professionals and organisations (for example higher education institutions) interested in providing CPD opportunities for their colleagues can find clear guidelines for submissions and specific suggestions about methods of delivery currently required by the BPS such as webinars and workshops, as well as specific topics of interests, such as Coaching, Autism, Safeguarding, Public Mental Health, Obesity, Research Excellence Framework, Suicide, Work and Health, Writing for Publication and many others.

With regard to Counselling and Psychotherapy there are a number of centres, agencies and higher education institutions across the UK, usually registered as organisations' members with the main professional bodies (BACP, UKCP, Counselling and Psychotherapy in Scotland, etc) that offer accredited training in these professions and also regular workshops, seminars and CPD events. Specific national portals have been recently created to inform and update counsellors and psychotherapists about all the CPD events and opportunities that run over the calendar year in the UK. The offer of online CPD events and webinars have also become more common, creating a whole new path of distance learning opportunities, such as interviews with specialists in specific areas of mental health and therapeutic approaches, training and conferences that can be attended live (with the possibility to participate actively accessing live forum, spaces for questions and debates) or watched retrospectively.

Regular conferences are also offered annually by the main professional bodies such as the BPS, BACP or the UKCP and addressed to cover specific themes and research updates. Among CPD opportunities for psychologists, counsellors and psychotherapists, training to become a supervisor is an example of the possible offers. The BPS, UKCP and BACP have specific frameworks to accredit training courses in supervision that relate to their professional standards. Usually supervision training is delivered by higher education, further education and private training providers. Training providers in this field can be quite flexible in terms of curriculum to be covered (within different theoretical approaches, including integrative) but they have to meet specific assessment criteria to meet the requirements of the Framework for Higher Education Qualification (FHEQ) and the (NQF) National Qualification Framework/ Qualifications and Credit Framework Levels.

In order to maintain a good standard of CPD courses, providers are encouraged to remain familiar with the constant update of ethical frameworks of the various professional bodies, research development and learning outcomes required, and to offer a chance to participants to evaluate the training and its different aspects at the end of each course. The following vignette illustrates an example where the journey of a practitioner's CPD evolved over time.

Vignette I

Samantha is a Chartered Clinical Psychologist working in a NHS Trust at a mid-management level. She is mid-career and has been a member of BPS for ten years. She has always enjoyed participating in professional development activities, but has not until recently had a particular focus to her learning for future career plans. Two years ago, she completed a skills audit at her place of work, which identified a number of areas she could investigate further for learning opportunities. She successfully completed the BPS Supervision Skills workshops and as a result joined RAPPS (Register of Applied Psychology Practice Supervisors) in order to enhance her skills and career prospects. She has continued to engage in professional development activities periodically, including attendance at a number of BPS and other conferences, in both a delegate and presenting capacity. She has used the BPS MyCPD system to plan, record and reflect on her professional development. Her reflections have demonstrated the implementation of new skills and knowledge and the impact of these on herself and her career, her employers and service users. This is through a range of activities, which she has linked together to form a clearly defined 'journey' of interactions. She has recently

joined a BPS Member Network Committee to further support her development and is part of a mentoring pilot through her workplace, acting as
a mentor for early career clinical psychologists. In following the CPD cycle

and engaging in a range of both formal learning and informal activities, Samantha has been able to demonstrate the benefits of engagement and appreciate the mixed model of activities approach. This approach has been
sought, due to time and resource constraints, which mean she cannot
always take time off work to attend face to face and looks for alternative
material and modes of delivery to continue her participation.

Samantha in her reflection has made reference to the impact, not only in
her career and future work plans, but also in her more positive outlook on
lifelong learner and how the professional achievements have reaped rewards
in personal ambitions.

Challenges and limitations

The areas covering opportunities for CPD in psychology, counselling and psychotherapy are constantly expanding and evolving, as discussed so far. This
section is intended to focus on what are still the main challenges and limitations within this dimension of professional learning and reflect on possible
ways forwards.

As highlighted previously, for example illustrating the CPD cycle, it is clear
that this is a self-reflective process where the individual identifies their needs,
selects specific training and development opportunities and evaluates them. We
have also explained how professional bodies have regular audit processes to
monitor and evaluate the standards of activities undertaken by the individual
practitioners. However, because often in CPD there is not a formal assessment
of learning, one could argue that there is a very limited evidence about the
actual impact that CPD activities have on the practitioner's learning, clinical
practice or clients' outcomes, in contrast to the perceived value of evidence-
based practice often stressed within the profession (Neimeyer et al., 2009,
2010; Rossouw & Hatty, 2013). This could potentially be an interesting area to
develop in terms of research as it would fill a gap in the current knowledge
around CPD.

Another challenging aspect of CPD for practitioners is that, when talking
about professional services, the system or employer's agenda and needs in
providing CPD for employees can bypass the individual's motivation and
personal interest with potential consequent tensions within the system itself
(Rossouw & Hatty, 2013). It is important then to make sure that within professional services there is an open dialogue between organisations and individual members of staff, to discuss openly needs, expectations and learning

outcomes (Mulvey, 2013). Moreover, there are obvious financial implications that represent an open issue between systems and individuals. CPD activities and courses can be very expensive, for example, in the case of accredited and certificated training courses or when international leading experts run workshops and seminars and charge high fees. The question of whether the costs need to be covered by the organisations or by the individual practitioners is a very important one and has been part of the discussions around CPD for some time (Green, 2000). Organisations usually have allocated budgets for covering CPD activities for their employees but it is not always enough to cover the employees' needs and interests. Whereas, for example, the introduction of online CPD activities (sometimes free) may have alleviated some of the financial burdens for practitioners, the overall question about financial responsibilities for professional's CPD, remains an open debate.

Conclusion

This chapter has presented the case for Continuous Professional Development (CPD) in the professional areas of psychology, counselling and psychotherapy and its ethical value for individual practitioners, professional services and wider communities. The 'CPD cycle' has been presented and discussed as the main current model adopted by professional bodies such as BPS, BACP and UKCP to inform and support individual practitioners in the process of identifying suitable CPD activities for their personal and professional development and to evaluate the outcomes. In illustrating the current opportunities available in UK at the moment, it appears that the approved activities offered to professionals vary in terms of content and of modality of delivery, trying to meet different layers of needs, not just in terms of personal interests or identified areas for development, but also style of learning, time availability and financial resources. One direction that is expanding more and more, for example, is that of e-learning through online courses, events and webinars. Thanks to constantly updated technology, these opportunities offer participants the opportunity to engage with the event through live forum, chats and group discussions but also allow those who cannot attend the event 'live', to watch the recorded event via streaming. It is also now possible to access specific websites that offer an updated list of CPD national and international events, making it much easier for organisations and individuals to have a sense of what is currently on offer. In terms of challenges and limitations around CPD for these professions, some possible gaps in evidencing the actual impact of practitioner's learning through CPD activities on their clinical practice and clients' outcomes and experience exist. Another possible challenge is for professional services to find the balance between the system's needs and the individual's interest and specific benefit, as they not always coincide (Mulvey, 2013). Research, pedagogical theories and methods of delivery are constantly evolving in order to respond to an increasing multicultural, often distance learning population of students with different needs and styles of learning (Nind & Lewthwaite, 2018). Similarly, the opportunities offered to professional trainers and practitioners, in any field, including psychology, counselling and psychotherapy, need to keep expanding and developing to assure a sustainable support of their competences, personal and professional skills and ethical practice.

Reflective questions

1. What is the most effective process, for you to identify goals and make a plan for CPD this year?
2. What evidence do you have to demonstrate the impact that CPD activities have on my professional development?
3. How do you evaluate the impact that each of these activities has on my clients?
4. What would be the best tip you could offer to a colleague about how to plan and evaluate their CPD activities?

References

Association for Project Management. (2017) The growing significance of CPD: Ensuring professionalism in a dynamic and changing workplace. Available at: bit.ly/2sufj6.

Earley, P., & Porritt, V. (Eds.). (2008). *Effective Practices in Continuing Professional Development: Lessons from Schools.* Availabe at: https://discovery.ucl.ac.uk/id/eprint/10018638/3/RB15_Effective_CPD_practices_EarleyPorritt.pdf on the 25th of August 2018.

Friedman, A., & Tinner, L. (2016) *CPD Support and Compliance Challenges.* Bristol: PARN.

Golding, L., & Gray, I. (2006) Continuing professional development: A brief guide. *The Psychologist*, 19(9), 530–532.

Green, D. (2000) Who pays for CPD in clinical psychology? *Division of Clinical Psychology Information Leaflet No. 3, Produced by the Continuing Professional Development Subcommittee, BPS.* Available at: https://www.bps.org.uk/member-microsites/division-clinical-psychology accessed 27th August 2018.

Health and Care Professions Council: Glossary of Terms. Available at: https://www.hcpc-uk.org/standards/standards-of-conduct-performance-and-ethics 25th of August 2018.

Mulvey, R. (2013) How to be a good professional? Existentialist continuing professional development (CPD). *British Journal of Guidance and Counselling*, 41(3), 267–276. doi: 10.1080/03069885.2013.773961.

Neimeyer, G.J., Taylor, J.M., & Philip, D. (2010) Continuing education in psychology: Patterns of participation and perceived outcomes among mandated and non mandated psychologists. *Professional Psychology: Research and Practice*, 41(5), 435–441.

Neimeyer, G.J., Taylor, J.M., & Wear, D.M. (2009) Continuing education in psychology: Outcomes, evaluations, and mandates. *Professional Psychology: Research and Practice*, 40(6), 617–624.

Nind, M., & Lewthwaite, S. (2018) Methods that teach: developing pedagogic research methods, developing pedagogy. *International Journal of Research & Method in Education*, 22(1), 74–88.

Nursing and Midwifery Council. (2015) How to revalidate with the NMC: Requirements for renewing your registration. Availabel at: www.nmc.org.uk/globalassets/sitedocuments/nmc-publications/nmc-code.pdf accessed 23rd of August 2018.

Rossouw, P.J., & Hatty, M.A. (2013) Continuing professional development in psychology: requirements, assumptions and the lack of evidence. *Neuropsychotherapy in Australia*, 20, 8–9.

TDA (Training and Development Agency for Schools). (2007) *What does Good CPD Look Like?* London: TDA.

Chapter 22

Clinical vignettes and reflective questions

Jean Morrissey and Rachel Smith

This chapter presents a range of clinical scenarios that represent 'everyday' clinical situations together with various reflective questions based on the respective chapters within the text. Using fictional characters and creative writing strategies, each scenario presents the reader with different professional and ethical issues. The aim of the chapter is to provide the reader with material that will inspire, challenge and act as a springboard for ongoing reflection, discussion and learning concerning the professional and ethical challenges that may confront any trainee, clinician, supervisor and/or trainer within an ever-changing clinical context. Different audiences may be guided by different ethical codes, cultures of practice and training, among which there are many similarities and differences. For each scenario, the reader is asked to focus on the particular professional and ethical issues presented while paying particular attention to his/her code of practice and ethical principles underpinning safe, ethical and legal practice.

Vignette 1

Roslyn works as a part-time psychotherapist at a psychological services unit. She has a good working relationship with Joan, the administrator for the unit. Knowing that Roslyn also sees patients in her private practice, Joan asked Roslyn if she could make an appointment to see her for one or two sessions, saying, 'it's not a serious issue, not like the patients that come to see you here – it's just, I trust you so it will be much easier for me to talk about some personal things, you understand, don't you?'

1. What do you think are the key professional/ethical issues in this scenario?
2. Putting yourself in Roslyn's position, how would you respond to Joan's request?
3. What ethical and professional considerations would inform your response?

4. Imagine Joan asks you 'what should I consider when looking for a therapist?' What would you suggest to her and for what reasons?

5. During your discussion with Joan, she asks you 'which therapeutic approach would you recommend'? What would you say?

6. If you have had, or were going to have, personal therapy what factors were or might be significant for you when choosing a therapist and deciding whether to engage (or not) in therapy?

7. What chapter(s) in this book might assist you to consider the professional and ethical issues in this vignette further?

Vignette 2

Mike, an experienced Humanistic therapist and clinical supervisor, was asked by a local reputable college to supervise a group of four trainee counsellors who are undertaking a three-year degree programme in Integrative counselling. The trainees have just completed their second year and are about to commence their clinical placements whereby each trainee will take on a small case load of two clients.

Before deciding whether to accept this supervision contract, what questions might Mike need to ask the College in reference to the following issues and why?

1. Supervisees' theoretical training

   • The type of clinical placement and client group
   • Professional responsibility and accountability
   • Indemnity cover
   • Modes of communication between college, placement, supervisor and supervisee
   • Supervisee progress reports
   • Fitness to practice issues

2. What do you think are the key professional/ethical issues in this scenario?

3. What chapter(s) in this book might assist you to consider the professional and ethical issues in this vignette further?

Vignette 3

Bernadette works as an accredited CBT counsellor in a voluntary organisation. She has taken on a new client Liza in her early twenties, who sought counselling for 'panic attacks and low mood'. Bernadette and Liza contracted to meet initially for four sessions and then review. On the third session, Liza disclosed with some trepidation 'she was eight weeks pregnant and was considering having a termination'. Following Liza's disclosure, Bernadette was aware of her own discomfort and at the end of the session began to think about ending her contract with Liza on the next session. She recognised that the fit between maintaining professional and ethical practice and her own value and moral position on abortion presented her varying degrees of discomfort. As a peer co-worker, Bernadette shares her predicament with you and asks for your advice and guidance.

1. What would you initially say to Bernadette to assist her in examining her conflict?
2. What codes of practice and ethical principles should Bernadette refer to – to inform her decision about ending with Liza at this time?
3. Is there any other information you would like to have from Liza?
4. Should Bernadette decide that she is unable to work with this client, what would be a therapeutic and helpful way of terminating the counselling work?
5. What sources of supports are there for Bernadette? Where can she turn to for help with this issue?
6. What are your views about premature termination with a client?
7. What do you think are the key professional/ethical issues in this scenario?
8. Reflecting on your own clinical experience, have you ever experienced a situation whereby your own values or position on a certain issue challenged you in your clinical work? If so, what were the issues and how did you approach reconciling them?
9. What chapter(s) in this book might assist you to consider the professional and ethical issues in this vignette further?

Vignette 4

Dylan, a Narrative Therapist in an Adult Mental Health service received a referral from a GP requesting help for Mr and Mrs El-Salahi originally from the Sudan, following the sudden death of their 16-year-old son, Mustapha. According to the referral letter, Mrs El-Salahi speaks limited English and communicates mainly through her husband. In order to provide an important link between him and both clients, Dylan decides to conduct the initial consultation with an interpreter.

1. What does Dylan need to consider before undertaking clinical work using an interpreter concerning the following?

    *   Advising the client(s) and seeking their permission for the interpreter to be present
    *   Choosing an interpreter
    *   Allocating time for interpretation and the pre-briefing
    *   Preparing for interpretation
    *   The bilingual meeting
    *   Debriefing after the meeting

2. The addition of an interpreter will change the dynamics of the meeting, what challenges and opportunities might this present for you in your area of practice?
3. In the consulting room, how might your beliefs, values and reactions reflect your own culturally determined view of the world?
4. How do you feel hearing people say specific things about your own culture?
5. What aspects of your cultural background would you like people to be more informed about and for what reason?
6. What do you think are the key professional/ethical issues in this scenario?
7. What chapter(s) in this book might assist you to consider the professional and ethical issues in this vignette further?

Vignette 5

Zariah is a senior clinical psychologist working in Adult Mental Health services. Part of her role involves facilitating trainees from different helping professional backgrounds to get the most from their placement and maximise their professional learning. Zariah is particularly interested in helping trainees to develop their knowledge and practice especially concerning professional and ethical clinical issues. On meeting each new trainee, she asks him/her the following questions.

1. How would you answer these questions either as a trainee or in your role a trainer/facilitator to trainees?

    a. What professional or ethical issue(s) has been the most challenging for you to date and for what reason(s)?
    b. What factors help and/or hinder you to examine professional or ethical issue(s) and facilitate new understanding and learning?

c. In the consulting room, how might having a greater awareness of professional, legal and ethical considerations improve your clinical practice and outcome?
d. How does your code of practice and ethical principles assist you in providing safe ethical practice?
e. How might you help a junior colleague to develop a greater awareness of professional, legal and ethical considerations in clinical practice?
f. What would you do if you witnessed a colleague saying or doing something that you considered unprofessional and/or unethical?
2. What do you think are the key professional/ethical issues in this scenario?
3. What chapter(s) in this book might assist you to consider the professional and ethical issues in this vignette further?

Vignette 6

Due to organisational restructuring, Paul a part-time counselling psychologist in Adult Mental Health, has been asked to take up a full-time position in CAMHS (Children and Adolescent Mental Health Service). While looking forward to broadening his knowledge and skills in this specialist area of practice, he is anxious about his new position especially since he has minimal clinical experience working with this client group. Before starting his new post, he arranges a meeting with Louise, an experienced therapist who has worked for many years in CAMHS. On meeting Louise, Paul asks the following questions. How would you answer these questions if you were Louise?

1. In what way do professional, ethical and legal issues in CAMHS differ from those in Adult Mental Health?
2. What particular professional, ethical and legal issue(s) might I be faced with when working with children, adolescents and their families? Can you give examples?
3. What do you need to think about with regard to confidentiality when you are working with a four-year-old and how do you explain this to the child?
4. How would you explain issues relating to boundary setting and the limits of confidentiality to a 14-year-old?

5. How do you approach the challenges of working with teenagers while respecting parents' needs and requests to be informed of their child's progress?
6. What do you think are the key professional/ethical issues in this scenario?
7. What chapter(s) in this book might assist you to consider the professional and ethical issues in this vignette further?

Vignette 7

Raziya a trainee clinical psychologist was completing her Older Adult placement. Before ending, she met with Simon, her clinical mentor, to reflect on her placement, experiences and learning. Raziya stated that she had really enjoyed working with Older Adult clients despite the fact that she 'was dreading this placement' at the outset. Reflecting on her beliefs prior to starting the placement, she acknowledged her preconceptions and how she had believed that 'older clients might not be receptive or willing to discuss their personal problems, and particularly with someone who was young enough to be their daughter or indeed granddaughter'. During further discussion, Simon asked Raziya the following questions. How might you answer these questions if you were Raziya?

1. What do you think are the key professional/ethical issues in this scenario?
2. How might ageism manifest in the consulting room?
3. What particular professional, ethical and legal issue(s) have you encountered when working with older clients or clients with long-term needs? Can you give examples?
4. What might it be like for you working with clients who may be the same age as your parents/grandparents and how might you approach it?
5. How has your clinical training helped you [or not] to develop a greater awareness of professional, legal and ethical considerations when working with older clients or clients with long term needs?
6. What chapter(s) in this book might assist you to consider the professional and ethical issues in this vignette further?

Vignette 8

George has just successfully completed his two-year postgraduate psycho-therapy programme. During his training, he worked as an unpaid therapist in two voluntary organisations and a GP practice. Sally, a colleague, informed him that there was a vacancy coming up for a full-time counsellor/therapist in a nearby Primary care setting.

1. Sally who works in Primary care offers to help George by arranging a mock interview and asking the following questions. How would you answer these questions if you were being interviewed?

   • How does your theoretical orientation fit with short-term work?
   • What professional/ethical challenges might you encounter when working in Primary care?
   • Please give an example of a piece of work where you felt you had to work outside of the model you are predominantly inclined towards, and why? What did you learn about yourself from this experience?
   • In your opinion, what factors enhance/hinder effective MDT work in Primary care?
   • How might 'being paid' for your clinical work impact on you and your clinical work?

2. What do you think are the key professional/ethical issues in this scenario?
3. What chapter(s) in this book might assist you to consider the professional and ethical issues in this vignette further?

Vignette 9

Kajori, an experienced clinician and researcher, is Jeanie's research supervisor for her Doctorate in Clinical Psychology. Jeanie is undertaking a qualitative (interview-based) study in the area of female self-harm within a forensic setting. Having received ethical approval, Jeanie and Kajori arrange a meeting to discuss potential professional and ethical issues that might occur while conducting research interviews and explore how Jeanie might best manage them. Imagine you are Jeanie, how would you respond to the following questions posed by her supervisor?

1. What are the issues that you need to consider in terms of the context of this research study?
2. What is your understanding of research on 'sensitive' topics?

3. What professional and ethical issues do you need to consider in reference to promising confidentiality to research participants?
4. How will you ensure that your needs as a researcher do not cause or contribute to distress for the participants?
5. What self-care strategies could you use to ensure your own well-being while undertaking data collection/analysis and how might they assist you in your dual role as researcher and clinician?
6. What do you think are the key professional/ethical issues in this scenario?
7. What chapter(s) in this book might assist you to consider the professional and ethical issues in this vignette further?

Vignette 10

Abdul has just successfully completed his Doctorate in Counselling Psychology. During his training, he worked in various voluntary organisations and NHS mental health settings. A colleague, Andrew, informed him, that there was vacancy coming up for a full-time therapist in a nearby Secondary care setting. Andrew, an experienced psychotherapist who works in Secondary care, offers to help Abdul to prepare by arranging a mock interview and asking the following questions. How would you answer these questions if you were being interviewed?

1. How does your theoretical orientation fit with medium-to-long-term work?
2. What professional/ethical considerations and challenges might you encounter when working in Secondary care?
3. Please give an example of a piece of work where you felt you had to work outside of the model you are predominantly inclined towards, and why. What did you learn about yourself from this experience?
4. In your opinion, what factors enhance/hinder effective MDT work in Secondary care?
5. As the NHS moves towards a 'payment by results' (PRB) economy, how might this impact on your clinical work and possibly conflict with your professional and ethical beliefs that inform your work?
6. What do you think are the key professional/ethical issues in this scenario?
7. What chapter(s) in this book might assist you to consider the professional and ethical issues in this vignette further?

Vignette 11

Mary is a third-year student on a four-year Masters programme in Integrative psychotherapy. She works as an unpaid counsellor for a large charity. She recently started work with Edward, a 50-year-old man who has cerebral palsy. At the outset, Mary discussed with her clinical supervisor and the centre manager her concerns about taking on Edward who has severe difficulties in verbal expression/articulation and whether she was 'skilled enough to work with someone with a disability'. Over time, Mary learnt from Edward about the importance of stating when she does not understand what he is saying and above all not to do what so many people do – 'pretend they understand'. In supervision, Andrea has discussed how she has become aware of her skills and development needs in this area. At the same time, she is mindful that she is required to complete a recorded process report as part of her course requirement. Reflecting on this, Mary considers which client to approach to seek his/her permission. She wants to ask Edward; however, she is concerned that his speech impediment would interfere with the audibility of the recording. Although uncomfortable with her decision, Mary decided to approach another client. She feels guilty about her decision and recognises that she is also discriminating against Edward on the grounds of his disability. Thinking about this scenario:

1. What do you think are the key professional/ethical issues in this scenario?
2. What are your thoughts/views about Mary's decision? How might you have handled it and for what reasons?
3. Reflecting on your own experience as a therapist, supervisor or trainer, have you ever experienced a situation whereby your own values or position on a client's, supervisee's or trainee's disability challenged you in your clinical work? If so, what was the issue and how did you reconcile it?
4. What is your organisation's policy on disability and how is it operationalised in practice?
5. What chapter(s) in this book might assist you to consider the professional and ethical issues in this vignette further?

Vignette 12

James, an experienced systemic therapist, endeavours to keep himself physically fit; yet he questions whether he pays as much attention to maintaining his emotional well-being. Thinking about this further, he reflected on whether he had been 'fit to practice' the previous year when his long-standing relationship with his partner ended. Although he only took a few days off work, he recalled feeling anxious and low in mood for several months. He wondered if his clients noticed and to what extent had impacted on the therapeutic relationship and his effectiveness as a family therapist. His manager, Ken, was very supportive at the time and asked if he needed time off work. He declined his offer, believing that it was best to 'keep busy'; he recognised this was his old pattern during times of stress. He had done the same several years ago when his best friend, Shane, died by suicide. James decided to think about 'fitness to practice' further and discuss it at his next reflecting team meeting. How might you answer these questions if you were a member of that peer group?

1. What are your thoughts/views about James's decisions to keep on working? How might you have handled a similar situation – the same/differently? In addition, for what reasons?
2. What criteria do you use to determine whether you are 'fit to practice'?
3. What issues might help/hinder/you from acknowledging that you are 'unfit to practice'?
4. What issues might help/hinder you from acknowledging that a peer co-worker is 'unfit to practice'?
5. What is your organisation's policy/procedures on fitness to practice and how is it implemented?
6. What do you think are the key professional/ethical issues in this scenario?
7. What chapter(s) in this book might assist you to consider the professional and ethical issues in this vignette further?

Vignette 13

A study day on 'The Role of Social Media: Challenges and Opportunities for Counsellors, Psychologists & Psychotherapists' is being advertised and you are interested in attending. Imagine you have enrolled to attend this study day, how you would respond to the following questions as part of the study day requisite?

1. What training/education have you received to date on social media and therapy?
2. What do you hope to learn from attending this study day? Identify three specific things.

3. What professional/ethical challenges have you encountered in your area of practice concerning social media? Illustrate your answer with examples.
4. What is your organisation's policy on The Role of Social Media and Therapy and how is it implemented in practice?
5. What chapter(s) in this book might assist you to consider the professional and ethical issues in this vignette further?

Vignette 14

Cameron, an experienced cognitive behavioural therapist works as a senior clinician/co-ordinator for a large charity that offers low-fee counselling for clients with a range of psychological problems. The charity is a popular placement for trainees from diverse training backgrounds and theoretical orientations. Although there are policy guidelines concerning clients' notes (e.g. regarding security and confidentiality), Cameron has become aware that there is wide disparity in what trainees – and indeed some experienced practitioners – write in clients' notes. While Cameron does not want to be prescriptive, he believes that some key principles need to be drawn up on 'writing client notes' as part of achieving good practice. With the agreement of the supervisor and the centre director, Cameron decided to research the area of note taking and invited all staff and trainees to attend a meeting to discuss the topic and consider the following questions in preparation for the forthcoming discussion. How would you answer the following questions?

1. What do you think are the key professional/ethical issues in this scenario?
2. What should be included in client notes?
3. What should not be included in client notes?
4. How should contact records be structured/arranged?
5. What is your organisation's practice placement criteria for what is to be written in clients' notes?
6. Has your approach to clinical notes changed over the years, if so, in what way?
7. What chapter(s) in this book might assist you to consider the professional and ethical issues in this vignette further?

Vignette 15

Kay, an experienced psychotherapist, works on part-time basis in a Secondary care setting. As part of the staff's Continuing Professional Development (CPD), a member of the MDT presents a paper/clinical case for discussion at their monthly 'Journal Club'. Having a keen interest and many years of experience working in the area of self-harm, Kay agreed to present the following paper 'Working in Particular Settings with People who Self-Injure' (Babiker & Arnold, 1997). She also presented a clinical case of a young man called Tom who cuts himself when he feels 'angry', 'really bad' or 'full of guilt'. As he cuts, 'he physically feels no pain, but feels a sense of relief when he sees his blood'. Tom attends to see Kate weekly and always brings his blades with him, just in case he 'might feel bad after the session'. After Kay's presentation, much discussion ensued about self-harm and the harm-reduction (harm-minimisation) approach as opposed to harm-prevention strategies. Imagine that you are the therapist in this scenario:

1. What do you think are the key professional/ethical issues in this scenario?
2. How would you feel during and after the session, knowing that Tom had immediate access to his blades after each session?
3. In your experience, in what ways, and for whom, is self-injury (harm) a problem? How might identifying this help you in your clinical work?
4. In your clinical role, how do you balance reducing risk to client and reducing risk to self?
5. What has been your experience of working in organisations/institutions whereby the model of care for self-harm is a preventative/cure approach. What challenges does it present for the client, the therapist, MDT and the organisation?
6. Reflecting on your own clinical experience, have you ever experienced a situation whereby your own values or position on a client's self-harming behaviour challenged you in your clinical work? If so, what was the issue and how did you reconcile it?
7. What chapter(s) in this book might assist you to consider the professional and ethical issues in this vignette further?

Vignette 16

Madeline, an experienced CBT therapist, thought about the pending loss of many experienced colleagues who were retiring in the coming year. She thought about their wealth of experience, the numerous changes they had encountered in clinical practice and the many clients, trainees, supervisees, colleagues they had work with over the years. She asked her colleague Peter who had retired recently, 'what sustained him to be able to work for nearly 30 years in clinical practice?' He replied, 'I've learnt about the importance of good self-care'. Reflecting on Peter's response, she thought about specific situations where she now recognises that she compromised her self-care and as result suffered both professionally and personally. With some difficultly, she recognises that this has been a long-standing issue over the course of her career. Wanting to implement change, she wonders how she might begin to develop better self-care strategies. Reflecting on this scenario, how might you respond to the following questions?

1. What do you think are the key professional/ethical issues in this scenario?
2. What suggestions would you offer to Madeline to help her consider and implement better self-care?
3. Why do you think self-care is important in counselling and psychotherapy work?
4. Reflecting on your own practice, what personal, professional, organisational factors might enhance and/or hinder your self-care?
5. How might you know if you have neglected/compromised your self-care?
6. What chapter(s) in this book might assist you to consider the professional and ethical issues in this vignette further?

Vignette 17

For nearly two years, Ricardo, a 22-year-old, has been seeing Peter, a gay therapist, who has not disclosed his sexuality to Ricardo. One evening when attending an LGBTQIA event with his friends, Ricardo meets Peter. Ricardo questions his therapist about his sexuality at the next session. Reflecting on this scenario, how might you respond to the following questions? Imagining you are Peter; how might you respond to Richardo's challenge about his sexuality?

1. Under what circumstances (if any) might you disclose your sexuality to a client/supervisee/trainee?
2. Reflecting on how it would be to work with an LGBT client; what preconceptions, if any, would emerge for you?
3. As a LGBT client, therapist, supervisor or trainer what preconceptions, if any, have you encountered from clients, supervisees, trainees, colleagues or your professional organisation?
4. How comfortable are you when discussing issues of sexuality with your clients, supervisees, trainees?

5. What do you think are the key professional/ethical issues in this scenario?
6. What chapter(s) in this book might assist you to consider the professional and ethical issues in this vignette further?

Vignette 18

An experienced psychotherapist, Robert works in a Secondary care setting. As a clinician, supervisor and trainer he is always mindful of the importance of confidentiality and boundaries but particularly so since moving to live and work in a rural setting. A year ago, Robert took on a new patient, Charles, who was married to Carol and has two teenage children. Charles described feelings of self-hatred and guilt about 'living a lie' with his wife, Carol, and their two children. While he did not think he was gay, Charles stated, 'He had enjoyed sex with men for many years'. A few months later, Robert met up with his colleagues for their bimonthly peer supervision. A colleague, Barbara, began to present a couple, Charles and Carol, whom had recently started therapy. She stated that she was finding it hard to engage Charles in therapy who had cancelled on a few occasions. His wife, Carol, was quite depressed and feared that her husband was having an affair with another woman. Based on what Barbara has said – it suddenly became clear to Robert that she was discussing his client, and at that point, he immediately excused himself. Reflecting on this scenario, how might you respond to the following questions?

1. What do you think are the key professional/ethical issues in this scenario?
2. What should Robert say/or not to Charles about their next appointment?
3. What process or transferential issues are you aware of when reading this vignette and how might they affect you if Charles was your patient/client?
4. Have you experienced a similar situation, if so, how did you approach it and what did you learn from the experience?
5. What chapter(s) in this book might assist you to consider the professional and ethical issues in this vignette further?

Vignette 19

Shamir is a senior psychiatrist in a Community Adult Mental Health Team, with a particular interest in developing services to maintain high ethical standards and become more appropriate and relevant to the populations they are there to serve. Part of his role involves facilitating trainees from different helping professional backgrounds to get the most from their placement and maximise their professional learning particularly concerning working collaboratively with service users and their families/carers, and to find a way around the issues to make user involvement a practical reality. On meeting each new trainee, he asks them the following questions.

1. What is your understanding of co-production?
2. What is the difference between co-production and collaborative practice?
3. Identify three concerns that you have about sharing power and decision-making with your clients in clinical therapy services?
4. Identify three potential benefits of service user involvement in clinical therapy services?
5. What factors might enhance practitioners to proactively take up user involvement and seek open communication and feedback in counselling and therapy services?
6. What factors might hinder practitioners to proactively take up user involvement and seek open communication and feedback in counselling and therapy services?
7. What three things could you do in your area of practice to raise awareness and promote open discussion so that a way forward for user involvement may be found in clinical therapy services?
8. In your area of practice, how might having a greater awareness of service user involvement improve your clinical practice and client satisfaction?

Vignette 20

Tobias an experienced Integrative therapist and clinical supervisor, was asked by a local reputable college to give a half-day training on 'The Adverse effects of Therapy' to trainees who are undertaking a four-year MSc programme in Integrative Psychotherapy. As part of the workshop, Tobias asks the trainees to get into small groups and answer the following questions in relation to the statement:

It is often said in jest that therapy should come with a health warning. The discomfort so often associated with the psychotherapeutic process may be experienced as injurious in the moment and deleterious in the long term if not handled well.

(Cross & Wood 2015: 47)

1. Thinking about the adverse effects of therapy, what do you think are the key professional/ethical issues for you, your organisation and professional body? Give examples.

2. How do you prepare your clients for the likelihood of adverse effects from counselling/psychotherapy?
3. When might you advise a client *not* to engage in counselling psychotherapy and for what reason(s)?
4. How do you respond to clients who state, 'I feel worse since coming here [therapy]'?
5. How do you manage clients/families who report adverse effects because of counselling/psychotherapy?
6. What chapter(s) in this book might assist you to consider the professional and ethical issues in this vignette further?
7. Reflecting on your own experience of personal therapy, what thoughts/feelings, does the above statement evoke?

Vignette 21

Aisha, a senior social worker in Adult Mental Health, has been asked to take up a part-time position in supporting and facilitating trainees from different professional backgrounds during their Adult Mental Health placement. While looking forward to taking on this tutoring role, she arranges a meeting with Tina, a clinical psychologist who previously undertook this role for many years. On meeting, Tina helps Aisha to reflect and consider her new role by asking the following questions. How would you answer these questions if you were Aisha?

1. What professional, ethical and legal issue(s) might you be faced with when working with trainees from different professional backgrounds? Can you give examples?
2. How does your professional code of practice help you to support and educate trainees in thinking through dilemmas? Give examples.
3. How might you support trainees to work with complex presentations? when trying to negotiate and balance their duties and responsibilities?
4. How might you respond to a trainee who discloses an issue of unsafe practice?
5. How might you enhance trainees' awareness of ethical and professional consideration to ensure best practice?
6. What chapter(s) in this book might assist you to consider the professional and ethical issues in this vignette further?

Vignette 22

Emeka, a trainee clinical psychologist, was undertaking his child and family placement. As part of his learning agreement, he met with Sarah, his clinical mentor, to reflect on his placement, experiences and learning. Emeka stated that he was enjoying working with young people and their families/carers, although at times he had some concern that risk management was disproportionately focused on client inadequacies, which further marginalised people who had mental health difficulties. While discussing examples of risk aversive methods to prevent harm, he acknowledged wider societal trends in risk avoidance and that the team's fear of complaints and blame may explain the staff's behaviour. During further discussion, Sarah asked Emeka the following questions. How might you answer these questions if you were Emeka?

1. What do you think are the key professional/ethical issues in this scenario?
2. What do you understand as 'defensive practices'? Give examples.
3. Reflecting on your own area of work, have you witnessed or carried out risk aversive practices in your area of work? Give examples.
4. What do you understand as 'positive–risk taking'? Give examples.
5. Give examples of organisational practices that might promote and reinforce a culture of defensive rather than defendable practice?
6. Give examples of organisational practices that might support a culture of positive risk taking?
7. How has your clinical training helped you [or not] to develop a greater awareness of positive risk taking with clients at times in their well-being and recovery?
8. What chapter(s) in this book might assist you to consider the professional and ethical issues in this vignette further?

Vignette 23

Amira, a consultant psychologist with a particular interest in community psychology and social justice, was asked by a local university to be part of a Re-Accreditation team for a Professional Doctorate in Counselling Psychology curriculum. In preparing, Amira writes some questions to ask the curriculum team at the meeting. How would you respond to the following questions if you were a member of the curriculum team?

1. Community psychology asserts a commitment to social justice and empowerment of communities yet faces some distinctive ethical issues and dilemmas. Can you give an example of some?

2. What are some of the tensions that exist between the professionalisa-
    tion of community psychology and the aim of 'giving away psychology'
    and being accountable to the most marginalised?
3. What are the potential challenges in applying ethical codes conceived
    within an individualistic framework to community psychology?
4. What are the criticisms of professional curricula for not equipping its
    practitioners with a clearer framework and skill set to work directly
    from a social justice agenda?
5. What are the different ways in which practitioners can demonstrate
    their commitment to social justice values and action?
6. What chapter(s) in this book might assist you to consider the profes-
    sional and ethical issues in this vignette further?
7. In your own area of clinical practice, what do you do to raise aware-
    ness, share knowledge, challenge old ways of thinking and empower
    clients?

Conclusion

There is little doubt that 'everyday' clinical situations present a range of professional, ethical and legal challenges for the trainee, clinician, supervisor
and/or trainer within an ever-changing clinical context. Professional codes
and guidelines offer some guidance and support; however, they are by no
means intended to be conclusive. In addition, as with all professional and
ethical challenges, there are no absolutes, each situation needs to be given
careful ethical and professional consideration to ensure best practice. It is
hoped that having the opportunity to reflect on and discuss the above
vignettes in a safe and supportive context will contribute to enhancing the
trainee's/clinician's capacity to be constantly ethically mindful in undertaking
their challenging work and roles.

Reflective questions

1. Which scenario(s) have you found the most relevant and for what
    reasons?
2. Which scenario(s) have you found the least relevant and for what
    reasons?
3. What professional/ethical issues would you add and why?
4. What professional/ethical issues would you like to learn more and
    for what reasons?

References

Babiker, G., & Arnold, L. (1997) *The Language of Injury, Comprehending Self-Mutilation*, Leicester, UK: BPS Blackwell, pp. 127–143.

Cross, M., & Wood, J. (2015) The Person in ethical decision-making: living with our choices. In R. Tribe & J. Morrissey (Eds.). *The Handbook of Professional and Ethical Practice*, Hove, UK: Brunner-Routledge, pp. 47–59.

Part 6

Social Inclusion

Chapter 23

Social justice theory and practice

Haneyeh Belyani and Claire Marshall

'Social' comes from the Latin '*socialis*' meaning 'Of companionship or allies' (Online etymology dictionary, 2018a), while the etymology of 'Justice' originates from the Latin '*iustitia*' meaning 'Righteousness or equity' (Online etymology dictionary, 2018b). Social justice then, is virtue, fairness and decency between individuals, groups or communities. The human rights agenda assigns principles to the individual, relating to certain standards (Mayblin, 2017), hence the notion of an individual's 'right' was tied to law and the Universal Declaration of Human Rights was created, asserting that 'All human beings are born free and equal in dignity and rights. They are endowed with reason and conscience and should act towards one another in a spirit of brotherhood' (UN General Assembly, 1948). In contemporary literature, social justice has been defined in many ways, including:

> Social justice is one way of thinking about addressing social inequalities and encouraging inclusion. It incorporates a human rights perspective and promotes a just society by challenging injustice and valuing diversity. It accepts that there has not been a level playing field, power has not been equally distributed and that self-determination and opportunities for some individuals and groups remains an aspiration as opposed to a reality. It attempts to move away from an individualised model of blame or causation which psychology has often unwittingly followed. For example, mental health has often been seen as an exclusively individual issue, without any relation to the wider context and societal factors which may predispose a person to poor mental health.
>
> (Tribe & Bell, 2017: 20)

On this basis:

> Social justice involves promoting access and equity to ensure full participation in the life of a society, particularly for those who have been systematically excluded on the basis of race/ethnicity, gender, age, physical or

mental disability, education, sexual orientation, socioeconomic status, or other characteristics of background or group membership.

(Courtland, 2007: 2)

These are not discreet social stratifications: they are often inextricably inter-twined (Rosenthal, 2016). Indeed, identities are formed based on these factors and one's experience in society hinges on how it conceptualises and responds to such givens. However, the very fact that these categories have traditionally been presented as binary categories (black/white, male/female, young/old, able/disable, educated/uneducated, heterosexual/homosexual), says something quite concretely about those who categorise in this way. Social justice issues are cur-rently being addressed in the therapies, from training (Flores et al., 2014; Gainor, 2005; Koch & Juntunen, 2014; Lago & Smith, 2017; Palmer & Parish 2008; Spanierman & Smith, 2017) to practice (as will be discussed later in this chapter). While interrogation of the specificities of how issues pertaining to social (in)justices should be highlighted to therapists in training and discus-sions around the implications for clinical practice are invaluable, the context from which such injustices arises first needs more thought. Thus, the opening section of this chapter seeks to not only define social justice and the codifica-tions associated with it but also what such definitions and the paradigms used to conceptualise social (in)justice implies about societies as a whole. In the second half of the chapter, implications for clinical practice will be explored.

In contemporary society, identity politics has been codified using legal, pol-itical and economic systems of value. It has been argued that neoliberalism affects the individual person, as they contend and adapt within employment motivated by individualism. It is this conformity to capitalism and the work place that has come to dictate our own value and worth (Pallotta-Chiarolli & Pease, 2014). The economy has reduced institutions and individuals to money making machines, caught in transactional relationships that are only assigned value in terms of economic output or productivity. Meanwhile, the accelerated pace of life facilitated by technology, the flows of global migration and the endless possibilities for success presented as attainable for those who apply themselves correctly, along with a climate of self-authorship where identity is presented as something that can/should be constantly re-invented (and commu-nicated to the world in affirmation-seeking sound bites) leads to an implicit instability. The narrative around one's response to this instability is often defined as the requirement to develop resilience. 'To be resilient the subject must ... accept ... an understanding of life as a permanent process of continual adaptation to threats and dangers that are said to be outside of its control' (Chandler & Reid, 2016: 53).

Issues of social injustices are inherently tied with territories of experience that the mainstream has organised as divergent (Jun, 2017). 'Ife (2010) locates the normative framework that entrenches privileges a legacy of the Enlightenment and Western humanism, whereby the human was exalted over and above nature. As he points out, it was a particular construction of the human that was idealised, namely European, white, adult, able-bodied and highly educated males. Thus, humanism was used to defend a Western, patriarchal and colonialist world view' (Pease, 2010: 7). Communities and individuals define themselves not only by what they are but what they are not; the theory of the Other is one useful way to understand this (Dalal, 2012; Jensen, 2011). Lacan (2001) suggested humans *come into being* in relation to Otherness. Otherness shows itself in society's rules, and expectations, as well as the things it agreed on and the things that are offensive, forbidden or banned. He also thought Otherness appeared in language. For Lacan, our relationship with the Other tells us a lot about who we are. This is to say that the way we talk about and organise our communities reveals our views, prejudices, biases, ethics, morals and so on. Language and conceptual frameworks say a great deal about the individual and collective psychology of those who want or need to reduce some peoples experience in this way (Baldwin, 2017; Fanon, 2017; Kristeva, 1991; Žižek, 2016). First, we must interrogate the psyches of those who have created the categories by which people are marginalised, delegitimized and disregarded.

It has been argued that 'To surmount the situation of oppression, people must first critically recognize its causes, so that through transforming action they can create a new situation' (Freire, 1970: 21). This view is challenging when engaging with issues of social (in)justice, as the problem is so often located within the individual rather than the systems themselves and much less with those who silently partake in upholding these systems (Herman, 1997). As others have argued:

> The reproduction of oppression does not require active consciousness on the part of the privileged … People in privileged groups feel that their lives are normal. In fact, they have become the model for idealised human relations and this partly explains why most do not want to know about the experiences of the oppressed.
>
> (Pease, 2010: 12)

From this normative stance, ways of relating become codified in pre-assigned symbolic values that people replicate and reinforce by operating within systems of subjugation. In other words: 'Internalized privilege and oppression are sometimes manifested as prejudice and stereotypes. Prejudice and stereotypes are activated automatically and influence individuals' perception and judgment, and oftentimes individuals are not aware of this influence' (Chung & Bemak, 2012: 112–113).

If we are to engage truly with the subject of social (in)justice, we must not confuse 'symptom' (response) and cause. Understanding the contextual factors is paramount. We must consider the client's context – both in terms of the options available, the opportunities they have been afforded and the resources that are accessible to them. But we must go further. We must radically critique the systems of power that give rise to inequality. We must then go further still and interrogate the motives, drives and intentions behind these. It is only in so doing that we might adequately appreciate the social ontology and therein truly empathise, articulate and begin to engage therapeutically with issues of social (in)justice. What follows now is an exploration of how psychologists and psychotherapists might engage with social (in)justice issues in practice.

Social justice in practice

The question of whether we should be concerned with social justice in our practice has been largely answered by writers who have positioned practitioners as having a duty and responsibility to acknowledge and address social justice issues. 'The psychologist who stands by silently while oppression occurs', has been identified as engaging in 'Passive collusion' (Brown, 1997: 59). Shklar (1990) also points to 'Passive injustice', noting that it is easier to mislabel injustice as misfortune than acknowledge it. Aldarondo (2007) maintains the necessity to address clients' social realities if we are to address their distress. This is in line with the view that wellness is interconnected with the meeting of personal, relational and collective needs and that 'Wellness cannot flourish in the absence of justice' (Prilleltensky, et al., 2007: 19).

There has been a growing amount of literature 'Focussed on translating the field's social justice values into social justice action' (Cutts, 2013: 10). Examples include professional practice guidelines (e.g. British Psychological Society, 2017); the Draft Code of Ethics proposed and under consultation by the UK Council for Psychotherapy (2018) and the British Association of Social Worker's Code of Ethics (2014).

Different levels of action in practice

In 2016, a referendum on whether the UK should stay or leave the European Union (EU), resulted in 52% of voters choosing to leave the EU. London, where the majority of voters had cast their vote to remain, became a hotspot for discussion and analysis, which followed clients into the therapy room as they expressed their views and feelings on the matter. January 2017 saw the inauguration of Donald Trump as America's forty-fifth president. At the time, despite having no American clients, this controversial and divisive new president often visited the therapy room through client accounts. Then in November 2017, The Global Wealth Report by Credit Suisse identified that more than half of the world's wealth was in the hands of the richest 1% of the population, which promoted an Oxfam press release highlighting a 'Huge gulf' between those who have wealth and those who do not (Kramers, 2017, para. 1). Yet, despite its significance, this piece of news was surprisingly absent from our consulting rooms, leaving us to question why, when the consequences are arguably further reaching.

This description of the impact social injustice can have on individuals may help us start to understand this silence:

> Every oppression and injustice tries to convince people to swallow its message about what to expect from life. It adjusts persons to take their place in an unjust social world without complaining (and often enlists counselling for this purpose) … people are convinced that injustice is the natural order and there must be something wrong with them if they do not accept it.
>
> (Winslade, 2017: 19)

Reynolds and Hammoud-Beckett (2017) stress the importance of clinicians making an intentional move away from neutrality and towards the adoption of an activist and 'Justice-doing' stance. Social justice advocacy has been promoted by identifying a 'Responsibility to be role models in word and deed' (Arredondo & Perez, 2003: 288). Winslade (2017) acknowledges that social justice is often associated with advocacy, however he points to the importance of helping clients find alternative discourses to narrate their experiences and identifies therapeutic conversation as a form of action in and of itself.

We wish to highlight a dichotomy between 'being' and 'doing', as this split positions the former as passive and the latter as active. Instead, we wish to emphasise that action towards social justice can take many nuanced forms that can encompass both aspects of how practitioners position themselves in relation to discrimination and inequality as well as how they work with clients. This flexibility allows the socially conscious practitioner to intervene across different levels, including working with the individual, shaping policy and impacting on service delivery. The rest of the chapter will highlight some of the ways this can be done in clinical practice and seeks to ground these examples in clinical case studies.

A phenomenological stance

Assuming oppression and injustice become internalised (Winslade, 2017), how can we enable clients to recognise and express such experiences? We suggest that within a therapeutic context, this empowerment begins at assessment. Gerber (2007) reflects on clients' internal and external worlds, noting that clients often believe that therapy is concerned with their internal world, leaving out details relating to their external world. He reports specifically asking clients about their feelings in regards to their community and social or political events during the assessment sessions. Gathering this information in the initial phases allows the practitioner to get a fuller picture of the client in context. While asking specifically about such events can communicate that this material has a place in therapy and may prevent harmful social conditions being mistaken for interpersonal or psychological difficulties (Aldarondo, 2007), we also wish to draw attention to the significance of exploring the meaning attributed to these experiences.

A commitment to phenomenology involves continual efforts to suspend 'Previous knowledge' in order to concentrate on 'Subjectivity and phenomenon as experienced' (Finlay, 2016: 175). The importance of phenomenology has been highlighted, emphasising the 'Respect for the personal, subjective experience of the client over and above notions of diagnosis, assessment and treatment, as well as the pursuit of innovative, phenomenological methods for understanding human experience' (Lane & Corrie, 2007: 120). We posit that a phenomenological stance is in line with social justice values, as it provides clients with the opportunity to examine the labels that have been used to construct their experience and explore the meanings attributed to them. Through questioning the implicit truth claims of the associations to these labels, clients can find the freedom to construct their own meaning making and narrative. In essence, we believe that matters relating to oppression can only be expressed in spaces that are non-oppressive and as far as possible agenda-free, which conversely may include suspending our own social justice agenda.

To ground this notion in practice, we take the vignette example of 71-year-old Sam.

Vignette I

An unexpected deterioration in Sam's health led to the sudden amputation of his leg while he was in surgery – a medical decision that had not been discussed with him but seen as necessary to save his life. Two years later, feeling depressed and isolated, Sam started therapy after much encouragement by his family. Described as an active man who was once 'full of life', Sam now described himself as a 'disabled old fool' and apologised for wasting precious resources. The therapeutic work focussed on Sam's view of self and identity, staying close to the way that Sam made sense of his loss and his conceptualisations of masculinity and strength. This phenomenological stance allowed Sam to suspend societal narratives, labels and expectations (or lack of) around age and disability, allowing more freedom to explore his own meanings and create alternative ones if he so wished. Sam reflected that he had believed the 'expected and dignified response' to the amputation of his leg was to accept he was aging, had health complications and should expect less from himself and life. Sam chose to reject these labels and barriers, choosing to define himself on his own terms, looking forward to a fuller future that could still be meaningful.

The therapeutic gaze

The work with Sam demonstrates how therapy can enable clients to explore society's role in constructing their identity and provide a space to renegotiate these constructions. The therapeutic value in enabling clients to explore alternative identities and versions of the self is emphasised as the 'Social availability of these accounts of personhood is no less a matter of justice than the distribution of other goods and services throughout society' (Paré, 2014: 210). We suggest that in addition to the renegotiations of discourses of self, therapy can provide an opportunity to have a different relationship with oneself. In much the same way that individuals who experience themselves as likeable or even lovable in the eyes of the therapist can come to believe that they are in fact worthy of love; clients who consistently feel respected and worthy through the therapeutic gaze, may come to view themselves as such. Furthermore, we suggest that a more positive and compassionate view of self lends itself to treating others in the same way.

Commitment to social justice, therefore, involves a commitment from the practitioner to reflect on their own processes, biases and reactions. These reflections can help practitioners consider their stance in relation to social justice issues, their responses to difference and privilege and how this positioning impacts upon their working relationships and their responses to themselves and clients.

Accessibility and engagement

The most effective therapy is rendered useless if inaccessible. As providers of services, we have a responsibility to work towards bridging gaps and removing barriers, particularly as many vulnerable individuals face more barriers to accessing services. The importance of 'Access' and 'Participation' for individuals to live in a fairer world is highlighted, whereby they have equal access to 'Resources, services, power, information' and are 'Consulted on decisions that impact their lives as well as the lives of other people in their contexts and systems' (Lane & Corrie, 2007: 319).

In its simplest form, accessibility can involve thinking about how to remove barriers that may be created through the existing structures of many services. Examples include:

- The time and day that services are available and whether they disadvantage those who can't take time off during office hours.
- The physical properties and location of services and their accessibility.
- The expectation that parents of young children attend therapy services without their child but without any provisions of support.
- The cost of services and travel to services.
- Availability of information in different languages and for those who may struggle to read or understand the information presented.

- Service thresholds and waiting times.
- Blanket policies around missed sessions and withdrawal of services.

Without careful consideration of these issues, there is the danger that services become accessible only to the majority, further marginalising those who may need the service the most.

Practitioner's own position in relation to power

Proctor (2002) draws attention to a high correlation between feeling powerlessness and suffering psychological distress, stressing the importance of being aware of power so clients are not subjected to further abuses of power. Proctor (2002) identifies three categories of power: role power relates to the power differentiations that can be implied and created through the differing roles of client and therapist. Societal power relates to the power that can be inherited through societal structures such as gender, age or culture and historical power, which involves the client and therapist's own personal experiences of feeling powerful or powerless. Like Proctor, many writers have written about power, emphasising the importance of sharing power (Goodman et al., 2004) and increasing accountability around the use of power (Reynolds & Hammoud-Beckett, 2017). Massor (1989) warns that imbalances of power are always present within the therapeutic relationship and indeed any behaviour can be justified once the therapist is set up as the 'expert'.

We believe that as practitioners, we hold a privileged position, aligned between both individuals and services. In our view this position allows unique access and influence with the potential to intervene in different ways. For example, practitioners may decide to readdress inequality by making important changes in the way they work individually, such as through conversations with colleagues and peers and through research and publications. Others may work to implement change through policy development and service delivery. Regardless of the level, we believe that an exploration of the practitioner's own relationship with power and privilege is needed (Reynolds & Hammoud-Beckett, 2017) to promote non-oppressive practice and enable deliberate decisions around the type of action they wish to take.

Vignette 2: listening to Tina's story

Tina (aged twenty-two) was raising Samuel (aged five) and Jack (aged three) on her own. Tina had grown up in care and described being isolated with little support. Samuel had been diagnosed with a rare physical condition whereby his muscles were not developing sufficiently and he was increasingly immobile. Samuel's additional needs brought Social Service's involvement who became concerned that Samuel was showing symptoms of stress, such as head banging. Jack was also showing behavioural difficulties. As the pressure mounted, Tina found it increasingly difficult to cope, which led to Social Services temporarily placing Samuel and Jack with respite foster carers. The foster carers who were much older than Tina, with grown-up children of their own, were well supported and financially comfortable. With the support of friends and family, they shared the emotional and physical pressures of caring for the children and gradually Samuel stopped head banging and Jack's behaviour improved.

Tina came into therapy feeling dejected and described herself as a 'terrible mother'. Through the non-judgemental phenomenological contact in therapy, she was able to give voice to wider aspects of her subjective experience and consider herself within her wider context and beyond discourses such as 'single mother', 'Looked after Child' and 'bad mother'. The compassionate gaze of the therapist who sought to understand Tina, holding the view that she deserved support instead of condemnation, enabled Tina to move towards a more compassionate view of herself. Accessing alternative discourses enabled Tina to focus on her resilience and determination.

At points Tina was unable to afford the travel to therapy. During these occasions, Skype sessions were offered instead to continue to support her and to preserve continuity. Where possible, alternative appointments were offered when Tina was unable to attend sessions due to commitments with other professionals. At one stage, panicked by the prospect of not being able to have her children returned to her care, Tina plunged into despair and hopelessness, missing a number of consecutive sessions. At this time, she was not discharged but supported to return and continue with her sessions.

Tina discussed the lack of trust she had in practitioners and the powerlessness she felt within the system. We reflected on our own position within that same system and our own sense of power and powerlessness. Individually and with Tina, we thought about the impact of power in our work. Eventually, Tina seemed to feel respected and empowered enough to have a less defensive, more open conversation with social services about her and her family's needs.

Conclusion

This chapter has considered the theoretical and historical roots of social justice and examined its relevance to clinical practice. The discipline has been criticised for not equipping its practitioners with a clearer framework and skillset to work directly from a social justice agenda (Cutts, 2013), which could result in social justice becoming a 'Buzzword' (Speight & Vera, 2004: 111). Although we agree that a clearer framework and further training is useful, we have wanted to illustrate that therapeutic work is nuanced and there are many different ways in which practitioners can demonstrate their commitment to social justice values and action. This flexibility allows each of us to play our own part in raising awareness, sharing knowledge, challenging old ways of thinking and empowering clients.

Reflective questions

1. What are your experiences in relation to power and discrimination and how does this shape the stance that you take towards social justice?
2. Do you feel that practitioners should incorporate social justice values and action in their practice? Why?
3. What do you already do in pursuit of social justice and should you do more?
4. This chapter has discussed different types of action concerning social justice; what type of action are you comfortable with?

References

Aldarondo, E. (2007) Rekindling the reformist spirit in the mental health professions. In E. Aldarondo (Ed.). *Advancing Social Justice Through Clinical Practice*. New York: Routledge, pp. 3–18.

Arredondo, P., & Perez, P. (2003) Expanding multicultural competence through social justice leadership. *The Counseling Psychologist*, 31, 282–289.

Baldwin, J. (2017) *I Am Not Your Negro*. London: Penguin Classics.

British Association of Social Workers. (2014) The code of ethics for social work. Available at: www.basw.co.uk/about-basw/code-ethics [accessed 12 June 2018].

British Psychological Society. (2017) *Practice Guidelines*, 3rd edition. Leicester: BPS.

Brown, L.S. (1997) Ethics in psychology: Cui bono? In D. Fox, & I. Prilleltensky (Eds.). *Critical Psychology: An Introduction*. London: Sage, pp. 51–67.

Chandler, D., & Reid, J. (2016) *The Neoliberal Subject: Resilience, Adaptation and Vulnerability*. London: Rowman & Littlefield Ltd.

Chung, R.C.Y., & Bemak, F. (2012) *Social Justice Counselling: The Next Step Beyond Multiculturalism*. London: Sage.

Courtland, L. (2007) *Social Justice: A Moral Imperative for Counsellors (ACAPCD-07)*. Alexandria, VA: American Counseling Association.

Cutts, L.A. (2013) Considering a social justice agenda for counselling psychology in the UK. *Counselling Psychology Review*, 28(2), 8–16.

Dalal, F. (2012) *Thought Paralysis: The Virtues of Discrimination*. London: Karnac.

Fanon, F. (2017) *Black Skin White Masks*. (1967). London: Pluto Books.

Finlay, L. (2016) *Relational Integrative Psychotherapy: Processes and Theory in Practice*. Chichester: Wiley.

Flores, M., De La Rue, L., Neville, H., Santiago, S., Rakemayahu, K., Garite, R., Spankey, B.M., Valgoi, M., Brooks, J., Lee, E.S., & Ginsburg, R. (2014) Developing social justice competencies: A consultation training approach. *The Counseling Psychologist*, 42(7), 998–1020.

Freire, P. (1970) *Pedagogy of the oppressed*. New York: Seabury Press.

Gainor, K. (2005) Social justice: The moral imperative of vocational psychology. *The Counseling Psychologist*, 33(2), 180–188.

Gerber, L.A. (2007) Social justice concerns and clinical practice. In E. Aldarondo (Ed.). *Advancing Social Justice Through Clinical Practice*. New York: Routledge, pp. 3–18.

Goodman, L.A., Liang, B., Helms, J.E., Latta, R.E., Sparks, E., & Weintraub, S.R. (2004) Training counselling psychologists as social justice agents: Feminist and multi-cultural principles in action. *The Counseling Psychologist*, 32(6), 793–837.

Herman, J.L. (1997) *Trauma and recovery: From Domestic Abuse to Political Terror*, New York: Basic Books.

Ife, J. (2010) *Human Rights from Below: Achieving Rights Though Community Development*, Cambridge: Cambridge University Press.

Jensen, S.Q. (2011) Othering, identity formation and agency. *Qualitative Studies*, 2(2), 63–78.

Jun, H. (2017) *Social Justice, Multicultural Counselling, and Practice: Beyond a Conventional Approach*. London: Sage.

Koch, J., & Juntunen, C. (2014) Non-Traditional teaching methods that promote social justice: Introduction to the special issue. *The Counseling Psychologist*, 42(7), 894–900.

Kramers, M. (2017, November 14). Reaction: Credit Suisse global wealth report highlights huge gulf between haves and have nots. [Press release]. Available at: https://www.credit-suisse.com/about-us/en/reports-research/global-wealth-report.html [accessed 20 March 2018].

Kristeva, J. (1991) *Strangers to Ourselves*. Trans by Roudiez, L. S. New York: Colombia University Press.

Lacan, J. (2001) *Ecrits*. Trans. Alan Sheridan. (1966). London: Routledge.

Lago, C., & Smith, B. (2017) *Anti-Discriminatory practice in Counselling & Psychotherapy*. London: Sage.

Lane, D.A., & Corrie, S. (2007) *The Modern Scientist Practitioner: A Guide to Practice in Psychology*. London: Routledge.

Masson, J. (1989) *Against Therapy*. London: Harper Collins Publishers.

Mayblin, L. (2017) *Asylum after Empire: Colonial Legacies of Asylum Seeking*. London: Rowman & Littlefield Ltd.

Online etymology dictionary. (2018a) Social. Available at: www.etymonline.com/word/social. [Accessed 19 June 2018].

Online etymology dictionary. (2018b) Justice. Available at: www.etymonline.com/word/justice. [Accessed 19 June 2018].

Pallotta-Chiarolli, M., & Pease, B. (Eds.) (2014) *The Politics of Recognition and Social Justice: Transforming Subjectivities and New Forms of Resistance*. London: Routledge.

Palmer, A., & Parish, J. (2008) Social justice and counselling psychology: Situating the role of graduate student research. *Canadian Journal of Counselling*, 42(4), 278–293.

Paré, D. (2014) Social Justice and the Word: Keeping Diversity Alive in Therapeutic Conversations La justice sociale et le discours: assurer la diversité dans les conversations thérapeutiques. *Canadian Journal of Counselling and Psychotherapy/Revue canadienne de counseling et de psychothérapie*, ol. 48(3), 206–217.

Pease, B. (2010) *Undoing Privilege: Unearned Advantage in a Divided World*. London: Zed Books.

Prilleltensky, I., Dokecki, P., Frieden, G., & Wang, V.O. (2007) Counseling for wellness and justice: Foundations and ethical dilemmas. In E. Aldarondo (Ed.). *Advancing Social Justice Through Clinical Practice*. Mahwah, NJ, US: Lawrence Erlbaum Associates Publishers, pp. 19–42.

Proctor, G. (2002) *The Dynamics of Power in Counselling and Psychotherapy: Ethics, Politics and Practice*. Ross-on-Wye: PCCS Books.

Reynolds, V., & Hammoud-Beckett, S. (2017) Social justice activism and therapy: Tensions, points of connections and hopeful scepticism. In C. Audet, & D. Paré (Eds.). *Social Justice and Counselling: Discourse in Practice*. London: Routledge, pp. 3–15.

Rosenthal, L. (2016) Incorporating intersectionality into psychology: An opportunity to promote social justice and equity. *American Psychologist*, 71(6), 474–485.

Shklar, J. (1990) *The Faces of Injustice*. New Haven: Yale University Press.

Spanierman, L.B., & Smith, L. (2017) Confronting white hegemony: A moral imperative for the helping professions. *The Counseling Psychologist*, 45(5), 727–736.

Speight, S.L., & Vera, E.M. (2004) A social justice agenda: Ready or not? *The Counseling Psychologist*, 32, 109–118.

Tribe, R., & Bell, D. (2017) Social justice, diversity and leadership. *The European Journal of Counselling Psychology*, 6(1), 1–9.

UK Council for Psychotherapy. (2018) *UKCP Draft Code of Ethics*. London: UKCP.

UN General Assembly. (1948) Universal declaration of human rights. Available at: www.un.org/en/universal-declaration-human-rights/ [accessed 29 June 2018].

Winslade, J. (2017) Counselling and social justice: What are we working for? In C. Audet, & D. Paré (Eds.). *Social Justice and Counselling: Discourse in Practice*. London: Routledge, pp. 16–28.

Žižek, S. (2016) *Disparities*. London: Bloomsbury.

Chapter 24

Ethical and professional issues in community psychology

Angela Byrne

Values are seen as central to community psychology and it is often defined, among other features, by a stance for social justice and solidarity with marginalised communities. This stance does not mean that community psychology is free from ethical challenges. On the contrary, working within a community psychology framework poses many ethical dilemmas as practitioners attempt to implement these values. Therefore, it is essential that those working within this approach engage in critical self-reflection. This chapter will begin with a brief consideration of the stated values and principles of community psychology. It will then outline some key ethical issues and dilemmas, including dilemmas posed by the professionalisation of community psychology.

Community psychology has many roots and influences, including social psychology, liberation psychology, feminism, Marxism and decoloniality theory and has developed in different parts of the world at different times and with different emphases. Given the context of this book, the emphasis will be on community psychology in the UK. It is beyond the scope of this chapter to give a history of the development of and influences on community psychology in the UK; however, a comprehensive account is provided by Burton et al. (2007) and Kagan et al. (2011) and a list of relevant resources and links are provided after this chapter.

What is community psychology?

Community psychology is defined not by location but rather by how it conceptualises problems and by a set of values, principles and practices. Therefore, it is not simply about taking a traditional psychological or academic research model and locating it in a community setting, such as a charity, community organisation or faith group. The following sections outline some of the key features of a community psychology approach.

An alternative understanding

Community psychology provides an alternative understanding to the individualising and internalising approaches more usually found in Euro-American psychology, where the focus tends to be on the individual and their inner world, behaviours or immediate relationships. Community psychology takes an ecological perspective, seeing people in their social context and considers how social systems operate and interact. Community psychology views distress health and well-being as connected to people's social, material and political contexts, for example, the stability they are afforded by their economic position and the intersecting forms of discrimination and oppression they may face. The focus therefore moves away from internal, biomedical and individual psychological explanations of people's distress towards an understanding of the impact that oppressive political and social environments have on people and communities and on how people and communities can influence these structures.

A stance for social justice

Community psychology approaches have been described as underpinned by values of social justice, liberation, empowerment and inclusion of marginalised people (e.g. Kagan & Burton, 2001). Community psychologists do not attempt to take a stance of neutrality or detachment but actively oppose neutrality since neutrality in the face of social injustice and inequality is seen as colluding with those systems of injustice. Community psychologists generally position themselves as being on the side of the oppressed and marginalised Within community psychology, social justice includes distributive justice which refers to fair and equitable allocation of resources and procedural justice, which comprises fairness, transparency and inclusion in decision making and genuine collaboration (Evans et al., 2014). Patel (2016) argues that we should also be aiming beyond social justice and towards legal justice and reparation.

Praxis

Community psychologists use the term 'praxis' to highlight the interconnected nature of theory and practice. Following Freire's concept of praxis as a process of 'reflection and action upon the world in order to transform it' (e.g. Freire 1996: 33) community psychologists attempt to engage in a cycle of reflection research and social action from the value base of social justice (e.g. Prilleltensky, 2001).

Collaboration

Collaboration is a key principle of community psychology. Community psychologists attempt to engage with communities and work collaboratively, negotiating ways of working and shared goals and ensuring meaningful participation There is an emphasis on 'working alongside', rather than 'working on behalf of'. Community psychologists talk of 'giving psychology away', sharing knowledge and skills with community members. However, true collaboration also involves acknowledging the expertise of community members and mutual exchange of knowledge (British Psychological Society (BPS), 2018a). Collaboration also encompasses working together with other disciplines; community psychology is often described as interdisciplinary and an approach that promotes theoretical and methodological pluralism.

Participatory research

According to Patel (2003: 34), 'ethical research should be empowering research, whereby the development of the research questions lies with the very people to whom the research pertains'. In line with the stated values and principles of community psychology, research strategies aim to be participatory with active involvement of people at all stages from the formulation of research questions, conducting the research, analysing and interpreting results, producing the reports and deciding on methods of dissemination. As community psychologists are also interested in bringing about change they often adopt a participatory action research (PAR) approach, involving cycles of research, action and reflection.

The degree of participation varies and can be seen on a continuum, from being controlled and managed by community members without professional involvement to being controlled by professional researchers. A review of publications arising from community-based participatory (CBPR) research found that the majority fall into the latter category of being controlled by professional researchers, with varying degrees of participation (Durham Community Research Team, 2011). This type of research is often claimed to be inherently more ethical than more traditional types of research, because it is seen as more egalitarian and focused on community concerns, however, as outlined below, this type of research has its own ethical challenges.

Prevention and social action

Community psychology interventions often focus on prevention rather than treatment and this entails working at different levels, attempting to bring about change in the environment or at policy level. Community psychology is concerned with change beyond the individual and attempts to address structural inequalities and material resources. The focus also moves from the individual to the role of the group in bringing about social change. The strengths and resources of a community are acknowledged and built upon and the approach aims to strengthen connections between community members. Drawing on concepts associated with liberation psychology, such as *concientización* (e.g. Freire, 1996), it is argued that, in building connections with each other and in understanding their experiences and distress in their social and political contexts, people come to find ways to take collective action to tackle these forces.

The following vignette illustrates these principles and practices in an example of how participatory action research contributed to a campaign to address homelessness and mental health in London and supported the establishment of the Housing and Mental Health Network.

Vignette 1

The Focus E15 campaign was founded in 2013 by a group of young mothers who came together following eviction from the hostel where they were living in the East London Borough of Newham. On seeking help from the council, they were told that they would have to take private rented accommodation far from London and thus be separated from their families and support networks. The women organised themselves, protested and undertook a series of actions to highlight the problems of homelessness and social cleansing in Newham. This included occupying a block of flats on a housing estate from which the residents had been moved so that the land could be sold to private developers. They also established a weekly street stall in a busy shopping area where they could bring their campaign to the local community and talk with people about the impact of the housing crisis. Hearing the stories of others in this way led Focus E15 to collaborate with researchers Kate Hardy and Tom Gillespie (Hardy & Gillespie, 2016) on a piece of participatory action research exploring the experiences of people facing actual or threatened homelessness in Newham. They worked together to formulate the research questions and women from the Focus E15 campaign became peer researchers, conducting structured interviews with people affected by the housing crisis. Their findings highlighted the significant numbers of people being told they had to leave London and that this disproportionately affected women and children and people with disabilities. The insecurity, displacement and housing conditions had a significant impact on people's mental health, including suicidal thoughts and self-harm. The research team worked with illustrators to create drawings of participants to show the human face of the problem but in a way that preserved people's anonymity. These are now part of an exhibition in the Museum of Homelessness, which travels around the UK staging exhibitions and events. The team held workshops and events to disseminate the research and launched the Housing and Mental Health Network of activists, artists, local charities, community psychologists, NHS and social care workers, academics and many other groups working together to highlight the links between austerity, housing and mental health and campaign for housing justice.

Professional issues in community psychology

There have been various moves towards professionalisation of community psychology in the UK and internationally. In the UK, these include the establishment of a community psychology section of the BPS and academic journals. There are also increasing numbers of undergraduate and postgraduate courses in community psychology, which are subject to systems of accreditation and pressure to develop competency frameworks. The establishment of standards and competencies are often seen as necessary for protection of the public, indeed competence is one of the four key ethical principles laid down by the BPS (2018b). However, such developments also create dilemmas and challenges. These developments increase the status of community psychology, while also restricting entry to the profession. Academic conferences and journals, with their paywalls and registration fees, can make the work inaccessible to the very people they aim to benefit. This tendency towards professionalisation appears therefore to be at odds with the principle of 'giving away' psychology.

How have community psychologists attempted to address these tensions? Hadjiosif and Desai (in press) describe how the Community Psychology Section of the BPS have tried to create accessible and inclusive alternatives to professional conferences with the community psychology festivals, which have taken the dissemination of community psychology praxis out of traditional conference venues and into community settings, creating events that are interdisciplinary and co-produced with artists and community and activist groups. Social media have created new opportunities, such as Twitter discussions and the online platform communitypsychologyuk.ning.com where people can interact and exchange ideas. Nevertheless, the professionalisation of community psychology reinforces the power differentials between community psychologists and those with whom they aim to work and create ethical challenges when trying to implement the stated values and principles of a community psychology approach.

Ethics and community psychology

When we discuss ethics in relation to community psychology, we are not simply talking about the ethical codes of professional bodies but also how we enact the values and principles of a community psychology approach. Ethics are informed by values and involve the establishment of norms to guide how we conduct our work. According to Campbell (2016), community psychology has yet to develop a well-articulated ethical framework to guide research and practice and there is surprisingly scant literature on ethics in community psychology. However, this does not mean that consideration of codes of ethics for research and professional practice is not relevant to the discussion of community psychology. Individual disciplines develop ethical principles which stipulate guidelines for professional practice and ethical standards, which may be enforced, and community psychologists adhere to the ethical guidelines of their profession as well as the ethical principles for research. Adherence to these guidelines can create challenges for those working within community psychology approaches. For example, how does a community give informed consent to interventions? How do we reconcile professional guidance on relationship boundaries while being truly collaborative? However, before turning to the challenges of working within existing ethical codes, it is important to consider more fundamental issues to do with power.

Patel (2016) has written about how liberation psychology approaches neglect the fundamental question of power and her reflections can also be applied to community psychology. Patel (2016: 45) questions 'whether psychologists can ever "liberate" people whose difficulties are rooted in pervasive social, economic and political structural inequalities and social injustices using psychology as a tool'. Patel has written extensively about the harms of psychology and the extent to which it can serve to reinforce social inequalities (e.g. Patel, 2003, 2011). Applying this to a discussion of ethics in community psychology, we cannot assume that, because we are attempting to collaborate with communities in pursuit of social justice that we cannot create harm for those we are working with. Therefore, we need to consider the iatrogenic effects of taking part in community psychology initiatives for communities.

Doing no harm

The first and most fundamental ethical principle is to do no harm (non-maleficence). What might this look like in relation to community psychology?

Distribution of power and resources

Community psychologists are good at analysing the problems of communities in terms of access to resources but also need to look at their role in relation to inequalities in distribution of resources. The current systems of commissioning services and projects in the UK can often pitch different groups and sectors against each other as rivals. The professionalisation of community interventions means that those with professional identities who can navigate the systems, speak the language of evidence-based practice and have the backing of statutory sector institutions are more likely to be funded and this can actively take funding away from grassroots community projects. 'Partnership projects' can involve very unequal partnerships in which university departments, NHS services or large charities become the budget holders, subcontracting and deciding on allocation of funds to the community groups, with the inherent power imbalances that this implies. This may be accompanied by imposition of targets, practices and methods of evaluation. Holmes and Newnes (2004) note psychologists' 'instincts for colonisation', creating roles for ourselves that position us as experts, such as supervising others, with the associated professional standing and salaries. Community psychologists need to consider the impact their interventions might have for local community groups, both those they choose to collaborate with and others who may lose out in the process. Potential benefits and harms should be weighed up and deciding not to initiate projects should always be an option.

Imposition of values and understandings

Psychology as a discipline has often been criticised for the Eurocentrism of its assumptions and the unrepresentativeness of its practitioners (e.g. Patel, 2003, 2011). As Holmes and Newnes (2004) note, psychologists are overwhelmingly white and middle-class and often do not live in the communities where they work. The community psychology literature and guidance often assumes that the psychologist is from outside the community, an academic, researcher or professional clinician entering a community to work alongside marginalised, often racialised communities. For example, there are often discussions of how to 'engage with communities'. Therefore, we need to be aware of the risk of imposition of the understandings and the values of the psychologists, for example, as to what constitutes wellness, empowerment or justice as well as creating space for those working within their own communities.

At the 2017 Community Psychology Festival, I was privileged to chair a symposium entitled 'Working outside the box: Building on the strength of our communities', which involved presentations from psychologists working within their own communities, including their own Temples, Mosques and grassroots community organisations (Mustafa, 2017; Patel & Patel, 2017; Qureshi, Ahmad, Tahir & Noor, 2017; Toki, 2017). What united most of the presenters was that they were doing this work in their own time, unpaid and outside of the 'box' of professional psychology – a situation that enabled them to draw on their knowledge, understanding and membership of the community without the structural and ideological barriers that have made psychology so inaccessible to many communities, particularly those from Black and minority ethnic communities. However, this also presented many challenges, including access to resources. Avoiding harm, therefore, requires consideration of how to avoid undermining such initiatives and enabling them to flourish.

Responsibility for change

Community psychologists have critiqued mainstream psychology for promoting the idea that responsibility for change lies with the individual. However, there is also a risk with community psychology that, while acknowledging the influence of social and political factors, we can end up locating responsibility for change with the most marginalised groups. Therefore, we must also look to challenging oppressive structures and practices, including within our own professions. According to Patel (2003) social action can begin with the acknowledgement that psychologists have played powerful roles historically in adversely influencing social policy, for example, in education and health services and even in sustaining systems of oppression, such as apartheid. This is of course, not only a historical problem, for example, the current participation of UK psychologists in 'psycho compulsion' within the welfare system (e.g. Friedli & Stearn, 2015). The following vignette illustrates how a group of psychologists in the UK have responded to the impact of austerity policies mobilising psychologists and psychological knowledge to challenge these policies.

Vignette 2

Since 2010, successive UK governments[1] have pursued austerity policies, involving cuts to public services and welfare benefits. This has involved cuts to NHS budgets, social services and local government. So-called welfare reforms have included the bedroom tax, cuts to disability benefits, the two-child limit for child benefit and the introduction of universal credit. These measures have been linked to increases in poverty and inequality (e.g. Oxfam, 2013) and the impact has been intersectional with other forms of inequality, with women, people from Black and minority ethnic communities and older people being among those most affected. The impact on disabled people has been especially acute and cuts to services and welfare benefits have been linked to increased deaths, including suicides (e.g. Mills, 2017). At the same time, UK psychologists have been criticised for participating in what Lynn Friedli and colleagues have termed 'psycho-compulsion' (e.g. Friedli & Stearn, 2015), which involves the promotion of psychological explanations for unemployment and the provision of mandatory activities to modify attitudes, beliefs and motivation for work and making work an outcome of psychological therapy. Psychologists Against Austerity have attempted to mobilise psychologists and use psychological knowledge in order to challenge austerity policies, describing this as their 'public and professional duty' as applied psychologists. They produced a briefing paper on the psychological impact of austerity in which they identified five 'austerity ailments' (Psychologists Against Austerity, 2016) and used this as a basis for their ongoing campaign against austerity policies and challenge to the narratives that support them.

Accountability

A key question when working within a community psychology framework is 'Who decides on the process and outcome of community interventions?' and this raises the important question of accountability. In an article entitled 'Responsible to whom? Responsible for what?', O'Neill, 1989) presents some of the ethical dilemmas inherent in situations in which the community psychologist has responsibilities towards funders, community organisations and marginalised communities and particularly where there appear to be differing agendas or divided loyalties. He argues for focusing on the most vulnerable or marginalised groups but notes that this creates an 'accountability gap' in which the group to whom we owe primary loyalty are the least likely to be able to hold us to account. Therefore, we need to create mechanisms and cultivate relationships in which we can be held to account by community members.

In developing partnership working, building trust is essential. Given the history of psychology contributing to the oppression and marginalisation of many communities, mistrust of psychologists is entirely understandable. We need to acknowledge how our theories and practices have contributed to racism, disempowerment of women, oppression of LGBT communities, people with disabilities and many other marginalised groups and to avoid replicating these. Spending time, transparency, reliability, respect and humility are key. Structures such as project steering groups must include representatives of the community who are in a position to question and challenge, without fear of repercussion. Where there are very unequal power relations between psychologists and other stakeholders, community members might nominate someone independent they trust to be alongside them in this regard. Attention should also be paid to ensuring representation for those who may be marginalised or excluded within the community group.

Reflexivity and the avoidance of harm

Some questions to consider in the planning of interventions might include:

- How has the need for research or intervention been constructed?
- Whose interests are being served?
- Who is likely to benefit?
- Who might be harmed and what kind of harm might arise? Consider the risks of imposing ideas or practices; impact on resources and sensitivity of findings
- How do we know that what we can bring is wanted or needed?
- How can we ensure accountability to those we aim to benefit? Who can hold us to account and how?

Potential challenges of ethical codes

Ethical codes for research and practice are based on a set of principles and are mainly concerned with individual rights, whereas community psychology requires thinking about collective rights. Communities and community groups may have their own ethical frames that differ from those of professional bodies and research ethics committees. Participatory research is concerned with process as outcome and the process itself is supposed to be empowering. In reviewing ethical issues in community-based participatory research, Banks et al. (2013) advocate the approach of 'everyday ethics' which is relationship-based, focusing on care and responsibilities within relationships and encompassing issues such as building trust and negotiating power. Some key challenges relating to ethical codes include:

Relationships and boundaries

Codes of conduct governing research and professional practice in psychology recommend that practitioners are aware of the harms that can arise from 'dual relationships'. Dual relationships are often spoken about as potentially harmful and to be avoided. According to Everett et al. (2013) 'This speaks to the privilege of some practitioners' distance from the lives of clients and normalizes this distance as a measure of professionalism' (p. 17). When working within a community psychology framework, relationships and boundaries are generally not so clear cut as people often have multiple relationships as co-researchers, clients, colleagues and fellow activists. In discussing her model of Social Action Psychotherapy, Holland (1992) relates how some of her clients became her closest colleagues and that this was seen as unorthodox and even unethical by those working within more formal structures. In addressing the dilemmas that may be raised by multiple relationships, Everett et al. (2013) draw on the work of Tomm (2002) who argues that codes of ethics should remain centred on the avoidance of exploitation, not shifted onto avoidance of dual relationships. It is important to aim for clarity of roles, to discuss transitions in relationships and confidentiality of information.

Confidentiality

Ethical codes usually stress the importance of privacy and confidentiality, however this presents challenges for participatory research where anonymity is often not possible as researchers are members of community in which they are conducting the research. As above, what is important is the avoidance of harm and the importance of confidentiality and informed consent to participate.

Informed consent

The principle of informed consent is generally thought of in relation to individuals so how might we think of it in relation to communities? Some of the challenges include the fact that participatory action research and community work evolves in ways that make it difficult to specify in advance what the experience and outcomes might be like and thus, what people are consenting to

Thus, consent may need to be an ongoing process as the work evolves. A further challenge includes the fact that we may not be able to reach all of those who might be affected in the wider community in order to obtain consent, thus relying on groups or organisations as representatives. In this, we need to consider who may not be represented and also to consider mechanisms by which we can present the outcomes of the work to the wider community and consult them about dissemination and action.

In order to address some of the issues outlined above, community psychologists and those with whom they are collaborating may develop explicit agreements prior to undertaking the work. This could include the risks and benefits of the initiative as well as the rights and responsibilities of all those involved. Such agreements should cover ownership and dissemination of findings and publications. These should be co-constructed and subject to ongoing review. Finally, we need to address the institutional ethical review process so that it can accommodate this kind of work.

Conclusion

Community psychology asserts a commitment to social justice and empowerment of communities yet faces some distinctive ethical issues and dilemmas. Tensions exist between the professionalisation of community psychology and the aim of 'giving away psychology' and being accountable to the most marginalised. There are also potential challenges in applying ethical codes conceived within an individualistic framework to community psychology. In order to be truly accountable to communities we need to develop ethical frameworks and practices that encompass our responsibilities within relationships and to engage in critical reflection on issues of power and the potential for causing harm through the imposition of values and understandings and reinforcing unequal distribution of power and resources.

Reflective questions

1. Considering the regulation of community psychology, what redress should be available to community members who have been harmed or let down by community psychology projects or research?

2. How could you go about devising a competencies framework for the practice of community psychology, while adhering to the values of community?

3. How would you ensure that an event or publication which aims to disseminate community psychology praxis is accessible to all members of the community?

4. A number of longstanding local mental health peer support projects are losing their funding as commissioners want to move to a 'recovery model', defined by time-limited support, working 'towards independence' and using 'evidence-based practice'. How could a community psychology approach work ethically to support those affected?

Note

1 Conservative and Liberal Democrat coalition: 2010–2015 and Conservative: 2015–present.

References

Banks, S., Armstrong, A., Carter, K., Graham, H., Hayward, P., Henry, A., Holland, T., Holmes, C., Lee, A., McNulty, A., Moore, N., Nayling, N., Stokoe, A., & Strachan, A. (2013) Everyday ethics in community-based participatory research. *Contemporary Social Science*, 8(3), 263–277.

BPS. (2018a) *Guidance for Psychologists on Working with Community Organisations*. Leicester: British Psychological Society.

BPS. (2018b) *Code of Ethics and Conduct*. Leicester: British Psychological Society.

Burton, M., Boyle, S., Harris, C., & Kagan, C. (2007) Community Psychology in Britain. In S.M. Reich, M. Riemer, I. Prilleltensky, & M. Montero (Eds.). *International Community Psychology*. Boston, MA: Springer, pp. 219–237.

Campbell, R. (2016) 'It's the Way that You Do It': Developing an ethical framework for community psychology research and action. *American Journal of Community Psychology*, 58, 294–302.

Durham Community Research Team. (2011) *Community-based participatory research: Ethical challenges*. Available at: https://ahrc.ukri.org/documents/project-reports-and-reviews/connected-communities/community-based-participatory-research-ethical-challenges/ Accessed 30 September 2018.

Evans, S.D., Rosen, A., & Nelson, G. (2014) Community psychology and social justice. In C.V. Johnson, H.L. Friedman, J. Diaz, Z. Franco, & B.K. Nastasi (Eds.). *Praeger Handbook of Social Justice and Psychology*. Santa Barbara, CA: Praeger, pp. 143–163.

Everett, B., MacFarlane, D.A., Reynolds, V.A., & Anderson, H.D. (2013) Not on our backs: Supporting counsellors in navigating the ethics of multiple relationships in queer, two spirit and/or trans communities. *Canadian Journal of Counselling and Psychotherapy*, 47(1), 14–28.

Freire, P. (1996). *Pedagogy of the Oppressed*. London: Penguin Books.

Friedli, L., & Stearn, R. (2015) Positive affect as coercive strategy: Conditionality, activation and the role of psychology in UK government workfare programmes. *Medical Humanities*, 41, 40–47.

Hadjiosif, M., & Desai, M. (in press). The Evolution of the community psychology festival. In C. Walker, S. Zlotowitz, & A. Zoli (Eds.). *New Ideas for New Times: A Handbook of Innovative Community and Clinical Psychologies*. London: Palgrave.

Hardy, T., & Gillespie, T. (2016) *Homelessness, health and housing: Participatory action research in East London*. Available at: www.e15report.org.uk Accessed 30 September 2018.

Holland, S. (1992) From social abuse to social action: A neighbourhood psychotherapy and social action project for women. In J.M. Ussher, & P. Nicolson (Eds.). *Gender Issues in Clinical Psychology*. London: Routledge, pp. 68–77.

Holmes, G., & Newnes, C. (2004) Thinking about community psychology and poverty. *Clinical Psychology*, 38, 19–221.

Kagan, C., & Burton, M. (2001) *Critical Community Psychology Praxis for the 21st Century*. Manchester: Interpersonal and Organisational Development Research Group, IOD Occasional Papers: Number 2/01. Manchester Metropolitan University.

Kagan, C., Burton, M., Duckett, P., Lawthom, R., & Siddiquee, A. (2011). *Critical Community Psychology*. Oxford: Wiley Blackwell.

Mills, C. (2017) Dead people don't claim: A psychopolitical autopsy of UK austerity suicides. *Critical Social Policy*, 38(2), 302–322.

Mustafa, S. (2017) *Faith in Recovery: Making talking therapy relevant to Muslim communities*. Paper presented at 3rd Community Psychology Festival, Bristol, England. 15–16 September 2017.

O'Neill, P. (1989) Responsible to whom? Responsible for what? Some ethical issues in community intervention. *American Journal of Community Psychology*, 17, 323–341.

Oxfam. (2013) *The true cost of austerity and inequality: UK case study*. Available at: https://policy-practice.oxfam.org.uk/publications/a-cautionary-tale-the-true-cost-of-austerity-and-inequality-in-europe-301384 Accessed 30 September 2018.

Patel, N. (2003) Clinical psychology: Reinforcing inequalities or facilitating empowerment? *The International Journal of Human Rights*, 7(1), 16–39.

Patel, N. (2011) The psychologization of torture. In M. Rapley, J. Moncrieff, & J. Dillon (Eds.). *De-medicalising Misery: Psychiatry, Psychology and the Human Condition*. Basingstoke: Palgrave MacMillan, pp. 239–255.

Patel, N. (2016) Commentary on Afuape and Hughes. Looking further at liberation: A critical Perspective. In T. Afuape, & G. Hughes (Eds.). *Towards Emotional Wellbeing through Liberation Dialogue*. London: Routledge, pp. 43–47.

Patel, N., & Patel, S. (2017) *Harnessing strengths: Working Together with the Gujarati Community*. Paper presented at 3rd Community Psychology Festival, Bristol, England, 15–16 September 2017.

Prilleltensky, I. (2001) Value-based praxis in community psychology: Moving towards social justice and social action. *American Journal of Community Psychology*, 29(5), 747–778.

Psychologists Against Austerity. (2016) *The psychological impact of austerity: A briefing paper*. Available at: https://psychagainstausterity.files.wordpress.com/2015/03/paa-briefing-paper.pdf Accessed 30 September 2018.

Qureshi, M., Ahmad, N., Tahir, M., & Noor, M. (2017) *Love for all, hatred for none: Drawing on the resources of our community*. Paper presented at 3rd Community Psychology Festival, Bristol, England. 15–16 September 2017.

Toki, R. (2017) *Strengthening the Heritage - working with British Bangladeshi young people*. Paper presented at 3rd Community Psychology Festival, Bristol, England. 15–16 September 2017.

Tomm, K. (2002) The ethics of dual relationships. In A.A. Lazarus (Ed.). *Dual Relationships and Psychotherapy*. New York: Springer, pp. 32–43.

Resources and links

Community psychology UK: www.compsy.org.uk
Community psychology section of the British Psychological Society: http://cps
   bps.org.uk/
Focus E15 Campaign: www.focuse15.org
Psychology in the real world http://www.psychologyintherealworld.co.uk/
Psychologists for Social Change (formerly Psychologists Against Austerity
   http://www.psychchange.org

Conclusion

As stated at the outset, our aim for writing this 3rd edition of the *Handbook of Professional, Ethical and Research Practice for Psychologists, Counsellors, Psychotherapists and Psychiatrists* has been to update the book and examine the developments in a fast-changing, complex and litigious landscape. As editors, we believe that the need to be an effective, ethical and socially responsible practitioner is a central requirement of clinicians, irrespective of their professional grouping. To do this, we asked counsellors, psychologists, psychotherapists and psychiatrists, to address a range of professional, ethical and research practice issues, which are of concern to all practitioners and service users/experts by experience, regardless of the therapeutic or clinical context or the modality used. Each chapter aimed to provide readers with the knowledge, understanding, reflection and clinical vignettes of a particular professional, ethical and research practice issue. This was undertaken so that practitioners may enhance their knowledge and skills to work more effectively and be more ethically aware and socially responsible. While professional codes and guidelines offer some guidance and support, they are by no means intended to be conclusive. Also, as with all professional and ethical challenges, there are no absolutes, each situation must be given careful ethical and professional consideration to ensure best practice. We hope that readers will come away with a better understanding of the issues raised and have the opportunity to reflect on and discuss these issues in a safe and supportive context which will contribute to enhancing the trainee's/clinician's capacity to be constantly ethically mindful in undertaking their challenging work and roles in clinical practice, training, research and beyond.

Index

Pages in *italics* and **bold** refer to images and tables, respectively.

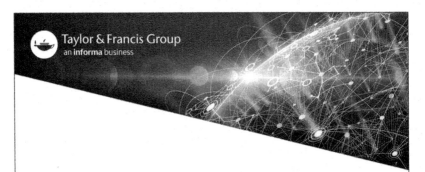